The Other Gospels

The Other Gospels

Accounts of Jesus from Outside the New Testament

EDITED AND TRANSLATED BY
BART D. EHRMAN AND ZLATKO PLEŠE

OXFORD
UNIVERSITY PRESS

OXFORD
UNIVERSITY PRESS

Oxford University Press is a department of the University of Oxford.
It furthers the University's objective of excellence in research,
scholarship, and education by publishing worldwide.

Oxford New York
Auckland Cape Town Dar es Salaam Hong Kong Karachi
Kuala Lumpur Madrid Melbourne Mexico City Nairobi
New Delhi Shanghai Taipei Toronto

With offices in
Argentina Austria Brazil Chile Czech Republic France Greece
Guatemala Hungary Italy Japan Poland Portugal Singapore
South Korea Switzerland Thailand Turkey Ukraine Vietnam

Oxford is a registered trademark of Oxford University Press
in the UK and certain other countries.

Published in the United States of America by
Oxford University Press
198 Madison Avenue, New York, NY 10016

Library of Congress Cataloging-in-Publication Data
The other Gospels : accounts of Jesus from outside the New Testament / edited
and translated by Bart D. Ehrman and Zlatko Pleše.
pages cm
Concise edition with English text only.
Rev. ed. of: The Apocryphal Gospels : texts and translations. c2011.
ISBN 978-0-19-933521-3 (hardcover : alk. paper)—ISBN 978-0-19-933522-0 (pbk. : alk. paper)
1. Apocryphal Gospels. 2. Apocryphal books (New Testament).
I. Ehrman, Bart D., editor of compilation. II. Plese, Zlatko, editor of compilation.
BS2850.A3A66 2013
229'.8052—dc23 2013020110

To our faculty colleagues in the Department of Religious Studies at the University of North Carolina at Chapel Hill

CONTENTS

PREFACE

Two years ago we published a four-language edition of the various Gospels that did not make it into the New Testament, *The Apocryphal Gospels: Texts and Translations.* It included all of the early accounts of Jesus' words and deeds found in Greek, Latin, and Coptic; for each of these texts we provided a new English translation, with the original language on the left-side page and the English translation on the right. Our goal was to make these valuable works available to scholars, graduate students, and even advanced undergraduates who had facility with one or another of these ancient languages. Altogether the collection contained some forty different documents—Gospels down to the Middle Ages, and several important ones from later times, as they could be found in our three target languages.

Sometimes these books are called the "apocryphal" Gospels. The term is not altogether apt, as "apocrypha" means "hidden things," and these books are not especially hidden, although some of them are indeed hard to find, either in the original languages or in English translation. But the term apocrypha eventually came to refer to the books that did not come to be included in the canon of Scripture, and it is in that sense that they are best applied to these other Gospels. In any event, Oxford University Press published our book in 2011.

It then occurred to us that by creating a new edition with just the English translations of these valuable, noncanonical texts we could perform a service to the reading public at large, which, alas, is not, as a rule, trained to read the ancient languages. This would be an edition for lay readers who want to know what the Gospels from outside the New Testament have to say. And that's what the current book is—a translation of the Gospels down to the Middle Ages (and some from beyond that time) from outside the New Testament, which survive either in their entirety or only in fragments. Our definition of "Gospel" is reasonably broad: by it we mean a book that records the words, deeds, and experiences of the earthly Jesus (or of others, such as Pontius Pilate, who are important only because of their connection to him). We do not include books that are concerned only with revelations that Jesus allegedly delivered after his resurrection (for example, the Apocryphon of John) or those that happen to be entitled "Gospels" but are not, in some way, about Jesus' earthly life (e.g., the Gospel of Truth). In this English-only version of our book we have included a couple of additional texts not found in the four-language edition: a new translation of the Gospel of the Savior, and of the Discourse Upon the Cross (sometimes called the "Stauros" [= Cross] Gospel) that is closely aligned with it, and of new fragments that have turned up of the Gospel of Judas.

Some of the Gospels we include here are relatively well known to students of the Apocrypha: the Gospel of Thomas, the Gospel of Peter, and the Gospel of Mary, for example. But others are very difficult to find in English translations, such as the Gospel of Nicodemus, the Story of Joseph the Carpenter, and the Death of Pilate. Our collection includes Gospels that survive from antiquity in a complete form, with beginning, middle, and end (e.g., the Proto-Gospel of James and the Gospel of Nicodemus), those available only in fragments (e.g., the Gospel of Peter; Papyrus Egerton 2), and those known not from surviving manuscripts but by quotations in the writings of the church Fathers (e.g., the Gospel of the Egyptians; the Greater Questions of Mary).

We should point out that similar collections of noncanonical texts do exist, but none exactly like the one we present here. Some of these others are intended only for scholars and are not widely used by those without scholarly aspirations, such as the two-volume *New Testament Apocrypha* by W. Schneemelcher or the one-volume *Apocryphal New Testament* by J. K. Elliott. Other collections present just a fraction of the available Gospel texts. This is true both of the somewhat misnamed book *The Complete Gospels* by Robert Miller, a very nice collection which contains, however, just thirteen of the over forty texts we provide here, and one of the editors' (Ehrman's) own *Lost Scriptures,* which contains seventeen of these Gospels (out of the forty-seven texts that it includes—the others being epistles, and apocalypses, and so on, rather than Gospels).

The forty some Gospels we give here are in our own translations, and the translations have not been altered from our earlier book, *The Apocryphal Gospels* (with the exception of the fore-mentioned Gospel of Judas). Each text is also provided with an Introduction that has been modified somewhat from its earlier incarnation. Essentially, we have tried to make the Introductions more accessible to lay readers by eliminating most of the technical discussions that are not of broader interest and by rephrasing some of the corresponding jargon. There are several technical terms and symbols that we simply have to use on occasion, however, and these are defined in the Table of Technical Terms that follows this Preface. In addition, we have tried to keep the bibliographies as simple as possible, giving non-English titles only if they are mentioned in the Introduction itself.

Readers should be alert to the fact that some of these Gospels are highly fragmentary. In the four-language edition of our book we indicated precisely where there are lines, words, and even parts of words missing in a manuscript (these gaps in a manuscript are called "lacunae"). We did this, however, only on the original language side of the page, choosing not to burden the English translation with numerous brackets and ellipses [. . .] that could detract from the reading (so that anyone interested in such matters could simply consult the original language side of the page). We have chosen to reproduce those translations precisely here for ease of reading. Scholars and others who want to see where the lacunae and hypothetical reconstructions occur can revert to that other edition.

But we have made one exception here in the English-only edition. Since we did not present the text of the Gospel of the Savior in that other edition, and since this text comes from manuscripts that are very fragmentary indeed, in this one instance we have resorted to the use of brackets and ellipses to allow a reader to recognize the extend of the text that actually survives.

In conclusion, we would like to extend our heartfelt thanks to Cynthia Read, Executive Editor at Oxford University Press, for her willingness and enthusiasm both in accepting this book for publication and in seeing it through its journey into print.

We dedicate the book to our learned, interesting, and generous colleagues in the Department of Religious Studies at the University of North Carolina at Chapel Hill.

TABLE OF TECHNICAL TERMS AND SYMBOLS

Manuscript A manuscript is any "hand-written" copy of a text.

Papyrus Papyrus is a reed that grows in the marshy areas around the Nile; it was used in antiquity to produce a writing material (before the invention of paper) on which many of the most ancient surviving texts can be found.

Parchment Parchment is a writing material manufactured out of animal skins (cattle, sheep, goats, and so on); eventually it came to replace papyrus as the writing material of choice.

Roll/Scroll A roll was the ancient form of book in which a number of sheets of writing material were combined (e.g., by being pasted together) and then written on (one side only) and rolled up.

Codex A codex is a "book" in the form we are accustomed to using today, in which different leaves are folded together and bound at the spine, with writing on both sides. (Plural: "codices")

Recto For papyrus and parchment codexes recto refers to the "right"-hand of two facing pages; for papyrus rolls, the recto refers to the side of a roll in which the fibers from the papyrus plant run horizontally.

Verso For papyrus and parchment codices verso refers to the left-hand of two facing pages; for papyrus rolls, the verso refers to the side of a roll in which the fibers from the papyrus plant run vertically. (In a papyrus roll, as opposed to a codex, this would be the underside that was normally not written on.)

→ A right arrow indicates the side of a papyrus fragment on which the fibers run horizontally.

↓ A down arrow indicates the side of a papyrus fragment on which the fibers run vertically.

The Other Gospels

INFANCY GOSPELS

1

The Infancy Gospel of Thomas

The so-called Infancy Gospel of Thomas presents some of the most complicated textual and historical problems of the entire corpus of early Christian literature. On the most basic level, we do not know the extent and contents of the original version of the book. This Gospel, in its various forms, presents a number of self-contained narratives about the young Jesus, between the ages of five and twelve. It was probably written, originally, in Greek. But the Greek manuscripts that contain the account differ radically from one another, with entire chapters missing from some witnesses and present in others. Of the fourteen Greek manuscripts that attest the Gospel, fully eight have never been published or made available to scholarly scrutiny. Moreover, these manuscripts are all very late—most of them from the fourteenth or fifteenth centuries, well over a millennium removed from the earliest attested form of the text. We do have, on the other hand, earlier manuscripts in other languages. There are Syriac copies from the fifth and sixth centuries and at least one fragmentary Latin witness from about the same date. But these translations also differ significantly both among themselves and from what can be found in the Greek, so that some scholars have even argued that the version of the Gospel found in the Syriac, or as attested in a combination of various versions—Syriac, Latin, Georgian, and especially Ethiopic—better represents the "original" than the Greek. Whatever its oldest form, there can be no doubt that this Gospel was one of the most popular of the early Christian apocrypha down through the ages. We have copies of it in an astonishing number of late antique and medieval languages—thirteen altogether.

J. A. Fabricius was the first to publish a version of the Gospel in 1703 (Greek and Latin), but for the past century and a half it has been best known from the two Greek versions produced by Constantine von Tischendorf in 1853. The longer of his two versions contained nineteen chapters and has commonly been called Greek A; Tischendorf based it, principally, on two fifteenth-century manuscripts, supplemented in places by two other manuscripts of about the same date. His shorter version (Greek B) contained just eleven chapters, and was based on just one fourteenth- or fifteenth-century manuscript. Since Tischendorf's day, other Greek manuscripts have come to light, in particular one published by DeLatte in 1927, which contains an additional three chapters at the beginning of the narrative portraying some of Jesus' miraculous activities already as a two-year old in Egypt, and a longer version of one of the child Jesus' speeches (ch. 6; this ms also ascribes the account to James rather than Thomas). These differences make DeLatte's Athenian manuscript much closer to the Latin form of the text that Tischendorf had published.

But there were other forms of the text used by other translators into other languages, centuries earlier, making it well nigh impossible to know in some cases which of the disputed stories of Tischendorf's fuller Greek A derive from the oldest traceable form of the tradition and which are later (medieval?) additions. The most recent detailed study of the manuscript tradition has been by Chartrand-Burke, who convincingly argues that the oldest form of Greek text is found in an eleventh-century Jerusalem manuscript.

With this variety of ancient manuscript evidence available, it is difficult to know *what* to translate in making a version of this Gospel available in English. It is not even clear that the best policy would be to translate the oldest surviving form of the text; there is no reason to privilege the earliest form of the text over other forms. All of the stories found in the account—in whatever version one finds it—are apocryphal, and all can contribute to our understanding of how different Christian storytellers in different times and places told stories about the young Jesus prior to his experience in the temple as a twelve-year-old. Various story tellers (and authors) added some incidents to the narrative and deleted others; they edited the stories they inherited and put their own stamp upon them. For contemporary readers of the apocryphon, a case can be made that a fuller version rather than some kind of posited "original" is of the greatest interest. And so, in the text that follows we have given the fuller form of the narrative, roughly in Tischendorf's Greek A version. The following chapter will provide the additional stories found in the opening narrative of the Athens manuscript published by DeLatte.

The textual problems posed by our manuscripts affect such basic issues as what this Gospel (or these various versions of this Gospel) should even be called. Until the middle of the twentieth century it was most widely known simply as the "Gospel of Thomas," or the "Gospel of Thomas the Israelite." Since the discovery of the Nag Hammadi Library in 1945 (the so-called Gnostic Gospels), it has become customary to refer to it as the "Infancy Gospel of Thomas," to differentiate it from the Coptic Gospel of Thomas that is now more familiar (and which we also include in this collection). Both titles are derived from the late Greek manuscripts used by Tischendorf (none of which actually calls the book a "Gospel"). The most ancient translations of the book do not attribute it to Thomas (whether "doubting Thomas" or "Thomas the Twin," the alleged author of Coptic Thomas); Stephen Gero has argued that the ascription to Thomas is no older than the Middle Ages. De Santos Otero has argued that the oldest ("original") title was "The Childhood Deeds of Our Lord Jesus Christ."

When was the first account of these "childhood deeds" written? Any range of dates from the first to the sixth centuries (whence our earliest manuscripts derive) has been proposed, with the majority of scholars opting for an earlier date. In part this is based on the assumption that early Christians would have been interested in knowing what their miracle-working Savior was like as a child, and no doubt would have told stories about his various escapades, encounters, and miracles from an early period. And in part the early dating is based on the circumstance that one of the most familiar stories—where the young Jesus confronts and confounds a potential teacher by explaining to him the mysteries of the alphabet (see ch. 14)—is attested already in the writings of Irenaeus from around 180 CE (*Against Heresies,* 1. 20. 1) and in the book known as the *Epistle of the Apostles* (the *Epistula Apostolorum*) (ch. 4), which dates possibly several decades earlier. Even though neither source indicates that the story derives from a "Gospel of Thomas," Irenaeus does intimate that he found it in a "heretical" book (rather than having simply heard it from an oral source). Possibly this was an early version of what is now the collection of stories familiar to us in Infancy Thomas. As Irenaeus was writing in Greek, the story was evidently already in that language. Where the first version of the book was first produced is anyone's guess, though it must have been somewhere in the Greek-speaking east.

In part because Irenaeus indicates that the story was used by a group of Gnostics called the Marcosians, some scholars have considered whether the Infancy Gospel of Thomas is a gnostic production. On the one hand, one of the overarching themes of the Gospel could lend itself to a gnostic construal, for here Jesus is shown to be full of divine knowledge from an early age—on three occasions, for example, besting teachers who presumed to provide him with instruction. On the other hand, there is nothing particularly gnostic about the desire to portray Jesus as superior to other humans, and there is no trace of sophisticated gnostic cosmology or mythology in the text. Moreover, there is nothing docetic about the portrayal of Jesus (that is, it does not portray him as a divine being who was not really human): he appears to experience pain when hit on the shoulder (ch. 4) or pulled by the ear (ch. 5). It is probably better, therefore, not to see this as a specific gnostic set of tales.

What, then, was the function of the Gospel in its earliest forms? The individual accounts of the Gospel are self-contained stories. They may have well circulated independently of one another prior to being written down, much like the stories of the New Testament Gospels. But only the loosest organizational patterns can be found in the book. Occasionally stories are linked by theme (e.g., Jesus' household miracles in chs. 11–13), and the collection is carried forward by periodic indications of Jesus' advancing age (five years old, 2:1; six, 11:1; eight;

12:4; and twelve, 19:1). Taken as a whole, the stories are clearly designed to show the amazing miracle-working abilities of Jesus already as a child: he did not wait for his public ministry to begin doing wondrous deeds. But many of the accounts do not seem to portray Jesus—at least to modern eyes—in a favorable light. As a child he uses his supernatural powers in a way that seems capricious, mean-spirited, and vicious—killing off playmates who irritate him and withering teachers who discipline him. Is this the loving Savior of the canonical tradition?

Many readers do not think so. And so Paul Mirecki indicates that the entire narrative simply focuses on the "sensational nature of the precocious child's activities"; Oscar Cullmann thinks the editor of the text was "lacking in good taste, restraint, and discretion"; and J. K. Elliott states that "the main thrust of the episodes is to stress in a crudely sensational way the miraculous powers of Jesus." Ronald Hock and others, however, have seen something more historically and theologically significant in these accounts of Jesus as the miracle-working Wunderkind. As has long been recognized by scholars of classical antiquity, ancient biographers typically told stories about their protagonists' childhoods in order to adumbrate the outstanding features of their personalities that came to full expression in deeds during their adulthoods. Ancient writers (and readers) knew nothing of "psychological development" (in our post-Freudian terms). For them, a person's character (personality) was fixed at birth, and could be seen in their activities from an early age. The Infancy Gospel of Thomas is designed to show who the Savior was and to show in clear terms what his character was.

This view accounts for the effortless miracles done by the child Jesus, as he heals the sick, raises the dead, and proves remarkably handy around the home (ch. 11), the farm (ch. 12), and the carpenter shop (ch. 13). But how can this view explain the apparent evil streak in the child? It may be that the modern reading of Jesus' interactions with his playmates and teachers would not have occurred to ancient readers. These were Christians who revered Jesus as their all-powerful Lord and Savior, who thought that unbelievers and opponents of Christ would be subject to dire consequences. This is seen already in the stories of the youthful Jesus. He is opposed by a Jewish man for violating the Sabbath (as he will be later in life) and shows that he is in fact superior to the Sabbath (ch. 2); he is opposed by the son of a scribe (as he would eventually be opposed by the scribes), and he demonstrates his power to judge the living and the dead (ch. 3). Those who think themselves superior in knowledge are shown to be fools by comparison (the three accounts of Jesus and a teacher; chaps. 6–7, 14, 15). Those who harm him are subject to his divine wrath (ch. 3), a foreshadowing of what will happen—in the view of Christian storytellers—at the end of time (see Matthew 25:31–46 and the book of Revelation).

In short, in the Infancy Gospel of Thomas we have stories of the child Jesus that indicate the character of the Christian Savior. He is a powerful miracle worker, the all-knowing Son of God; he is one who stands above the law of the Jews, who has the power of life and death; he is one who heals those in desperate need yet who violently opposes all who fail to believe in him or who try to gainsay his mission.

The following translation is based on Tischendorf Greek A, used here for reasons explained above, with only minor textual alterations.

Bibliography

Chartrand-Burke, T. "The Greek Manuscript Tradition of the *Infancy Gospel of Thomas*," *Apocrypha* 14 (2003): 129–51.

Cullmann, O. "The Infancy Gospel of Thomas," in *New Testament Apocrypha*, ed. W. Schneemelcher; trans. R. McL. Wilson. Louisville: Westminster/John Knox, 1991; vol. 1, pp. 439–52.

Elliott, J. K. *The Apocryphal New Testament*. Oxford: Clarendon, 1993; pp. 68–83.

Gero, S. "The Infancy Gospel of Thomas: A Study of the Textual and Literary Problems," *Novum Testamentum* 13 (1971): 46–80.

Hock, R. *The Infancy Gospels of James and Thomas*. Santa Rosa, CA: Polebridge, 1995.

Mirecki, P. "Thomas, Infancy Gospel of," in *The Anchor Bible Dictionary*, ed. D. N. Friedman et al. New York: Doubleday, 1992; vol. 6, pp. 540–44.

von Tischendorf, C. *Evangelia Apocrypha*. Leipzig: H. Mendelssohn, 1853 (2nd ed. 1876); pp. xxxvi–xlviii; 140–56.

The Infancy Gospel of Thomas

1

I, Thomas the Israelite, make this report to all of you, my brothers among the gentiles, that you may know the magnificent childhood activities of our Lord Jesus Christ—all that he did after being born in our country. The beginning is as follows:

Jesus Makes Sparrows on the Sabbath

2

(1) When this child Jesus was five years old, he was playing by the ford of a stream; and he gathered the flowing waters into pools and made them instantly pure. These things he ordered simply by speaking a word. (2) He then made some soft mud and fashioned twelve sparrows from it. It was the Sabbath when he did this. There were also a number of other children playing with him. (3) When a certain Jew saw what Jesus was doing while playing on the Sabbath, he left right away and reported to his father, Joseph, "Look, your child is at the stream and he has taken mud and formed twelve sparrows. He has profaned the Sabbath!" (4) When Joseph came to the place and looked, he cried out to him, "Why are you doing what is forbidden on the Sabbath?" But Jesus clapped his hands and cried to the sparrows, "Be gone!" And the sparrows took flight and went off, chirping. (5) When the Jews saw this they were amazed; and they went away and reported to their leaders what they had seen Jesus do.

Jesus and His Young Playmates

3

(1) Now the son of Annas the scribe was standing there with Joseph. He took a willow branch and scattered the water that Jesus had gathered. (2) Jesus was irritated when he saw what happened, and he said to him: "You unrighteous, irreverent idiot! What did the pools of water do to harm you? See, now you also will be withered like a tree, and you will never bear leaves or root or fruit."[1] (3) Immediately that child was completely withered. Jesus left and returned to Joseph's house. But the parents of the withered child carried him away, mourning his lost youth. They brought him to Joseph and began to accuse him, "What kind of child do you have who does such things?"

1. See Psalm 1:3.

4

(1) Somewhat later he was going through the village, and a child ran up and banged into his shoulder. Jesus was aggravated and said to him, "You will go no further on your way." Right away the child fell down and died. Some of those who saw what happened said, "Where was this child born? For everything he says is a deed accomplished!" (2) The parents of the dead child came to Joseph and blamed him, saying, "Since you have such a child you cannot live with us in the village. Or teach him to bless and not to curse[2]—for he is killing our children!"

Joseph Rebukes Jesus

5

(1) Joseph called to the child and admonished him privately, "Why are you doing such things? These people are suffering, they hate us and are persecuting us!" But Jesus replied, "I know these are not your words; nevertheless, I also will keep silent for your sake. But those others will bear their punishment." And immediately those who were accusing him were blinded. (2) Those who saw these things were greatly frightened and disturbed; they were saying about him, "Everything he has said, whether good or bad, has become an amazing deed." When Joseph saw what Jesus had done, he rose up, grabbed his ear, and yanked it hard. (3) The child was irritated and said to him, "It is enough for you to seek and not find; you have not acted at all wisely. Do you not know that I am yours? Do not grieve me."

Jesus' First Encounter with a Teacher

6

(1) Standing off to the side was an instructor named Zachaeus, who heard Jesus say these things to his father. He was greatly amazed that he was speaking such things, though just a child. (2) After a few days he approached Joseph and said to him, "You have a bright child with a good mind. Come, hand him over to me that he may learn his letters, and along with the letters I will teach him all knowledge, including how to greet all the elders and to honor them as his ancestors and fathers, and to love children his own age." (3) And he told him all the letters from Alpha to Omega, clearly and with great precision. But Jesus looked at the instructor Zachaeus and said to him, "Since you do not know the true nature of the Alpha, how can you teach anyone the Beta? You hypocrite! If you know it, first teach the Alpha, and then we will believe you about the Beta." Then he began to interrogate the teacher about the first letter, and he was not able to give him

2. See Rom. 12:14.

the answers. (4) While many others were listening, the child said to Zachaeus, "Listen, teacher, to the arrangement of the first letter of the alphabet; observe here how it has lines, and a middle stroke crossing both lines which you see, how they converge with the top projecting and turning back, three marks of the same kind, each principal and subordinate, of equal proportion.[3] Now you have the lines of the Alpha."[4]

7

(1) When the teacher Zachaeus heard the child setting forth so many such allegorical interpretations of the first letter, he was at a complete loss about this kind of explanation and his teaching, and he said to those standing there, "Woe is me! I am wretched and at a complete loss; I have put myself to shame, taking on this child. (2) I beg you, brother Joseph, take him away. I cannot bear his stern gaze or make sense of a single word. This child is not of this world; he can even tame fire. Maybe he was born before the world came into being. I cannot fathom what kind of uterus bore him or what kind of womb nourished him. Woe is me, friend. He befuddles me; I cannot follow his reasoning. I have fooled myself and am miserable three times over. I was struggling to have a student and have been found to have a teacher. (3) My friends, I know all too well my shame: though an old man, I have been defeated by a child. I may grow weak and die because of this child, for at this moment I cannot look him in the face. When everyone says that I have been defeated by a young child, what can I say? How can I explain the things he told me about the lines of the first letter? I have no idea, my friends, for I do not know its[5] beginning or end. (4) And so I ask you, brother Joseph, take him back home. What kind of great thing he could be—whether a divine being or an angel, I do not know even what to say."

8

(1) While the Jews were giving Zachaeus advice, the child laughed aloud and said, "Now let what is yours bear fruit, and let the blind in heart see. I have come from above to curse them and call them to the realm above, just as the one who sent me for your sake commanded." (2) When the child stopped

3. The Greek passage may be corrupt. For the cursive technique of joining the three constituent movements of the capital Alpha as a single sequence, see E. G. Turner, *Manuscripts of the Ancient World*. London: Institute of Class. Studies, 1987; pp. 1–3.

4. Irenaeus indicates that a gnostic group known as the Marcosians had an apocryphal writing in which the young Jesus disputed with his teacher over the meaning of the Alpha and the Beta. It is difficult to know if Irenaeus was referring to the Infancy Gospel of Thomas. See Irenaeus, *Adv. Haer.* 1. 20. 1.

5. Or: his

speaking, immediately all those who had fallen under his curse were healed. No one dared to anger him from that time on, fearing that he might cripple them with a curse.

Jesus' Healing Powers
9

(1) Some days later Jesus was playing on a flat rooftop of a house, and one of the children playing with him fell from the roof and died. When the other children saw what had happened, they ran away, so that Jesus stood there alone. (2) When the parents of the one who died arrived they accused him of throwing him down. But Jesus said, "I certainly did not throw him down." But they continued to abuse him verbally. (3) Jesus leapt down from the roof and stood beside the child's corpse, and with a loud voice he cried out, "Zenon!" (for that was his name) "Rise up and tell me: did I throw you down?" Right away he arose and said, "Not at all, Lord! You did not throw me down, but you have raised me up!" When they saw this they were astounded. The parents of the child glorified God for the sign that had occurred, and they worshiped Jesus.

10

(1) A few days later there was a young man who was splitting wood in a secluded spot. The axe fell and split open the sole of his foot. He lost a lot of blood and was dying. (2) There was a disturbance and a crowd started to gather. The child Jesus also ran to the spot. Forcing his way through the crowd, he grabbed the young man's injured foot and immediately it was healed. He said to the young man, "Rise now, split the wood, and remember me."[6] When the crowd saw what had happened it worshiped the child, saying, "The Spirit of God truly resides within this child."

Jesus' Miracles at Home
11

(1) When he was six years old, his mother gave him a water jug and sent him to draw some water and bring it back home. But he was jostled by the crowd, and the water jug was shattered. (2) So Jesus unfolded the cloak he was wearing and filled it with water, and brought it to his mother. When his mother saw the sign that had happened, she kissed him. She kept to herself the mysterious deeds that she saw him do.[7]

6. See Gospel of Thomas 77.
7. See Luke 2:19, 51.

12

(1) When it later became time for sowing, the child went out with his father to sow wheat in their field. When his father sowed, the child Jesus also sowed a single grain of wheat. (2) When he harvested and threshed the grain, it produced a hundred large bushels.[8] He called all the poor people of the village to the threshing floor and gave them the wheat; and Joseph took what was left of it. He was eight years old when he did this sign.

13

(1) Now his father was a carpenter, and at that time he used to make plows and yokes. He received an order from a certain rich man to make a bed for him. But when one of the bars, the so-called crossbeam, came out too short, he did not know what to do. The child Jesus said to his father Joseph, "Place the two pieces of wood on the floor and line them up from the middle to one end." (2) Joseph did just as the child said. Then Jesus stood at the other end, grabbed the shorter board, and stretched it out to make it the same length as the other. His father Joseph saw what he had done and was amazed. He embraced the child and gave him a kiss, saying, "I am blessed that God has given me this child."

Jesus' Second Encounter with a Teacher

14

(1) When Joseph observed the mind of the child and his age, and saw that he was starting to mature, he again resolved that he should not be unable to read, and so took him out and gave him over to another teacher. The teacher said to Joseph, "First I will teach him to read Greek, and then Hebrew." For the teacher knew of the child's learning and was afraid of him. Nonetheless, he wrote out the alphabet and practiced it for him for a long time; but the child gave him no response. (2) Then Jesus said to him, "If you are really a teacher and know the letters well, tell me the power of the Alpha, and I will tell you the power of the Beta." The teacher was aggravated and struck him on the head. The child was hurt and cursed him; and immediately he fainted and fell to the ground on his face. (3) The child returned to Joseph's house. Joseph was smitten with grief and ordered his mother, "Do not let him out the door; for those who anger him die."

8. See Matt. 13:3–9; Mark 4:3–9; Luke 8:5–8; Gospel of Thomas 9.

Jesus' Third Encounter with a Teacher

15

(1) Some time later there was another instructor, a close friend of Joseph, who said to him, "Bring the child to me at the school. Maybe I can use flattery to teach him his letters." Joseph said to him, "If you are that courageous, brother, take him along with you." He took him with great fear and much anxiety, but the child went along gladly. (2) He entered the school with confidence and found a book lying on the reading desk. He picked it up, but instead of reading the words in it, he opened his mouth and began to speak in the Holy Spirit, teaching the Law to those who were standing there. A great crowd gathered and stood there listening to him; they were amazed at the beauty of his teaching and his carefully crafted words[9]—amazed that he could speak such things though still an infant. (3) But when Joseph heard about this he was frightened. He ran to the school, concerned that this instructor may also have proved inexperienced. But the instructor said to Joseph, "You should know, brother, that I took the child as a pupil; but he is filled with great grace and wisdom. Now I ask you, brother, take him home." (4) When the child heard these things, he immediately laughed at him and said, "Since you have rightly spoken and rightly borne witness, for your sake that other one who was struck down will be healed." And right away the other instructor was healed. Joseph took the child and returned home.

Additional Healings

16

(1) Now Joseph sent his son James to bundle some wood and bring it home. The child Jesus also followed him. While James was gathering the firewood, a snake bit his hand. (2) When he was stretched out on the ground dying, Jesus came up to him and breathed on the bite. The pain immediately stopped, the animal burst, and straight away James was returned to health.[10]

17

(1) After these things, an infant in Joseph's neighborhood became sick and died; and his mother was weeping loudly. When Jesus heard the outburst of sorrow and the disturbance, he ran up quickly and found the child dead.[11] He touched its breast, saying "I say to you, young child, do not die but live, and be with your

9. See Luke 4:16–22.
10. See Acts 28:1–6.
11. See Mark 5:22–43; Luke 7:11–17.

mother." Immediately the child opened its eyes and laughed. Jesus said to the woman, "Take him, give him milk, and remember me." (2) When the crowd standing there saw what had happened, it was amazed. The people said, "Truly this child is either a god or an angel of God, for his every word is an accomplished deed." Jesus then left from there to play with the other children.

18

(1) Some time later a house was being built and there was a great disturbance. Jesus got up and went out to the place. He saw a man lying down, dead. Taking his hand he said, "I say to you, O man, rise up and do your work." Immediately he rose up and worshiped him. (2) When the crowd saw this, it was amazed and said, "This child comes from heaven. For he has saved many souls from death—for his entire life he is able to save them."

Jesus as a Twelve-Year-Old in the Temple

19

(1) When he was twelve years old his parents made their customary trip to Jerusalem, in a caravan, for the Passover feast.[12] After the Passover they returned home. While they were returning, the child Jesus went back up to Jerusalem. But his parents thought he was in the caravan. (2) After their first day of travel, they began looking for him among their relatives and were upset not to find him. They returned again to the city to look for him. After the third day they found him sitting in the temple in the midst of the teachers, both listening and asking them questions. Everyone was attending closely, amazed that though a child, he silenced the elders and teachers of the people, explaining the chief points of the Law and the parables of the prophets. (3) When his mother Mary came up to him she said, "Why have you done this to us, child? See, we have been distressed, looking for you." Jesus replied to them, "Why are you looking for me? Don't you know that I must be doing my Father's business?"[13] (4) The scribes and Pharisees said, "Are you the mother of this child?" She replied, "I am." They said to her, "You are most fortunate among women, because God has blessed the fruit of your womb.[14] For we have never seen or heard of such glory, such virtue and wisdom." (5) Jesus got up from there and followed his mother, and he was obedient to his parents. But his mother kept to herself all these things that had happened. And Jesus grew in wisdom and stature and grace.[15] To him be the glory forever and ever. Amen.

12. Luke 2:41–52.

13. Or: with those who are my Father's; or: in my Father's house.

14. Luke 1:42.

15. Luke 2:51–52.

2

The Infancy Gospel of Thomas C

An Alternative Beginning

The following is a translation of the three additional chapters, similar to those found in the Latin version, that occur at the beginning of the narrative of Infancy Thomas in the fifteenth-century manuscript edited by A. Delatte in 1927 (Ms 355; Bibliothèque National, Paris).

Bibliography

DeLatte, A. "Évangile de L'enfance de Jacques: Manuscrit No. 355 de la Bibliothèque Nationale." In *Anecdota Atheniensia*. Paris: Édouard Champion, 1927; vol. 1, pp. 264–71.

The Infancy Gospel of Thomas C

1

When a disturbance occurred Jesus was being sought after by Herod the king.[1] Then an angel of the Lord said to Joseph, "Rise, take the child and his mother and flee to Egypt, away from Herod, for he is seeking to destroy the child."[2] Jesus was two years old then, when he went into Egypt. As they were passing through the wheat fields they began plucking the ears of grain and eating them. When they reached Egypt they came to the house of a certain widow and stayed there for a year. When Jesus saw the children of the Hebrews playing, he played with them; and he took a salted fish and cast it into the water, saying, "Shake off the salt and swim in the water."[3] When the people in the neighborhood saw what happened, they immediately reported to the widow with whom Mary was living. When the woman heard these things, she hastened outside and chased them away.

2

As Jesus was walking with his mother along the streets of the city, he saw a teacher instructing a group of children. Twelve sparrows came down off the wall, fighting with one another, and suddenly they fell into the teacher's lap. When Jesus saw this he laughed. But when the teacher saw him laughing he was filled with anger and said, "What have you seen that is so funny?" He said to him, "Listen teacher: a widow is coming to you carrying some wheat that she has had a hard time purchasing. When she arrives here she will stumble and scatter her wheat. That is why these sparrows are fighting, to see how much grain each one of them can get." Jesus did not leave until the matter that he had spoken of came to fulfillment. But when the teacher saw that Jesus' words actually happened, he ordered him to be chased from the city, along with his mother.

3

An angel of the Lord met Mary and said to her, "Take the child and return to the land of Judea; for those who were seeking the child's life have died."[4] Mary arose with Joseph and Jesus, and they came to Capernaum, in the region of Tiberius,

1. See Matt. 2:1–16.
2. Matt. 2:13.
3. See Acts of Peter, 5.13.
4. See Matt. 2:20.

in their own homeland. When Jesus knew he had come out of Egypt, he withdrew into the wilderness after the death of Herod, until the disturbance in Jerusalem had died out. And I myself, James, began to glorify God, who gave me the wisdom I found before him to write his story. Amen! I also thought it necessary to make known to all the brothers from the gentiles all the things done by our Lord Jesus Christ. He was born in our region of Bethlehem and in the village of Nazareth. The beginning of these things is as follows.

3

The Proto-Gospel of James

(The Birth of Mary, the Revelation of James)

Of all the early Christian apocrypha, none played a larger a role in the theology, culture, and popular imagination of late antiquity and the Middle Ages than the Proto-Gospel of James (often referred to by its Latin name, the Protevangelium Jacobi). This title is not original or even ancient—it comes from the first publication of the book in the sixteenth century (see below)—but it is in some respects appropriate: this is the Gospel "prior to" the Gospel, an account of the events leading up to and immediately following the birth of Jesus. The focus of attention is on Jesus' mother Mary, on her own miraculous birth, upbringing, young life, and engagement to Joseph. In addition, the account narrates, as a kind of Christian expansion and interpretation of the infancy narratives of Matthew and Luke, the circumstances of Jesus' birth, Mary's continued virginity (demonstrated famously by a midwife's postpartum inspection), and the opposition to the Christ child by King Herod, leading to the miraculous protection of John the Baptist and his mother, and the murder of his father, Zacharias, the high priest of the Jews, in the temple.

The account was probably written in the late second century (see below) and became particularly popular in the eastern part of Christendom. Largely on the basis of episodes found in its narrative, the eastern church instituted feast days to honor the Virgin Mary throughout the year. The book now survives in some 150 Greek manuscripts and a range of eastern versions: Coptic, Syriac, Ethiopic, Armenian, Georgian, and Slavonic. This is not to say that it was completely unknown in the western world; there are still fragments of a Latin version, and more important, it was taken over by the widely read Gospel of Pseudo-Matthew, which popularized most of its stories. But for the most part the Proto-Gospel was not transmitted in the West because its portrayal of Jesus' "brothers" as sons of Joseph from a previous marriage was roundly condemned by no less an authority than Jerome. In Jerome's forcefully stated view, Jesus' alleged brothers were in fact his cousins. This interpretation was closely tied to Jerome's ascetic agenda: for him, not only was Mary a perpetual virgin, but Joseph—the earthly father of the Lord—was as well. The account of the Proto-Gospel was explicitly condemned in 405 CE by Pope Innocent I and eventually in the sixth-century document known as the Gelasian Decree (No. 8).

The book was reintroduced in the West by G. Postel in 1552, in a Latin translation of a now unidentified Greek manuscript. Postel entitled the work *Protevangelium sive de natalibus Jesu Christi et ipsius Matris virginis Mariae, sermo historicus divi Jacobi minoris,* a title traditionally shortened to Protevangelium Jacobi. It is not called this in the manuscripts, however, which have a bewildering array of long and explanatory titles for the work, such as "Narrative and History Concerning How the Very Holy Mother of God was Born for Our Salvation" or "Narrative of the Holy Apostle James, the Archbishop of Jerusalem and Brother of God, Concerning the Birth of the All Holy Mother of God and Eternal Virgin Mary." Our earliest manuscript, however, Bodmer V of the third or fourth century, simply calls it "The Birth of Mary, the Revelation of James." In this context, "revelation" does not refer to the literary genre ("apocalypse"), but either to the nature of the account (it is revelatory) or to the ultimate source of the author's information: even though he claimed to be James—presumably the brother of Jesus—he received his information by divine revelation.

In earlier times the book may simply have been called the Book of James. This appears to be its title in our earliest certain reference to the account, by the church father Origen (died 254 CE), who indicates in his *Commentary on Matthew* 10.17 (on Matt. 13:55) that James was the son of Joseph from a previous marriage, claiming that this is taught either in "the Gospel of Peter" or the "Book of James," the latter of which, he says, stresses the ongoing virginity of Mary. As the latter is a key theme of the Proto-Gospel, there is little doubt that Origen is referring to our text. More questionable are possible references in Clement of Alexandria (died 215 CE), who knows the story of Mary's postpartum inspection by a mid-wife, but does not indicate the source of his knowledge (*Stromateis,* 7, 16, 93), and in Justin Martyr (died 165 CE), who knows the tradition that Jesus was born in a cave outside Bethlehem but also does not reference the text of the Proto-Gospel itself (see *Apology* 1. 33).

The Greek text of the Proto-Gospel was first published by M. Neander in Basel in 1563. For the past century and a half, the most influential and widely translated edition has been the Greek text constructed by Constantine von Tischendorf in 1853 on the basis of eighteen late medieval manuscripts. Just over a century later our first truly early manuscript, Bodmer V, was published by Testuz; this became the basis of what is now the best available edition of the Gospel, E. de Strycker's *La forme la plus ancienne du Protévangile de Jacques.*

Our earliest full manuscript, Bodmer V, is interesting in part because it demonstrates that enormous textual alterations have been made in the course of the transmission of the text. Among other things, this papyrus manuscript lacks one of the most fascinating passages of the entire Gospel, the account in chapter 18 in which Joseph, in the first person, describes how time stood still when the Son of God entered into the world. Indeed, our surviving witnesses attest wide-ranging textual differences, both great and small. This makes it particularly difficult to speak about an "original" form of the text. Like many of the other early Christian Gospels, the Proto-Gospel is based on oral traditions that had long been in circulation among Christian story tellers. These oral traditions affected the written texts, just as the written texts affected the oral accounts.

Any quest for an original text is complicated by the circumstance that the Proto-Gospel gives clear signs of being based on yet earlier sources available to the author. Not only is chapter 18 narrated in the first person (Joseph's perspective); so too is the postscript: "I James, the one who has written this account" (chap. 24). What is most striking, of course, is that the first person of chapter 24 is different from the first person of chapter 18. Clearly the two parts of the narrative come from different sources. What has struck scholars even more, however, is that the Gospel appears to contain three self-contained narratives with only slight ties to one another. This led Adolf Harnack to posit three older sources that had been incorporated into the longer account: (a) a kind of "biography of Mary" in chapters 1–17, beginning with the circumstances of her miraculous birth to the wealthy Jerusalemite Joachim and his hitherto barren wife, Anna; through her holy and protected infancy; to her upbringing in the Jerusalem temple, where she was daily fed by an angel; through her engagement to the elderly Joseph and then her virginal conception; (b) an account of Joseph and the birth of Jesus in chapters 18–20, including the trip to Bethlehem, the first-hand description of his vision of time standing still, and the narrative of the postpartum inspection of Mary, which showed her to be a virgin even after giving birth; and (c) an account of the death of Zacharias, the father of John the Baptist, in the wake of Herod's wrath, in chapters 22–24.

More recent scholars such as de Strycker have argued for an original unity of the text, largely on the grounds of literary style and vocabulary. What is clear, in any event, is that the subject matter does shift in the final chapters of the book, where Mary, the key figure of the narrative as a whole, disappears from sight, and the family of John the Baptist assumes center-stage. Even if this latter account was "original" to the text, it probably came from a different oral or written source from the rest of the account, as did the vision of Joseph in chapter 18.

The various sources of the author's information are, of course, lost in the mists of Christian antiquity. But it is not difficult to reconstruct the driving force that led to their creation (this is true of many of the apocryphal Gospels, especially the so-called Infancy Gospels). Our canonical texts are largely silent about the events prior to and leading up to Jesus' birth, but his unique standing as the Son of God led Christians to wonder about parts of the story left out. If he was special, as shown by the fact that he was conceived by a virgin—what can we say about his mother? Who was Mary? What made her special? How was she herself born? How did she maintain her own purity, to make her a worthy "vessel" for the Son of God?

It would be a mistake, however, to see this account driven exclusively by biographical concerns, or even by the impulse to provide a story in praise of Mary, the mother of Jesus. Scholars have long recognized that there is an apologetic impulse behind the account as well—that is to say, the account attempts to dispel charges leveled against the Christians by its learned opponents ("apology" in this context means "reasoned defense"). In the late second century, the probable date of this work, pagan and possibly Jewish enemies of Christianity attacked the "credentials" of Jesus as the Son of God. One of the earliest and best known opponents was the pagan Celsus, who voiced the widespread charges that Jesus came from the lower class, that his parents were poor and not of royal blood, that his "father" was a common laborer (a carpenter), and that his mother had to spin for a living. Moreover, the circumstances of his birth were highly suspect: his mother, according to Celsus, had been seduced by a Roman soldier and given birth out of wedlock. With this kind of pedigree, Jesus could surely not be the Son of God (see Origen, *Against Celsus* 1. 28–39).

Celsus was answered by no less an apologist than Origen, one of the great intellectuals among the early Christians (early third century), in his work *Against Celsus*. But the apologetic task was not only taken up in tractates that directly engaged the polemics, it also came to color the ways Christians told their stories about Jesus, precisely in order to highlight the aspects of his life and background that would counter the pagan charges leveled against him. This apologetic goal may explain many of the emphases of the Proto-Gospel. Here Mary is not an impoverished Jewish peasant. Her father is the richest man in Israel and of royal blood. She herself is of impeccable morals and purity. Her purity is safeguarded from the time of her birth and demonstrated in her unusual upbringing, as she spends her young life, literally, in the temple, day and night, fed by the hand of an angel. The stories of the account demonstrate in particular her sexual purity. Not only is she a virgin at the time of her conception; she also remains a virgin, even after giving birth, as shown by the physical inspection of a skeptical midwife. Joseph himself never lays a finger on her. Moreover, he is not a poor carpenter, but an established building contractor. Finally, Mary's spinning activity is not for money, it is to provide a curtain for the sacred temple of God.

The apologetic need to establish Jesus', and Mary's, credentials eventually waned, of course, as Christianity spread throughout the Roman world and became, near the end of the fourth century, the religion of the Empire. But the theological emphases sprouted in the apologetic discourse of the second century came to bear considerable doctrinal fruit in these later years, as the purity and perpetual virginity of Mary became central issues in the theological discussions of the fifth century and on into the middle ages. For many of these discussions, the Proto-Gospel played a central role—either itself or in its revised form in the Gospel of Pseudo-Matthew and later texts.

The Proto-Gospel is written in such a way as to encourage its "authoritative" nature. Even though it was probably not written by a Jew in Palestine—or if it was, it was by a Jew who was remarkably ignorant of both Palestinian geography (he evidently did not realize that Bethlehem was in Judea) and Jewish customs (such as the "water of purity" ritual)—it was written in a style self-consciously imitative of the Septuagint, the Greek translation of the Hebrew Bible. In particular, themes from 1 Samuel 1–4 (the miraculous birth of Samuel to the barren Hannah; see the miraculous birth of Mary to the barren Anna) and Susannah (whose father was also "a very rich" Joachim) predominate. It appears that this pseudonymous author wanted to give his account a biblical feel and resonance. That he claims to be none other than James—presumably Jesus' older "brother"—provides credibility to his account, as does his claim to have written the Gospel soon after the death of Herod (the Great): the account, that is, is to be taken as nearly contemporaneous with the events it describes.

It is impossible to say where the text was originally written. As it appears to have been composed in Greek, it must have been somewhere in the Christian east. Given the apologetic concerns that drive much of the narrative, and the knowledge of the account by the late-second / early third century Origen, it appears to have been written some time in the second half of the second century.

The translation here is of the text provided by de Strycker (used with permission, and with only occasional changes), including the longer version of 18.1–21.3, which is (secondarily) shortened in our oldest witness, the manuscript Bodmer V.

Bibliography

Beyers, R., and J. Gijsel. *Libri de Nativitate Mariae: Pseudo-Matthaei Evangelium. Textus et Commentarius*. CCSA 9. Turnhout: Brepols, 1997.

Bovon, F. "The Suspension of Time in Chapter 18 of Protevangelium Jacobi," in *The Future of Early Christianity: Essays in Honor of Helmut Koester*, ed. B. Pearson. Minneapolis: Fortress Press, 1992; pp. 393–405.

Cullmann, O. "The Protevangelium of James," in *New Testament Apocrypha*, ed. W. Schneemelcher; trans. R. McL. Wilson. Louisville: Westminster/John Knox, 1991; vol. 1, pp. 421–38.

Elliott, J. K. *Apocryphal New Testament*. Oxford: Clarendon, 1993; pp. 48–67.

Hock, R. *The Infancy Gospels of James and Thomas*. Santa Rosa, CA: Polebridge, 1995.

Smid, H. R. *Protevangelium Jacobi: A Commentary*. Assen: van Gorcum, 1965.

de Strycker, E. *La forme la plus ancienne du Protévangile de Jacques*. Brussels: Société des Bollandistes, 1961.

von Tischendorf, C. *Evangelia Apocrypha*. Leipzig: H. Mendelssohn, 1853 (2nd ed. 1876); pp. xii–xxii; 1–50.

Testuz, M., ed. *Papyrus Bodmer V: Nativité de Marie*. Geneva: Bibliotheca Bodmeriana, 1958.

Vorster, W. S. "James, Protevangelium of," in *The Anchor Bible Dictionary*, ed. D. N. Friedman et al. New York: Doubleday, 1992; vol. 3; pp. 629–32.

Van Stempvoort, P. A. "The Protevangelium Jacobi, the Sources of Its Theme and Style and Their Bearing on Its Date," in *Studia Evangelica III*, ed. F. Cross. Berlin: Akademie Verlag, 1964; pp. 410–26.

The Proto-Gospel of James (The Birth of Mary, the Revelation of James)

The Rich Joachim and His Self-Exile

1

(1) In the "Histories of the Twelve Tribes of Israel" there was a very wealthy man Joachim, who used to offer a double portion of his gifts to the Lord, saying to himself, "The portion that is my surplus will be for all the people, and the portion that is for forgiveness will be for the Lord God as my atonement." (2) Now the great day of the Lord drew near, and the sons of Israel were offering their gifts. Reuben stood before him and said, "You are not allowed to offer your gifts first, since you have not produced any offspring in Israel."

(3) Joachim was very upset and went away to consult the book of the twelve tribes of the people, saying to himself, "I will examine the Book of the Twelve Tribes of Israel to see if I am the only one not to produce offspring in Israel." And he searched and found that everyone who was righteous had raised up offspring in Israel. Then he remembered the patriarch Abraham, that at the end of his life the Lord God had given him a son, Isaac.

(4) Joachim was very upset and did not appear to his wife, but went out to the wilderness and pitched his tent there. Joachim fasted for forty days and nights, saying to himself, "I will not come down for either food or drink until the Lord my God visits me. My prayer will be my food and drink."[1]

The Lamentation of Anna

2

(1) Now his wife Anna wailed and mourned twice over, saying "I mourn for being a widow, I mourn for being childless." (2) The great day of the Lord drew near, and her servant Judith said to her, "How long will you humble your soul? See, the great day of the Lord is drawing near, and you are not allowed to lament. But take this headband that my supervisor gave me; I am not allowed to wear it, since I am your servant and it is of royal quality." (3) Anna replied, "Go away from me. I did none of these things and yet the Lord God has severely humbled me. For all I know, some scoundrel has given this to you, and you have come to implicate me in your sin."[2] Judith, her servant, said, "Why would I curse you, just

1. See John 4:34.
2. The meaning of the exchange is obscure.

because you have not listened to me? The Lord God has closed your womb to keep you from bearing fruit in Israel."

(4) Anna was very upset, and took off her clothes of mourning; she then washed her face and put on her bridal clothes, and in mid-afternoon went down to walk in her garden. She saw a laurel tree and sat beneath it, and after resting a bit she prayed to the Master, saying, "O God of my fathers, bless me and hear my prayer, just as you blessed the womb of Sarah and gave her a son, Isaac."[3]

3

(1) While Anna was gazing at the sky she saw a nest of sparrows in the laurel tree, and she mourned to herself, "Woe is me. Who gave me birth? What kind of womb bore me? I have been born as a curse before the sons of Israel and have been despised; they have mocked me and banished me from the temple of the Lord my God. (2) Woe is me, what am I like? I am not like the birds of the sky, for even the birds of the sky are productive before you, O Lord. Woe is me, what am I like? I am not like the senseless living creatures, for even the senseless living creatures are productive before you, O Lord. Woe is me, what am I like? I am not like the wild beasts of the earth, for even the wild beasts of the earth are productive before you, O Lord. (3) Woe is me, what am I like? I am not like these waters, for even these waters are tranquil yet prance about, and their fish bless you, O Lord. Woe is me. What am I like? I am not like this soil, for even this soil produces its fruit in its season and blesses you, O Lord."

Some Angelic Visitations

4

(1) Then, behold, an angel of the Lord appeared and said to her, "Anna, Anna, the Lord has heard your prayer. You will conceive a child and give birth,[4] and your offspring will be spoken of throughout the entire world." Anna replied, "As the Lord God lives, whether my child is a boy or a girl, I will offer it as a gift to the Lord my God, and it will minister to him its entire life."[5]

(2) Behold, two angels came, saying to her, "See, your husband Joachim is coming with his flocks." For an angel of the Lord had descended to Joachim and

3. Gen. 21:1–3.
4. See Luke 1:13.
5. See 1 Sam. 1:11, 28; 2:11.

said, "Joachim, Joachim, the Lord God has heard your prayer. Go down from here; see, your wife Anna has conceived a child." (3) Joachim immediately went down and called his shepherds and said, "Bring me here ten lambs without spot or blemish, and the ten lambs will be for the Lord God; and bring me twelve young calves and the twelve calves will be for the priests and the council leaders, and bring a hundred male goats for all the people."

(4) And behold, Joachim came with his flocks and Anna stood beside the gate and saw Joachim coming with his flocks; and running up to him she hung on his neck and said, "Now I know that the Lord God has blessed me abundantly. For see, the widow is no longer a widow and I who am childless have conceived a child." Then Joachim rested the first day in his home.

The Birth of Mary
5

(1) On the next day he brought his gifts as an offering, saying to himself, "If the Lord is gracious to me, the leafed plate of the priest's mitre[6] will make it known to me." And Joachim offered his gifts and looked closely at the priest's leafed mitre as he went up to the altar of the Lord; and he saw no sin in himself. Joachim then said, "Now I know that the Lord God has been gracious to me and forgiven me all my sins." He went down from the temple of the Lord justified and came to his house.[7]

(2) Some six months came to completion for Anna; and in the seventh month she gave birth. She asked the midwife, "What is it?" The midwife replied, "A girl." Anna said, "My soul is exalted today."[8] And she laid the child down. When the days came to completion, Anna washed off the blood of her impurity, gave her breast to the child, and named her Mary.

Mary's Early Life
6

(1) The child grew stronger every day. When she was six months old, her mother set her on the ground, to see if she could stand. She walked seven steps and came to her mother's bosom. Her mother lifted her up and said, "As the Lord my God lives, you will not walk at all on this ground until I have taken you up to the temple of the Lord." Then she made a sanctuary in her bedroom and did not

6. Literally: the priest's leaf. The meaning is obscure. See de Strycher, *Protévangile,* p. 85., n. 1.
7. See Luke 18:14.
8. See Luke 1:46.

allow anything impure or unclean to pass through her lips. And she called the undefiled daughters of the Hebrews and they entertained her.

(2) When the child had her first birthday, Joachim held a great feast and invited the chief priests, priests, scribes, council leaders, and all the people of Israel. Joachim brought the child out to the priests and they blessed her, saying, "O God of our fathers, bless this child and give her a name that will be famous forever, to all generations." And all the people replied, "Let it be so! Amen." They brought her to the chief priests, and they blessed her, saying, "O Most High God, look upon this child and bless her with an ultimate blessing, equal to none."

(3) Her mother took her back to the sanctuary in her bedroom and nursed the child. And Anna made a song to the Lord God, saying, "I will sing a holy song to the Lord my God, for he has visited me and removed from me the reproach of my enemies.[9] The Lord my God has given me the fruit of his righteousness, unique and abundant before him. Who will report to the sons of Reuben that Anna is now nursing a child?[10] Listen closely, you twelve tribes of Israel: Anna is nursing a child!" And she laid her down to rest in the bedroom of her sanctuary and went out to serve the others. When the feast ended they descended happy, and they gave glory to the God of Israel.

7

(1) Months passed for the child. When she became two, Joachim said, "Now we should take her up to the temple of the Lord, to fulfill the promise we made;[11] otherwise the Master may send some harm our way and our gift be deemed unacceptable." Anna replied, "Let's wait until she is three; otherwise she may be homesick for her father and mother." Joachim agreed, "Let us wait."

(2) When the child turned three, Joachim said, "We should call the undefiled daughters of the Hebrews and have each take a torch and set them up, blazing, that the child not turn back and her heart be taken captive away from the temple of the Lord." They did this, until they had gone up to the Lord's temple. And the priest of the Lord received her and gave her a kiss, blessing her and saying, "The Lord has made your name great among all generations. Through you will the Lord reveal his redemption to the sons of Israel at the end of time."

(3) He set her on the third step of the altar, and the Lord God cast his grace down upon her. She danced on her feet, and the entire house of Israel loved her.

9. See 1 Sam. 2:1.
10. See Gen. 21:7.
11. See 1 Sam. 1:21–28.

Joseph Becomes Mary's Guardian

8

(1) Her parents went away marveling, praising and glorifying God, the Master, that the child did not turn back. Mary was in the temple of the Lord, cared for like a dove, receiving her food from the hand of an angel.

(2) But when she reached her twelfth birthday, the priests held a council and said, "See, Mary has become twelve years old in the Lord's temple. What then shall we do with her, to keep her from defiling the sanctuary of the Lord our God?" They said to the chief priest, "You have stood on the Lord's altar. Go in and pray about her, and we will do whatever the Lord God reveals to you." (3) The chief priest went in, taking the robe with twelve bells into the Holy of Holies; and he prayed about her. And behold, an angel of the Lord appeared and said to him, "Zacharias, Zacharias, go out and gather the widowers of the people, and have each of them bring a rod; she will become the wife of the one to whom the Lord God gives a sign."[12] The heralds went out to all the countryside of Judea and the trumpet of the Lord was blown, and see, everyone came running.

9

(1) Joseph cast aside his carpenter's axe and went to their meeting. When they had gathered together they went to the chief priest, bringing their rods. When he had received the rods from them he went into the temple and prayed. When he finished his prayer, he took the rods, went outside, and gave them back. And no sign appeared among them. But Joseph took the last rod, and behold! A dove came out of the rod and flew onto Joseph's head. The priest said to Joseph, "You have been chosen to take the Lord's virgin into your safe-keeping." (2) But Joseph refused, saying, "I have sons and am an old man; she is but a child. I do not want to become a laughingstock to the sons of Israel." The priest replied, "Fear the Lord your God, and remember everything that he did to Dathan, Abeira, and Core, how the earth split open and they were all swallowed up because of their dispute.[13] Now, Joseph, you should be afraid of this happening to your house as well."

(3) Joseph was afraid and took her into his safe-keeping. He said to her, "Mary, I have received you from the temple of the Lord. Now I am leaving you in my house, for I am going out to construct some buildings; later I will come back to you. The Lord will watch over you."

12. See Num. 17:1–9.
13. See Num. 16:1, 31–33.

Mary Spins for the Curtain in the Temple
10

(1) Then the priests held a council and said, "We should make a curtain for the Lord's temple." The priest said, "Call to me the undefiled virgins from the tribe of David." The servants went out looking for them and found seven virgins. The priest then remembered that the child Mary was from the tribe of David, and that she was undefiled before God. The servants went out and led her back. (2) And they brought them into the Lord's temple. And the priest said, "Cast lots before me to see who will spin the gold, the asbestos, the fine linen, the silk, the sapphire blue, the scarlet, and the true purple." Mary drew the lot for the true purple and the scarlet, and taking them she returned home. At that time Zacharias became silent.[14] Samuel took his place, until Zacharias spoke again. And Mary took the scarlet and began to spin it.

The Annunciation
11

(1) Mary took a pitcher and went out to fetch some water. And behold, she heard a voice saying, "Greetings, you who are favored! The Lord is with you. You are blessed among women."[15] Mary looked around, right and left, to see where the voice was coming from. She then entered her house frightened and set the pitcher down. Taking up the purple she sat on her chair and began to draw it out. (2) And behold, an angel of the Lord stood before her and said, "Do not fear, Mary. For you have found favor before the Master of all. You will conceive a child from his Word."[16] But when she heard this she asked herself, "Am I to conceive from the living Lord God and give birth like every other woman?" (3) The angel of the Lord said to her, "Not so, Mary. For the power of God will overshadow you. Therefore the holy one born from you will be called the Son of the Highest.[17] And you will name him Jesus, for he will save his people from their sins."[18] Mary replied, "Behold the slave of the Lord is before him. May it happen to me as you have said."[19]

Mary Visits Elizabeth
12

(1) She made the purple and the scarlet, and brought them to the temple. The priest took them and blessed her, "Mary, the Lord God has made your name great; you will be blessed among all the generations of earth."

14. See Luke 1:20–22, 64.
15. See Luke 1:28.
16. See Luke 1:30–31.
17. See Luke 1:35.
18. See Matt. 1:21.
19. See Luke 1:38.

(2) Full of joy, Mary went off to her relative Elizabeth.[20] She knocked on the door; and when Elizabeth heard she cast aside the scarlet and ran to the door. When she opened it she blessed Mary and said, "How is it that the mother of my Lord should come to me? For see, the child in me leapt up and blessed you." But Mary forgot the mysteries that the archangel Gabriel had spoken to her, and gazed at the sky and said, "Who am I, Lord, that all the women of earth will bless me?"

(3) She stayed with Elizabeth for three months. Day by day her own belly grew. Mary then returned home in fear, and hid herself from the sons of Israel. She was sixteen when these mysteries happened to her.

Joseph Discovers Mary's Condition

13

(1) When she was in her sixth month, behold, Joseph returned from his buildings. As he came into the house he saw that she was pregnant. Striking his face he cast himself to the ground on sackcloth, weeping bitterly and saying, "How can I look upon the Lord God? How can I utter a prayer for this young girl? For I received her from the temple of the Lord God as a virgin, but I did not watch over her. Who has preyed upon me? Who has done this wicked deed in my home and defiled the virgin? Has not the entire history of Adam been summed up in me? For just as Adam was singing praise to God, when the serpent came and found Eve alone, and led her astray,[21] so too has this now happened to me."

(2) Joseph rose up from the sackcloth, called Mary, and said to her, "You who have been cared for by God: why have you done this? Have you forgotten the Lord your God? Why have you humiliated your soul—you who were brought up in the Holy of Holies and received your food from the hand of an angel?" (3) But she wept bitterly and said, "I am pure and have not had sex with any man."[22] Joseph replied to her, "How then have you become pregnant?" She said, "As the Lord my God lives, I do not know."

14

(1) Joseph was very afraid and let her be, debating what to do about her. Joseph said, "If I hide her sin, I will be found to be fighting the Law of the Lord; if I reveal her condition to the sons of Israel, I am afraid that the child in her is angelic, and I may be handing innocent blood over to a death sentence.

20. See Luke 1:39–45.

21. See Gen. 3:13.

22. See Luke 1:34.

What then should I do with her? I will secretly divorce her."[23] Then night overtook him.

(2) Behold, an angel of the Lord appeared to him in a dream and said, "Do not be afraid of this child. For that which is in her comes from the Holy Spirit. She will give birth to a son, and you will name him Jesus. For he will save his people from their sins."[24] Joseph rose up from his sleep and glorified the God of Israel who had bestowed favor on him; and he watched over her.

The Authorities Discover Mary's Condition
15

(1) But Annas the scribe came to see him and said, "Joseph, why have you not appeared before our council?" Joseph replied, "I was tired from my journey and rested on my first day back." Annas then turned and saw that Mary was pregnant. (2) He left and ran off to the priest and said to him, "Joseph, the one you have vouched for, has committed a great sin." The priest replied, "What has he done?" He said, "He has defiled the virgin he received from the Lord's temple and has stolen her wedding rights.[25] And he has not revealed this to the sons of Israel." The priest asked, "Joseph, has done this?" Annas the scribe replied, "Send some servants, and you will find that the virgin is pregnant." The servants went off and found her just as he had said. They brought her back to the judgment hall, along with Joseph.

(3) The high priest said to her, "Mary, why have you done this? Why have you humiliated your soul and forgotten the Lord your God? You who were brought up in the Holy of Holies and received your food from the hand of an angel, and heard his hymns, and danced before him—why have you done this?" But she wept bitterly and said, "As the Lord my God lives, I am pure before him and have not had sex with any man."

(4) The priest then said, "Joseph, why have you done this?" Joseph replied, "As the Lord my God lives, I am pure toward her." The priest said, "Do not bear false witness, but speak the truth. You have stolen her wedding rights[26] and not revealed it to the sons of Israel; and you have not bowed your head under the mighty hand that your offspring might be blessed." Joseph kept his silence.

23. See Matt. 1:19.
24. See Matt. 1:20–21.
25. Or: eloped with her.
26. Or: eloped with her.

16

(1) The priest said, "Hand over the virgin you received from the Lord's temple." And Joseph began to weep bitterly. The priest said, "I will have both of you drink the Lord's 'water of refutation,' and it will reveal your sin to your own eyes."[27] (2) The priest gave it to Joseph to drink, and sent him away to the wilderness. But he came back whole. He then gave it to Mary to drink and sent her off to the wilderness. And she came back whole. All the people were amazed that their sin was not revealed.

(3) The priest said, "If the Lord God has not revealed your sin, neither do I judge you." And he released them. Joseph took Mary and returned home, rejoicing and glorifying the God of Israel.

The Journey to Bethlehem

17

(1) An order went out from the king, Augustus, that everyone from Bethlehem of Judea was to be registered for a census.[28] Joseph said, "I will register my sons. But what should I do about this child? How should I register her? As my wife? I would be too ashamed. As my daughter? The sons of Israel know that she is not my daughter. This day of the Lord will turn out as he wishes."

(2) He saddled the donkey and seated her on it; and his son led it along, while Samuel followed behind. When they approached the third milestone, Joseph turned and saw that she was gloomy. He said to himself, "Maybe the child in her is causing her trouble." Then Joseph turned again and saw her laughing. He said to her, "Mary, why is it that one time I see you laughing and at another time gloomy?" She replied, "Because my eyes see two peoples, one weeping and mourning and the other happy and rejoicing."

(3) When they were half way there, Mary said to him, "Joseph, take me down from the donkey. The child inside me is pressing on me to come out." He took her down from the donkey and said to her, "Where can I take you to hide your shame? For this place is a wilderness."

Joseph Watches Time Stand Still

18

(1) He found a cave there and took her into it. Then he gave his sons to her and went out to find a Hebrew midwife in the region of Bethlehem.

27. See Num. 5:11–31.

28. See Luke 2:1.

(2) But I, Joseph, was walking, and I was not walking.[29] I looked up to the vault of the sky, and I saw it standing still, and into the air, and I saw that it was greatly disturbed, and the birds of the sky were at rest. I looked down to the earth and saw a bowl laid out for some workers who were reclining to eat. Their hands were in the bowl, but those who were chewing were not chewing; and those who were taking something from the bowl were not lifting it up; and those who were bringing their hands to their mouths were not bringing them to their mouths. Everyone was looking up. I saw a flock of sheep being herded, but they were standing still. The shepherd raised his hand to strike them, but his hand remained in the air. I looked down at the torrential stream, and I saw some goats whose mouths were over the water, but they were not drinking. Then suddenly everything returned to its normal course.

The Birth of Jesus and the Witness of the Midwives
19

(1) I saw a woman coming down from the hill country, and she said to me, "O man, where are you going?" I replied, "I am looking for a Hebrew midwife." She asked me, "Are you from Israel?" I said to her, "Yes." She asked, "Who is the one who has given birth in the cave?" I replied, "My betrothed." She said to me, "Is she not your wife?" I said to her, "She is Mary, the one who was brought up in the Lord's temple, and I received the lot to take her as my wife. She is not, however, my wife, but she has conceived her child by the Holy Spirit." The midwife said to him, "Can this be true?" Joseph replied to her, "Come and see." And the midwife went with him.

(2) They stood at the entrance of the cave, and a bright cloud overshadowed it. The midwife said, "My soul has been magnified today, for my eyes have seen a miraculous sign: salvation has been born to Israel." Right away the cloud began to depart from the cave, and a great light appeared within, so that their eyes could not bear it. Soon that light began to depart, until an infant could be seen. It came and took hold of the breast of Mary, its mother. The midwife cried out, "Today is a great day for me, for I have seen this new wonder."

(3) The midwife went out of the cave and Salome met her. And she said to her, "Salome, Salome, I can describe a new wonder to you. A virgin has given birth,[30] contrary to her natural condition." Salome replied, "As the Lord my God

29. The Bodmer Papyrus V gives a much shorter version of chaps. 18–21; the longer form of the text, generally regarded as older than the Bodmer version, is followed here, as reconstructed by de Strycher. Several witnesses report the vision of Joseph in chapter 18 in the third person.

30. See Isa. 7:14.

lives, if I do not insert my finger and examine her condition,[31] I will not believe that the virgin has given birth."

20

(1) The midwife went in and said to Mary, "Brace yourself. For there is no small controversy concerning you." Then Salome inserted her finger in order to examine her condition, and she cried out, "Woe to me for my sin and faithlessness. For I have put the living God to the test, and see, my hand is burning, falling away from me." (2) She kneeled before the Master and said, "O God of my fathers, remember that I am a descendant of Abraham, Isaac, and Jacob. Do not make me an example to the sons of Israel, but deliver me over to the poor. For you know, O Master, that I have performed my services in your name and have received my wages from you."

(3) And behold, an angel of the Lord appeared and said to her, "Salome, Salome, the Master of all has heard your prayer. Bring your hand to the child and lift him up; and you will find salvation and joy." (4) Salome joyfully came and lifted the child, saying, "I will worship him, for he has been born as a great king to Israel." Salome was immediately cured, and she went out of the cave justified. And behold a voice came saying, "Salome, Salome, do not report all the miraculous deeds you have seen until the child enters Jerusalem."

The Visit of the Magi and the Slaughter of the Innocents

21

(1) And behold, Joseph was ready to go into Judea. But there was a great disturbance in Bethlehem of Judea. For magi came saying, "Where is the king of the Jews? For we saw his star in the east, and we have come to worship him."[32] (2) When Herod heard, he was troubled; and he sent servants to the magi. He then summoned the high priests and asked them in the praetorium, "What does Scripture say about where the messiah is to be born?" They replied, "In Bethlehem of Judea, for that is what is found in Scripture." He then released them and asked the magi, "What sign did you see concerning the king who has been born?" The magi said, "We saw a magnificent star shining among these stars and overshadowing them, so that the other stars disappeared. And thus we knew that a king had been born in Israel, and we came to worship him." Herod replied, "Go and look for him. If you find him, let me know, that I too may come to worship him."

31. See John 20:25.
32. See Matt. 2:1–12.

(3) The magi then left, and behold, the star they had seen in the east preceded them until they entered the cave, and it stood over the entrance of the cave. The magi saw the child with its mother, Mary, and they took from their packs gifts of gold, frankincense, and myrrh. (4) When they were warned by a revelation from an angel not to enter Judea, they went home another way.

22

(1) When Herod realized that he had been duped by the magi, he grew angry and sent his murderers, saying to them, "Kill every infant, two years and under."[33]

(2) When Mary heard that the infants were being killed, out of fear she took her child and wrapped him in swaddling clothes and placed him in a cattle manger.[34] (3) But when Elizabeth heard that they were looking for John, she took him and went up into the hill country looking for a place to hide him. But there was no hiding place. Then Elizabeth moaned and said, "Mountain of God, receive a mother with her child." For Elizabeth was not able to climb the mountain. And straight away the mountain split open and received her. And the mountain was shining a light on her, for an angel of the Lord was with them, protecting them.

The Death of Zacharias
23

(1) Herod was looking for John, and he sent servants to Zacharias, saying, "Where have you hidden your son?" He answered them, "I am a minister of God, constantly attending his temple. How could I know where my son is?" (2) The servants left and reported everything to Herod. Herod became angry and said, "His son is about to rule Israel." He sent his servants back to him to say, "Tell me the truth: where is your son? For you know that I can shed your blood with my hand." The servants went to report these things to him. (3) Zacharias responded, "I am God's witness if you shed my blood. For the Master will receive my spirit, since you will be shedding innocent blood in the forecourt of the Lord's temple."[35] Zacharias was murdered around dawn, but the sons of Israel did not know that he was murdered.

24

(1) But the priests came out at the time of greeting, and Zacharias did not come out to meet them with his blessing, as was the custom. The priests stood, waiting to greet Zacharias with a prayer and to glorify the Most High God.

33. See Matt. 2:16–18.
34. See Luke 2:7.
35. See Matt. 23:35.

(2) When he did not come, everyone grew afraid. One of them took courage, entered the sanctuary, and saw blood congealed beside the altar of the Lord. He then heard a voice, "Zacharias has been murdered, and his blood will not be wiped away until the avenger comes." When he heard this word he was afraid and went outside to report to the priests what he had seen and heard. (3) Taking courage they entered and saw what had happened. The paneling around the temple cried out and they ripped their clothes from top to bottom. They did not find his corpse, but they found his blood turned to stone. They left in fear, and reported to all the people that Zacharias had been murdered. All the tribes of the people heard and grieved for him, mourning for three days and nights. (4) After three days the priests deliberated whom to appoint in Zacharias's place, and the lot fell to Simeon. For this is the one who learned from a revelation of the Holy Spirit that he would not see death until he should see the Christ in the flesh.[36]

Epilogue
25

(1) But I James, the one who has written this account in Jerusalem, hid myself away in the wilderness when there was a disturbance at the death of Herod, until the disturbance in Jerusalem came to an end. There I glorified God, the Master, who gave me the wisdom to write this account.

(2) Grace be with all those who fear the Lord. Amen.

36. See Luke 2:26.

4

The Gospel of Pseudo-Matthew

The designation of this Gospel as Pseudo-Matthew is modern, originating with the 1853 edition of Constantine von Tischendorf, who wrongly thought the book's false attribution to the disciple Matthew formed part of the original text. Recent scholarship has shown, however, that the attribution entered into the manuscript tradition centuries after the book itself was composed. For the sake of convenience, however, the now traditional name continues to be used.

The book is a Latin reworking of the (Greek) Proto-Gospel of James, based probably on one or more Latin editions of that work that have long since been lost. There are numerous differences from the Proto-Gospel, in both contents and emphases. In terms of contents, Pseudo-Matthew lacks the account of Joseph's observation of time standing still at the birth of Jesus (ch. 18; lacking in some manuscripts of the Proto-Gospel as well), as well as the entire final section of the Proto-Gospel, which directly concerns neither Mary nor Jesus but instead describes how John the Baptist and his mother, Elizabeth, were divinely protected from the wrath of Herod, and how his father, the priest Zacharias, was murdered in the temple (chs. 22–24). In place of these stories, Pseudo-Matthew tells of the holy family's flight to Egypt, during which the infant Jesus performs numerous miracles—taming dragons, lions, and leopards; making a palm tree bend down to deliver its fruit to a famished Mary; causing idols in an Egyptian pagan temple to bow down in worship before him. These were some of the most familiar stories of the Christ child throughout the Middle Ages.

The attribution of the account to Matthew is found only in later versions of the text, in two letters that serve as a kind of preface: one from two bishops, Cromatius and Heliodorus, to the famous scholar and translator Jerome, and the other his response to them. The first letter indicates that the bishops have learned that Jerome had discovered a Hebrew Gospel written by Matthew about the birth of the virgin Mary and the infancy of Jesus; they would like him to translate it for them into Latin. In Jerome's reply he affirms that he does in fact have this Gospel, and that he is translating it so as to counter false claims made about such matters by heretics.

That this correspondence was not originally part of the Gospel has been shown by the most recent full study of the book by Jan Gijsel; the apocryphal letters were tacked on two centuries after the book had been in circulation, in order to authenticate its account by no less a figure than Jerome—whose criticism of the views of the Proto-Gospel ultimately led to its condemnation in the West. And so, whereas the Proto-Gospel itself was not (extensively) promulgated in Latin translation, its legacy lived on in the reworking and expansion of Pseudo-Matthew.

Portions of the Gospel of Pseudo-Matthew were first printed in an edition of the Letters of Jerome by G. A. Bussi in 1468. But the first scholarly edition of the Gospel was by Thilo in 1832, on the basis of one fourteenth-century and one fifteenth-century manuscript, both of the Bibliothèque Nationale in Paris. The former provided the book's title: *Incipit liber de ortu virginis et de infantia Christi* ("Here Begins the Book Concerning the Origin of the Virgin and the Childhood of Christ").

The most influential edition until very recent times has been Tischendorf's. In addition to the manuscripts used by Thilo, Tischendorf had access to two others of the fourteenth century. One of them bears the title *Incipit liber de ortu beatae Mariae et infantia Salvatoris a beato Mattaeo evangelista hebraice scriptus et a beato Hieronymo prebytero in latinum translatus* ("Here Begins the Book Concerning the Origin of the Blessed Mary and the Childhood of the Savior, from the Gospel written by the Blessed Matthew in Hebrew and translated by the Blessed Elder Jerome Into Latin). This title is what led Tischendorf to call the book "Pseudo-Matthew."

Tischendorf's limited exposure to manuscripts of the book led to one other far-reaching result. Three of his four manuscripts, like many other late manuscripts in the tradition, tacked an additional section onto the narrative, a Latin reworking of the Infancy Gospel of Thomas. Recognizing that this section must have derived from a different source, Tischendorf labeled it the "altera pars" (i.e., "the other part"). What he could not have realized was that this "other part" in fact was not an original component of the Gospel but was added only in some elements of the tradition long after the Gospel itself had been in circulation. Since a version of the Infancy Gospel of Thomas is already translated in the present collection, this "altera pars" will not be included here.

The manuscript attestation of the Gospel has increased exponentially since Tischendorf's day. Gijsel provides an exhaustive and compelling analysis in which he examines 187 manuscripts, classifying the great bulk of them (150) into four major family groups. The earliest surviving manuscripts of the Gospel date from the early ninth century. Gijsel therefore dates the archetype of this group of manuscripts to around 800 CE and sees the proliferation of manuscripts as deriving from the general reflection on and devotion to Mary during the Carolingian Age. This was also a period that saw a revival of interest in the writings of the "great" church fathers of the fourth and fifth centuries, which accounts for the correspondence of Jerome forged, then, at this time, and appended to the Gospel.

There continue to be debates concerning when the Gospel itself was composed. E. Amman produced one of the most influential studies nearly a century ago. Amman's most significant argument was that one of the distinctive changes that Pseudo-Matthew made to the Proto-Gospel was the description of Mary's ascetic existence in the temple as a child, in which she is said to have devoted herself to prayer and work. This description, Amman argues, is dependent on the Rule of Benedict from the mid-sixth century. Amman, then, dates the Gospel to the end of that century. The problem is that the changes Amman notes could have been made at just about any date after the mid-sixth century. More recently, M. Berthold has argued that Pseudo-Matthew shows evidence of literary dependence on the *Vita Agnetis* of Pseudo-Ambrose, which itself was used in the *De Virginitate* of Aldhelm of Malmesbury in 690 CE. On these grounds, Pseudo-Matthew must obviously date to some time in the mid-seventh century, at the earliest.

In the most thorough analysis to date, Gijsel has maintained that even though direct literary dependence on the Rule of Benedict cannot be demonstrated, there are enough general similarities to suggest that the book was written when monastic orders were beginning to expand in the West, by someone invested in them. Largely on these grounds he makes a convincing argument that the text was produced in the first quarter of the seventh century, by a monk in the Latin-speaking West who was enchanted by the account of the Proto-Gospel and its potential for conveying homage to Mary as a model virgin embracing the monastic ideal. This author was not well versed in Jewish customs or biblical traditions—there are even more "mistakes" here than in the Proto-Gospel—and he was not a particularly gifted writer, hence the rough and occasionally slovenly character of the older form of the text.

In reworking his model, the Proto-Gospel, this pseudonymous author ("James") made numerous changes, great and small. In addition to the major omissions and additions mentioned above, the author has minimized references to Jewish customs and practices, even dubious ones, such as Joachim's perusal of the "Book of the Twelve Tribes of Israel," and his later consultation of the "leafed plate of the priest's mitre." Moreover, he made several more plausible narrative claims (Anna is upset after her husband has been gone five months, instead of right away; she gives birth after nine months instead of seven). In addition, he clarified the miraculous nature of Mary's virginal state. She is explicitly said to have remained a virgin, not just at her conception of Jesus but even after giving birth, as the mid-wife Salome now explicitly proclaims: "I dared to tempt your virgin, who brought forth the light, and remained a virgin after giving birth" (13:4).

Possibly the most striking differences from the Proto-Gospel, however, involve Mary's voluntary commitment to a state of virginal purity. To be sure, in the second-century Proto-Gospel Mary is and remains a virgin. But that is because of external circumstances: she has been protected by others and has, as a result, never touched a man. Revising the account some five hundred years later, the Latin author of Pseudo-Matthew makes Mary's virginity a matter of deliberate choice and commitment from her earliest years. When the priests in the temple tell her that "God is cherished in children and is worshiped in posterity, just as has always been among the people of Israel," she replies: "Above all, God is recognized and worshiped through chastity. . . . This is what I learned in the temple of God from my infancy: a virgin can be most precious to God. For that reason I determined in my heart that I would never know a man." In addition, as we have seen, she is committed to do nothing but pray and work, all day long; and what food she receives she distributes to the poor. Here is a Mary who is the model of the monastic life as practiced in the sixth and seventh centuries in the West.

Not only was Pseudo-Matthew itself popular in such circles for nearly a millenium, its message was spread even further abroad as its reworked stories were themselves edited for incorporation in the eleventh-century book, *Libellus de nativitate sanctae Mariae* ("Book on the Birth of Saint Mary") and by Jacob of Voragine in *The Golden Legend* (written 1260 CE), which was the most widely read and influential book of the late middle ages, down to the Reformation.

The following translation is of Gijsel's A text, altered in only a handful of places based on the manuscript evidence.

Bibliography

Beyers, R. *Libri de nativitate Mariae: Libellus de nativitate sanctae Mariae: Textus et commentarius.* CCSA 10. Brepols: Turnhout, 1997.

Elliott, J. K. *Apocryphal New Testament.* Oxford: Clarendon, 1993; pp. 84–99.

Gijsel, J. *Libri de nativitate Mariae: Pseudo-Matthaei Evangelium Textus et Commentarius.* CCSA 9. Turnhout: Brepols, 1997.

Klauck, H.-J. *Apocryphal Gospels: An Introduction.* London: T&T Clark, 2003; pp. 78–81.

von Tischendorf, C. *Evangelia Apocrypha.* Leipzig: H. Mendelssohn, 1853 (2nd ed. 1876); pp. xxii–xxxi; 51–112.

The Gospel of Pseudo-Matthew

Prologue

I, James, son of Joseph the carpenter, who have lived in the fear of God, have carefully recorded everything I have seen with my own eyes that occurred at the time of the birth of the holy Mary and of the Savior. And I give thanks to God who has given me wisdom to tell the accounts of his advent, and who has shown the fullness of time to the twelve tribes of Israel.

The Wealthy and Pious Joachim

1

1 In those days there was a man in Israel named Joachim, from the tribe of Judah. He was a shepherd of his own sheep, and he feared the Lord with a simple heart. He had no concerns apart from his flocks, from which he would feed all those who feared God, making a double gift to those who labored in the fear of God and in teaching, and making a single gift to those who ministered to them. He used to divide everything into three parts—whether his lambs, his goats, his wool, or anything else he owned. One part he would give to the widows, orphans, sojourners, and the poor; another part to those engaged in serving God; and the third part to himself and his entire household.

2 Because he did these things, God multiplied his flocks, so that there was no one like him among the people of Israel. He began doing these things when he was fifteen years old. When he was twenty he took as his wife Anna, daughter of Isachar, from the tribe and family of David. He lived with her for twenty years, but had no children.

Joachim Goes into Self-Exile

2

1 And it came to pass during the days of the festival that Joachim was standing among those who were offering incense to the Lord, preparing his own gifts in the presence of the Lord. A scribe of the temple named Ruben approached him and said to him, "You are not allowed to stand among the sacrifices being offered to God, because God has not blessed you by giving you offspring in Israel." And so, being put to shame in the presence of the people, he left the temple of God weeping and did not return to his own home, but went off to his flocks. He took his shepherds with him into the mountains far away, so that his wife heard no word from him for five months.

The Promise to Anna

2 As she was weeping in prayer, she said, "Lord, you have already not given me children; why have you taken my husband from me? Behold, five months have passed and I have not seen my husband; I do not know where he might have died or where I should construct his tomb." While she was weeping profusely in the garden of her house, she lifted her eyes in prayer to the Lord and saw a nest of sparrows in a laurel tree. She sent up her voice to the Lord with a sigh and said, "Lord God Almighty, who has given children to all your creatures, to wild animals, beasts of burden, reptiles, fish, and birds—all of whom rejoice over their children: have you excluded me alone from the gift of your bounty? You know, O Lord, that from the beginning of my marriage I vowed that if you would give me a son or daughter, I would offer the child in your holy temple."[1]

3 And while she was speaking, an angel of the Lord appeared before her and said, "Do not fear, Anna, for your offspring is in the plan of God. The child you will bear will be marveled at in all ages, until the end of time." When he said these things, he disappeared from her sight. But she was filled with trembling, having seen such power and having heard such words. She entered her room and threw herself on her bed, and stayed in prayer, as if dead, all day and night.

4 After this she called in her servant and said to her, "You have seen me bereaved and in distress, but you did not even want to come to me?" She replied by murmuring, "If God has closed your womb and taken your husband from you, what can I do for you?" When Anna heard these words, she wept even more.

An Angel Visits Joachim
3

1 At that time a young man appeared in the mountains where Joachim was shepherding his flocks; and he said to him, "Why do you not return to your wife?" Joachim replied, "I have been married to her for twenty years. But now, since God has not wanted to give me children from her, I have come out of the temple God in shame, under reproach. Why should I return to her, now that I have been cast out? I will stay here with my sheep, for as long as God wants me to live, but through the hands of my servants I will bestow their portions again to the poor, the widows, the orphans, and those who serve God."

2 When he had said these things, the young man replied to him, "I am an angel of God; today I appeared to your wife, who was weeping and praying, and I consoled her. You should know that she has conceived a daughter from your seed. This one will be the temple of God, and the Holy Spirit will rest within her,

1. See 1 Sam. 1:11, 28; 2:11.

and she will be blessed above all holy women, so that no one will be able to say that there has ever been anyone like her, nor will there be anyone like her after her. And so go down from the mountains and return to your wife, and you will find her pregnant. For God has animated a seed in her and has made her the mother of an eternal blessing."

3 Joachim worshiped him and said, "If I have found favor before you, sit for a while in my tent and bless your servant." The angel said to him, "Do not call yourself a servant, but a fellow servant with me; for we are servants of one Lord. For my food is invisible and my drink cannot be seen by mortals.[2] For that reason, you should not ask me to enter your tent, but what you were about to give to me, offer up as a burnt offering to God." Then Joachim took a spotless lamb and said to the angel, "I would not have dared to offer a burnt offering to God if your commandment had not given me the authority to make a priestly offering." The angel replied to him, "Nor would I have urged you to make an offering, if I did not know the will of the Lord." Now when Joachim offered the sacrifice, the angel returned to heaven along with the odor of the sacrifice, as if with the smoke.

4 Then Joachim fell on his face from noon until evening. But when his servants and paid workers came, not knowing what had happened, they were frightened; and thinking that he might want to kill himself, they forced him to get up. When they heard his explanation, they were struck with great wonder and astonishment; and they urged him to do as the angel had commanded without delay and to return quickly to his wife. When Joachim wavered and debated within himself whether he should return, he was overpowered by sleep. And behold, the angel who had appeared to him while he was awake appeared to him in a dream, and said, "I am the angel God has given you as a guardian. Go down with confidence and return to Anna, for the compassionate deeds that you and your wife have done have been recited in the presence of the Highest. Such an offspring has been given to you as neither the prophets nor the saints have had from the beginning—nor ever will have." Then when Joachim awoke, he summoned all of his servants and told them his dream. They then worshiped God and said, "Be careful not to spurn the angel of God any further; but get up; let us go and shepherd the flocks at a slow pace."

5 When they had arrived, after walking for thirty days, the angel of the Lord appeared to Anna while she was standing in prayer and said to her, "Go to the door that is called 'golden' to meet your husband, for he is coming to you today." And she went out her servants and began to pray, standing in the door and waiting for a long time. Just when she was becoming disheartened by her long wait, she raised her eyes and saw Joachim coming with his flocks. Anna ran out to him and hung onto his neck, giving thanks to God and saying, "I was a widow, and behold I am no longer; I was sterile and behold, I have conceived." Then there

2. See John 4:34.

was joy among all their friends and family, so that the entire land and people from all around rejoiced at this news.

The Birth, Infancy, and Upbringing of Mary

4

1 After these things, when her nine months were completed, Anna brought forth a daughter and named her Mary. When Anna finished nursing her in her third year, Joachim and Anna his wife went up together to the temple of the Lord. They offered sacrificial victims to the Lord and handed over their little girl Mary to the company of virgins, who continuously praised God, day and night. When she was placed before the temple, she ascended the fifteen steps of the temple so quickly that she did not look back at all or seek after her parents, as infants customarily do. When this happened everyone was struck with wonder, so that the priests of the temple themselves were amazed.

5

1 Then Anna was filled with the Holy Spirit in the presence of all, and she said, "The Lord God of hosts has remembered his word, and God has visited his people with his holy visitation to turn back to himself the hearts of those who have risen up against us, the lowly. He has opened his ears to our prayers and removed from us the insults of our enemies. The one who was sterile has become a mother, and has brought forth exultation and joy in Israel. Behold, I will be able to offer gifts to the Lord, and my enemies will not be able to stop me—for the Lord has turned them away from me and given me an eternal joy."[3]

6

1 Now everyone stood in admiration of Mary. Even though she was only three years old, she walked with such a firm step and spoke so perfectly and was so devoted to the praise of God that she seemed not to be a little girl but an adult. She dedicated herself to prayer as if she were already thirty years old. Her face shown so brightly that it was barely possible for anyone to look straight at her. She was dedicated to working in wool; and whatever the old women were unable to do, she could untangle, even though she was of such a tender age.

2 Moreover, she established this rule for herself, that she would dedicate herself to prayer from the early morning until nine o'clock; then from nine until three she engaged in weaving. From three o'clock onwards, again, she did not

3. See 1 Sam. 2:1.

stop praying until an angel of God appeared to her and she received some food from his hand. And so she advanced more and more in the fear of God. Finally when she was trained by the older virgins to offer praise to God, she was energized by such a zeal for goodness that she was found to be the first at the vigils, more learned in the wisdom of the law God, more deeply humble, more elegant in singing the songs of David, more generous in giving, more pure in heart, and more perfect in every virtue. For she was stable and unmoveable; and she daily progressed, becoming better and better.

3 No one saw her irritated; never did anyone hear a word of abuse from her. Her every word was so full of grace, that God could be detected in her speech. She always persevered in prayer and the study of the law of God. And she was anxious for her companions, lest any of them should sin even through a single word, lest any raise her voice in laughter, lest any should be hurtful or proud toward a companion. She blessed God without ceasing; and in order to avoid being drawn from her praise of the Lord even when meeting someone, she would respond to one who greeted her with the words, "Thanks be to God." And so it was from her that the saints first acquired the habit of greeting one another by saying, "Thanks be to God." Every day she was refreshed only by the food she received from the hand of an angel, and what she received from the priests of the temple she gave to the poor. Angels were frequently seen speaking with her, and they attended to her as to a most esteemed loved one. And any sick person who touched her was immediately restored to health by her.

Mary's Commitment to Chastity

7

1 At that time, the priest Abiathar offered countless gifts to the priests that he might take Mary for his son as a wife. But Mary forbade them by saying, "It is not possible for me to know a man or for a man to know me." The priests and all her family said to her, "God is cherished in children and is worshiped in a posterity, just as has always been among the people of Israel." Mary responded by saying, "Above all, God is recognized and worshiped through chastity."

2 "For before Abel, no human was just before God. He pleased God through his sacrifice; and he was violently murdered by the one who was displeasing to God.[4] But he received two crowns—one for his sacrifice and the other for his virginity—because he allowed no pollution to enter his flesh. Then Elijah, for the same reason, was taken up to heaven while in his flesh, because he kept his flesh virgin.[5] Thus, this is what I learned in the temple of God from my infancy:

4. Gen. 4:1–16.
5. See 2 Kings 2:11–12.

a virgin can be most precious to God. For that reason I have determined in my heart that I will never know a man."

Joseph Is Chosen as Mary's Guardian
8

1 Then Mary reached the age of fourteen. On this occasion the Pharisees said, "Now that the way of women has come upon her, she can no longer stay in the temple." They came up with a plan to send a herald to all the tribes of Israel, so that everyone should convene at the temple of the Lord on the third day. When all the people had convened, Isachar the high priest rose up and climbed to the highest step so that he could be heard and seen by all the people. When there was a great silence, he spoke: "Hear me, children of Israel, and give ear to my words. Since the day this temple was constructed by Solomon, there have lived in it daughters of kings, of prophets, of chief priests, and of high priests—women known to be both great and admirable. Nonetheless, when they reached the legal age, they have taken men in marriage, followed the custom of their predecessors, and so pleased the Lord. But Mary alone has a new arrangement appeared, since she has vowed to God to remain a virgin. For this reason, it seems to me that we should seek to learn to whom she should be given as her guardian, by asking God and awaiting his answer."

2 This word pleased the entire assembly, and a lot was cast by the priests over the twelve tribes, and the lot fell on the tribe of Judah. They all then admonished the tribe of Judah, telling them that everyone who did not have a wife was to come on the following day and bring a branch in his hand. This is how it came about that Joseph, even though he was an old man among youngsters, brought a branch. When they handed their branches over to the high priest, he made a sacrifice to God and inquired of the Lord. And the Lord said to him, "Bring everyone's branches into the holy of holies, and let everyone's branch remain there. And instruct them to come to you in the morning in order to receive their branches. From the tip of one of the branches a dove will emerge and fly up to heaven. Whoever is holding the branch that has produced this sign should be given to Mary as her guardian."[6]

3 It happened that very early on the next day, everyone came together; and after making an offering of incense, the high priest entered the holy of holies and brought out the branches. When he distributed them to each one, no dove emerged from any of the branches. Then Abiathar the high priest put on his priestly robe with twelve bells, entered the holy of holies, burned a sacrifice, and poured forth a prayer. An angel appeared and said to him, "Here is a very short

6. See Num. 17:1–9.

branch which you counted as nothing and did not bring out with the others. When you bring it out and give it away, it will reveal the sign that I told you." This was the branch that Joseph had held, which had been considered worthless, since he was an old man and was not able to take Mary; nor did he want to ask for his branch. And since he stood at the very back of the crowd, humbly, the high priest Abiathar called out with a great voice and said, "Come and take your branch, for we are waiting for you." Joseph went up full of fear, since the high priest called him with a very loud voice. And just as he reached out his hand and took the branch, immediately from the tip of the branch a dove emerged, brighter than snow, very beautiful, and after flying a long time around the top of the temple, it went up to the heavens.

4 Then all the people congratulated the old man, saying, "You have been blessed in your old age, for God has shown you worthy to receive Mary." But when the priests said to him, "Receive her, because from all your tribe, you alone have been chosen by God," Joseph began to entreat and ask them, speaking out of shame, "I am an old man and I have sons; why are you handing this little girl over to me? She is my granddaughter's age and is younger than my grandsons." Then Abiathar the high priest said, "Remember, Joseph, how Dathan, Core, and Abiron perished when they despised the will of the Lord. So also it will happen to you, if you insist on despising what God has commanded you."[7] Joseph said to him, "Indeed, I do not despise the will of God, but I will be her guardian until this too can be learned from the will of God—which of my sons is able to have her as a wife. Let several virgins from among her companions be given over for her to spend time with in the meanwhile." Abiathar the high priest responded, "Indeed virgins will be given to comfort her until the day arrives that has been fixed for you to receive her. For she cannot be united to another in marriage."

5 Then Joseph received Mary into his home, along with the five other virgins who were to be with her, namely Rebecca, Sephora, Susanna, Abigea, and Zahel. The high priest gave them silk, hyacinth, scarlet, flax, purple, and linen. They cast lots among themselves to see what each virgin should do. And this is how it happened that Mary came to receive the purple, to weave for the curtain in the temple of the Lord. And when she received it, the virgins said, "You are the youngest and from humble origins: how have you deserved to get the purple?" And when they said this, they began to call her, in derision, "Queen of Virgins." But while they were acting this way among themselves, an angel appeared in their midst and said to them, "This word will not be spoken in vain; for you have made the truest prophecy." Terrified by the appearance of the angel and by his words, they began to ask Mary to forgive them and to pray for them.

7. See Num. 16:1, 31–33.

The Annunciation
9

1 On the next day while Mary was standing beside the fountain to fill her small pitcher, an angel appeared to her and said, "You are blessed, Mary, for you have prepared a dwelling place for God in your spirit. Behold, a light will come from heaven in order to dwell in you, and through you it will enlighten all the world." Likewise on the third day while she was working the purple with her fingers, a young man of indescribable beauty came in to her. When Mary saw him she was afraid and began to tremble. He said to her, "Do not fear, Mary; you have found favor with God.[8] Behold, you will conceive and bring forth a king who will rule not only on earth but also in heaven; and he will reign forever and ever."

Joseph Discovers Mary's Condition
10

1 While these things were happening, Joseph was in Capernaum beside the sea, occupied with his work, for he was a carpenter. He had stayed there for nine months. And so, when he returned to his house, he found Mary pregnant and he began to tremble all over; and out of anguish he cried out and said, "Lord, Lord, receive my spirit, for it is better for me to die than to live." The virgins who were with Mary said to him, "We know that no man has ever touched her. We know that innocence and virginity have been constantly kept immaculate in her. She has always abided in God, always in prayer. Daily an angel of the Lord speaks with her; daily she receives food from the hand of an angel. How could there be any sin in her? If you want us to lay out our suspicion to you—no one but an angel of God has made her pregnant!"

2 Joseph said, "Why are you misleading me, making me believe you—that an angel of God has made her pregnant? It could be that someone disguised himself as an angel and seduced her." When he said this he wept and said, "How will I be able to approach the temple of God? How can I see the priests of God? What am I to do?" And when he said these things he thought he should go into hiding and send her away.

11

1 When he had decided to rise up at night and flee from home, behold, in that night an angel of the Lord appeared to him in his sleep and said, "Joseph, son of David, do not fear to take Mary as your wife, for the child that is in her is from

8. Luke 1:28.

the Holy Spirit. She will bear a son who will be named Jesus; for he will save his people from their sins."[9] Rising from his sleep Joseph gave thanks to his God and spoke to Mary and the virgins who were with her, and he told them his vision. And feeling relieved about Mary, he said, "I have sinned, for I held you in some suspicion."

Mary and Joseph Put on Trial
12

1 Now the rumor spread that Mary was pregnant, and she was arrested by the ministers of the temple, along with Joseph; and they were taken to the high priest. Together with the priests he began to reproach Joseph, "Why have you wronged this virgin, who is so great and respected that an angel of God used to feed her like a dove in the temple of the Lord? She never even wanted to see a man, and she was so learned in the law of the Lord! If you had not done her violence, she would have remained a virgin to this day." But Joseph swore a solemn oath that he had never even touched her. Abiathar the high priest then said to him, "As the Lord lives, now I will make you drink the water of the Lord's drinking, and your sin will immediately be revealed."[10]

2 Then the entire multitude, greater than could be numbered, gathered together; and Mary was again brought to the temple of the Lord. The priests, her parents, and her relatives were weeping and saying to Mary, "Confess your sin to the priests! You were like a dove in the temple of God, and you received food from the hand of an angel!" But Joseph was summoned to the high altar and was given the "water of drinking." If a liar tastes this water, and then goes around the altar seven times, God gives a certain sign in his face. When, therefore, Joseph drank confidently, and went around seven times, no sign of sin appeared in him. Then all the priests and ministers and people declared that he was pure, saying "You are blessed, because no guilt has been found in you."

3 They called Mary and said to her, "What excuse are you able to give? Or what greater sign can appear in you besides what is already clearly seen, that you have conceived a child in your womb? This is all we ask of you: since Joseph is pure with respect to you, confess who has seduced you. For it is better for you to admit what you have done than to have the Lord's anger expose you through a sign on your face, in full public view." Then Mary said, with firm conviction, "If there is any stain on me, or any sin, or if any lustful act has been committed, let the Lord unmask me before all the people, so that I can be corrected by all as an example of correction." She then went up to the altar of the Lord and received

9. Matt. 1:20–21.

10. See Num. 5:11–31.

the "water of drinking." After tasting it she walked around seven times, and no sign or trace of any sin was found in her.

4 When the entire crowd was amazed—for it saw her pregnant belly—it began to be disturbed, everyone saying different things at once. One said she was holy, another accused her of having a bad conscience. Then Mary, seeing that the crowd was suspicious that she had not been entirely vindicated, spoke with a clear voice to all who would listen: "As the Lord of all hosts lives, in whose presence I stand, I have never known a man; indeed, I decided long ago, while still a young child, never to know one. And this is the vow I made to God from my childhood, that I would remain in the purity of the one who created me. By this vow I am confident that I will live for him alone, and serve him alone, and abide in him alone, without any pollution, as long as I live."

5 Then everyone began kissing her knees, asking her to forgive their evil suspicions. And all the crowd, along with the priests and all the virgins, led her home with exaltation and joy, crying out and saying to her, "May the name of the Lord be blessed, for he has revealed your holiness to all the people of Israel."

The Journey to Bethlehem
13

1 And then, after some time, a census was ordered by an edict of Caesar Augustus, so that everyone had to hurry to their native land.[11] This census was the first made while Cyrinus was the governor of Syria, and it compelled Joseph to go with Mary to Bethlehem, because Joseph and Mary were from the tribe of Judah and from the house and ancestry of David. While, therefore, Joseph and Mary were going on the road that led to Bethlehem, Mary said to Joseph: "I see two peoples before me, one weeping and the other rejoicing." Joseph responded to her, "Sit and hold onto the donkey, and do not speak any unnecessary words to me." Then a beautiful child appeared before them, dressed in bright clothing; and he said to Joseph, "Why do you say that these words that you have heard about the two peoples are unnecessary? For she has seen the Jewish people weeping because they are moving away from God, and she has observed the gentile people rejoicing, because they are coming to the Lord, as he promised to your fathers, Abraham, Isaac, and Jacob. For the time is coming when in the seed of Abraham the blessing will be bestowed on all people."

2 When he said these things, he commanded the donkey to stop and he instructed Mary to come down from the animal and to enter a cave which had always been dark, since it had never seen the light of day. But when Mary entered, the entire cave began to shine with great splendor. It was as if the sun

11. Luke 2:1.

were inside, so the whole cave began to produce a brilliant light; and it was like noontime inside, so the divine light lit up that cave. This light did not diminish day or night, until Mary brought forth a son, whom the angels surrounded at birth. And once he was born and standing firmly on his feet, they worshiped him, saying, "Glory to God in the highest and on earth, peace among people of good will."[12]

Mary Is Inspected by the Midwives

3 When Joseph found Mary with the infant she had borne, he said to her, "I have brought Zahel, a midwife, to you. Look, she is standing outside the entrance to the cave, unable to enter because of the great brightness." When Mary heard this she smiled. But Joseph said to her, "Do not smile, but take care so that she can examine you, to see if you may need her medicine." And Mary ordered her to come in to her. When Mary allowed herself to be inspected, the midwife cried out with a great voice, "Great Lord, have mercy! Before now, nothing like this has been heard of or even suspected—the breasts are full of milk and the boy who has been born shows the virginity of his mother. No stain of blood can be found on the child, and no pain has appeared in the mother. A virgin has given birth and after giving birth she has remained a virgin!"

4 Another midwife named Salome heard her say this and said, "Certainly I will not believe this unless I examine her myself." Salome came in to Mary and said to her, "Allow me to inspect you, so that I might know if what Zahel told me is true." Mary permitted herself to be inspected; but as soon as Salome pulled her right hand away from the examination, her hand withered and she began to be greatly distressed by the pain and to cry out, weeping and saying, "Lord, you know that I have always feared you and have taken care of the poor asking for nothing in return. I have accepted nothing from the widow and the orphan, and I have never sent the impoverished away empty handed. Behold, I have become wretched because of my disbelief, because I dared to put your virgin to the test, who brought forth the light, and remained a virgin after giving birth."

5 While she was saying this, a luminous young man appeared next to her and said, "Go up to the child and worship him; touch him with your hand and he will heal you, for he is the savior of all who hope in him." Salome immediately went up and worshiped the child; she touched the fringe of the swaddling clothes that covered him, and right away her hand was healed. She then went outside and began to cry out, speaking about the great miracle that she had seen, about what she had suffered and how she had been cured, so that many came to believe by her proclamation.

12. Luke 2:14.

Witnesses to Christ's Character

6 There were also some shepherds who were claiming to have seen angels in the middle of the night, singing a hymn to God; from them they heard that the savior of humans had been born, who is Christ the Lord, in whom the salvation of Israel would be re-established.[13]

7 And also a gigantic star was shining from evening until morning. This star was signaling the birth of Christ, who would restore not only Israel but also all the nations, as he promised.

14

1 On the third day after the Lord's birth, Mary left the cave and came into a stable, and she placed the child in a manger. And an ox and an ass bent their knees and worshiped him. Then was fulfilled what was spoken by Isaiah the prophet, who said, "The ox has recognized its owner and the ass the manger of its lord."[14] These animals were around him, constantly worshiping him. Then was fulfilled what was spoken by Habbakuk the prophet, who said, "Between the two animals you will make yourself known."[15] Joseph and Mary stayed in the same place with the child for three days.

15

1 On the sixth day he entered Bethlehem, where he spent seven days. On the eighth day he brought the child to the temple of the Lord. And when the child received circumcision, they offered up for him a pair of turtle doves and two young doves.[16]

2 There was a man of God in the temple, a prophet who was righteous, whose name was Simeon, who was 112 years old.[17] He had received from God an answer to prayer: he would not taste death until he saw Christ, the Son of God, in the flesh. When he saw the child he exclaimed with a loud voice, "God has visited his people; God has fulfilled his promise." And he hastened to worship the child. After this he took him up in his garment and worshiped him and kissed the soles of his feet, saying, "Now send your servant away in peace, O Lord; for my eyes have seen your salvation, which you prepared in the view of all the people, a light for a revelation to the nations and glory to your people, Israel."

13. Luke 22:15–19.

14. Isa. 1:3.

15. See Hab. 3:2 in the Latin version; the Hebrew reads differently.

16. Luke 2:21–24.

17. Luke 2:25–35.

3 Also in the temple of the Lord was Anna, the daughter of Phanuel.[18] She had lived with her husband seven years from the time of her virginity. She was now a widow, eighty-four years old. She never left the temple of the Lord, but devoted herself to fastings and prayers. She also came up to the child and worshiped him, saying that in him would be the redemption of the age.

The Visit of the Magi
16

1 Two years later, magi came from the East to Jerusalem, bringing great gifts; and they fervently asked the Jews: "Where is the king who has been born to us? For we saw his star in the East and we have come to worship him."[19] When this news reached King Herod, it so terrified him that he summoned the scribes, Pharisees, and teachers of the people and inquired from them where the prophets had predicted the Christ would be born. They told him, "In Bethlehem, for so it is written, 'And you Bethlehem, land of Judah, you are not least among the leading lands of Judah, for from you will go forth a leader who will rule my people Israel.'" Then King Herod summoned the magi and carefully inquired from them how the star had appeared to them; and he sent them to Bethlehem saying, "Go, and when you find him report back to me, so I may also come to worship him."

2 As the magi advanced on the road the star appeared, and as if providing them guidance it preceded them until they came to the place where the child was. And when the magi saw the star they rejoiced with a great joy, and entering in they found the child Jesus sitting on Mary's lap. Then they opened their treasures and gave expensive gifts to Mary and Joseph (and to the infant himself a piece of gold). One offered gold, another incense, and the third myrrh. When they wanted to return to King Herod, they were warned in a dream what Herod was planning. They then worshiped the infant again and with great joy they returned to their own region by a different way.

The Wrath of Herod and the Flight to Egypt
17

1 When King Herod saw that he had been deceived by the magi, his heart was inflamed and he sent his soldiers out on every path, wishing to capture them. When he was not able to find a trace of them, he sent soldiers to Bethlehem and

18. Luke 2:36–38.
19. Matt. 2:1–12.

killed every infant from two years and under, according to the time that he had solicited from the magi.[20]

2 One day before Herod had done this, Joseph was warned by an angel of the Lord, "Take Mary and the child and go, take the desert route to Egypt."[21]

Baby Jesus Is Worshiped by Dragons and Other Wild Beasts
18

1 When they arrived at a certain cave where they wanted to cool themselves off, Mary came off the donkey and sat down, and held Jesus on her lap. There were three male servants with them on the road, and one female servant with Mary. And behold, suddenly many dragons came out of the cave. When the servants saw them they cried out. Then the Lord, even though he was not yet two years old, roused himself, got to his feet, and stood in front of them. And the dragons worshiped him. When they finished worshiping him, they went away. Then was fulfilled what was spoken by the prophet in the Psalms, who said, "Praise the Lord from the earth, O dragons and all the places of the abyss."[22]

2 The Lord Jesus Christ, though just a small child, walked along with them so that he might not be a burden to anyone. Mary and Joseph were saying to one another, "It would be better for those dragons to kill us than to harm the child." Jesus said to them, "Do not think of me as a young child, for I have always been the perfect man, and am now; and it is necessary for me to tame every kind of wild beast."

19

1 So too both lions and leopards were worshiping him and accompanying him in the desert, wherever Mary went with Joseph. They went before them showing them the way and being subject to them; and bowing their heads with great reverence they showed their servitude by wagging their tails. But on the first day that Mary saw lions, leopards, and various other wild beasts surrounding them, she was terrified. The young child Jesus smiled in her face and spoke to her with a consoling word, saying, "Do not fear, Mother, for they are hastening along, not to hurt you but to serve you." With these words he removed the fear from their hearts.

2 And so lions, asses, oxen, and beasts of burden carrying their baggage were all walking together with them, and whenever they made a stop, they would

20. Matt. 2:16–18.
21. Matt. 2:13–15.
22. Ps. 148:7.

graze. There were also tame goats who came out with them and followed them from Judah; these were walking among the wolves with no fear. One was not afraid of another, and none of them was harmed by another in any way. Then was fulfilled what Isaiah said, "Wolves will pasture with sheep and the lion and ox will eat straw together."[23] There were two oxen used as pack animals with them on the way; lions guided them on the way of our Lord Jesus Christ, whose baggage they were carrying.

The Miracle of the Palm Tree
20

1 Then, after these things, on the third day after they had started out, Mary was weary from too much sun in the wilderness, and seeing a palm tree she wanted to rest awhile in its shade. Joseph hastened to lead her to the palm and he had her descend from the donkey. When Mary sat down, she looked to the foliage on the palm and saw that it was full of fruit, and she said, "If only I could get some of that fruit from the palm!" Joseph said to her, "I am surprised that you're saying this, when you can see how high the palm is. You are thinking of the fruit of the palm; but I am thinking about the water that we no longer have in our water skins; we have nowhere to replenish them to quench our thirst."

2 Then the young child Jesus, sitting in the lap of his mother, the virgin, cried out to the palm tree and said, "Bend down, O tree, and refresh my mother from your fruit." Immediately when he spoke, the palm tree bent its top down to Mary's feet. Everyone gathered the fruit in it and was refreshed. After all its fruit had been gathered, the tree remained bent, expecting that it would rise up at the command of the one who had ordered it to bend over. Then Jesus said to it, "Stand erect, O palm, and be strong, and become a companion of my trees that are in the paradise of my Father. And open up from your roots the hidden springs, that water may flow from them to quench our thirst." Immediately the palm stood erect, and from its roots springs of water began to come forth, clear, cold, and very sweet. When they saw the springs of water flowing, they all rejoiced with a great joy and drank, together with their beasts and companions, giving thanks to God.

21

1 They set out on the next day. But as they started their journey, Jesus turned to the palm tree and said, "I give you this privilege, O palm: one of your branches will be taken by my angels and planted in the paradise of my Father. Moreover,

23. Isa. 11:6.

I will bestow this blessing on you, that whoever emerges victorious from a contest will be told, 'You have attained to the palm.'" While he was saying this, behold an angel of the Lord appeared, standing above the palm tree. Removing one of its branches it went flying away. When everyone saw this they fell on their faces to the ground as if dead. Then Jesus spoke to them and said, "Why has fear seized your hearts? Do you not know that this palm that I have had moved will be available to all the saints in the place of delights, just as it was available to you in this desert?"

The Shortcut to Egypt
22

1 Joseph said to him, "Lord, since this great heat is burning us up, if you wish let us take the route by the sea, so that we can pass through the coastal cities in order to rest." Jesus said to him, "Do not fear Joseph; I will shorten the stages along the way for you, so that you will reach your humble abode in this single day, when it would normally take you thirty days of haste." While he was saying this, they looked up and saw the mountains of Egypt and its plains.

2 While rejoicing and exulting, they entered one of the cities, called Sohennen. Since they knew no one there to provide them with hospitality, they went into a temple which is called the capitol of this city in Egypt. In this temple were placed 365 idols, to each of whom the impious were paying divine honors on a separate day.

Jesus Is Worshiped by the Pagan Idols
23

1 Then, when Mary entered the temple with her young child, all the images fell, and every idol, cast on its face, showed itself clearly to be nothing. Then was fulfilled what the prophet said, "Behold, the Lord will come on a swift cloud, and all the handiwork of the Egyptians will be moved from before his face."[24]

24

1 When word reached Afrodisius, he came to the temple with his entire army and all his friends and companions. But all the priests of the temple were hoping that he would say nothing against those who had caused the idols to fall. When he entered the temple and saw that what he had heard was true, he immediately went up to Mary and began to worship the young child Mary was holding in her

24. Isa. 19:1.

lap as the Lord. And after he worshiped him, he spoke out to his entire army and all his friends, and said, "If this one were not the Lord of these our gods, they would not have prostrated themselves before him; nor would they lie prostrate in his presence and declare him to be their Lord. And so, if we ourselves do not very carefully do what we have seen our gods do, we are all in great danger of incurring his wrath and being destroyed, just as happened to Pharoah, king of Egypt, who lived in those days when God performed great miracles in Egypt and led forth his people by his mighty hand."

5

The Latin Infancy Gospels (J Composition)

Arundel Form

The Latin Infancy Gospel, more recently labeled the "J Composition" (for reasons explained below) is a later account of the births and early lives of Mary and Jesus, based largely (though not exclusively) on a reworking of the Proto-Gospel of James (from a lost Latin translation) and of the Gospel of Pseudo-Matthew. Included in the narrative are the events surrounding the birth of Mary, her early life, her betrothal to Joseph, her conception, the birth of Jesus, the trip to Egypt, and Jesus' miracles as a young boy. Also included here, however, is unique material drawn from an otherwise unknown Latin source, including accounts of the conversations of Joseph and his son Symeon both before and after Mary gives birth (ch. 66), declarations by the midwife and the wise men about Mary and Jesus (chs. 70–76; 93–94); and a story of a compassionate robber (chs. 111–25).

The text was first edited by M. R. James in 1927, who recognized that it survived in two different recensions, one preserved in a fourteenth-century manuscript in the British Library (Arundel 404, ms. A) the other in a thirteenth-century manuscript found in the Hereford Cathedral Library (Hereford 0. 3. 9, ms. H). Since James's edition more manuscripts of each recension have been discovered; the most recent edition has been produced by J.-D. Kaestli and M. McNamara, who have replaced James's vague title ("The Latin Infancy Gospels") by designating the work as the J Composition, in honor of James himself.

The earliest manuscript of the Gospel in either form is from Montpellier, dating from around 800. It preserves the first twenty-one paragraphs of the Arundel recension (known as JAr). Even though this manuscript is at least three hundred years older than any of our other witnesses, Kaestli and McNamara judge that it does not preserve the earliest form of the text but represents a later, more heavily edited version.

Since the Gospel heavily utilizes Pseudo-Matthew, it must have been composed some time after the mid-seventh century and, obviously, before the end of the eighth century (the date of ms M). Its place of origin is not known.

There is some question about the Special Source (that is, for the material not drawn from the Proto-Gospel or Pseudo-Matthew), especially for the traditions found in chs. 59–97. James believed these materials contained a docetic Christology (in which Jesus only "appeared" to be human) and so he assigned the source to the one docetic Gospel with which he was familiar, the Gospel of Peter. This view has not met with widespread assent. Some scholars have been more persuaded by a quotation by Sedulius Scottus, allegedly drawn from "The Gospel according to the Hebrews," which coincides closely with the Special Source. P. Vielhauer and J. Gijsel have suggested that the Source was therefore the Gospel of the Nazareans, which now survives otherwise only in fragments (as later presented in this collection). This view too has not won many supporters. The reality is that we simply cannot know where the unknown author of the J Composition derived his unique traditions.

The translation that we provide here follow the more famous Arundel recension, as reconstructed by Kaestli and McNamara and used with permission.

We do not reproduce the entire Gospel here, since the earlier chapters closely parallel the Proto-Gospel and Pseudo-Matthew, but only selections from chapter 59–97 and 111–25. These portions of the Gospel contain much of the unique material, although even here there are overlaps with the earlier traditions, especially Pseudo-Matthew.

Bibliography

Enslin, M. "Hagiographic Mistletoe," *Journal of Religion* 25.1 (1940): 10–24.

Gijsel, J. "Les 'Évangiles latins de l'Enfance' de M. R. James," *AnBoll* 94 (1976): 289–302.

James, M.R. *Latin Infancy Gospels. A New Text, with a Parallel Version from the Irish.* Cambridge: Cambridge University Press, 1927.

Kaestli, J.-D. and M. McNamara, eds. *Latin Infancy Gospels: The J Compilation.* Appendix of *Apocrypha Hiberniae I. Evangelia Infantiae.* Vol. 2. CCSA 14. Turnhout: Brepols, 2001; pp. 619–880.

McNamara, M., et al., eds. *Apocrypha Hiberniae I. Evangelia Infantiae.* Vol. 1. CCSA 13. Turnhout: Brepols, 2001; pp. 41–134.

De Strycher, É. *La forme la plus ancienne du Protévangile de Jacques. Recherches sur le Papyrus Bodmer 5 avec une édition critique du texte grec et une traduction annote.* Brussels: Société des Bollandistes, 1961; pp. 364–71.

The Latin Infancy Gospels (J Compilation: Arundel Form)

[. . .]

The Journey to Bethlehem for the Census

59 But in those days an edict went out from Augustus Caesar that everyone should register[1] by hurrying to their own native land[2] and making a transcript of all their belongings, both for themselves and for their wives and children, as well as for their male and female servants. They were also to declare their estates, cattle, money owed to them, and their household possessions. And so they all returned to the places where they had been born to file for the census and taxes.[3]

60 When therefore that decree had gone out to all Judea under the governor of Syria, Cyrinus, it was necessary that Joseph, who was a carpenter,[4] and who was formerly called Moab,[5] set out for Bethlehem with his sons and with Mary, who was betrothed to him, and whom he had received from the temple of the Lord[6] because Joseph and Mary were from the tribe of Judah and the land of David.[7]

Mary's Vision of Two People

61 As they thus traveled on the road, Mary said to Joseph, "I see two people before me, one weeping and the other rejoicing." Joseph replied to her, "Sit on the donkey and do not speak any unnecessary words to me!" Then a beautiful child appeared before them, clad in bright clothing, saying to Joseph, "Why did you say that the words you had heard about the two people are unnecessary? For she has seen the people of the Jews weeping because they have departed from God, and she sees the people of the gentiles rejoicing because they have come to God, according to what God promised to your fathers, Abraham, Isaac, and Jacob. For the time is come that a blessing should be bestowed on all nations in the seed of Adam."[8] And saying this he withdrew from their sight.

1. See Luke 2:1.
2. See Ps.-Mt. 13.1.
3. See Luke 2:3.
4. See Matt. 13:55.
5. The name Moab may be related to Joseph's lineage from the house of David (Luke 2:4): see the beginning of the *Book of Ruth*, where a relative of David's grandfather emigrates from Bethlehem to Moab. See McNamara et al. (2001) 13:79, 218–19.
6. See Prot. Jas. 19.3.
7. See Luke 2:4; Ps.-Mt. 13.1.
8. See Gen. 12:3; the whole chapter reproduces almost verbatim the text of Ps.-Mt. 13.1.

Joseph in Search for a Lodging Pllace

62 (1) But Joseph went forward to the city, while Mary remained behind with his son Symeon because she was pregnant and walked slowly. (2) Having entered Bethlehem, his native land, standing in the center of the city he said, "There is nothing more fitting than that one should love one's city. Indeed, the true repose for every human being is to repose in one's own tribe. Now I see you after a long time, Bethlehem, the fair house of David the king and God's prophet."

63 And marching around he saw a solitary little house and said, "I should stay in this place because it seems to me to be an abode for visiting strangers; for I do not have any lodging here or a guest-chamber where we could rest." And looking around it he said, "This is a humble dwelling indeed, but fitting for poor people, particularly because it is so far from human clamor that it cannot harm a woman in labor. In this place, therefore, I must take rest with all who are mine."

The Arrival of Mary

64 (1) And when he was saying this, he went outside and looked down the road, and there he saw Mary approaching with Symeon. (2) When they had thus arrived to him, Joseph said, "Symeon, my son, why have you been long in coming?" He responded, "If it were not for me, lord father, then Mary would have delayed because of her pregnancy, as she often paused on the way and grew tired; for I was worried all the time that she would go into labor on the road. But I thank the Most High for giving her endurance; for as far as I can guess, and as she herself is saying, she is about to give birth." When he had said these things, he commanded the donkey to stand still, and Mary came down from the animal.[9]

65 Then Joseph said to Mary, "My child, you have had great exertion because of me. Go inside, therefore, and take care of yourself. And you, Symeon, fetch water and wash her feet, and give her food and, should she need anything else, do as her heart wishes." So Symeon did what his father ordered and led her to a cave which, upon Mary's entrance, welcomed the daylight and began to shine as if it were noon.[10]

66 (1) But once inside, she herself did not remain at rest, but she was unceasingly giving thanks within herself. Symeon said to his father, "Father, what are we to think this maiden is experiencing, for she is speaking to herself all the

9. This sentence is taken from Ps.-Mt. 13.2.

10. See Ps.-Mt. 13.2.

time?" Joseph said to him, "She cannot speak to you because she is tired from the journey. For this reason she speaks to herself—in fact, she is giving thanks." (3)[11] And he approached her and said, "Arise, lady daughter, climb into bed and rest."

The Visit and Witness of the Midwife

67 Saying these things he went outside. After a little while, Symeon followed him and said, "Hurry, lord father, come quickly. Mary is asking for you; for she is very much in want of you. Indeed, I think her delivery is near." Joseph said to him, "I will not leave her; you rush quickly, since you are young, go into the city and look for a midwife to come in to the girl, for a midwife is a great help for a woman in labor." Symeon replied, "I am not known in this city. How can I find a midwife? But hear me, lord father: I know, indeed I am certain, that the Lord cares for her and will give her a midwife and a nurse, and everything else she needs."

68 (1) And as they spoke these things, behold, a young woman was coming with a chair on which it was customary to assist women in labor, and she began to wait. When they thus saw her, they were amazed, and Joseph said to her, "My child, where are you going with this chair?" The maiden responded, "My mistress sent me to this place because a youth came to her in a great hurry, saying to her, 'Come quickly to pull out a new baby, for the maiden is about to give birth to her first offspring'. Hearing this, my mistress sent me on ahead of her. For behold, she herself is following me." (2)[12] Joseph looked about and indeed saw her coming, and he went out to meet her and they greeted one another. And the midwife said to him, "Man, where are you going?" He replied, "I am looking for a Hebrew midwife." The woman said to him, "Are you from Israel?" And Joseph said to her, "I am from Israel." The woman said to him, "Who is the maiden who is giving birth in this cave?" Joseph replied, "Mary, who has been betrothed to me, and who was reared in the temple of the Lord." The midwife said to him, "Is she not your wife?" "She has been betrothed to me," replied Joseph, "but she has conceived by the Holy Spirit." The midwife said to him, "Is it true what you are saying?" Joseph replied to her, "Come and see."

69 They entered the cave, and Joseph said to her, "Go and visit her." As she wanted to move deeper into the cave, she became afraid because a great light shone in it, which did not diminish day or night, as long as Mary remained there.[13] Joseph then said to Mary: "Behold, I have brought Rachel, a midwife, to

11. 66(2) is omitted here, as it is found only in the Irish Infancy gospels (*Liber Flavus Fergusiorum* and *Lebhear Breac*). The Latin "J compilation", of which the Arundel text is one of the main representatives, has already narrated a similar episode about Mary's vision of the two peoples, in this case borrowed from Ps.-Mt. 13.1, in chap. 61. See above, n. 8.

12. For the whole second paragraph see the parallel text in Prot. Jas. 19.1.

13. See Ps.-Mt. 13.2.

you; look, she is standing outside in front of the cave and she dares not enter here because it is too bright, nor indeed can she." When Mary heard this, she smiled. Joseph said to her, "Do not smile, but be wary; for she has come to examine you, in case you need medicine." And she instructed her to come in to her, and she began to stand before her. After Mary allowed herself to be inspected for hours, the midwife cried out with a loud voice and said, "Great Lord God, have mercy, for this has so far never been heard of or seen, or even suspected, that the breasts are full of milk yet the newborn boy declares her a virgin: no stain of blood has befallen the child, and no pain has appeared on her while delivering. A virgin has conceived, a virgin has given birth, and after giving birth has remained a virgin!"[14]

70 (1) Since the midwife was delaying in the cave, Joseph entered. The midwife ran to meet him, and they both proceeded outside and found Symeon waiting. (2) Symeon questioned her, saying, "Mistress, what is happening with the girl? Can she have some hope for her life?" The midwife said to him, "What is that you say, man? Sit down and I will tell you about a marvelous event." (3) And raising her eyes to heaven, the midwife said with a clear voice, "Almighty Father, what is this great marvel I have seen, by which I am astounded? What are my deeds that have made me worthy to see your holy sacraments, so that you have prepared your handmaid to come here and to see the wonders of your blessings, my Lord? What should I do? How can I relate what I have seen?" (4) Symeon said to her, "I entreat you to reveal to me what you have seen." The midwife said to him, "This thing will not be hidden from you because it has many blessings. So attend to my words and keep them in your heart.

71 When I came in to inspect the girl, I found her with her face upward, gazing up into heaven and talking to herself—though I suspect that she prayed and gave blessings to the Most High. When I had thus come to her, I said to her, 'Daughter, tell me, do you not feel some pain, or is there not some spot on your body seized with pain?' But as if she had not heard anything, she remained as still as a solid rock, gazing up into heaven.

72 In that hour all became quiet with deep silence and awe. For even winds stopped and gave no breeze, and not a single leaf on trees was stirred nor sound of waters heard; rivers did not flow, nor did the sea wave, and all the gushing waters grew silent; no human voice made a sound, and there was great silence. For indeed, from that hour on even the heavenly firmament had ceased its rapid course and the measures of hours all but passed away. All things had become silent in a great awe and stupefied, while we were attending on the coming of the Highness, the end of the ages.[15]

14. See Ps.-Mt. 13.3.
15. See Heb. 9:26.

73 (1) When therefore the hour came near, the power of God went forth openly. (2) And the girl, standing and gazing into heaven, became as white as snow. For the determined time of the blessings was already coming forth. When the light had thus come forth, she adored the one she saw she had borne. And the child himself was radiating intensely round about like the sun,[16] clean and most pleasant to look at, because he appeared alone as peace bringing calm to everything. (3) Now in that hour in which he was born, the voice of many invisible ones was heard, saying 'Amen' in unison. And that same newborn light was multiplied, and the clarity of its brightness darkened the brightness of the sun. And this cave was filled with clear brightness, together with a most sweet odor. Thus, in fact, was this light born as the dew that comes down from heaven to the earth. For its odor gives off a fragrance that is stronger than any scent of ointments.

74 (1) Now I stood stupefied and marveling, and fear gripped me; for I was looking upon the astounding clarity of the brightness that was born. But that light, little by little withdrawing into itself, assimilated itself to the child, and in a moment the child came to be as children are normally born.[17] (2) And I put on boldness and bent down and touched him, and lifted him up in my hands with great fear, and I was frightened because there was no weight in him as of a newborn person. (3) And I inspected him, and there was no defilement in him,[18] but it was as if he was bathed in the dew of God the Most High, shining in his body, light to carry, and brilliant to look at. And while I was greatly amazed that he was not crying, as newborn children normally do, (4) and while I held him looking into his face, he smiled at me with a most pleasant smile, and opening his eyes he gazed at me intently; and immediately a great light came forth from his eyes like a great lightning."

75 When Symeon heard these things, he replied, "O blessed woman, who was worthy to see and proclaim this new and holy sight! I am fortunate because I heard these things and, even though I did not see, nevertheless believed."[19] The midwife said to him, "I have yet to reveal to you a marvelous event for your amazement." Symeon replied, "Reveal, O mistress, for I rejoice hearing these things." The midwife said to him, "In that hour in which I carried the child in my hands, I saw that he had a clean body, which was not defiled like other humans who are born with impurity. And I was concerned in my heart lest perchance

16. "Like the sun" renders M. R. James's conjecture *solis modo,* based on the Hereford reading *ad modum solis* (JHer 73.2); the Arundel manuscript has *solummodo,* "in a unique fashion."

17. This nondocetic rendering of the passage stands at odds with James translation, p. xxi: "But that light by little and little withdrawing into itself, *made itself like to an infant,* and in a moment *it became an infant* as infants are wont to be born."

18. Cf. supra 69 and Ps.-Mt. 13.3.

19. See John 20:29.

there might remain inside the girl's womb some residues[20] to be cut free. For this sometimes happens to women at childbirth, and for this reason they are in peril and feel disheartened. And straightaway I called up Joseph and gave the child into his hands. And I approached the girl, touched her, and found her clean from blood. But what should I relate? What should I say? I am confused. I do not know how I could explain such great brightness of the living God. But you, O Lord, are my witness that I have touched her with my hands and found the girl who had given birth a virgin, not only from childbirth but also from having sex with a man. In that very hour I cried out with a mighty voice and glorified God, and I fell on my face and worshiped him. After this I went outside. And Joseph, for his part, wrapped the child in swaddling clothes and laid him in a manger."[21]

76 Symeon said to her, "Has he given you some reward?" The midwife replied, "I rather owe a reward and a debt of gratitude and prayer. Indeed I have promised to offer a flawless sacrifice to God, who has deemed me worthy to be the examiner and witness of this mystery. For instead of the gifts that are offered in the temple of the Lord, I am offering the gift on my own.[22] Saying this, she told her apprentice, "Little daughter, pick up the chair and let us go. For today my old age has seen that the pregnant woman has given birth without pangs and as a virgin—if indeed this ought to be called birth. For I suspect in my mind that she has abandoned herself to the will of the everlasting God." And saying this, she left with her.

Salome's Incredulity[23]

77 Now it came to pass that, while they traveled, another midwife met them, Salome by name,[24] and they greeted one another. The midwife said to her, "I have some news to tell you, Salome." She replied, "What sort of news?" The midwife said, "A virgin has given birth to a boy, and her nature as a virgin has remained intact, which has hardly ever been seen." Salome said to her, "Is it a male that the virgin has given birth to? The midwife responded, "A virgin gave birth to a male." Salome said to her, "As surely as the Lord lives, I will not believe unless I examine her myself,[25] and unless I put my hand in and look her over

20. Lit. "fetuses."

21. See Luke 2:7.

22. The Hereford form (JHer) has instead: "And since I have promised to offer a flawless sacrifice in the temple of the Lord, I am rather offering myself as a gift instead of the gifts to Almighty God."

23. The Salome episode is preserved only in the Latin versions of the Infancy narrative (77–80), in a form that is based on Prot. Jas. 19.3–20.3 and further enriched with the borrowings from Ps.-Mt. 13.4–5.

24. See Ps.-Mt. 13.4.

25. See Ps.-Mt. 13.4.

carefully, I will not believe that the virgin has given birth."[26] The midwife said to her, "Let us go to her together." When they came in to Mary, Salome said to her, "My child, allow me to inspect you to learn if that which Rachel said to me is true."[27] When Mary permitted this, she gave her a full inspection and thus found it to be as the midwife had told her.

78 But as soon as she pulled her hand away from the examination, it withered from the excessive splendor. And because of the pain she began to be greatly distressed, and weeping she cried out and said,[28] "Woe to my wickedness and disbelief, for I have put the Lord to the test, and see, my hand is withering by fire."[29] She kneeled before the Lord and said, "Lord, God of my fathers, remember me, for I am of the seed of Abraham, Isaac, and Jacob. You should not make this a portent to the sons of Israel,[30] but rather deliver me over to your poor. Lord, you know that I have always feared you; that I have provided every care for them in your name and cured all of the poor without receiving anything; and that I have inflicted no pain on anyone and expected my reward from you. From the widow and orphan I have accepted nothing, and I have not let the poor go empty handed. Behold, I have become wretched because of my disbelief, because I boldly came to test your virgin who had given birth to the great light, and remained a virgin after giving birth."[31]

79 While she was saying these things, a splendid young man appeared before her, saying to her, "Salome, approach the boy and worship him; bring your hand and touch him, and he will heal it, for he is the one who will save you, the Savior of the world, a hope for all who believe in him."[32] Salome immediately approached the boy and said, "Lord, should I touch you or worship you first?"[33] And worshiping the child she touched the fringe of the swaddling clothes in which he was wrapped, and immediately her hand was healed. She went outside and began to proclaim the great miracles she had seen, and what she had suffered and how she had been cured, so that many came to believe her proclamation,[34] saying, "This boy, who is the son of God, has been born a king in Israel."[35]

26. See Prot. Jas. 19.3.

27. See Prot. Jas. 20.1. In chap. 69 as well as in the parallel passage in Ps.-Mt. 13.4 the midwife is identified as Zachel.

28. See Ps.-Mt.13.4.

29. See Prot. Jas. 20.1.

30. See the Hereford form ad loc. "You should not make me a portent in Israel . . ."

31. See Ps.-Mt. 19.4.

32. See Ps.-Mt. 19.5 and Prot. Jas. 20.3.

33. See Prot. Jas. 20.4.

34. See Ps.-Mt. 19.5.

35. See Prot. Jas. 20.4.

80 Now as the midwife and Salome journeyed on the road, a voice came saying, "Salome, mind you don't talk further about the wonders you have seen until the boy enters Jerusalem."[36]

The Visit and Witness of the Shepherds[37]

81 Now Joseph came out of the cave into the forecourt and said, "O new order of things! O strange childbirth! How I have become a father I know not; for, behold, today a son has been born to me who is Lord of all." While he was saying this, he went to the road outside and said, "Today it is fitting for me to search for some food, especially since it is the birthday of this boy. For I believe that today a great glory is celebrated in heaven and that all the archangels and all the heavenly powers are rejoicing. And it is therefore fitting for me to do justice to this very day in which the glory of God has appeared for the whole earth."

82 (1) While he was saying this, he saw the shepherds coming and speaking to each other, "Behold, we have gone around the whole of Bethlehem and we have not found what has been said to us outside the city. Let us enter, then, and search in these places nearby." (2) Joseph said to them, "Do you have any lamb or kid for sale, or hens or eggs?" They said to him, "We have none of these here with us." Joseph said to them, "Not even country herbs or cheese?" They replied to him, "O man, why are you making fun of us? We have come for another great thing, yet you keep asking us about things for sale." Joseph said to them, "What is it that you have come for?" They said, "If you hear, you will be amazed." Joseph said to them, "If you tell me, then I will also tell you about a wonder that I have in my guest-house."

83 (1) The shepherds said to him, "Last night we sat watching on a hill, and the moon rose bright as a clear day. Now we were keeping watch over our flock,[38] as is our custom, because of thieves and wolves. And we were telling stories to one another, while some were singing and playing hide-and-seek, and we were very happy at that hour.[39] (2) But as these things were happening among us, suddenly a large and powerful man appeared to us, coming from the east. He came to us, then, shining round in the glory of God, and round about him we saw a great multitude of chariots. When we saw it, we fell on our faces smitten with great fear. (3) But he said to us with a loud voice, 'Fear not, O shepherds! For behold, I have come to you to proclaim to you the glory of God

36. See Prot. Jas. 20.4.

37. For a similar yet more detailed and expanded version of this section see the parallel text in the Irish Leabhar Breac infancy narrative (InfLB), 81–85, ed. McNamara et al. (2001) 13:324–42.

38. See Luke 2:8.

39. See the variant "in that joy," instead of "in the same region" (Luke 2:8), in the Greek column of Codex Bezae.

and a great joy, not only to you but also to all nations, because today is born Christ the Lord, who is the Savior of all the heavenly powers and humans. Behold, today he has been made manifest in Bethlehem, the city of David. Go, therefore, and you will find him wrapped in swaddling clothes and lying in a manger. Indeed, he is the Son of God, who has come to give eternal life to the nations and to all who believe in him.'[40] (4) When he had said this to us, we heard the voices of many angels singing and saying, 'Glory to God in the highest, and on earth peace to people of good will.' They said these words while singing, as well as many others. We have therefore come here to look for these things, and also to see the gift of God according to what has been said to us."

84 (1) When Joseph heard this, he said, "I am not able to hide this mystery from you. Come, then, and see. For behold, the child who has been born is here in my guest-house. He is indeed Christ the Lord." The shepherds said to him, "Blessed man, show us that child." Joseph said to them, "Come and see where he is lying in a manger." They left at once, and when they looked into the manger and saw the child, they fell prostrate and worshiped him. (3)[41] And they said to Joseph, "We have seen the child filled with God's grace; we adored his arcane secret while he looked at us and smiled most pleasantly in manifold appearances, constantly changing form. For at first he revealed himself to us as most pleasant, as stern and fearsome, and also as most sweet and human, and then again as both small and large. And as soon as he opened his eyes, the great light emanated from his eyes and the sweetest odor from his mouth." (4) They said therefore to him, "O most blessed man, what a son has been born to you, one who is able to save you! And since you have deigned to accept us in peace and permitted us to enter your house and see the glory of God, we invite you to come to our meeting that we may rejoice together, for today all of us shepherds are offering gifts to the almighty God. And so we ask you to agree to come and feast with us today."

85 (1) Joseph replied to them, "You have done well indeed for asking me. Thank you, but it is not right for me to come with you and leave the child alone with his mother. Be assured, however, that I am entirely with you." The shepherds said to him, "Since you have thus decided, then we will go on and send to you the fat of milk and fresh cheeses." (2) Joseph replied to them, "Go in peace." They left rejoicing and glorifying God, claiming that they had seen angels in the middle of the night singing a hymn to God, and that they had heard from them that the Savior of humans had been born, who is Christ the Lord, in whom the salvation of Israel would be restored.[42]

40. See Luke 2:9–12.

41. The second paragraph, which contains the conversation between Joseph and his son Symeon (Semion) while the shepherds are inside the house, is preserved only in the Irish Leabhar Breac Infancy narrative.

42. claiming . . . restored: see Ps.-Mt. 13.6.

86[43] And then there was the third day: an ox and an ass bent their knees at that manger and worshiped him. Then was fulfilled what was said through Isaiah the prophet, "The ox has recognized its owner and the ass the manger of its lord."[44] Now these animals, having him between themselves, bent their knees and worshiped him so that what was spoken by Habakkuk the prophet might be fulfilled, who said, "Between the two animals you will make yourself known."[45] They stayed in the same place with the child for three days. But on the sixth day they entered Bethlehem and spent the seventh day there. And on the eight day, after circumcision was done, the child received the name by which the angel had called him. And when the day of purification had dawned, they made offerings[46] of the poor, for they did not possess the supplies of the rich.

The Visit and Witness of the Magi

87 After many days, that is, after three years of days, Joseph looked out on the journey road and saw a band of wayfarers coming to the cave.

88 For an enormous star was shining over the cave from evening until morning, whose magnitude had never been seen since the beginning of the world. For even the prophets who were in Jerusalem were saying that this star was signaling the birth of Christ, who, as it was promised, would restore not only Israel but also all the nations.[47]

88a[48] And they came to Jerusalem from the East, bringing great gifts, and they earnestly asked the Jews, saying, "Where is the king of the Jews who has been born? For we have seen his star in the East and sensed of his aroma, and so we have come to pay him homage." When this rumor reached King Herod, it disturbed and so terrified him that he sent for the scribes, Pharisees, and teachers of the people and inquired from them where the prophets had predicted the Christ would be born. They told him as it was written: that in Bethlehem of Judah, which is not least among the rulers of Judah, a leader would go forth who would rule the people of Israel.[49] Then King Herod summoned them and carefully inquired from them how the star had appeared to them. And he sent them

43. The chapter draws heavily on Ps.-Mt. 14.1–15.1.

44. See Isa. 1:3.

45. See Hab 3:2 (LXX).

46. the child . . . called him: see Luke 2:21–24.

47. The chapter is a slightly revised version of Ps.-Mt. 13.7.

48. This section, a slightly revised version of Ps.-Mt. 16.1–2 (see also Matt. 2:1–12), is completely absent in the Hereford form (JHer).

49. See Matt. 2:5–6.

away, asking that they search diligently and, when they find out, report back to him so that he also might come and worship him upon collecting a great number of the best possible gifts of all kinds. When they thus went out on the road, the star appeared and, as if providing guidance, moved ahead of them until they came to the place where the child was. When they saw the star, they were overwhelmed with a great joy.

89 (1)[50] But when Joseph saw them, he said, "Who do you think are those coming here to us? It seems to me that they have drawn near after coming a long way. I should therefore get up and meet them." While he thus moved forward, he said to Symeon, "I think that those who are coming are diviners. For behold, they do not rest even for a moment, and they are looking around and arguing among themselves. I also think that they are strangers, for even their appearance differs from ours—indeed, their attire is flowing and its color is purple. Furthermore, they have pointed caps on their heads and shoes on their feet, as those who are free from work.[51] Look, they have stopped and are looking at me. Look again, they are coming here!" (2) When they had thus reached the cave, Joseph said to them, "Who are you? Tell me!" But they rashly wanted to get inside, and indeed they said that they would enter. And Joseph said to them, "For your salvation's sake, tell me who you are, and why you are heading toward my guest-house?" They replied, "Because our guide[52] has entered here before us. (3) Why are you asking us where we are from? We have come from the East because God has sent us here." Joseph said to them, "I ask you to tell me why you have come here." They replied to him, "We are going to tell you, for salvation is for all.

90 (1) We have seen in the sky the star of the King of the Jews, and we have come to worship him; for thus it is written in the old books about the sign of this star, that, when this star appears, the eternal King shall be born and grant immortal life to the just." (2) Joseph said to them, "You should have first searched through Jerusalem, for the sanctuary of God is there." They responded to him,[53] "We have been to Jerusalem and announced to the king that the Christ was born and that we are searching for him. But he said to us, 'I do not know where he has

50. Along with the parallel texts in the Hereford form (JHer) and the Irish Leabhar Breac Infancy Narrative (InfLB), there are two external witnesses to the dialogue between Joseph and his son Symeon at the arrival of the 'magi' in the Arundel ms. (JAr) 87 and 89.1. One is preserved by the mid-ninth-century Irish writer Sedulius Scottus in his *Commentary on Matthew*, and the other is quoted by the glossator of the twelfth-century Irish Gospel-Book of Máel Brigte, ad Matt. 2:11.

51. The Irish Leabhar Breac Infancy Narrative has the following text: "The manner of their aspect is that of a king or leader." The phrase *velud opere deficientes*, "as those free from work," probably indicates a royal way of life.

52. That is, the star. JHer has *dux itineris nostri*, the guide of our journey.

53. For the content of the Magi's report to Joseph (90.2 *Fuimus* to 90.4 *adorem eum*), a vivid elaboration of the reworking of Matt. 2:1–12 in *Ps.-Mt.* 16.1–2, see *above*, 88a.

been born.' (3) Yet he kept sending for all who search the scriptures, and for all the wise men and the chief priests and the teachers, and they came to him. He inquired of them where the Christ was to be born. And they said, 'In Bethlehem of Judah, for thus it is written about him: "And you, Bethlehem, in the land of Judah, shall not be least among the rulers of Judah; for from you shall come forth a leader who is to rule my people Israel."' As soon as we had heard this, we understood it and have come to worship him. For this star appeared, too, and preceded us ever since we set out. (4) But when Herod heard these reports, he was frightened and secretly inquired of us the time when the star had appeared. (5) As we were about to leave, he said, 'Search diligently, and when you have found him, bring word back to me so that I may also come and worship him.'

91 (1) Herod himself gave us his diadem, which he used to wear on his head—this diadem has a white headband—and the royal ring holding a gem, an incomparable token which the king of the Persians had sent him as a gift and which Herod, in his turn, bid us to give as a gift to this child. For Herod himself has promised to bring him a gift if we return to him. (2) We accepted the gifts and departed from Jerusalem. And behold, the star that had appeared to us preceded us from the time we had left Jerusalem all the way to this place. See, it entered this cave in which you stand; and you do not allow us to come inside." (3) Joseph said to them, "I will no longer hinder you. Follow it, for God is your guide—not only yours but also of all those to whom he wanted to reveal his glory." (4) When the Magi heard this, they entered and saluted Mary, saying, "Hail, full of grace!"[54] And when they approached the manger, they looked inside and saw the child.

92 (1) But Joseph said, "Symeon, my son, pay attention and see what these strangers are doing inside; for it is not proper for me to spy on them." (2) And thus he did. He said to his father, "Behold, they entered and saluted the boy, and fell facedown to the ground, and according to the custom of the barbarians they now adore him, one at a time kissing the child's feet. I do not know what it is they are doing." Joseph said to him, "Watch, watch intently." Symeon responded, "Behold, they are opening their treasure chests and offering him gifts." (3) Joseph said to him, "What are they offering?" Symeon, replied, "I think that they are offering those gifts which King Herod sent. For, look, from their purses they have offered to him gold, incense, and myrrh. And they have given many gifts to Mary." (4) Joseph said to him, "These men have done well indeed, for they have not kissed the child without payment—not like those shepherds of ours, who came here without any gifts."[55] (5) Again, he said to him, "Watch more intently and see what they are doing!" So Simeon watched them and said, "Behold, they adore the boy again and, look, they are coming out here!"

54. See Luke 1:28.

55. See *above*, 82.2.

93 (1) They came out and said to Joseph, "O most blessed man, now you know who this boy is whom you are rearing." Joseph said to them, "I believe that he is my son." They said to him, "His name is greater than yours. Yet perhaps you are still worthy to be called his father, for you serve him not as your son but as God and your Lord, and whenever you touch him with your hands, take note of him with great fear and attention. Do not therefore regard us as though we were ignorant, but learn this from us: the one to whom you have been assigned as foster-father is himself the God of gods and the Lord of lords, the God and king of all rulers and powers, God of the angels and of the just. (2) He is the one who will deliver all nations in his name, for his is the majesty and the dominion, and he will crush death's sting and overthrow the power of hell. All kings will serve him, and all the tribes of the earth will worship him, and every tongue will make confession to him,[56] saying, 'You are the Christ Jesus, our redeemer and savior. For you are God, the power and brilliance of the eternal Father.'"

94 (1) Joseph said to them, "Whence have you learned these things you are telling us?" The Magi said to him, "There are, among you, old writings of God's prophets in which it is written about Christ, how his coming is to take place in this age. Likewise, there are even older scriptural writings among us in which it is written about him. (2) And as for the rest of it, since you have asked us how we are able to know this, listen to us. (3) We have learned about it from the sign of the star; for it has appeared to us brighter than the sun. (4) About its brightness nobody has ever been able to say anything. Now this star which has risen indicates that God's offspring will reign in the splendor of daylight. And it did not move about in the center of the sky as the fixed stars are wont to do, or even the planets which, even though they observe a determined course of time, are always said to be wandering—the former ones moving about although they are immobile, and the latter in spite of their undetermined forecast. Yet this one alone is not wandering about. For neither the whole firmament, that is, the sky, seemed to us to be able to contain it in its greatness, nor could the sun darken it by the brilliance of its light as it does with the other stars. The sun itself grew weaker having seen the splendor of its arrival. Indeed, this star is the Word of God; for there are as many words of God as there are stars, but the Word of God is the indescribable God, just as this star is indescribable. (5–7) And it was our companion on the road we traveled as we were coming to Christ."

95 (1) Joseph therefore said to them, "You have delighted me immensely with all these words you have spoken. Now I ask that you deign to stay with me today." (2) They said to him, "We request that you permit us to set out on our journey. For the king has commanded us to return rather swiftly to him." But he detained them.

56. See Phil. 2:9–11.

96 Then they opened their treasure chests and bestowed expensive gifts upon Mary and Joseph. And when they wanted to return to King Herod, that same night they were warned in dreams by an angel of the Lord not to return to Herod. They adored the child with great joy and returned to their own country by another road.[57]

Herod's Massacre and the Flight to Egypt

97 But when Herod saw that he had been tricked by the Magi, his heart was inflamed and, in his great anger, he sent his people out on every road to search them out and capture them. And since he was not able to find them at all, he sent soldiers to Bethlehem and killed all the children according to the time he had learned from the Magi. Now, one day before this had happened, an angel of the Lord appeared to Joseph in dreams and said, "Take the boy and his mother and flee on the desert road to Egypt, for Herod is after the child's life." Then Joseph got up from sleep and did as the angel of the Lord had commanded him.[58]

[. . .]

The Story of the Compassionate Robber[59]

111 When Jesus had thus granted a magnificent reward to the palm of Christ, as told in the story about the place where they spent the night,[60] they began to traverse a solitary desert plain that was both long and wide. Now twelve merciless robbers were frequenting this plain, sparing neither possessions nor lives of those who were passing through. To those traveling with guards they used to say—for they were unable to exercise violence against them—that they had received the permission from the authorities of the neighboring lands to escort

57. See Ps.-Mt. 16.2, based on Matt. 2:11–12.

58. In the two basic manuscript witnesses of the Arundel form of the J compilation, viz. A and V, the narrative of Herod's massacre and the flight to Egypt is followed by (i) Herod's attempt to kill John the Baptist (98) and the murder of the priest Zacharias (99–101), both based on Prot. Jas. 22.3–24.4; (ii) the life and teaching of John the Baptist (102), inspired by the canonical Gospels; (iii) the miracles of the child Jesus during the flight to Egypt and in Egypt (103–109), including the miracle of the bowing palm tree and that of the animals worshiping Jesus (103–106), the fall of the idols, and the conversion of Afrodosius (107.2–109)—all borrowed from Ps.-Mt. 18–24; (iv) the end of the sojourn in Egypt and the subsequent settling in Nazareth (110), based on Ps.-Mt. 25 (see 24.1, 17–19 Gijsel).

59. The story of the holy family's encounter with the compassionate robber is preserved only in the two most important manuscript witnesses of the Arundel form (A and V), and is absent from the Hereford form, which finishes near the end of the preceding section (108).

60. See 106, not translated in this selection. The special privilege granted to the bowing palm (the "palm of Christ") consisted in having one of its branches planted in Paradise. The story is borrowed from Ps.-Mt. 21.

people in this desert for a fee and to protect them from wanderers. It is by trifles of this sort and by robberies that they procured their living, and they inflicted whatever harm they could on those passing through. Yet it often happened that they argued so much among themselves over the division of spoils for the sake of a greater share that they injured each other severely. For this reason, they made an agreement that the total gain of one day would belong to one person and the gain of another day to another, and so on in an orderly sequence. In this way, each one of them could enjoy his allotted daily gain without disquieting his accomplices.

112 One day, however, while they stood in the places of ambush and hoped to acquire something in their abominable way, they saw Joseph with the blessed virgin and their servants coming from afar. Thinking that these were merchants because the cattle that walked with them seemed to be loaded, they kept saying that they would greatly enrich themselves with these people's possessions. For these people, they claimed, were advancing at a slower pace because their load was so heavy. Yet he to whom the gain of that day was due replied to the rest, "Stop and give up your hope, for you will accomplish nothing with such words! Surely, I have never broken the sequence that we all accepted, and so I will enjoy the gain that is due to me on this day. Once I receive it, I wish thereafter to improve my life, and I no longer want to take part in the heinous work done so far. For both my wife and my children are grieved that I have persisted so long in such an ignominious life."

113 While the robbers were thus conversing about these and other things, the blessed company was drawing near. When they noticed the scarcity of the incomers' possessions, the robber was ridiculed by the others for obtaining this sort of booty, as the rest of them were saying, "If you refuse to share this great gain with us, we will retaliate against you when such an opportunity arises again. For it is customary for fellows to recompense one another." They pointed their fingers at him saying, "O worthy sir, you really should depart from our beneficial company in favor of such an honorable gain, which has remained hidden from the ignorant under the semblance of poverty!"

114 He, however, as if stirred into madness by all sorts of sneers and nettling remarks made by the others, gnashed his teeth and said, "I will avenge my immense pain on this old man, whom the Devil has brought to such an advanced age. My little children will be nourished with milk from his flock. As for the boy, since he is of a comely appearance, I will make him serve my son. The mistress and her servants, too, I will put out for sale as quickly as possible. But I still do not know what to do with the old man. I do not see how to make any use of him. The best thing for him is to die; for having already been wasted by old age, he is wasting bread for nothing."

115 Thus, therefore, did the impious robber march with displeasure in front of the most precious treasure, thinking about its value. And grinding his teeth as he hastened toward his dwelling, with his dreadful and grim face he looked now at the boy, now at the mother, and now at the old man. During all that time, the boy did not cease to smile at him; but the old man he found never holding back his tears, for he was overly distressed with concerns not over his own life, but over those of the boy and his mother.

116 But when it seemed fitting to him, who makes both lions and dragons tame (as was confirmed by very clear proofs during that same journey),[61] who is merciful, and who with his might brought back the Israelites from Egypt after taming the fury of the Egyptian king—he suddenly turned the wolf-like robber into a tame lamb. He besprinkled him with the dew of his piety, to the point that the robber showed the feelings of pure compassion and kindness toward those on whom he had earlier pronounced such a cruel sentence. For he said to Joseph, "My dearest, do not wail, but comfort the boy, his mother, and the servants! For, from now on, you will experience only good things from me."

117 After they had exchanged comforting words, the robber said, "Follow me. I will lead the way and prepare a suitable place for your reception." And so, around evening time, Joseph was received with his family into the robber's house and, at the husband's command, laudably provided with all necessary things by the hostess. And since the household took the utmost care of its guests, a bath had already been prepared for the boy. While the boy sat in it, clapping hands at the matron who was holding him, and splashing water in the bath with his hands as children are wont to do, a most pleasant odor arose like a vapor above the water. When the whole house had been filled with the odor of this sort, foam as white as snow appeared on the surface, more fragrant than could be said. As this foam went over the top of the bath and began to flow down on the ground, the lady of the house, who was holding the boy in the bath, gathered it with diligence and respectfully found a place for it, attributing what had happened to divinity rather than to a human force.

118 Next morning after breakfast, the lady of the house exchanged multiple embraces with the guests and then, pressing the boy upon her breast, declared that the mother who had given him birth was blessed since the child of such sweetness had never been seen on earth. When the hostess thus commended them to the Lord, their host took them to the safe place for resuming their journey, and after they thanked their host in many ways for such a friendly hospitality, he commended them to the Creator of All. When they thus parted from one another, Joseph said to Jesus, "Lord, the excessive heat is wearing us down."

119 Joseph was therefore ordered through an angel to return from Egypt,[62] where the gods of the gentiles had been broken into pieces and the wood of

61. See 103–104, borrowed from Ps.-Mt. 18–19.

62. See Matt. 2:19–20.

error cast down,[63] and where Joseph had next revealed the commandments of the Law to those Egyptians who had requested it out of the desire of their pure heart. And taking along his family, he went back the same way he had come so that what had been spoken might be fulfilled, "Out of Egypt I have called my son."[64]

120 When they arrived at the place where they had departed from their host, who on that other occasion had received them so harshly and then sent them away after being stirred up to such a great piety, they took counsel together, saying that they should visit the host and the hostess. So they got off the public road and entered the same narrow path they had taken with the host. Meanwhile, the same host had experienced an event that should not be consigned to oblivion.

121 For one day, when he and his accomplices cruelly attacked certain strong people wanting to pass through the desert, in order to plunder them and kill them, they were so prudently defending their possessions and their lives that a great number of the robbers were killed. Some of them were also afflicted with so many different wounds that they would never be restored to health. Among them all, the aforementioned host was wounded more seriously than the rest, and was delivered back to his house as if he were to be buried. His wife wailed over him with loud cries and ineffable laments, and the robbers who stood by, seeing that no remedy could cure him, left the house at his wife's command.

122 And so, having closed all windows and doors, the wife most devoutly approached the remedy she had collected on that earlier occasion during the boy's bath;[65] for in the meantime she had often used it to drive away the afflictions of her own body. And when she had daubed all of her husband's wounds with great confidence and exuberant prayers, every single wound was healed instantly and without delay. The husband was so fully restored to his previous health that there were no visible scars from the wounds. So when his wife realized by what sort of power the husband had become healed, she gave thanks to God.

123 The wife then summoned all who could be there in person and, when asked about what had happened, she retold in the exact order both the event and the manner in which this ointment had been obtained. When other robbers saw it, they implored that this ointment be sold to them at howsoever high a price. Yet the wife refused and said that she did not want to sell the gift received from God's power. She nevertheless promised that she would bestow some of it for

63. The text refers back to the episode describing the fall of the idols in Sothenen (107.2–109).

64. See Hos. 11:1; for the whole sentence see Matt. 2:13–15, 21.

65. See *above*, 117.

free upon those who made a pious request under extreme necessities. And so each robber, in order to find favor with the wife—so that he might get a share of the remedy should the necessity arise for it—began to serve her with so fervent a zeal that every single hour he would bring to her abode whatever valuable thing he could seize. For this reason, the husband and wife in the end became rich beyond belief; but now they were even more resolved to engage only in good deeds, returning gratitude for their life and riches to God alone and the child whom they had hosted, and from whom also that ointment came.

124 When they had grown rich with a great many goods, as said above, Joseph arrived to their house for a visit, exhausted by his many toils. As the husband saw him there with his family, full of immense joy he hastily called up his wife, and they both ran to meet the visitors and received them in a most cheerful manner, declaring that the cause of all their prosperity was come. After most friendly greetings, while they continued to enjoy one another's company, the host narrated in detail everything that had happened to him since their departure, recounting how he had been healed and made rich on account of that remedy. Having thanked God for all these things, they began to proceed with cheer toward the dining room. There they consumed various dishes, along with an ever increasing number of all sorts of drinks, and they frequently made all kinds of jokes that were not offensive to God before they went to bed in order to rest. The household staff carefully attended to their wellbeing. Next morning, after breakfast, they did not wish to tarry there longer; and although the host assented to their wish, it is impossible to express how much the hostess and her husband were sorry about their hasty departure. The husband himself showed them the road on which they might proceed safely and find food for sale.

125 So when he returned home, commended by them to God, he toiled so hard to do good works that afterwards, hanging on the cross with the Lord, he deserved to obtain pardon for all his sins.[66] May God deign to lead us to them, he who lives and rules forever and ever! Amen.

66. See Luke 23:39–43.

6

History of Joseph the Carpenter

Like other infancy gospels, the History of Joseph the Carpenter attempts to fill the narrative gaps in the opening chapters of Matthew and Luke by shedding more light on the life of and death of "the father of Christ according to flesh." Framed as a revelation given by Jesus to his disciples on the Mount of Olives (1, 30–32), this first-person 'homily' outlines the central moments in Joseph's biography: his background (ch. 2), his relationship with Mary (3–4), his role in Jesus' birth and growing to manhood (chs. 5–14), and his death at the age of hundred and eleven (chs. 15–29). As indicated by its opening section ("This is the departure from the body of our father Joseph"), the text focuses on the circumstances accompanying Joseph's death and on Jesus' miraculous preservation of Joseph's body, followed by the proclamation of his feast-day. Besides its clear purpose for Christian liturgy, the text tries to clarify the ambiguous status that Jesus' adoptive father has in the canonical Gospels. Here Joseph is straightforwardly portrayed as an old widower with children from his previous marriage; this clarifies the New Testament references to Jesus' brothers (chs. 2–4). Joseph's initial doubts about Mary's virginity (ch. 5) are immediately countered by his readiness to register Jesus as the legitimate son (ch. 7), and is further explained by human incapacity to understand divine mysteries (ch. 17). Finally, Jesus' curious reluctance to promise immortality to Joseph during his lifetime, which created a stir among the apostles (chs. 30–31), is amended by a passionate filial care for the father's post-mortem fate: at Jesus' instigation, the soul of Joseph is delivered to heaven (ch. 23) and his body is preserved both from corruption (chs. 25–27) and from end-times tribulations (ch. 31).

The History of Joseph the Carpenter is a complex mixture of ancient literary genres. The "revelatory dialogue" (in which Jesus delivers a revelation, as in other Gospel texts) serves as a narrative frame for two distinct literary units: (1) the biography of Joseph, a kind of Christian midrash on the canonical infancy narratives, which seems heavily indebted to the Proto-Gospel of James, and (2) the account of Joseph's death, to which the text itself refers as a "testament", and which exhibits a number of striking similarities with the

Jewish-Hellenistic genre of "testament' literature" (e.g., the *Testament of Abraham*). The section is also quite similar in form and content to various sixth- and seventh-century Coptic accounts of the passing of the Virgin Mary (the dormition traditions), including the *Sermon on the Virgin's Dormition* delivered by Theodosius of Alexandria in 565. In its present form, the *History of Joseph the Carpenter* is thus a compilation of various traditions concerning Mary and the "holy family," most likely composed in Byzantine Egypt in the late sixth or early seventh century. Some earlier scholars proposed Greek as the original language of this composition, but their linguistic arguments have been rejected by other specialists in favor of a Coptic original.

The text of the History of Joseph the Carpenter is preserved in three different versions: one in Arabic and two in the regional dialects of Coptic—Sahidic and Bohairic, respectively. The Arabic version, attested by a number of both complete and fragmentary manuscript witnesses dating from the fourteenth century onward, was first published by G. Wallin in 1722 along with his own Latin translation. In 1808, E. Quatremère reported his discovery of the complete Bohairic version in an eleventh-century manuscript from the Vatican Library, at that time stored in the Royal Library in Paris. Eventually, P. de Lagarde produced an authoritative critical edition of the Vatican Bohairic manuscript.

The translation here is of de Lagarde's edition, with occasional changes based on a careful examination of photographs of the manuscript. The most significant variants in the other Coptic version (the Sahidic fragments) are given in footnotes.

Bibliography

Aranda Perez, G. "Joseph the Carpenter," in *The Coptic Encyclopedia*, A. S. Atiya, gen. ed. New York-Toronto: Macmillan, 1991; vol. 5, pp. 1371–74.

Boud'hors, A. "Histoire de Joseph le Charpentier," in *Écrits apocryphes chrétiens*, ed. P. Geoltrain and J.D. Kaestli. Paris: Gallimard, 2005; vol. 2, pp. 25–59.

Boud'hors, A. "Origine et portée du récit apocryphe copte intitulé *Histoire de Joseph le Charpentier*," in Marie dans les *récits apocryphes chrétiens* 1. Bulletin de la Société française d'études mariales. Paris: Mediaspaul, 2004; pp. 139–54.

Lagarde, P. de., ed. *Aegyptiaca*, Göttingen: Hoyer, 1883, pp. 1–37.

Lefort, L.-Th. "À propos de l'*Histoire de Joseph le Charpentier, Le Muséon* 66 (1953): 201–23.

Robinson, F. *Coptic Apocryphal Gospels*. Texts and Studies 4.2. Cambridge: Cambridge University Press, 1896; pp. xxvii–xxix, 130–59, and 220–35.

Suciu, A. "New Fragments from the Sahidic Version of the *Historia Josephi Fabri Lignarii*," *Le Muséon* 122 (2009): 279–89.

Suciu, A. "A Coptic Fragment from the *History of Joseph the Carpenter* in the Collection of Duke University Library," *HTR* 106 (2013): 93–104.

History of Joseph the Carpenter

Prologue

This is the departure from the body of our father Joseph, the carpenter, the father of Christ according to flesh, who lived one hundred and eleven years, and whose entire life our Savior related to the apostles on the Mount of Olives. The apostles, for their part, wrote down these words and deposited them in the Library at Jerusalem. And the day when the holy old man laid down the body was the twenty-sixth day of the month of Epiphi,[1] in the peace of God. Amen.

Frame Story: Jesus Addresses His Disciples

1 (1) One day, when our good Savior was sitting on the Mount of Olives and his disciples were assembled before him, he spoke with them saying: "Beloved brothers and children of my good Father, whom he chose from among the whole world, (2) you know that I have told you many times that I must be crucified and taste death for the entirety,[2] and rise from the dead and give you the preaching of the gospel, so that you may preach it in the whole world, and that I would clothe you with power from on high[3] and fill you with a holy spirit, so that you may preach to all the nations saying to them, 'Repent, (3) for it is better for a person to find a cup of water[4] in the age that is coming than all the goods of the entire world.' (4) And again, 'Better is a single footstep in the house of my father than all the wealth of this world.'[5] (5) And again, 'Better is a single moment of the righteous rejoicing than a thousand years of the sinners crying and mourning: their tears cannot be wiped away, nor are they heeded at all.'[6] (6) Now then, my honorable members, when you go to them, preach to them that it is with right balance and right measure that my Father will draw an account with you.[7] And again, 'A single careless word that you utter will be required from you.'[8] (7) Just as no one can escape death, so no one also can escape what he has done, be it good or evil.[9] (8) Yet all these words have I told you already, that is, 'No mighty one can be saved by his power, nor can a person be saved by the size of his riches.'[10] Listen now, I will tell you the life of my father Joseph, the blessed old carpenter.

1. July 20 in the Julian, or August 2 in the Gregorian calendar.
2. See Heb. 2:9.
3. See Luke 24:49.
4. See Mark 9:41.
5. See Mark 10:23–25.
6. See Rev. 21:3–4; Isa. 25:8.
7. See Ezek. 45:10; Matt. 7:2; Mark 4:24; Luke 6:38.
8. See Matt. 12:36.
9. See Eccl. 12:14; 2 Cor. 5:10.
10. See Ps. 32:16.

Joseph's First Marriage

2 (1) There was a man Joseph from a city called Bethlehem, which belonged to the Jews and is the city of King David.[11] (2) He became well versed in the knowledge and craft of carpentry. (3) This man Joseph took to himself a wife in the union of a holy matrimony, and she bore him sons and daughters, four male sons and two female daughters, whose names are Judas and Joset, James and Simon; the names of his daughters are Lysia and Lydia.[12] (4) And the wife of Joseph died as it is appointed to all people[13] and left James still at young age.[14] (5) Joseph was a righteous man[15] glorifying God in all things, and he went on working at the craft of carpentry, he and his two sons, living by the work of their hands according to the Law of Moses. (6) And this righteous man of whom I speak, this is Joseph my father according to flesh, to whom my mother Mary was betrothed for a wife.[16]

Mary in the Temple

3[17] (1) While my father Joseph remained a widower, my mother Mary, for her part, good and blessed in every manner, dwelled in the temple and served there in purity, having grown up to twelve years: she spent three years in the house of her parents and another nine years in the temple of the Lord. (2) Then the priests, as they saw the virgin live reverently and dwell in the fear of the Lord, spoke to one another, saying, 'Let us search for a good man and betroth her to him until the time of the wedding, lest we let the custom of women befall her in the temple and we come to be under a great sin.'

Joseph the Safe-Keeper of Mary

4. (1) Immediately they called up the tribe of Judah and chose from it twelve people corresponding to the names of twelve tribes of Israel. (2) The lot fell upon the good old man Joseph, my father according to flesh. (3) Then the priests spoke and said to my blessed virgin mother, 'Go with Joseph and obey him until

11. See Luke 2:4.

12. For the names of Joseph's sons, see Mark 6:3 (James, Joses, Judas, Simon) and Matt. 13:55 (James, Joseph, Simon, Judas). In Mark 15:40, Mary is "the mother of James the younger and of Joses, and Salome." Epiphanius, *Panar.* 78.8 names Joseph's two daughters "Mary and Salome"; according to the Coptic *Synaxarion*, Joseph had three daughters.

13. This phrase, used throughout the text, is probably borrowed from Heb. 9:27.

14. See Mark 15:40.

15. See Matt. 1:19.

16. See Matt. 1:18; Luke 1:27.

17. See parallel passages in Prot. Jas. 7.2–8.3.

the time comes that we make the wedding.'[18] (4) My father Joseph received Mary my mother into his house. She found the little boy James in the sadness of orphanage and began to foster him; for this reason she was called Mary of James.[19] (5) After Joseph had brought her into his house, he next took to the road to work in carpentry. (6) Mary my mother spent two years in his house until the right time.

Mary's Pregnancy and Joseph's Dream Vision

5 (1) Now in the fourteenth year of her life I came out of my own will and resided in her, I who am Jesus, your life. (2) And when she was three months pregnant, the guileless Joseph came from the place where he worked in carpentry and found my virgin mother pregnant. Disturbed and fearful, he planned to dismiss her secretly.[20] (3) And because of grief he did not eat or drink.

6 (1)[21] But in the middle of the night, behold Gabriel, the archangel of joy, came to him in a vision by the order of my good Father and said to him, 'Joseph, son of David, do not be afraid to take Mary your wife to yourself; for he whom she is about to bear is from the Holy Spirit. (2) She shall bear a son and you shall call his name Jesus:[22] it is he who will rule all nations with a rod of iron.'[23] (3) And the angel left him. Joseph awoke from sleep and did as the angel of the Lord commanded him: he took Mary to himself.[24]

The Birth of Jesus

7 (1) After these things a decree went out from Emperor Augustus that all of the world should be registered, each person after his city. (2) The good old man also went, and he took Mary, my virgin mother, to his city of Bethlehem—for she was about to deliver—and had his name recorded by the scribe: 'Joseph, the son of David, and Mary his wife, and Jesus his son are of the tribe of Judah.'[25] (3) And Mary my mother bore me on the way back to Bethlehem, near the tomb of Rachel,[26] the wife of Jacob the patriarch, who is the mother of Joseph and Benjamin.

18. For the alternative account of Joseph's election as the guardian of Mary, see Prot. Jas. 8.3–9.2.

19. Mary the virgin is assimilated here to Mary of James from Luke 24:10; see Matt. 27:56; Mark 15:40.

20. See Matt. 1:18–19; see Prot. Jas. 13.1–14.1.

21. For 6.1–2 see Matt. 1:20–21; the whole chapter resembles Prot. Jas. 14.2.

22. See below 17.5–6.

23. See Ps. 2:9.

24. See Matt. 1:24.

25. See Luke 2:1–6; see also Prot. Jas. 17.1, where Joseph is at a loss as to how he should register Mary and her child.

26. See Gen. 35:19–20.

The Flight to Egypt

8 (1) Satan took counsel with Herod the Great,[27] the father of Archelaus, who beheaded John, my beloved kinsman.[28] (2) Thus he sought for me in order to kill me,[29] thinking that my kingdom was from this world.[30] (3) Joseph was informed by my Father in a vision; and he got up and took me and Mary my mother;[31] I was sitting on her arms with Salome walking behind us. We went down to Egypt and stayed there for a year, until the body of Herod was eaten by worms and died[32] because of the blood he shed of the sinless little children.[33]

The Settling in Nazareth

9 (1) When that lawless Herod died, we returned to the land of Israel and resided in a city of Galilee whose name is Nazareth.[34] (2) And my father Joseph, the blessed old man, worked at the craft of carpentry and we lived from the work of his hands. He never ate bread he did not earn, acting in accordance with the Law of Moses.

10 (1) And after this long period of time, his body did not remain without power, nor his eyes without light; not one tooth was missing in his mouth; and he did not lack in understanding and wisdom all that time, but was rather like a youth. His life had reached one hundred and eleven years in a good old age.[35]

11 (1) Now his two elder sons Joset and Symeon took wives and went to their house. His two daughters also took their husbands, as it is customary for all people; and Joseph stayed with James, his little son. (2) After the virgin bore me, I lived with them in a full obedience of childhood.[36] Indeed, I did all things human short of sin alone.[37] (3) And I called Mary my mother and Joseph my father, and I obeyed them in everything they told me. I never contradicted them, but I loved them dearly.

27. See Matt. 2:4, where Herod consults with all the chief priests and scribes.

28. Herod the Great (37–4 BCE), who ordered the massacre of the infants (Matt. 2:16–17), is confused here with Herod Antipas, the ruler of Galilee and Perea (4 BCE-39 CE), who had John the Baptist beheaded (Matt. 14:1–12, Mark 6:14–29).

29. See Matt. 2:13.

30. See John 18:36.

31. See Matt. 2:13–14.

32. See Acts 12:23, which describes the death of Herod Agrippa.

33. See Matt. 2:15–16.

34. See Matt. 2:19–23.

35. See Deut. 34:7: "Moses was one hundred twenty years old when he died; his sight was unimpaired and his vigor had not abated."

36. See Luke 2:51.

37. See Heb. 4:15.

Joseph's Death Draws Near

12 (1) But then the death of Joseph, my father, drew near, as is appointed to all people.[38] (2) When his body grew ill, his angel announced to him, 'In this year you will die.' (3) And as his soul was troubled, he went up to Jerusalem. He entered the temple of the Lord and repented in front of the altar. He prayed in this way, saying:

13 (1) 'God, the Father of all mercy[39] and the God of all flesh,[40] the Lord of my soul and body and spirit:[41] (2) If the days of my life you have allotted me in the world are completed, then I beseech you, Lord God, that you send me the archangel Michael to stand by me until my wretched soul come out from my body without trouble and torment. (3) For death is a great fear and trouble to all people, whether human, cattle, beast, reptile, or bird. (4) In short, every creature under heaven which has a living soul is fearful and troubled until their soul is separated from their body. (5) Now, then, my Lord, let your angel stand by my soul and my body until they are separated from one another without trouble. (6) Do not cause the angel, appointed to me from the day you created me until now, to fill his face with anger toward me in my path, as I am coming to you, but rather let him be at peace with me. (7) Let not those with changing faces give trouble to me in the path, as I am coming to you.[42] (8) Let not those who are at the gates retain my soul, and do not put me to shame at your fearful tribunal. (9) Let not the waves of the fiery river heave like beasts towards me, the river in which all souls are purified before seeing the glory of your Godhead. (10) O God who judges everyone with equity and righteousness,[43] let now your mercy, my Lord, become my solace; for you are the fountain of all good. Yours is the glory forever and ever. Amen.'

14 (1) After these things he returned to Nazareth, the town where he resided, and fell sick with the illness of which he was to die,[44] as it is appointed to all people.[45] (2) And his illness was very grave, more than all other times he was sick from the day he was born into the world.

38. See Heb. 9:27.
39. See 2 Cor. 1:3.
40. See Jer. 32:27.
41. See 1 Thess. 5:23.
42. See the Egyptian *Book of the Dead,* chap. 17. In *T. Ab.* 17, Death reveals to Abraham all of his frightening faces.
43. See Ps. 9:8.
44. See 2 Kings 13:14.
45. See Heb. 9:27.

Joseph's Biography Summarized

(3) This is the life-sketch of my beloved father Joseph. (4) He was forty when he took a wife. He remained in wedlock with his wife for another forty-nine years; she died, and he lived alone for a year. (5) My mother spent two years in his house when the priests gave her to him, after he was told by the priests, 'Guard her until the time for celebrating your marriage.' (6) At the beginning of the third year of her dwelling in his house, that is, the fifteenth year of her life,[46] she bore me on the ground in a mysterious fashion: no one understands it in the whole creation save me and my Father and the Holy Spirit, since we are in unity.

15 (1) Now all the days of the life of my father Joseph, the blessed old man, were one hundred and eleven years, as my good Father commanded. (2) And the day he departed from the body was the twenty-sixth of the month Epiphi. (3) Then began the transformation of the precious gold, which is the flesh of my father Joseph, and the change of the silver, which is the mind and wisdom.[47] (4) He forgot to eat and to drink, and the knowledge of his craft turned into error. (5) And when the light rose on that day, that is, the twenty-sixth of the month Epiphyte, my father Joseph became disturbed on his bed: he let a loud groan, clapped his hands, and cried out in great disturbance, speaking as follows:

The Lament of Joseph

16 (1) 'Woe to me today. Woe to the day my mother bore me to the world. (2) Woe to the womb in which my life was sown. Woe to the breasts whose milk I sucked.[48] (3) Woe to the knees on which I sat. (4) Woe to the hands that lifted me up until I grew up and came to live in sin. (5) Woe to my tongue and my lips, for oftentimes they have been implicated in violence, in calumny and false slander, and in idle words of distraction full of deceit. (6) Woe to my eyes, for they have looked at wrongdoings. (7) Woe to my ears, for they have loved to listen to empty talks. (8) Woe to my hands, for they have laid hold of things that are not theirs. (9) Woe to my stomach and my bowels, for they have craved for foods that are not theirs; whenever my stomach found something,

46. One of the Sahidic manuscript fragments (S'British Library, Or 3581B, chaps. 13.6–15.2) has after "the fifteenth year of her life" the following text: "and Joseph lived for yet another 18 years from the moment she gave birth by an inscrutable mystery." This detail supplements information about the length of Joseph's life in the prologue as well as in 10.1 and 15.1.

47. In ancient Egyptian texts, the flesh of gods is made of gold and their bones of silver.

48. See Job 3:11–16.

it burned it more than a burning fiery furnace and made it useless in all respect. (10) Woe to my knees, which have served my body ill, taking it to many a worthless path. (11) Woe to my body, for it has made my soul barren and estranged from God who created it. (12) What am I to do now? I am enclosed on all sides. (13) Truly woe to all who will sin. (14) Truly this is the same great trouble which I saw upon my father Jacob[49] when he was coming forth from the body, and which has also overtaken me, the wretched one, as of today. (15) But hurry, O God the arbitrator of my soul and my body, who do your will in me!'

Jesus at Joseph's Death-Bed

17 (1) While my beloved father Joseph was saying these things, I got up and approached him as he lay down. I found him troubled in his soul and his spirit, and I said to him, 'Hail, my beloved father Joseph, whose old age is good and blessed at once.' (2) He answered in great fear of death, saying to me, 'Hail many times, my beloved son. Behold, my soul has rested within me a little when I heard your voice. (3) Jesus my lord, Jesus my true king, Jesus my good and merciful savior, Jesus the redeemer, Jesus the steward, Jesus the protector, Jesus who are all goodness, Jesus whose name is sweet in the mouth of all and very soothing, Jesus the eye that sees, the ear that listens with righteousness: Hear me today, me your servant, as I beseech you, shedding my tears in your presence. (4) You are truly God, you are truly the Lord, just as the angel oftentimes said to me, and especially on the day that my heart was in doubt because of typically human thought about the blessed virgin—for she conceived a child—and I said: "I will dismiss her quietly."[50] (5) But as I was thinking about this, the angel appeared to me in a vision and said to me: "Joseph, son of David, do not be afraid and accept Mary your wife to yourself; for he whom she is about to bear is from the Holy Spirit. (6) Do not doubt at all about her conception, for she will bear a son and you shall call his name Jesus."[51] (7) You are Jesus Christ, the savior of my soul and my body and my spirit. Do not find fault with me, your servant and the work of your hands! (8) I did not understand, my Lord, nor do I know the mystery of your incredible birth; nor did I ever hear that a woman had conceived without a man, or that a virgin bore a child while sealed in her virginity. (9) My Lord, if this mystery had not been ordained, I would not

49. See Matt. 1:15–16.
50. See Matt. 1:19.
51. See Matt. 1:20–21; see *above* 6.1–2.

believe in you and your holy birth, nor would I glorify her who bore you, Mary the holy virgin.

Joseph Recalls an Episode from Jesus' Infancy[52]

(10) I remember also the day when the asp bit a boy and he died. (11) His people surrounded you in order to deliver you to Herod. (12) Your mercy laid hold of him: you raised him, even though they falsely charged you that it was you who killed him. And there was a great joy in the house of the one who had died. (13) I immediately took you by the ear and spoke with you saying: "Be prudent, my son!" You rebuked me at once and said, "If you were not my father according to the flesh, surely I would tell you what you did to me!" (15) Now then, my Lord and my God, supposing that you have settled accounts with me for that day and caused these fearful signs to fall upon me, I beseech your goodness not to bring me to your judgment. (16) I am your servant and the son of your servant. (17) If you break off my bonds, I will offer to you a sacrifice of praise, which is the confession of the glory of your Godhead, that you are Jesus Christ, truly the Son of God and the son of man at once.'

Jesus to Mary on the Inevitability of Death

18 (1) As my father Joseph was speaking, I could not refrain from shedding tears, and I cried, watching as death held sway over him and listening to the words of misery he was speaking. (2) After this, my brothers, remember my death on the cross for the life of the whole world. (3) Then my beloved mother Mary, whose name is sweet in the mouth of all who love me, got up and said to me in great pain, 'Woe to me, my beloved son. Is he perhaps going to die, Joseph of the good and blessed old age, your beloved and honorable father according to flesh?' (4) I said to her, 'My beloved mother, who is there ever among people who have worn flesh that will not taste death? (5) For death is the ruler of humankind, my blessed mother. (6) Indeed, you also must die like all people. (7) Whether it is Joseph my father or you my blessed mother, your death is not death but life eternal and unending. (8) For I am also going to die for the universe, because of the mortal flesh I wore in you. (9) So now, my beloved mother, get up and go inside to the blessed old man Joseph until you get acquainted with the ordinance which will come from on high.'

52. This whole section combines three episodes from the *Infancy Gospel of Thomas*, chaps. 4–5, 9 and 16.

19 (1) And she got up and entered the place where he lay, and she found him with the mark of death shown forth in him. (2) I, for my part, my beloved ones, was sitting at his head, and Mary my mother was sitting by his feet. (3) And he lifted up his eyes to my face, but was not able to speak, for the hour of death held sway over him. (4) He thus lifted up his eyes and released a loud groan. (5) And I held his hands and his knees for a long while, as he looked at me and beseeched me, 'Do not let me be taken away!' (6) And I placed my hand beneath his heart and found his soul brought to his throat, for it was about to be brought up from his body. But the last hour had not yet been completed for Death to come; otherwise it would not have refrained, for it was accompanied by Disturbance and preceded by Crying and Destruction.

Farewell and Lamentation by Joseph's Children

20 (1) When my beloved mother saw me touch his body, she likewise touched his feet and found out that the breath and heat had withdrawn and left them. (2) She said to me, guilelessly, 'Thank you, my beloved son, for since the moment you placed your hand on his body, the heat withdrew from him. (3) Look, his feet and his shins are cold like crystal.' And I called his sons and his daughters and said to them, 'Get up and speak with your father; for this is the time to speak, before the mouth that speaks fails and the wretched flesh becomes cold.' (5) Then his sons and his daughters spoke with Joseph. He was in peril because of the fatigue of dying, ready to depart from this world. (6) Lysia the daughter of Joseph[53] replied, saying to her brothers, 'Woe to me, my brothers, if this is not the disease of our beloved mother—we have not seen her until now! (7) And so it is also with our father, that we should not see him forever.' (8) Then the children of Joseph lifted up their voices and cried. I, too, and Mary my virgin mother cried with them, for surely the hour of death was come.

Jesus Wards Off the Powers of Darkness

21 (1) Then I looked towards the south, and I saw Death.[54] He arrived near the house followed by Amente, who is his instrument along with the Devil, and by a countless troop of officers clothed with fire, their mouths breathing out smoke and sulfur. (2) And my father Joseph looked and saw those who came after him, who were filled with wrath toward him, just as they usually fill their face with

53. S^D has "his older daughter Lydia, the purple seller," alluding to Lydia from Acts 16:14.

54. The arrival of Death with countless frightening forms or powers is a distinctive feature of the Jewish "testament" genre; see *T. Ab.* 16–20, where it is God who sends Death to the patriarch's deathbed.

rage against every soul coming forth from the body, and especially the sinners, in whom they find a little of their own. (3) When the good old man saw them in the company of Death, his eyes shed tears. (4) In that hour the soul of my father Joseph separated with a loud groan, seeking a way to hide so as to be saved. (5) When I saw the groaning of my father Joseph—for he saw authorities that he had never seen—I got up at once and reprimanded the Devil and all those who were with him. (6) And they departed in shame and in great disturbance. (7) And no one among those sitting around my father Joseph knew anything, not even Mary my mother, about all the fearful squads coming after the soul of humans. (8) But when Death saw that I had reprimanded the authorities of darkness and cast them out, for they had no authority over him, he became afraid.[55] (9) And I got up at once and raised a prayer to my Father of many mercies,[56] saying:

Jesus' Prayer for the Soul of Joseph

22 (1) 'My Father and the Father of all mercies, the Father of truth, the eye that sees, the ear that hears,[57] hear me, your beloved Son, as I beseech you for the work of your hands, namely my father Joseph: send me a great choir of angels, and Michael the steward of goodness, and Gabriel the herald of light, that they may walk with the soul of my father Joseph until it passes across the seven eons of Darkness,[58] and also that it may not pass through the narrow paths it is fearful to tread on and even more to see the powers upon them, the river of fire rushing there like waves of the sea. (2) And be merciful toward the soul of my father Joseph as it is ascending to your holy hands, for this is the hour when he needs mercy.'

(3) I say to you, my honorable brothers and my blessed apostles, that every person born into the world and acquainted with good and evil, if he has spent his time relying on his eyelids, has need of the mercy of my good Father when he comes to the hour of death, and to the passing of the path, and to the fearful tribunal, and to the making of his defense. (4) But I will turn back to how my father Joseph, the righteous old man, departed from the body.

55. For a similar outcome of Jesus' encounter with Death in the underworld (Amente), see *The Book of the Resurrection of Jesus Christ by Bartholomew (Res. Bart.)* 4.2–8.

56. See 2 Cor. 1:3.

57. See Joseph's invocation in 17.3.

58. For Boud'hors (2005) 51, *ad loc.*, the seven eons of darkness are the inversed image of the seven heavens of Paradise; but they can also stand for the seven planetary spheres that the soul must traverse during its post-mortem heavenly voyage.

Jesus Hands Joseph's Soul to the Angels

23[59] (1) When he thus gave up his spirit, I saluted him. (2) The angels took his soul and wrapped it in finest linen packages.[60] (3) I entered and sat by him; nobody noticed that he was dead among those sitting around him. (4) And I made Michael and Gabriel watch over his soul because of the authorities on the road; and the angels sang before it until they delivered it to my good Father.

Jesus Consoles Joseph's Family

24 (1) Now I turned to the body of my father Joseph, laid down like an empty jar. I sat, brought down his eyes, and tried to close them and his mouth. I stayed there looking upon him. (2) I said to the virgin, 'Mary, my mother, where are now all works of craftsmanship that this man had made from his youth until now? They have all passed away in this single hour as though he had never been born into the world.' (3) When his sons and his daughters heard me saying this to Mary, my virgin mother, they said to me with great weeping, 'Woe to us, our

59. The longest extant Sahidic manuscript fragment (S'Vatican Library, Borgia 109, no. 121, chaps. 14–24,1) contains a more detailed version of chap. 23, which runs as follows: "(1) When I said 'Amen,' my beloved mother Mary responded to me in the language of the heavenly beings. (2) And, behold, immediately Michael and Gabriel and the choir of the angels came forth from heaven. They came and stood upon the body of my father Joseph. (3) And straightaway his rattling and panting greatly increased, and I realized that his bitter hour was come. (4) And he kept laboring like a woman about to give birth, his affliction spreading over him as a violent wind and as a great fire that devours a great wood. (5) As for Death, however, fear did not let him enter unto the body of my beloved father Joseph and separate it away; for he looked in and saw me sitting by his head, having hold of his temples. (6) And when I realized that Death feared to enter because of me, I rose and went outside the gate, and I found him waiting there alone in great fear. (7) And straightaway I said to him, 'O you who have come from the places of the South, enter quickly and accomplish that which my Father has commanded you. (8) But watch over him like the light of your eyes; for he is my father according to flesh, and he suffered with me in the days of my youth, fleeing with me from place to place because of Herod's plot, and I was taught by him like all children, whom their fathers teach for their benefit.' (9) Then Abbaton went in and took the soul of my father Joseph, and he brought it forth from the body at the hour when the sun was about to rise in its course, on the twenty-sixth of the month of Epep, in peace. (10) All the days of the life of my beloved father Joseph amount to a hundred and eleven years. (11) Michael took hold of the two ends of a precious silken package, and Gabriel took hold of the other two ends. They greeted the soul of my beloved father Joseph and put it down into package. (12) But no one among those sitting beside him knew that he had died, nor did my mother Mary know. (13) And I had Michael and Gabriel watch over the soul of my beloved father Joseph because of the robbers on the roads. And I made the bodiless angels sing continually before him, until they took him to the heavens unto my good Father."

60. The way in which the angels handle Joseph's soul resembles the treatment of the viscera in the ancient Egyptian mummification procedures, where each of the inner bodily organs was wrapped in a separate linen package.

Lord; for surely our father is dead and we did not notice it, did we?' (4) I said to them, 'Indeed he is dead, and yet the death of Joseph my father is not death, but life forever.[61] (5) Great are the things which my beloved father Joseph is about to receive. For as soon as his soul came forth from the body, all trouble ceased for him. He went into the eternal kingdom; he left behind the burden of the body; he left behind this world full of all sorts of troubles and empty concerns. He went to the resting places of my Father, who is in the heavens that can never be destroyed.' (6) Now when I said to my brothers, 'Your father Joseph is dead, the blessed old man,' they got up and rent their garments and cried for a long while.

Jesus Preserves Joseph's Body from Corruption

25 (1) Then all the residents of the town of Nazareth and of Galilee, upon hearing about the mourning, gathered to the place where we were, according to the law of the Jews. They spent the whole day mourning for him until the ninth hour. (2) And at the ninth hour of the day[62] I had everyone leave. I poured the water on the body of my beloved father Joseph and anointed it with fragrant oil. I prayed to my good Father in the heavens with heavenly prayers, which I had written with my own fingers on the tablets of heaven[63] before I took flesh in the holy virgin Mary. (3) And right after I said the Amen of my prayer, there came a host of angels; and I ordered two of them to spread a robe and had them take up the blessed body of my father Joseph, deposit it amid the garments, and wrap it.

26 (1) And I laid my hands upon his body saying, 'No bad smell of death shall rule over you, nor shall your ears be foul-smelling; no waste shall ever flow forth from your body, and neither shall your shroud rot in the earth nor indeed your flesh, with which I have clothed you, but it shall stay in your body until the day of the thousand-year feast. The hair of your head, which I held in my hands so many times, shall not wither, my beloved father Joseph. And all will be well with you.

Jesus Establishes the Cult of Joseph

(2) Those who will provide an offering and deposit it in your shrine on your memorial day, which is the twenty-sixth of the month of Epiphi, I will also bless in the celestial offering, which is in the heavens. (3) And also whoever gives

61. See *above* 18.7.

62. This is also the hour of Jesus' death in the Synoptic Gospels; see Matt. 27:46; Mark 15:34; Luke 23:44.

63. See 1 Enoch 81.1, 93.2, 103.2, 106.19.

bread into the hand of a poor person in your name, I will not allow to lack in any good of this world in all the days of his life. (4) Those who give a cup of wine into the hand of a stranger, a widow, or an orphan on your memorial day, I will grant them to you to take them to the thousand-year feast. (5) Those who copy the book of your departure from the body and all the words that have come from my mouth today, I swear by your salvation, my beloved father Joseph, that I will grant them to you in this world; and also that, when they come forth from the body, I will tear the record of their sins so that they may not receive any torment, save the necessity of death and the fiery river[64] placed before my Father, which purifies every soul. (6) And if there is a poor person who has no means to do what I have said, when he begets a son and names him Joseph, glorifying your name, no famine or pestilence will happen in that house because your name dwells in it.'

The Burial of Joseph

27 (1) Afterward, the dignitaries of the town came accompanied by the corpse buriers to the place where my father's body had been laid, wanting to bury his body according to the burial custom of the Jews.[65] (2) And they found him already prepared for burial, with the shroud fitted to his body as if had been fastened with iron clasps; and when they touched him, they did not find any hole in the shroud. (3) Then they took him out to the tomb. (4) And while they dug at the cave's mouth to open up the entrance and place him next to his parents, I recalled the day when he had traveled with me down to Egypt and the great torments he had suffered because of me. And I spread myself over his body and wept over him[66] for a long while, saying:

Jesus Teaches About Death

28 (1) 'O Death, you stir plenty of tears and many a lament—but it is he who is over all things that gave you this marvelous authority! (2) But Death is not to be blamed like Adam and Eve, (3) and Death accomplishes nothing without my Father's command. (4) There is a man who had lived nine hundred years before he died, and many others even more than that. (5) Not a single one of them has said, "I have seen death," or "It comes at times, troubling anyone." (6) Rather, it does not trouble them save on a single occasion, and even then it is my good Father who sends it after the person. (7) And the moment it comes after him, he

64. See *above*, 13.9 and 22.1.
65. See John 19:40.
66. See Gen. 50:1.

hears the verdict coming from heaven. (8) If the verdict comes in haste and full of wrath, Death also comes in haste and anger so as to fulfill the command of my good Father, and to receive the person's soul and hand him to his Lord. (9) Death has no power to cast him into the fire or take him to the kingdom of the heavens. (10) Death, then, fulfills God's commands; Adam, however, did not do the will of my Father but rather committed transgression until my Father got angry with him—for he obeyed his wife and disobeyed my good Father until he brought death upon every soul. (11) Had Adam not disobeyed my good Father, he would not have brought death upon him. (12) What is it that prevents me from beseeching my good Father to send me a great chariot of light to place my father Joseph upon it, so that he does not taste death at all but is taken up in the flesh in which he was born to the places of rest, to dwell there with my incorporeal angels?[67] (13) But because of Adam's transgression these great troubles have come upon all mankind along with this great necessity of death. (14) Insofar as I myself wear the troubling flesh, it is necessary that I taste death in it for the creation I have made, in order that I may have mercy on them.'[68]

Jesus Concludes His Narrative

29 (1) As I was saying this, embracing my father Joseph and lamenting him, (2) they opened the door of the tomb and laid his body in it next to the body of Jacob, his father. (3) His end took place when he was a hundred and eleven years old; and not a single tooth was missing in his mouth, nor did his eyes remain without light, but his appearance was like that of a little child. (4) He never lost his strength, but was working at the craft of carpentry until the day he fell sick with the illness of which he was to die."

Frame Story Resumed: Apostles Ask About Enoch and Elijah

30. (1) Now we the apostles rejoiced while hearing these things from our Savior, and we got up at once and made our obeisance before his hands and his feet, rejoicing and saying, "We give thanks to you, our good Savior, for you have made us worthy to hear these words of life from you, our Lord. (2) Yet we wonder at you, our good Savior, as to why you have granted immortality to Enoch and Elijah, so that they till now reside amid the blessings while being in the flesh in which they were born, and their flesh never saw corruption.[69] (3) But the blessed

67. See Matt. 26:53.

68. The whole section 28.10–14 echoes both the images and themes of Rom. 4:12–19.

69. See Acts 2:27, 31; 13:35–37; for Enoch, see Gen. 5:24 and 1 En. 70.1–2; for Elijah, see 2 Kings 2:11.

old man, Joseph the carpenter, to whom you granted this great honor of calling him your father, and whom you obeyed in all things, and bid us saying, 'When I clothe you with power and send upon you the promise of my Father, that is, the Advocate, the Holy Spirit,[70] and send you to preach the holy gospel, preach also my beloved father Joseph'; (4) and again, 'Say these words of life to testify about his departure from the body'; (5) and again, 'Read this testament on the feast days and on the sacred days'; (6) and again, 'A person who has not been taught to read well shall not read this testament on the feast days'; (7) and again, 'Whoever takes away from these words or adds to them,[71] and so considers me a liar, I will soon take vengeance on him'—(8) we wonder why, since the day you were born in Bethlehem and called him your father according to the flesh, you have not promised immortality to him and granted him eternal life."

Jesus Replies by Invoking His Father's Omnipotence

31 (1) Our Savior answered and said to us, "The sentence which my Father pronounced upon Adam will not be annulled, inasmuch as he did not obey his commandments. (2) When my Father pronounces upon a person that he will be righteous, he becomes his chosen one. (3) When, on the contrary, the person loves the works of the Devil by his own will and sins, and the Father lets him live a long life, does he not know that he is about to fall into his hands unless he repents? (4) If again one lives a long life in good works, his actions make him an old person; (5) but when the Father sees one corrupting his way, he shortens his life. This is how he 'takes them away at the midpoint of their days.'[72] (6) Yet all the prophecies issued by my Father will be fulfilled upon humankind, and all things will befall them. (7) Also, you have told me about Enoch and Elijah that they are alive in the flesh in which they were born, but about Joseph, my father according to flesh, you ask: 'Why have you left him in the flesh till now?' (8) Even if he had lived ten thousand years, he still must die. (9) I say to you, my holy members, that every time Enoch and Elijah think of death, their wish is that they had already died so as to escape this great necessity which is laid down for them—especially since they will die in a day of torment and fear, of shouts and threats, and of grief. (10) For the Antichrist will kill these two men and shed their blood upon the earth for a jug of water, because of the rebukes they will give him when they denounce him."[73]

70. See John 14:26.

71. See Rev. 22:18–19.

72. See Ps. 101:25.

73. In this section, Enoch and Elijah are identified with the '"two witnesses' of the heavenly voice from Rev. 11:3–11.

Concluding Doxology

32 (1) We replied and said to him, "Our Lord and our God,[74] who are these two men of whom you have said, 'The son of perdition[75] will kill them for a jug of water'?" (2) Our Savior Jesus and our Life said to us, "They are Enoch and Elijah." (3) And when our good Savior said this to us, we were glad and rejoiced, and we gave thanks and glorified him, our Lord and our God,[76] our Savior Jesus Christ, through whom be all glory and all honor to the Father and Him and the life-giving Holy Spirit, now and for all time and forever and ever. Amen.[77]

74. See John 20:28.
75. See 2 Thess. 2:3.
76. See John 20:28.
77. The following text was added by the scribe: "Remember me, the sinner, the wretched, who stinks in the pit of his sins, Hapip. Lord, have mercy on him. Amen. I copied it on the twenty-eight of the month of Epiphi, in the year of the martyrs 783."

MINISTRY GOSPELS

7

The Jewish-Christian Gospels

There are no surviving manuscripts of the so-called Jewish-Christian Gospels. Information about what they contained and what they emphasized can only be inferred from quotations of them in hostile sources, the writings of the proto-orthodox church fathers. These quotations are in a hopeless state of confusion, so much so that scholars have long disagreed over the most basic issues, including whether these quotations derive from two, three, or more Gospels written by Christians concerned to portray Jesus in light of their own ongoing commitments to Jewish law and culture.

Part of the confusion resides in the fact that different patristic authors (and sometimes the same author) appear to call different Gospels by the same name (e.g., "the Gospel according to the Hebrews"). Moreover, in many instances authors understand these Gospels all to be versions of the Gospel according to Matthew, thought to have been originally written in Hebrew and then edited by "heretics" inclined to propagate a Jewish understanding of Jesus and his ministry.

The view that Matthew was originally written in Hebrew is very old, going back at least to the early second century. The proto-orthodox father Papias, whose works also are preserved only in quotations of later writers, wrote a five-volume work known as the *Expositions of the Sayings of the Lord,* in which he indicates that "Matthew composed the sayings [of Jesus] in the Hebrew tongue, and each one interpreted *[Or: translated]* them to the best of his ability." Traditionally this has been taken to indicate that the First Gospel originally appeared in Hebrew. A closer reading of Papias's quotation (preserved in Eusebius), however, suggests that he was not speaking of our Gospel of Matthew—or that if he was, he did not actually know about the origins and character of the book. Our Gospel of Matthew is much more than the sayings of Jesus; and it was almost certainly not originally written in Hebrew: it borrows stories verbatim from Mark, for example, a source that was written in Greek. Nonetheless, church fathers after Papias assumed that he was talking about our Matthew and concluded that since this book was written in Hebrew, it must have been the Gospel of choice among Christians who continued to hold allegiance to Jewish law and customs. And so any Gospel traditions that appeared to derive from a "Jewish" Gospel were thought to have come from this Hebrew form of Matthew—or a later redaction of it that incorporated even more fully Jewish ideas and concerns.

Compounding the confusion was the circumstance that various church fathers appear not to have realized that there were different Jewish-Christian groups with different theological views and liturgical practices living in different parts of the Christian world at different times. These different groups, of course, had different scriptural warrants for their religious commitments—including a range of different Gospels. Among other things, some of the church fathers did not realize that some Jewish-Christian groups (or at least one of them) derived from Palestine and continued to speak and read Aramaic, whereas others lived in the Jewish diaspora and knew only Greek.

As a result of all these factors, church fathers not infrequently confused one Jewish-Christian Gospel with another—all the time thinking that each of these Gospels was in fact the Hebrew version of Matthew. As it turns out, probably none of the Jewish-Christian Gospels known to us today was simply Matthew in Hebrew dress.

The early church fathers who quote the Jewish-Christian Gospels range from the late second to the early fifth centuries: Clement of Alexandria, Origen, Eusebius, Didymus the Blind, Epiphanius, and Jerome—not to mention later medieval sources. To give a sense of the confusion that reigned, we may consider just one reference in the writings of Jerome:

> In the Gospel according to the Hebrews, which was actually written in the Chaldean or Syriac language but with Hebrew letters, which the Nazareans use still today and which is the Gospel according to the Apostles, or, as most believe, according to Matthew—a Gospel that can also be found in the library of Caesarea—the following story is found. (Jerome, *Against the Pelagians*, 3, 2)

There are actually four different Gospels referred to by Jerome here: the Gospel according to the Hebrews, the Gospel according to Matthew translated into Hebrew, the Gospel used by the Nazareans, and the Gospel according to the Apostles. But he understands these four books to be one and the same. As it turns out, two of the books he refers to are problematic: it appears that Jerome never did know a form of Matthew written in Hebrew, and there is debate today over whether or not the Gospel according to the Apostles is simply a different name for one of the other known Gospels. The other two books he refers to are confused, because now there is reason to think that the Gospel according to the Hebrews and the Gospel of the Nazareans were different texts, written in different languages, with different views, and different contents.

The state of confusion witnessed to by Jerome has created endless headaches for modern critics trying to reconstruct the true state of affairs. A. F. J. Klijn, who has done more than anyone to try to sort out the mess, has convincingly argued that Jerome himself spoke of, and understood, the nature of the Jewish-Christian Gospels differently at different points of his career. All modern scholars working on the problem have tried to separate the various lines of tradition out from one another. There is universal agreement that the various quotations in the church fathers cannot go back to an original Hebrew (or Aramaic) version of Matthew's Gospel—most of them have no parallel in the canonical traditions. Nor can they all go back, in their entirety, to a single Aramaic revision of Matthew: for among the quotations are two different accounts of the baptism of Jesus, and these clearly come from different Gospels. There must, then, have been at least two Jewish-Christian Gospels. Moreover, there are solid linguistic reasons for thinking that one of these books was transmitted in Aramaic (as a number of the Fathers, including Eusebius and Jerome, explicitly state), whereas the other was written in Greek, since some of the Fathers (e.g., Clement of Alexandria and Didymus) could not read Hebrew/Aramaic, and so could not have quoted the book if that was its language. Moreover, there are linguistic features of some of the quotations that clearly indicate they derive from a Greek source.

And so, there were at least two Jewish-Christian Gospels. The question has long been whether, at least in the early centuries of the church (up to, say, the fifth century) there were two such Gospels or three. Although the matter continues to be disputed most scholars have thought there were three, one in Aramaic/Hebrew and two (at least) in Greek. One group of quotations (found in Origen, Eusebius, and Jerome, along with a group of marginal notes in several medieval Greek manuscripts of the Gospel of Matthew) involve Gospel traditions closely aligned with Matthew that appear to have had their origin in a semitic-language Gospel. Another group of quotations (found in the Alexandrian writers Clement, Origen, and Didymus the Blind, along with his one-time student Jerome) presuppose a different perspective, are not closely tied to the Gospel of Matthew, and appear to derive from a Greek source. A final group of quotations (found only in Epiphanius) presuppose yet a different perspective and clearly derive from some kind of Gospel harmony that was originally composed in Greek.

And so we possibly have three Jewish-Christian Gospels to consider from our sources: (1) the Gospel of the Nazareans, written in Aramaic, closely connected to Matthew, and located by church fathers in the region of Berea, near Aleppo Syria; (2) the Gospel according to the Hebrews, written in Greek and propagated among Jewish Christians living in Egypt; and (3) the Gospel of the Ebionites, a Greek Gospel harmony in use among Christians known by Epiphanius to be living in the area East of the Jordan River.

The quotations from these writings that follow derive from the works of the early church fathers (up to the fifth century), but do not include the later, and even more confused, quotations from the middle ages (ninth century and later). We have drawn quotations from Klijn, *Jewish-Christian Gospel Traditions*.

Bibliography

Bauer, W. *Orthodoxy and Heresy in Earliest Christianity*. Philadelphia: Fortress, 1971 (German original, 1934); pp. 241–85.

Elliott, J. K. *Apocryphal New Testament*. Oxford: Clarendon, 1993; pp. 3–16.

Howard, G. "The Gospel of the Ebionites," *ANRW* 2/25.5 (1988); pp. 4034–53.

Klauck, H.-J. *Apocryphal Gospels: An Introduction*. London: T&T Clark, 2003; pp. 36–64.

Klijn, A. F. J. *Jewish-Christian Gospel Traditions*. Leiden: E. J. Brill, 1992.

Klijn, A. F. J., and G. J. Reinink. *Patristic Evidence for Jewish-Christian Sects*. Leiden: E. J. Brill, 1973.

Vielhauer, P., and G. Strecker. "Jewish-Christian Gospels," *New Testament Apocrypha*. W. Schneemelcher, ed; trans. R. McL. Wilson. Louisville: Westminster/John Knox, 1991; vol. 1: pp. 134–78.

The Gospel of the Nazareans

None of the ancient sources that quotes this Gospel refers to it as the Gospel of the Nazareans. Indeed, to our knowledge, no Gospel went by that name until the ninth century, when Haimor of Halberstadt quotes an apocryphal tradition which indicated that many thousands of Jews converted to believe in Jesus while standing near his cross (see the discussion in Klijn, *Jewish-Christian Gospel Traditions*, pp. 129–31). It was thought in our more ancient sources, however, that there was a Gospel originally written "in Hebrew Letters" that was used by the Jewish sect of the Nazareans (see quotation 8 from Jerome), a name used of Christians as early as the New Testament period (Acts 24:3), no doubt because Jesus himself was called "the Nazarene." In any event, as the various quotations from this Gospel answer to this description, modern scholars have customarily called it the Gospel of the Nazareans.

Among our surviving sources the Gospel is quoted once by Origen, twice by Eusebius, and several times by Jerome. The sources have often confused the issue by calling the book the Gospel of the Hebrews, or by maintaining that it was the original (or edited) Hebrew version of the Gospel of Matthew. The Gospel does, to be sure, show close ties to Matthew. And it is at least possible that it was a later translation of that Gospel into Aramaic (Matthew originally having been written in Greek); but it is more likely that the author of this apocryphon wrote his account in light of his knowledge of Matthew, or of the traditions that were known to Matthew (see Klijn, *Jewish-Christian Gospel Traditions*, 36).

In addition to the patristic citations, this Gospel is also attested in a series of marginal notes of a group of Greek New Testament manuscripts dating from the ninth to the thirteenth centuries. Two of these manuscripts have a subscription that refers to a Gospel preserved on Mount Zion, in Jerusalem, which is called "the Jewish Gospel": TO IOUDAIKON. All of the mss have marginal notes on sundry passages of the Gospel of Matthew, which indicate the alternative readings of this "Jewish Gospel." The variant readings include explanatory comments, expansions, and variant traditions.

Jerome claims that the Gospel written in Hebrew was preserved in the famous library of Caesarea. This would make sense, in light of the circumstance that both Origen and Eusebius (the other two authors who quote it) had strong connections there. Jerome also claims that he personally translated the text from Hebrew into Greek (see quotation 5). He may mean, however, that he translated *portions* of the text as quoted in one of his sources—for example, Origen; there is no evidence to suggest that Jerome actually translated the entire work.

In any event, the quotations of this apocryphon suggest that it was a Gospel comparable in many ways to the Synoptic Gospels of the New Testament, Matthew, Mark, and Luke. Like them, this Gospel at the least contained accounts of Jesus' baptism, teaching, healing, and passion. Since the Gospel was already known to Origen, it must have been written by the mid-second century at the latest. Since its language was Aramaic, it was probably written in Palestine. Some scholars have suggested that it originated in Berea of Syria near Aleppo. The Gospel enjoyed a long life: the sources attesting it range at least from the late second (Origen) to the thirteenth centuries (TO IOUDAIKON manuscripts).

Bibliography

See the bibliography in the general introduction to the Jewish-Christian Gospels.

The Gospel of the Nazareans

1

It is written in a certain Gospel that is called "according to the Hebrews" (if in any event anyone is inclined to accept it, not as an authority but to shed some light on the question we have posed) that another rich man asked [Jesus], "Master, what good thing must I do to have life?" He replied to him, "O man, you should keep the law and the prophets." He responded, "I have already done that." Jesus said to him, "Go, sell all that you have and distribute the proceeds to the poor; then come, follow me."[1]

But the rich man began to scratch his head, for he was not pleased. And the Lord said to him, "How can you say, 'I have kept the law and the prophets?' For it is written in the law, 'You shall love your neighbor as yourself.' And look, many of your brothers, sons of Abraham, are clothed in excrement and dying of hunger while your house is filled with many good things, not one of which goes forth to these others." He turned and said to his disciple Simon, who sat beside him, "Simon, son of Jonah, it is easier for a camel to pass through the eye of a needle than for a rich person to enter the kingdom of heaven." (Origen, *Commentary on Matthew*, 15, 14)

2

For the Gospel that has come down to us in Hebrew letters makes the threat not against the one who hid the (master's) money but against the one who engaged in riotous living.[2] For (the master) had threes slaves, one who used up his fortune with whores and flute-players, one who invested the money and increased its value, and one who hid the money. The one was welcomed with open arms, the other blamed, and only the third locked up in prison. (Eusebius, *Theophania*, 4, 22).

3

In the Gospel that is called "according to the Hebrews," for the words, "bread to sustain our lives" I found the word "Mahar," which means "[bread] for tomorrow."[3] (Jerome, *Commentary on Matthew*, 6, 11).

1. See Matt. 19:16–24; Mark 10:17–25; and Luke 18:18–25.
2. See Matt. 25:14–30.
3. See Matt. 6:11.

4

In the Gospel that the Nazareans and Ebionites use, which I recently translated from Hebrew into Greek, and which most people consider the authentic version of Matthew, the man with a withered hand[4] is described as a mason, seeking for help in words like these: "I was a mason who made a living with my hands; I beseech you, Jesus, restore my health so I do not have to beg for food shamefully." (Jerome, *Commentary on Matthew*, 12, 13).

5

In the Gospel the Nazareans use, we find it written "son of Johoiada" instead of "son of Barachia." (Jerome, *Commentary on Matthew* 23, 35)

6

The name of that one (i.e., Barabbas) is interpreted to mean "son of their master" in the Gospel written according to the Hebrews. (Jerome, *Commentary on Matthew* 27, 16)

7

In the Gospel we have often referred to we read that "the enormous lintel of the temple was broken and split apart." (Jerome, *Commentary on Matthew* 27, 51)

8

In the Gospel according to the Hebrews, which was actually written in the Chaldean or Syriac language but with Hebrew letters, which the Nazareans use still today and which is that according to the Apostles, or, as most believe, according to Matthew—a Gospel that can also be found in the library of Caesarea—the following story is found: "Behold, the mother of the Lord and his brothers were saying to him, 'John the Baptist is baptizing for the remission of sins. Let us go and be baptized by him.' But he replied to them, 'What sin have I committed that I should go to be baptized by him? Unless possibly what I just said was spoken in ignorance.'" (Jerome, *Against the Pelagians*, 3, 2).

4. See Matt. 12:9–14; Mark 3:1–6; Luke 6:6–11.

9

And in the same volume: "(Jesus) said, 'If your brother sins by speaking a word against you, but then makes it up to you, you should accept him seven times a day.' His disciple Simon said to him, 'Seven times in a day?' The Lord responded, "Yes indeed, I tell you—even up to seventy times seven![5] For even among the prophets, after they were anointed by the Holy Spirit, a word of sin was found.'" (Jerome, *Against the Pelagians,* 3, 2)

10
Variant Readings Noted in New Testament Manuscripts

- On Matthew 4:5. The Jewish Gospel does not have, "into the holy city," but "in Jerusalem." (MS 566)
- On Matthew 5:22. The words "without cause" are not present in some copies, nor in the Jewish Gospel. (MS 1424)
- On Matthew 7:5. In this place the Jewish Gospel reads: "Even if you are resting on my breast but do not do the will of my Father in heaven, I will cast you away from my breast." (MS 1424)
- On Matthew 10:16. The Jewish Gospel says, "more than serpents." (MS 1424)
- On Matthew 11:12. The Jewish Gospel reads, "plunders." (MS 1424)
- On Matthew 11:25. The Jewish Gospel says, "I give you thanks." (MS 1424)
- On Matthew 12:40. The Jewish Gospel does not read, "Three days and three nights." (MS 899)
- On Matthew 15:5. The Jewish Gospel says, "That which you would have had as a benefit from us is now an offering [to the temple?]." (MS 1424)
- On Matthew 16:2–3. The passages marked with an asterisk are not set forth in other copies, nor in the Jewish Gospel. (MS 1424)
- On Matthew 16:17. The Jewish Gospel says, "son of John." (MS 566)
- On Matthew 18:22. After the words "seventy times seven" the Jewish Gospel reads: "For even among the prophets, after they were anointed by the Holy Spirit, a word of sin was found." (MSS 566, 899)
- On Matthew 26:74. The Jewish Gospel says, "And he made a denial, and swore, and cursed." (MS 4, 273, 899, 1414)
- On Matthew 27:65. The Jewish Gospel says, "And he gave them armed men to sit opposite the cave, to keep watch over it day and night." (MS 1424)

5. See Matt. 18:21–22 and Luke 17:3–4.

The Gospel of the Ebionites

Christianity started out as a sect within Judaism that had come to understand Jesus as the Jewish messiah. Eventually, however, the religion became predominantly gentile, and the Jewish understandings of the faith came to be proscribed and condemned as heresy. Still, Jewish Christian communities existed throughout the Jewish diaspora for centuries, as Christian polemical sources amply attest.

From at least the time of Irenaeus (ca. 180 CE), Jewish Christian groups were known as the Ebionites. Evidently the name derives from the Hebrew EBYON, "the poor." Jewish followers of Jesus may have adopted this name because they, like the earliest Jewish Christian communities mentioned in Acts 2:43–47 and 4:32–37, took on voluntary poverty for the sake of the gospel. Their opponents sometimes claimed they were "poor in faith."

Irenaeus believed that the Ebionites used only one Gospel, a version of the Gospel of Matthew (*Adv. Haer.* 3, 11, 7), which Irenaeus maintained was originally written in Hebrew. This claim contributed to the confusion among later writers, who believed that quotations from a Jewish-Christian Gospel must have derived from this Hebrew version of Matthew. This confusion persisted all the way down to one of our latest independent witnesses to the Jewish-Christian Gospels, the church father and heresy-hunter Epiphanius, at the end of the fourth century, who quotes a Gospel of the Ebionites, but mistakenly thinks that it goes under the name Matthew, and that it was originally written in Hebrew.

In fact, unlike the Gospel of the Nazareans, the account quoted by Epiphanius shows clear evidence of having been composed in Greek. One of the "confusions" of the Gospel involves the diet of John the Baptist, who is said to have eaten "pancakes" (Greek EGKRIDES) rather than "locusts" (AKRIDES). While this word play involves simply a change of one letter into two in Greek, it does not work in Aramaic. It should not be thought, however, that this Gospel is the Gospel according to the Hebrews (the other Jewish-Christian Gospel written in Greek): both accounts describe Jesus' baptism, but in radically different ways. In the Gospel of the Ebionites, in fact, the baptism scene is a key passage for understanding how the narrative was constructed, for here the unknown author has combined the traditions of Matthew, Mark, and Luke (as found in several manuscripts of the NT). In each of these earlier sources, the voice from heaven at the baptism speaks different words; in the Gospel of the Ebionites it speaks *all* these words, by speaking on three different occasions. The Gospel of the Ebionites, in other words, was, in part, a Gospel harmony, a conflation of the accounts of the Synoptic Gospels, comparable to the Diatessaron created by the church father Tatian in the mid-second century (about the same time as this Gospel was composed; for the Diatessaron, see later in this collection), except that unlike Tatian, this author did not, so far as we know, use the traditions found in the Gospel of John. Like him, however, he does appear to have used some non-canonical traditions.

Epiphanius maintained that the Jewish-Christian group that used this Gospel was located in the region East of the Jordan River. It is he alone who gives us access to their Gospel traditions, in his polemical work *The Panarion* (i.e., the "Medicine Chest," which provided the antidote for the bites of the serpents of heresy). From his quotations, several distinctive features of this Jewish sect can be detected. In particular, it is clear that they maintained that Jesus was the perfect sacrifice for sins, so that there was no longer any need for the Jewish sacrificial cult (saying 7). Moreover, since meat in the ancient world was generally consumed in connection with its sacrifice to God (or the gods), the Ebionites, who no longer believed in sacrifice, evidently maintained a vegetarian cuisine. That appears to be the reason that Jesus shows a disinclination to eat the Passover lamb (saying 8) and why his forerunner ate pancakes instead of locusts (see saying 3). It is somewhat more difficult to establish the group's particular christological views, although it appears that they rejected the notion that Jesus was fully human, and thought instead that he was an angel made incarnate (so, at least, Epiphanius; see sayings 6 and 7). In any event, their Gospel did not narrate a virgin birth; according to Epiphanius it began (as does the Gospel of Mark) with Jesus' baptism.

In addition to the baptism narrative, the quotations of the Gospel refer to Jesus' call of the twelve, his public ministry, the Last Supper, and the passion. It was, in other words, a narrative Gospel much like the Synoptics, on which it appears to have been based. It is difficult to assign a precise date to the Gospel, since it is known only in the writings of a late-fourth century church father. At the least we can say that it must date no earlier than the end of the first century, since its author had at his disposal the Gospels of Matthew, Mark, and Luke. Some scholars have argued that since it shows no evidence of knowing the Gospel of John, it cannot easily be dated after 150 CE; this presupposes, however, that a Christian writer would feel compelled to use the Fourth Gospel if it was widely in circulation (note, for example, that Justin from the mid-second century also never quotes John explicitly). In any event, most scholars have dated the Gospel to the mid to late second century.

Bibliography

See bibliography in the general introduction to the Jewish Christian Gospels.

The Gospel of the Ebionites

1

The beginning of the Gospel they use reads as follows: "And so in the days of Herod, King of Judea, John came baptizing a baptism of repentance in the Jordan River. He was said to have come from the tribe of Aaron, the priest, and was the child of Zacharias and Elizabeth. And everyone went out to him."[6] (Epiphanius, *Panarion*, 30, 13, 6).

2

For by chopping off the genealogies of Matthew they make their Gospel begin as we indicated before, with the words: "And so in the days of Herod, King of Judea, when Caiaphas was high priest, a certain one named John came baptizing a baptism of repentance in the Jordan River." (Epiphanius, *Panarion*, 30, 14, 3)

3

And so John was baptizing, and Pharisees came out to him and were baptized, as was all of Jerusalem. John wore a garment of camel hair and a leather belt around his waist; and his food was wild honey that tasted like manna, like a cake cooked in olive oil.[7] (Epiphanius, *Panarion*, 30, 13, 4–5)

4

And after a good deal more, it goes on: "When the people were baptized, Jesus also came and was baptized by John. When he came up out of the water, the heavens opened and he saw the Holy Spirit in the form of a dove, descending and entering him. And a voice came from heaven, 'You are my beloved Son, in you I am well pleased.' Then it said, 'Today I have given you birth.' Immediately a great light enlightened the place. When John saw this," it says, "he said to him, 'Who are you, Lord?' Yet again a voice came from heaven to him, 'This is my beloved Son, with whom I am well pleased.'[8] And then," it says, "John fell before him and said, 'I beg you, Lord—you baptize me!' But Jesus restrained him by saying, 'Let it be, for it is fitting that all things be fulfilled in this way.'"[9] (Epiphanius, *Panarion*, 30, 13, 3–4)

6. See Matt. 3:1–12; Mark 1:4–8; Luke 3:1–20.
7. See Matt. 3:4–5; Mark 1:5–6.
8. See Matt. 3:17; Mark 1:11; and Luke 3:22 (in MS D and several Old latin witnesses).
9. Matt. 3:14–15.

5

In the Gospel that they call "according to Matthew"—which is not at all complete, but is falsified and mutilated—which they refer to as the Hebrew Gospel, the following is found:

"There was a certain man named Jesus, who was about thirty years old. He is the one who chose us. When he came to Capernaum he entered the house of Simon, also called Peter, and he opened his mouth to say, 'As I was passing by the lake of Tiberias I chose John and James, the sons of Zebedee, and Simon, Andrew, Thaddaeus, Simon the Zealot, and Judas Iscariot; and I called you, Matthew, while you were sitting at the tax collector's booth, and you followed me.[10] I want you, therefore, to be the twelve apostles as a witness to Israel.'" (Epiphanius, *Panarion,* 30, 13, 2–3).

6

Again they deny that he was a man, apparently based on the word the Savior spoke when it was reported to him, "See, your mother and brothers are standing outside." "Who," (he asked) "is my mother and brothers?" Stretching out his hand over his disciples he said, "These are my brothers and mother and sisters—those who do the will of my Father."[11] (Epiphanius, *Panarion,* 30, 14, 5)

7

They do not allege that he was born from God the Father, but that he was created as one of the archangels, yet was made greater than they, since he rules over the angels and all things made by the Almighty. And, as found in their Gospel, they say that when he came he taught, "I have come to destroy the sacrifices. And if you do not stop making sacrifice, God's wrath will not stop afflicting you." (Epiphanius, *Panarion,* 30, 16, 4–5).

8

They have changed the saying by abandoning its true sequence, as is clear to everyone who considers the combination of the words. For they had the disciples say, "Where do you want us make preparations for you to eat the Passover lamb?"[12] And they made him respond, "I have no desire to eat the meat of this Passover lamb with you." (Epiphanius, *Panarion,* 30, 22, 4).

10. See Matt. 4:18–22; 9:9–13; Mark 1:16–20; 2:13–14; Luke 5:1–11, 27–32.
11. See Matt. 12:47–50; Mark 3:32–35; and Luke 8:20–21.
12. See Matt. 26:17; Mark 14:12; and especially Luke 22:15.

The Gospel according to the Hebrews

The Gospel according to the Hebrews was known and used in Egypt. It is quoted there by Clement of Alexandria, Origen, and Didymus the Blind. Jerome may also have become acquainted with it during his time there, although it is also possible that he came to know of it through his extensive knowledge of the writings of Origen (many of which are now lost to us). The title of the Gospel, as found in many of the patristic sources, indicates that it was used by Jewish Christians. Confusion as to its relationship to the other Jewish-Christian Gospels is caused principally by the ways it is referenced by Jerome, who (wrongly) indicates that it was originally written in Hebrew and that it was in use by the Jewish sect known as the Nazareans.

Unlike the Gospel of the Nazareans, this Gospel appears to have been circulated in Greek. Otherwise it would be impossible to account for its quotation by Clement of Alexandria and Didymus the Blind. Moreover, it does not appear to have any particular ties to the Gospel of Matthew, or to Matthean traditions in particular. In fact, it does not appear that any of its surviving traditions are reworkings of canonical stories: they instead seem to have been drawn from independent sources.

It is difficult to detect any particular theological orientation of the Gospel, when all the quotations of it are viewed in their entirety. But the first quotation, from Clement, is more familiar to modern readers from the Gospel of Thomas. Could this Gospel have had a gnostic orientation? Possibly saying # 6 could be read in a gnostic way, as indicating the moment when the divine element entered into Jesus at his baptism, making possible his ministry of healing and teaching. A gnostic slant would make sense in light of an Egyptian provenance, but none of the other quotations is closely tied to gnostic ideas. Some scholars have instead preferred to see the Gospel as standing firmly within the tradition of Jewish wisdom literature.

Like the Gospel of the Nazareans, the Gospel according to the Hebrews appears to have been a narrative account of Jesus' entire public ministry, from beginning to end: the surviving quotations involve his baptism, temptation, teaching, (death,) and resurrection. Since the Gospel was known already to Clement, it must have been written by the early or mid-second century. If Jerome knew the Gospel in manuscript form (as opposed to drawing his information about it from Origen), then it was extant at least until the early fifth century.

Bibliography

See the bibliography in the general introduction to the Jewish Christian Gospels.

The Gospel according to the Hebrews

1

As it is also written in the Gospel according to the Hebrews, "The one who is amazed will rule, and the one who rules will find rest." (Clement, *Miscellanies* 2.9.45)

2

If anyone accepts the Gospel according to the Hebrews, where the Savior himself says, "Just now my mother, the Holy Spirit, took me by one of my hairs and carried me up to the great mountain, Tabor." (Origen, *Commentary on John* 2.12)

3

It seems that Matthew is named Levi in the Gospel of Luke.[13] But this is not he; it is Matthias, the one who replaced Judas, who is the same as Levi, known by two names. This appears in the Gospel according the Hebrews. (Didymus the Blind, *Commentary on the Psalms* 184.9–10)

4

As we also read in the Hebrew Gospel, the Lord speaking to his disciples: "You should never rejoice, he said, except when you look upon your brother in love." (Jerome, *Commentary on Ephesians* 5.4)

5

The Gospel that is called "according to the Hebrews," which I have recently translated into both Greek and Latin, a Gospel that Origen frequently used, records the following after the Savior's resurrection: "But when the Lord had given the linen cloth to the servant of the priest, he went and appeared to James. For James had taken a vow not to eat bread from the time he drank the cup of the Lord until he should see him raised from among those who sleep." And soon after this it says, "The Lord said, 'Bring a table and bread.'" And immediately it continues, "He took the bread and blessed it, broke it, gave it to James the Just,

13. See Mark 2:14, Matt. 9:9; and Luke 5:27.

and said to him, 'My brother, eat your bread. For the Son of Man is risen from among those who sleep.'" (Jerome, *Illustrious Men* 2)

6

It is stated in the Gospel written in Hebrew, which the Nazareans read: "The entire fountain of the Holy Spirit will descend on him. And the Lord is Spirit, and where the Spirit of the Lord is, there is liberty." Later in that Gospel that we have mentioned above we find the following written: "Then, when the Lord came up from the water, the entire fountain of the Holy Spirit descended and rested on him; and it said to him, "My Son, in all the prophets I have been expecting you to come, that I might rest on you. For you are my rest, you are my firstborn Son, who rules forever."[14] (Jerome, *Commenatry on Isaiah* 11.1–3)

7

And in the Gospel according to the Hebrews, which the Nazareans are accustomed to read, the following is described as among the worst offenses: that someone should make the spirit of his brother sad. (Jerome, *Commentary on Ezekiel* 18.7)

14. See Matt. 3:16–17; Mark 1:10–11; Luke 3:21–22; John 1:32–34; see Isa. 11:2.

8

The Gospel according to the Egyptians

The Gospel according to the Egyptians cannot be found in any surviving manuscript, but only in the citations of the late-second century church father, Clement of Alexandria. Several other church fathers mention the existence of the Gospel, and say disparaging things about it.

Clement's contemporary, Hippolytus of Rome (*Refutation* 5, 7), indicates that the Gospel was used by the gnostic group known as the Naasenes to validate their view of the complexity of the soul. It is difficult to know whether this information is reliable: most of the surviving quotations are susceptible to a gnostic interpretation, but none of them directly mentions the soul. Some decades later, Origen (*Homily on Luke* 1.2) indicates that the Gospel was not one of the "church's," but that it was among the "large number" of Gospels used by "the heretics." The fourth-century Epiphanius (*Panarion* 62.2) indicates that the book was used by the Sabellians to demonstrate that the Father, Son, and Holy Spirit were one and the same. As so often happens with Epiphanius, it is not clear whether he actually had seen the book, or if rather he knew of it as a heretical Gospel and chose to slur the Sabellians by claiming they made use of it.

It is Clement alone who gives us quotations from the book, six altogether. On two occasions (sayings 2 and 5) he mentions the Gospel by name: in both instances it involves a conversation between Jesus and a woman disciple named Salome, who is known to us from two passages in the New Testament (Mark 15:40; 16:1; also Gospel of Thomas 61 and Pistis Sophia 132). In four other instances, Clement cites Gospel quotations of a conversation between these two; by inference, these quotations are also generally understood as having come from the Gospel according to the Egyptians. All these quotations deal with the same basic issues: sexual abstinence, the relation of the genders, and the legitimacy of childbearing.

None of Clement's quotations of the Gospel is disparaging; on the contrary, he appears to hold it as an authority. But he does assert that the teachings of the Gospel have been twisted by those who take them in a literal way to denigrate sexual activities and procreation. Clement quotes the Gospel in order to provide his own allegorizing interpretation of it. A more straightforward reading of the Gospel suggests that it was indeed written to support an ascetic lifestyle that rejected the pleasures of sex and denied the value of procreation. Its views appear to be based on a close reading of the Adam and Eve stories of Genesis 2–3, where, for example, pain in childbirth is seen as a direct result of sin having entered into the world.

It is impossible to say anything definitive about the extent and character of the Gospel: it may have been a sayings Gospel like the Gospel of Thomas or, more likely, a dialogue narrative like the gnostic work, the Pistis Sophia. But it may just as well have been a full narrative Gospel such as those that made it into the canon. If the latter, there is no trace in any of our sources of the rest of the Gospel, just the conversation(s) Jesus had with Salome, presumably, but not necessarily, during his earthly ministry (it is also possible that it consisted of conversations from after the resurrection).

One of the sayings (5) has striking similarities to the words of Jesus preserved in 2 Clement 12:1–2, but also to sayings of the Gospel of Thomas (22, 37). It is not clear if one source is borrowing from another, or if, instead, the saying was independently known in a variety of forms to various authors of the second century, as it circulated freely through the oral tradition.

Some scholars of the nineteenth and twentieth centuries were keen to tie this Gospel to other, equally scarcely known documents: the Gospel of Peter; sayings of Oxyrhnchus papyri 1 and 655 (which are now known to have come from the Gospel of Thomas); the Gospel of the Hebrews; the apocryphal Epistle of Titus; and so on. The reality, though, is that we simply do not have evidence to make any of these suggestions plausible.

There have long been debates concerning both the name of the Gospel and what the name might signify. W. Bauer maintained that it was the Gospel used by gentiles in Egypt, and that it was called the Gospel according to the Egyptians to differentiate it from the other Gospel widely in use there, but by Jews, the Gospel of the Hebrews (*Orthodoxy and Heresy*, p. 50). Other scholars have seen this reasoning as faulty, since Jews also could be Egyptian, and there were other Gospels (many other Gospels!) in use by Christians (Jew and gentile) in Egypt. More likely is the view that the title was devised by non-Egyptians to designate a Gospel used by the Christians of Egypt.

The Gospel must date before the earliest known references to it, that is, prior to the writings of Clement of Alexandria in the late second century. Most scholars date it to around the middle of the century. Given its title and its early attestation by the Alexandrian church fathers Clement and Origen, it is widely assumed to have been written there, in Egypt. There is now another Gospel called "Egyptian," in the Nag Hammadi Library. These two books have nothing in common and are not to be confused with one another.

We have translated the texts of Clement's quotations from the editions of Früchtel (1970) and Früchtel and Treu (1985).

Bibliography

Bauer, W. *Orthodoxy and Heresy in Earliest Christianity*. Philadelphia: Fortress, 1971; German original 1934.

Elliott, J. K. *The Apocryphal New Testament*. Oxford: Clarendon, 1993; pp. 16–19.

Früchtel, L., ed. *Clemens Alexandrinus, Stromata Buch VII-XII, Excerpta ex Thedot*. 2nd ed. GCS, 17. Berlin: Akademie Verlag, 1970.

Früchtel, L., and U. Treu, eds. *Clemens Alexandrinus, Stromata Buch I-VI*. 4th ed. GCS, 15. Berlin: Akademie Verlag, 1985.

Klauck, H.-J. *Apocryphal Gospels: An Introduction*. London: T&T Clark, 2003; German original Stuttgart, 2002; pp. 55–59.

Schneemelcher, W., "The Gospel of the Egyptians." in *New Testament Apocrypha*, ed. W. Schneemelcher; trans. R. McL. Wilson. Louisville: Westminster/John Knox, 1991; vol. 1, pp. 209–15.

The Gospel according to the Egyptians

1

When Salome asked, "How long will death prevail?" the Lord replied "For as long as you women bear children." But he did not say this because life is evil or the creation wicked; instead he was teaching the natural succession of things; for everything degenerates after coming into being. (Clement of Alexandria, *Miscellanies* 3.45.3)

2

Those who oppose God's creation because of self-control—which sounds good—also quote the words spoken to Salome, some of which we have already mentioned, found, I think, in the Gospel according to the Egyptians. For they claim that the Savior himself said, "I have come to destroy the works of the female." By "the female" he meant desire and by "works" he meant birth and degeneration. (Clement of Alexandria, *Miscellanies* 3.63.1)

3

Therefore it is probably with regard to the final consummation, as the argument indicates, that Salome says, "How long will people continue to die?" Now Scripture refers to a human being in two senses: that which is visible and the soul, that is, one subject to salvation and one not. And sin is called the death of the soul. For this reason, the Lord also replied shrewdly, "For as long as women bear children"—that is to say, for as long as desires continue to be active. (Clement of Alexandria, *Miscellanies* 3.64.1)

4

Why do those who adhere more to everything other than the true gospel rule not cite the following words spoken to Salome? For when she said, "Then I have done well not to bear children" (supposing that it was not necessary to give birth), the Lord responded, "Eat every herb, but not the one that is bitter." (Clement of Alexandria, *Miscellanies* 3.66.1–2)

5

This is why Cassian says, "When Salome inquired when the things she had asked about would become known, the Lord replied: 'When you trample (pl) on the garment of shame and when the two become one and the male with the female is neither male nor female.'"[1] The first thing to note, then, is that we do not find this saying in the four Gospels handed down to us, but in the Gospel according to the Egyptians. (Clement of Alexandria, *Miscellanies* 3.92.2–93.1)

6

And when the Savior said to Salome, "Death will last as long as women give birth," he was not denigrating birth—since it is, after all, necessary for the salvation of those who believe. (Clement of Alexandria, *Excerpts from Theodotus* 67.2)

1. See Gospel of Thomas 22, 37.

9

A Gospel Harmony: The Diatessaron?

It is difficult to know whether or not to include the one (possible) surviving fragment of Tatian's enormously important Diatessaron in an edition of the apocryphal Gospels. On the one hand, the Diatessaron did not principally contain apocryphal tales about Jesus, but was a harmony of the four (eventually) canonical Gospels, which wove their various accounts into one long, continuous narrative. On the other hand, the Diatessaron was a Gospel text that did not finally make it into the canon, even in the Syrian church where it was (probably) written and (certainly) promulgated—and in that sense it is "apocryphal." Moreover, some scholars have argued that Tatian used one or more non-canonical Gospels in composing his work.

Tatian was a Christian philosopher-theologian from Eastern Syria who went to Rome in the mid-second century and studied under the great Christian apologist Justin. After Justin's martyrdom in 165 CE, Tatian returned to his homeland. Justin himself may have used some kind of harmony of the Synoptic Gospels—many of his Gospel quotations appear to embody conflated forms of the text—but there is no certainty that he used the Fourth Gospel. Tatian, on the other hand, created a new Gospel harmony with all four of the Gospels that were to become canonical—hence the name of his great work, the Diatessaron ("Through the Four").

It continues to be debated among scholars whether Tatian produced this Gospel harmony in Greek or Syriac. It was, in any event, "the" Gospel used in Syria for at least two centuries. And it became popular in other places in Christendom, where it was either translated or used as the basis of Gospel harmonies in local languages down through the middle ages. Eventually the Diatesseron was replaced in Syria with an edition of the "separate" Gospels in the Peshitta translation, and remarkably, copies of the Diatessaron were not reproduced or preserved, so that today its reconstruction is one of the most difficult tasks confronting textual scholars, who have to rely on such sources as the commentary written on the Diatessaron by the Syriac church Father Ephrem and the many vernacular harmonies that were more or less closely tied to it (in such languages as Arabic, Persian, Latin, Middle German, Middle Dutch, Middle Italian, Middle English).

In some small measure that changed when the ancient city, Dura on the Euphrates, was uncovered in one of the great archaeological finds of the twentieth century. Dura had been destroyed by war in 256–57 CE; it was then deserted and lost, until accidentally unearthed by British soldiers after the First World War. Among the significant finds in Dura were the remains of a house that had been converted for use as a church building (ca. 231 CE). This is the first hard evidence of a physical structure used as a church from the ancient world—some two hundred years after the days of Jesus himself.

Also found in the excavations in Dura were a number of manuscripts—including a small scrap of parchment (9 x 11 cm), written on one side, that contains a Greek Gospel account drawn from the Passion narrative (Dura Parchment 24). The fragmentary copy relates the passages in which women were said to have watched the crucifixion from afar, and in which Joseph of Arimathea requests the body of Jesus. This account has extensive verbal similarities with each of the Gospels of the New Testament, but is identical to none of them. This circumstance led the first editor of the text, Carl Kraeling, to suggest that it was in fact a portion of a Greek version of the Diatesseron.

That judgment is not altogether certain, given the fact that there were other Gospel harmonies produced in the early centuries of the church as well (see the Gospel of the Ebionites for another example). But this fragmentary text certainly presents at least one such account, whether from the hand of Tatian or not.

We have translated the text of the fragment from the edition of Lührmann.

Bibliography

Kraeling, C. H. *A Greek Fragment of Tatian's Diatessaron, from Dura*. London: Christophers, 1935.

Lührmann, D. *Fragmente apokryph gewordener Evangelien in griechischer und lateinischer Sprache*. Marburg: N. G. Elwert, 2000; pp. 102–5.

Metzger, B. M. *The Early Versions of the New Testament: Their Origin, Transmission, and Limitations*. Oxford: Clarendon, 1977; pp. 10–36.

Petersen, W. L. *The Diatessaron: Its Creation, Dissemination, Significance and History in Scholarship*. Leiden: E. J. Brill, 1994.

Petersen, W. L. "The Diatessaron," in the *Anchor Bible Dictionary*, ed. D. N. Freedman et al. New York: Doubleday, 1992; vol. 2, pp. 189–90.

Schmidt, U. "The Diatessaron," in *The Text of the New Testament in Contemporary Research: Essays on the Status Quaestionis*, ed. B. D. Ehrman and M. W. Holmes. Leiden: E. J., Brill, 2012; pp. 115–42.

A Gospel Harmony
Dura Parchment 24

. . . of Zebedee, and Salome, and the wives
of those who had accompanied him from
Galilee, to see the one who was crucified. But it was
the Day of Preparation. The Sabbath was dawning.
When evening came on the Day of Preparation,
which is the day before the Sabbath,
a man came, who was a council member
from Arimathea, a city of
Judea. His name was Joseph. He was a good
and righteous man, and a disciple of Jesus,
but in secret, because he feared
the Jews. He was waiting for
the Kingdom of God. This one had not
agreed with the council. . . .[1]

1. See Matt. 27:55–61; Mark 15:42–47; Luke 23:50–56; and John 19:38–42; see also Gospel of Peter 3–5, 23–24.

10

Papyrus Berlin 11710

First published in 1923 by H. Lietzmann, the "Berlin papyrus" fragment, P.Berl. 11710, contains a brief conversation between Jesus and his disciple Nathaniel, modeled, evidently, on John 1:49 and 29—or at least on traditions similar to those incorporated in John. The surviving manuscript consists of two very small papyrus leaves (6.5 x 7.5 cm) that are well preserved and written on front and back; they date from the sixth century, but there is no way of knowing more exactly when the Gospel account they contain was itself composed. Their diminutive size suggests that they may have been part of an amulet (a small text used for magical purposes), rather than a Gospel book for public (or private) reading.

Altogether twenty-one short lines of text are preserved, followed at the end with the Coptic words "Jesus Christ, God." Jesus is otherwise not named in the text; he is instead consistently called the "Rabbi," possibly in keeping with the account of John 1:38, 49. Our translation is based on the text of Bernhard.

Bibliography

Bernhard, A. E. *Other Early Christian Gospels: A Critical Edition of the Surviving Greek Manuscripts*. London: T & T Clark, 2006; p. 102.

Elliott, J. K. *The Apocryphal New Testament*. Oxford: Clarendon, 1993; pp. 42–43.

Papyrus Berlin 11710

Fragment a ↓

[. . .] and
said, "Rabbi,
Lord, you are the Son
of God."[1] The rabbi answered him
and
said, "Nathaniel,

Fragment a →

walk in
the sun."
Nathaniel answered him
and
said, "Rabbi,
Lord, you are the lamb

Fragment b ↓

of God, who takes away
the sins of
the world."[2]
The rabbi
answered him
and said . . .

Fragment b →

[in Coptic]
Jesus Christ,
God

1. See John 1:48–49.
2. See John 1:48–49; 1:29, 35.

11

Papyrus Cairo 10735

The Cairo papyrus, P.Cair. 10735, consists of one papyrus leaf, written front and back and dating from the sixth or seventh century. It was first published by Grenfell and Hunt in 1903 as the fragment of a lost Gospel. In the following year, A. Deissmann wrote an influential analysis arguing that the text was not a Gospel but a homily or commentary on a Gospel. If the text is a Gospel, it provides an expanded version of the infancy narratives of Matthew and Luke. It is also possible, then, that the text derives from an early Gospel harmony.

The lines on the recto side involve the flight of the holy family to Egypt, with close connections to Matthew 2:13; the lines on the verso relate to the birth of John the Baptist, as narrated in Luke 1:36. Both texts, especially the latter, differ from the biblical accounts. Whether the author actually knew these earlier Gospels or only knew of the traditions that they utilized cannot be determined. It is also impossible to know when the account may have originally been written.

We have based our translation of the fragment on the edition of Santos Otero.

Bibliography

Deissmann, A. "Das angebliche Evangelienfragment von Kairo," *AR* 7 (1904) 387–92; reprinted in *Light from the Ancient East.* 2nd ed. New York: George H. Dorah, 1927; pp. 430–34.

Elliott, J. K. *The Apocryphal New Testament.* Oxford: Clarendon, 1993; pp. 45.

Grenfell, B. P., and A. S. Hunt. *Greek Papyri.* Oxford: Oxford University Press, 1903; no. 10; p. 735.

Jeremias, J., and W. Schneemelcher. "Fragments of Unknown Gospels," in *New Testament Apocrypha,* ed. Wilhelm Schneemelcher; tr. R. McL. Wilson. Louisville: Westminster/John Knox, 1991; vol. 1, p. 101.

de Santos Otero, Aurelio. *Los Evangelios Apócrifos: Colección de textos griegos y latinos, versión crítica, estudios introductorios y comentarios;* rev. ed. Madrid: Biblioteca de Autores Cristianos, 2003; p. 82.

Papyrus Cairo 10735

→

The angel of the Lord said, "Joseph, Rise up,
take Mary your wife and
flee to Egypt, and . . .[1]
. . .
. . .
every gift and if . . .
his friends . . .
of the king . . ."

↓

. . . you should understand." Then
the leader of hosts said to the virgin, "Behold
Elizabeth your relative has also conceived
and it is the sixth month for her who has been called
barren."[2] In the sixth month of the year, which is called Thoth,
the mother of John conceived him.
But it was necessary that the leader of the hosts proclaim John in advance,
the servant who precedes
the coming of his Lord.

1. See Matt. 2:13.
2. See Luke 1:36.

12

Papyrus Egerton 2 (and Papyrus Köln 255)

One of the most significant publications of early Christian texts in the first part of the twentieth century was H. I. Bell and T. C. Skeat, *Fragments of an Unknown Gospel and Other Christian Papyri*. The "Unknown Gospel" is preserved in Papyrus Egerton 2, which consists of four fragmentary papyrus leafs, two of which are too fragmentary to be reconstructed (one of them has simply one letter on one side). The other two (9.2 x 11.5 cm and 9.7 x 11.8 cm) contain four narratives that have, in places, striking similarities with the Gospels of the New Testament. But there are few verbatim agreements with their New Testament parallels, and some significant differences in content—including one narrative otherwise unknown.

Half a century after Bell and Skeat's initial publication of the papyrus, M. Gronewald discovered a fragment among the Cologne papyri that he perceptively recognized as belonging to the same manuscript (P.Köln 255). This new fragment (6.5 x 3.0 cm) adds portions of six lines to both recto and verso of Fragment one.

The stories contained in P. Egerton 2 are as follows: (a) Jesus' exhortation to his Jewish opponents to "search the Scriptures" (see John 5:39–47 and 10:31–39); (b) a foiled attempt to stone and then arrest Jesus, followed by his healing of a leper (see, e.g., John 10:31ff; Matt. 8:1–4; Mark 1:40–45; Luke 5:12–16; and Luke 17:11–14); (c) the question of whether it is right to pay tribute to the ruling authorities (see Matt. 22:15–22; Mark 12:13–17; and Luke 20:20–26); and (d) the highly fragmentary account of a miracle Jesus performed by the Jordan River, possibly to illustrate his parable about the miraculous growth of seeds. This final story has no parallel in the canonical Gospels.

Bell and Skeat were inclined to date the manuscript to 150 CE. This was a sensational claim, as it made P.Egerton 2 the oldest surviving Christian manuscript of any kind—older than the earliest surviving copies of the books that later became the New Testament. But soon after its publication C.H. Roberts edited a papyrus that is now known as P^{52}, which contains portions of John 18:31–38 and is generally dated to the year 125 CE (+/- 25 years). This is now generally considered the oldest surviving copy of any Christian writing. Moreover, on the basis of his fresh examination of P.Egerton 2, Gronewald has argued that Bell and Skeat were overly generous in their dating, that the text more likely was produced around 200 CE. Even so, P.Egerton 2 remains one of our earliest manuscripts of any piece of Christian literature.

After its first publication there was a flurry of scholarly interest in the text, with some fifty scholarly articles devoted to it within three years. One of the leading questions was, and continues to be, the relationship of this "Unknown Gospel" to the Gospels of the New Testament. Did its author construct his account based on the stories found in the canonical four Gospels? If so, why are there only scattered verbatim agreements? Was he attempting to create a Gospel Harmony? This would explain the material agreements not only with the Synoptics, but also with John; on the other hand, the author must have doing more than creating a harmony, since the fourth story of the text has no parallel in the New Testament (or anywhere else). Had the author read the Gospels that later became canonical and used them to construct his account from memory, without looking at them carefully? Had the stories of the New Testament Gospels been circulating orally, and he based his narratives on these oral traditions? Or was he writing in complete independence of the canonical Gospels? Is it possible that his account actually antedates the canonical accounts, that it was one of the sources for, say, the Fourth Gospel?

Without page numbering on the surviving fragments of P.Egerton 2, it is impossible to know for certain which pages preceded the others, and which side, recto or verso, is to be read first. What follows is a plausible reconstruction of the original order. For the most part, we have followed the text as reconstructed in Lührmann, but we have taken the sequence of the fragments from Bell-Skeat.

Bibliography

Bell, H. I., and T. C. Skeat. *Fragments of an Unknown Gospel and Other Early Christian Papyri*. London: Oxford University Press, 1935.

Bell, H. I., and T. C. Skeat. *The New Gospel Fragments*. London: Oxford University Press, 1935.

Bernhard, A. E. *Other Early Christian Gospels: A Critical Edition of the Surviving Greek Manuscripts*. London: T&T Clark, 2006; p. 84–87.

Elliott, J. K. *The Apocryphal New Testament*. Oxford: Clarendon, 1993; pp. 37–42.

Gronewald, M. "255. Unbekanntes Evangelium oder Evangelharmonie (Fragment aus dem 'Evangelium Egerton')," in *Kölner Papyri (P. Köln)*, ed. M. Gronewald et al. Opladen: Westdeutscher Verlag, 1987; vol. 6; pp. 136–45.

Klauck, H.-J. *Apocryphal Gospels: An Introduction*. London: T&T Clark, 2003; pp. 23–26.

Lührmann, D. *Fragmente apokryph gewordener Evangelien in griechischer und lateinischer Sprache*. Marburg: N. G. Elwert, 2000; pp. 142–53.

Schneemelcher, W. "Fragments of Unknown Gospels," in *New Testament Apocrypha*, ed. W. Schneemelcher; tr. R. McL. Wilson. Louisville: Westminster/John Knox, 1991; vol. 1, pp. 96–99.

Papyrus Egerton 2 (and Papyrus Köln 255)

1 ↓

And Jesus said to the lawyers:
"Punish every wrong-doer and transgressor,
but not me. . . .
how he does what he does."
Then he turned to the rulers of the people
and spoke this word: "Search
the Scriptures; you think that in them
you have life. They are the ones
that testify concerning me.[1] Do not think
that I came to accuse
you to my Father. The one who
accuses you is Moses, in whom
you have hoped."[2] They replied,
"We know full well that God spoke
to Moses. But we do not know
where you have come from."[3] Jesus answered
them, "Now what stands accused
is your failure to believe his
testimonies. For if you
had believed Moses, you would have believed
me. For that one wrote
to your fathers about me.[4] . . ."

1 →

. . . to the crowd . . .
stones together so that they might stone
him. And the rulers sought to lay
their hands on him,
that they might arrest him and deliver him over
to the crowd. They were unable
to arrest him because the hour
for him to be delivered over had not yet come.[5]

1. See John 5:39.
2. See John 5:45.
3. See John 9:29.
4. See John 5:46.
5. See John 7:30, 44.

But the Lord himself went out through their midst
and escaped from them.[6]
And behold, a leper approached him
and said, "Teacher Jesus, while I was traveling with some lepers
and eating with them
at the inn, I myself contracted leprosy.
If, then, you are willing,
I will be made clean." Then the Lord said to him,
"I am willing: be clean." Immediately
the leprosy left him.
Jesus said to him, "Go,
show yourself to the priests
and make an offering for your cleansing
as Moses commanded; and
sin no more. . . ."[7]

2→

. . . [they came]

to him and began rigorously
testing him, saying,
"Teacher Jesus, we know that you have come from God.
For the things you do give a testimony
that is beyond all the prophets. And so, tell
us: is it right to pay the kings the things
that relate to their rule? Shall we pay them
or not?"[8] But Jesus, knowing their
mind, became incensed
and said to them, "Why do you call me
teacher with your mouth, when you do not listen
to what I say? Well did Isaiah
prophesy about you, 'This people
honors me with their lips,
but their heart is far removed
from me. In vain do they worship me,
commandments. . . .'"[9]

6. See John 10:39; 4:30.
7. See Matt. 8:2–4; Mark 1:40–44; Luke 5:12–16.
8. See Matt. 22:15–22; Mark 12:13–17; Luke 20:20–26.
9. Isa. 29:13; see Mark 7:6–7.

2 ↓

. . . enclosed in a secret place . . .
placed underneath inwardly . . .
its weight beyond measure. . . .
And when they were puzzled, as it were,
over his strange question,
Jesus walked and stood
on the bank of the Jordan
river; he reached out
his right hand, and filled it
. . . . And he sowed it on the . . .
. . . And then . . .
. . . water . . .
. . . and . . .
before their eyes; and it brought forth fruit
. . . many . . . for
joy . . .

13

Papyrus Merton 51

The papyrus fragment known as Papyrus Merton 51 consists of one papyrus leaf (3.9 x 5.3 cm), written on front and back, dating from the third century. It was first published by B. R. Rees in 1959. Rees was uncertain whether the fragment contained an unknown Gospel or a homily based on the Gospel of Luke. Given the fragmentary nature of the text, it is impossible to resolve the question.

The verso is the easier side to reconstruct as it appears to contain Jesus' discourse about good trees bearing good fruit and bad trees bad, as found in Luke 6:43–45 and Matt. 12:33–35. The recto is badly preserved, but it may to be tied to Luke 7:29–30, where the unrepentant and unrighteous Pharisees are contrasted with the tax collectors and (common) people who accompanied Jesus.

The Lukan parallel has been used extensively to help reconstruct the missing words of the fragment. It should be noted, for example, that the term "Pharisees" does not occur in the preserved text, but is part of the reconstruction. Our translation of the text is based on the edition of Lührmann.

Bibliography

Bernhard, A. E. *Other Early Christian Gospels: A Critical Edition of the Surviving Greek Manuscripts*. London: T&T Clark, 2006; p. 99.

Elliott, J. K. *The Apocryphal New Testament*. Oxford: Clarendon, 1993; pp. 45.

Lührmann, D. *Fragmente apokryph gewordener Evangelien in griechischer und lateinischer Sprache*. Marburg: N. G. Elwert, 2000; pp. 155–58.

Rees, B. R. "51. Christian Fragment," in *A Descriptive Catalogue of the Greek Papyri in the Collection of Wilfred Merton, F.S.A.*, ed. B. R. Rees, H. I. Bell, and J. W. B. Barns. Dublin: Hodges Figgis & Co., 1959; vol. 2, pp. 1–4.

Papyrus Merton 51

→

. . . and when all the people and the tax collectors
heard, they declared God righteous,
confessing their own sins.
But the Pharisees were not baptized
by John, and they rejected the counsel of God
and the commandment of God.[1]
So too God rejects them.
But a Pharisee asked him to eat with him. . . .[2]

↓

For the evil man, bringing forth from [his]
evil, brought forth evil fruit,
as an evil tree brings forth (evil fruit) from evil.
And when you send forth good things
from the good treasure of the heart,
its good fruit is not destroyed.[3]
Now you do not call me Lord, Lord,
and do not do the things I say, nor
listen to a prophet who speaks. . . .[4]

1. See Luke 7:29–30; Mark 7:9.
2. See Luke 7:36.
3. See Matt. 7:15–20; 12:33–35; Luke 6:43–45.
4. See Matt. 7:21; Luke 6:46.

14
Papyrus Oxyrhynchus 210

Papyrus Oxyrhynchus 210 is a highly fragmentary text that comprises two fragments, the second of which has portions of just five letters. The other is more substantial (8.7 x 17.3 cm), containing, among other things, a discourse of Jesus. The text was first published by Grenfell and Hunt in 1899 as a Gospel fragment. More recently, C. H. Roberts has maintained that it comes from a homily or commentary on the Gospel. The text dates to the third century.

The fragmentary nature of the text makes its reconstruction very difficult. The recto appears to relate the appearance of an angel; this may be a reference to the infancy narrative of Matt. 1:24. The verso is more complete and involves Jesus' saying about the good tree producing good fruit, as found for example in Luke 6:44–45 and Matt. 12:33–35. But then the tone changes and the speaker, presumably Jesus, begins to speak in the style of the "I am" discourses of the Fourth Gospel. Moreover, he appears to claim to be the "form of God" and the "image of God,"—phrases known not from the Gospels but from the Pauline corpus (see 2 Cor. 4:4; Phil. 2:6; and Col. 1:15). It is not clear whether, in the full text, these were self-attributions of Jesus or if they were comments on the text by a homilist or commentator. If the former, this would have been a Gospel incorporating both synoptic-like and Johannine-like features.

We have based our translation of the fragment on the edition of Lührmann.

Bibliography

Bernhard, A. E. *Other Early Christian Gospels: A Critical Edition of the Surviving Greek Manuscripts*. London: T&T Clark, 2006; p. 100.

Grenfell, B. P., and A. S. Hunt. *The Oxyrhynchus Papyri*. London: Egypt Exploration Fund, 1899; pp. 9–10.

Lührmann, D. *Fragmente apokryph gewordener Evangelien in griechischer und lateinischer Sprache*. Marburg: N. G. Elwert, 2000; pp. 159–63.

Porter, S. E. "POxy II 210 as an Apocryphal Gospel and the Development of Egyptian Christianity," in *Atti del XXII Congresso internazionale di papirologia: Firenze, 23–29 agosto 1998*, ed. I. Andorlini et al. Florence: Istituto papirologica "G. Vitelli," 2001; pp. 1095–1108.

Roberts, C. H. "An Early Christian Papyrus," in *Miscellània papirològica*. FS Ramón Roca-Puig, ed. S. Janerus. Barcelona: Fundaciò Salvador Vives Casajuana, 1987; pp. 293–96.

Papyrus Oxyrhynchus 210

→

. . . to wait. He did these things as the angel
commanded, taking Mary.[1] But what was
spoken concerning the angel. . . .
they are signs. . . .

this . . .
yet . . .

↓

good . . .
he was saying . . .
son of the Father . . .
good. . . .

good

God . . . but . . .
Jesus. And he will say . . .
brings forth good fruit. But the evil
brings forth evil. Good . . .
but the fruit of the good tree . . .
and he will do good.[2] I am . . .
I am the image of . . .[3]
in the form of God . . .[4]
as his image
to God, to God the . . .
to be . . .
visible . . .
the . . .
that . . .

human. . . .

1. See Matt. 1:24; 2:14.
2. See Matt. 7:16–20; 12:33–35; Luke 6:43–45.
3. See 2 Cor. 4:4; Col. 1:15.
4. See Phil. 2:6.

15

Papyrus Oxyrhynchus 840

Discovered by Grenfell and Hunt in 1905 and published in 1908, Papyrus Oxyrhynchus 840 consists of a single parchment leaf, written front and back. The leaf itself is largely complete (with a few gaps, especially at the top of each page), but the text both begins and ends in mid-sentence. This then was part of a larger text. It is impossible to determine how extensive this larger text was, but the portion that remains is clearly a Gospel account unknown to us from any other source. The leaf itself is quite small (7.4 x 8.8 cm), and the writing is virtually microscopic, though legible. Size considerations suggest that the leaf was part of an amulet (see P. Berl. 11710), although whether the amulet consisted of an entire Gospel narrative, or merely an abstract, cannot be determined. The fragment dates to the third or, more probably, the fourth century.

The text begins in the middle of a speech of Jesus, in which he warns against the wages of evildoing. It then moves into an account of a controversy between a certain high priest, a Pharisee evidently named Levi (by making the high priest a Pharisee, the author reveals his ignorance of Jewish history and customs, and possibly his Christian bias), who confronts Jesus for entering the temple along with his disciples, without observing the proper cleansing rituals. This dispute is reminiscent of Synoptic passages such as Mark 7:1–8 and Luke 11:37–41, but has no precise parallel in any other known Gospel text. In response to the high priest's rebuke, Jesus launches into a vituperative attack on the nature of the cleansing rituals and begins to pronounce a "woe" upon his interlocutor, in a fashion comparable to Matt. 23:25–28.

The controversy related by this text is thus in some ways comparable to those of the Synoptics in style and substance, but it is a unique event among the Gospel records of the life of Jesus. Some scholars have tried to identify the text as belonging to lost portions of other known Gospels, such as the Gospel of Peter or the Gospel according to the Hebrews. But all such attempts have faltered, in no small measure because they attempt, with almost no evidence, to explain the unknown (the origin of this fragment) by other unknowns (the missing portions of other fragments). F. Bovon has argued that the fragment does not reflect an incident from the life of the historical Jesus but controversies over water baptism rituals in the early church (second or third centuries, the presumed date of the original form of the Gospel text).

We have translated the text as found in the edition of Lührmann.

Bibliography

Bernhard, A. E. *Other Early Christian Gospels: A Critical Edition of the Surviving Greek Manuscripts*. London: T&T Clark, 2006; p. 101.

Bovon, F. "Fragment Oxyrhynchos 840, Fragment of a Lost Gospel; Witness of an Early Christian Controversy over Purity," *JBL* 119 (2000) 705–28.

Elliott, J. K. *The Apocryphal New Testament*. Oxford: Clarendon, 1993; pp. 31–34.

Jeremias, J., and W. Schneemelche. "Fragments of Unknown Gospels," in *New Testament Apocrypha*, ed. W. Schneemelcher; trans. R. McL. Wilson. Louisville: Westminster/John Knox, 1991; vol. 1, pp. 94–95.

Kruger, M. J. "P. Oxy. 840: Amulet or Miniature Codex?" *JTS* 53 (2002): 81–94.

Kruger, M. P. *The Gospel of the Savior: An Analysis of P.Oxy. 840 and Its Place in the Gospel Traditions of Early Christianity*. Leiden: E. J. Brill, 2005.

Lührmann, D. *Fragmente apokryph gewordener Evangelien in griechischer und lateinischer Sprache*. Marburg: N. G. Elwert, 2000; pp. 164–69.

Schwartz, D. R. "'Viewing the Holy Utensils,' P. Ox. V, 840," *NTS* 32 (1986): 153–59.

Papyrus Oxyrhynchus 840

↓

"... earlier, before acting unjustly, he argues every point subtly.
But take care lest you somehow also
suffer they way they do.
For human evil doers receive [their due]
not only among the living;
they also await punishment and great
torment." And taking them along
he brought them into the sanctuary itself and
began walking in the temple.[1] A certain
Pharisee, a high priest named Levi,
came and met them and said
to the Savior, "Who has permitted you to trample
this sanctuary and to view these
holy vessels, when you have not washed
nor indeed have your disciples bathed their feet?
Although you are defiled
you have trampled this temple,
a place that is clean, where no one else
walks or dares to look upon these holy vessels without
washing and changing his clothes."[2] Immediately the Savior stood
with his disciples and answered him,

→

"You therefore who are here in the temple,
are you clean?" That one said to him, "I am clean, for I washed
in the pool of David, and by
one set of steps I went down [into the water] and by another
I came up; and I put on clothes that are white
and clean. Then I came
and looked upon these holy
vessels." The Savior answered him
and said, "Woe to you blind who do not see.

1. See Mark 11:27.
2. See Matt. 15:1–20; Mark 7:1–23.

You have washed in these waters that have been poured out,
in which dogs and swine have wallowed
night and day. And when you washed
you scoured the outer skin, which
even prostitutes and flute girls
anoint, wash, scour,
and beautify for human lust.
But inside they are
full of scorpions and
every evil.[3] But
my disciples and I, whom you say
have not bathed, have been dipped in waters
of eternal life, which come from . . .
But woe to those . . ."

3. See Matt. 23:16–28; Luke 11:37–41.

16

Papyrus Oxyrhynchus 1224

Papyrus Oxyrhynchus 1224 is a fourth-century manuscript consisting of several papyrus fragments written front and back, the largest measuring 6.3 x 13.1 cm. Altogether, small portions of six different pages of text are preserved, and on three of the pages the page numbers are visible: pp. 139, 174, [1]76. Obviously these fragments came from a large codex, the complete contents of which, of course, are unknown. Moreover, since over thirty pages separate the first fragment from the second, it is impossible to determine whether they contain portions of the same literary work or of different works. The fragments date to the fourth century.

The text was first published in 1914 by Grenfell and Hunt, who thought that it belonged with that found in P.Oxy 1, 654, and 655. The publication of the Nag Hammadi Library, however, has shown that the latter three all belong to a Greek version (or versions) of the "Coptic" Gospel of Thomas. That is obviously not the case with P.Oxy 1224.

The early parts of the text are too fragmentary to be reconstructed. The remaining portions appear to contain four different passages: (a) a first-hand account of a dream in which the author speaks with Jesus (p. 173; this has no parallel in the NT Gospels); (b) a (hostile) question, presumably directed to Jesus, concerning his "new teaching" (p. 174; see Mark 1:27); (c) a controversy over Jesus' association with sinners (p. 175; see Mark 2:13–17, par.); (d) an exhortation, presumably by Jesus, to pray for one's enemies (p. 176; see Matt. 5:44; Luke 6:27; Didache 1:3).

We have translated the text as presented in the edition of Lührmann.

Bibliography

Bernhard, A. E. *Other Early Christian Gospels: A Critical Edition of the Surviving Greek Manuscripts*. London: T&T Clark, 2006; pp. 100–101.

Elliott, J. K. *The Apocryphal New Testament*. Oxford: Clarendon, 1993; pp. 35–36.

Lührmann, D. *Fragmente apokryph gewordener Evangelien in griechischer und lateinischer Sprache*. Marburg: N. G. Elwert, 2000; pp. 170–77.

Schneemelcher, W. "Fragments of Unknown Gospels," in *New Testament Apocrypha*, ed. W. Schneemelcher; trans. R. McL. Wilson. Louisville: Westminster/John Knox, 1991; vol. 1, p. 100.

Papyrus Oxyrhynchus 1224

Fragment 1 →

139
. . . in all
. . . truly
I say to you . . .

Fragment 1 ↓

will . . . you. . . .

Fragment 2 → Column 2

173
burdened me. And when Jesus appeared
in a vision he said
"Why are you (sg.) disheartened? For not . . .
You, but the . . .
Giving. . . .

Fragment 2 ↓ Column 1

174
you spoke without answering.
What then have you replied? What sort
of new teaching do they say you
teach? Or what new baptism
do you preach? Answer and . . .

Fragment 2 ↓ Column 2

175
But when the scribes, the Pharisees,
and the priests, saw him
they became aggravated, because
he was reclining in the midst of sinners.

But when Jesus heard this he said,
"Those who are healthy have no need
of a physician. . . ."[1]

Fragment 2 → Column 1

176
"And pray for
your enemies,[2] for whoever is not
against you is for you.[3]
They are far away; tomorrow
their hour will come, and in . . .
of the opponent . . .

1. See Matt. 9:10–12; Mark 2:15–17; Luke 5:29–31.
2. See Matt. 5:44; Luke 6:27–28; Didache 1:3.
3. See Mark 9:40; Luke 9:50.

17

Papyrus Oxyrhynchus 2949

Papyrus Oxyrynchus 2949, discovered by Grenfell and Hunt sometime between 1897 and 1906, was first published in 1972 by R. A. Coles. It consists of two small papyrus fragments, the larger (4.0 x 7.5 cm) with thirteen lines of text, the smaller (1.7 x 2.6 cm) with five. Both fragments are written on one side only, so that probably they come from a roll rather than a codex.

Coles immediately recognized that the text had striking parallels with the Akhmim fragment of the Gospel of Peter 3–5 (see "Gospel of Peter" later in this collection; note especially the unusual phrase "friend of Pilate"), but saw that there were numerous differences as well. It would be highly significant if the fragments did preserve a copy of the Gospel of Peter, since they date from "the early third or possibly the late second century" (Coles). This would show beyond doubt that the Akhmim fragment (see Gospel of Peter, below) did not represent an early medieval composition in circulation only in the sixth or seventh centuries, but that the text could date no later than 200 CE or so—some 300–500 years before the earliest extensive witness to it (on the vexed question of whether this Gospel is the one referred to by Serapion in the late second century, see the discussion of the Akhmim fragment).

Still, on the basis of this scant and fragmentary text, it is difficult to establish the relationship between P.Oxy. 2949 and the Akhmim fragment. The coincidences in wording might indicate that (1) they come from literarily related but distinct Gospels (just as Matthew and Mark are verbatim alike in places, but are different compositions); (2) that the earlier papyrus preserves one of the sources for the other; or (3) that it represents a distinct version or recension of the other. In view of the extensive similarities between the texts, however, possibly it may be best to understand that the Gospel of Peter was subject to the vagaries of textual corruption over the centuries, and that these two documents represent two different textual traditions of the same Gospel.

We have translated the text as found in the edition of Lührmann.

Bibliography

Bernhard, A. E. *Other Early Christian Gospels: A Critical Edition of the Surviving Greek Manuscripts*. London: T&T Clark, 2006; p. 52.

Coles, R. A., "2949. Fragments of an Apocryphal Gospel (?)," in *The Oxyrhynchus Papyri*, ed. G. M. Brown et al. London: Egypt Exploration Society, 1972; vol. 41, pp. 15–16.

Foster, P. "Are There Any Early Fragments of the So-Called *Gospel of Peter*?" *NTS* 52 (2006): 1–28.

Lührmann, D. *Fragmente apokryph gewordener Evangelien in griechischer und lateinischer Sprache*. Marburg: N. G. Elwert, 2000; pp. 72–93, esp. 85.

Papyrus Oxyrhynchus 2949

But Joseph, the friend of Pilate,
stood there, and . . .
And knowing that he ordered him to be crucified
he came to Pilate and asked
for his body, for burial.[1] Pilate
sent to Herod and asked him
to return the body, saying, "My friend
has asked for the body." Herod said,
"Pilate . . . him . . .
. . . someone him . . . because
we would bury . . ."[2]

1. See Matt. 27:57–58; Mark 15:43; Luke 23:50–52; John 19:38.
2. See Gospel of Peter 2:3–5.

18

Papyrus Oxyrhynchus 4009

One of the most interesting early Christian papyri to be published in recent years is Papyrus Oxyrhynchus 4009. It was edited by D. Lührmann and P. Parsons in 1994, but already in the previous year it had been identified by Lührmann as belonging to the Gospel of Peter. If he is right, this would be a spectacular find: not only is this record of an unusual conversation between Jesus and Peter intriguing on its own merits, but if it derived from the Gospel of Peter, we would know beyond reasonable doubt that the Gospel was not simply a Passion narrative, but contained sayings of Jesus as well (either after the resurrection or, more likely, from his public ministry).

The papyrus consists of a single leaf 2.9 x 9.0 cm, written front and back. It probably dates to the second century, although P. Foster dates it to the early third. It is so fragmentary that the verso cannot be reconstructed; but familiar words on the recto point to parallels in well-known passages in the Synoptic Gospels (Matt. 9:37–38 = Luke 10:2f; Matt. 10:16b; Matt. 10:16a = Luke 10:3; Matt. 10:27 = Luke 12:4–5). The wording of these passages enabled Lührmann to reconstruct the text. What matters more, however, is the striking parallel to an agraphon of Jesus otherwise known only from 2 Clement 5:2–4 (see entry under Agrapha), which records the bizarre conversation of Jesus with Peter about the wolves who rip apart the lambs (the followers of Jesus). What is most intriguing is that in the Oxyrynchus fragment, the conversation is recorded in the first person: instead of speaking to "Peter," Jesus speaks to "me." Since the one other Gospel that we have in which Peter speaks in the first person is the Akhmim fragment of the Gospel of Peter, Lührmann has argued that in P.Oxy 4009 we have an episode from the same Gospel.

Against this view, T. Krause and T. Nicklas have raised reasonable, but probably not compelling, counter-arguments: (1) The "I" in the Oxyrhynchus fragment is never identified as Peter (the identification comes only through a comparison with 2 Clement); (2) in other Petrine texts (besides the Gospel) Peter identifies himself in the first person (see 2 Peter); (3) there are plenty of other, non-Petrine, narratives also written in the first person (and this could be one of them); and (4) the passage in question, obviously, has no parallel in the Akhmim fragment, which is the only certifiable Gospel of Peter we have.

In evaluating this back and forth, one cannot help but remain impressed that in P.Oxy 4009 we find a first-person narrative that is otherwise recounted of Peter—just as happens in the Akhmim fragment, where Peter in the first person narrates events that in other sources, such as canonical John, are narrated in the third person, about Peter. Thus in this small fragment we have not only an intriguing discussion between Jesus and Peter, but also, possibly, an early remnant of the Gospel that bears Peter's name.

We have translated the text from the edition of Lührmann.

Bibliography

Bernhard, A. E. *Other Early Christian Gospels: A Critical Edition of the Surviving Greek Manuscripts*. London: T&T Clark, 2006; pp. 50–51.

Foster, P. "Are There Any Early Fragments of the So-Called *Gospel of Peter*?" *NTS* 52 (2006): 1–28.

Kraus, T. J., and T. Nicklas. *Die Petrusevangelium und die Petrusapokalypse: Die griechischen Fragmente mit deutscher und englischer Übersetzung*. Berlin: de Gruyter, 2004; pp. 59–63.

Lührmann, D. *Fragmente apokryph gewordener Evangelien in griechischer und lateinischer Sprache*. Marburg: N. G. Elwert, 2000; pp. 73.

Lührmann, D., and P. J. Parsons. "4009. Gospel of Peter?" in *The Oxyrhynchus Papri*, ed. R. A. Coles et al. London: Egypt Exploration Society, 1994; vol. 60, pp. 1–5.

Papyrus Oxyrynchus 4009

→

"... the harvest ...
But be as innocent as
doves and wise
as serpents. You shall be like
sheep among wolves."[1]
I said to him, "What if
we are torn apart?"
He replied and said to me, "When the
wolves tear apart
the sheep they can no long
do it any harm.[2] Therefore
I say to you, do not
fear those who kill
you and after
killing can no longer
do any thing ..."[3]

1. See Matt. 10:16; Luke 10:3; Gospel of Thomas 39.
2. See 2 Clement 5:2–4.
3. See Luke 12:4–5.

19

Papyrus Vindobonensis G 2325

(*The Fayûm Fragment*)

G. Bickell published a first account of the Fayûm Fragment in 1885, the year he discovered the manuscript in Vienna, among a collection of papyri owned by Archduke Rainer. Bickell's facsimile addition followed in 1887. The discovery created a sensation in the world of scholarship (this was years before the appearance of the Oxyrhynchus papyri)—especially among scholars who thought that this fragmentary account of Jesus' passion might predate the Synoptic Gospels.

The fragment is only 3.5 x 4.3 cm and is written on one side only, so that it probably comes from a roll rather than a codex. It is dated to the third century, possibly the first half, and was originally found in the southeast Fayûm (Egypt). It was, of course, part of a much larger manuscript, otherwise lost. It contains Jesus' prediction of the flight of the disciples and of the denials of Peter (see Mark 14:26–30 and Matt. 26:30–34). As in Mark (but not Matthew), Jesus predicts that Peter will deny him three times before the cock crows "twice"; but unlike Mark, Jesus does not intimate that the disciples will meet him in Galilee after he rises from the dead. Given the circumstance that the oldest form of the Gospel of Mark ends in 16:8, with the women fleeing the empty tomb and not telling anyone what they had learned there (so that the disciples never do go to Galilee to meet Jesus), some scholars argued that here we have a more ancient version of Jesus' words at his Last Supper. (The fragment could not simply be a manuscript of Mark [or Matthew] because of the many differences of wording.)

Today the fragment is more widely thought to be a reworking of the Synoptic accounts, which provides an alternative and truncated version of them (Schneemelcher). Still, interest in the fragment has now been renewed because of D Lührmann's suggestion of a different reconstruction of line 5. Rather than T]OU PETROU (= "Peter") Lührmann suggests EM]OU PETROU (= "me, Peter"), so that the words of the text were spoken in the first-person, by Peter. On this ground he suggests that it contains a narrative from the Gospel of Peter, earlier than our surviving account of the document in the Akhmim fragment (see below).

Lührmann's reconstruction has not received widespread support. T. Kraus in particular has argued that there is probably not enough space in the left edge of the text to accommodate the two letters required; and it is never safe to draw significant historical conclusions (that this formed part of the Gospel of Peter) on the ground of what we precisely do not know (the contents of a hole in a manuscript).

As a result, the most we can say is that the Fayûm Fragment appears to be from an early Synoptic-like Gospel, which otherwise remains unknown.

We have translated the text from the edition of Lührmann.

Bibliography

Bernhard, A. E. *Other Early Christian Gospels: A Critical Edition of the Surviving Greek Manuscripts*. London: T&T Clark, 2006; p. 99.

Bickell, G. "Ein Papyrusfragment eines nichtkanonischen Evangeliums," *ZKTh* 9 (1885): 498–504.

Elliott, J. K. *The Apocryphal New Testament*. Oxford: Clarendon, 1993; pp. 43–45.

Foster, P. "Are There Any Early Fragments of the So-Called *Gospel of Peter*?" *NTS* 52 (2006): 1–28.

Kraus, T. J., and T. Nicklas. *Das Petrusevangelium und die Petrusapokalypse: Die griechischen Fragmente mit deutscher und englischer Übersetzung*. Berlin: de Gruyter, 2004; pp. 65–68.

Kraus, T. J. "P.Vindob. G 2325: Das sogenannte Fayûm-Evangelium—Neuedition und kritische Rückschlüsse," *ZAC* 5 (2001): 197–212.

Lührmann, D. *Fragmente apokryph gewordener Evangelien in griechischer und lateinischer Sprache*. Marburg: N. G. Elwert, 2000; pp. 80–81.

Schneemelcher, W. "Fragments of Unknown Gospels," in *New Testament Apocrypha*, ed. W. Schneemelcher; trans. R. McL. Wilson. Louisville: Westminster/John Knox, 1991; vol. 1, p. 102.

Papyrus Vindobonensis G 2325 (The Fayûm Fragment)

". . . all.
In this night you will all stumble,
just as it is written: 'I will smite the shepherd,
and the sheep will be scattered.'"
Peter said. "Even if all do so, I will not.
Jesus said, "Before a cock crows twice, three times
today you will deny me. . . ."[1]

1. See Matt. 26:30–35; Mark 14:26–31; Luke 22:31–34.

SAYINGS GOSPELS AND AGRAPHA

20

The Gospel according to Thomas

The Coptic Gospel of Thomas is the best known, most studied, and most controversial of all the apocryphal Gospels. Before the full text had been discovered, scholars had access to portions of it, without realizing what they were. Among the earliest discoveries and publications made by Grenfell and Hunt at Oxyrhynchus in the late 1890s were several papyrus fragments, later numbered P.Oxy 1, 654, and 655, which contained isolated sayings of Jesus. Published in 1897 and then 1904, these sayings were not recognized as belonging to the Gospel of Thomas until the discovery of the Nag Hammadi Library in 1945, which contained a complete copy of the Gospel in Coptic, in what is now known as Codex 2 of the collection.

The details of Grenfell and Hunt's earlier discovery can be summarized as follows. P.Oxy. 1 is a papyrus leaf, 9.5 x 14.5 cm, written on front and back and dating to around 200 CE. Grenfell and Hunt published the fragment in 1897, the year of its discovery, as *LOGIA IESOU: Sayings of our Lord from an Early Greek Papyrus*. The manuscript contains sayings that are now numbered as 26–30, 77b, 31–33 of the Gospel.

The two other fragments were discovered in 1903. P.Oxy. 654 comes from a papyrus roll of the mid to late third century. Measuring 7.8 x 24.4 cm, the Gospel text is written on the verso of a land survey. It contains what are now numbered as Sayings 1–7. It dates to the third century and was published in 1904 as *New Sayings of Jesus and Fragment of a Lost Gospel from Oxyrhynchus*. The "Lost Gospel" of the title is P. Oxy. 655, which in fact is not a single fragment but eight fragments, from a roll, the largest of which is 8.3 x 8.2 cm. Two of the fragments have now been lost; two others contain too little text to be identified. The fragments date to the third century, and contain Sayings 24 (probably) and 36–39.

Since these three Oxyrhynchus papyri come from different manuscripts, they provide some indication of the popularity of the Gospel, at least in this part of Egypt (120 miles south of Cairo).

Prior to 1945, scholars knew of the existence of a Gospel of Thomas—which was known to be different from the Infancy Gospel of Thomas transmitted throughout the Middle Ages—only because of occasional references to it in the writings of the church fathers. The first certain reference is in the *Refutation* of Hippolytus of Rome, ca. 222–235 CE, who contends that the book was used by a group of Gnostics known as the Naasenes, and who cites the following saying (with obvious similarities to Saying 4 of the text as it is now known): "The one who seeks after me will find me in children from the seventh year onward; for it is there that I reveal myself, hidden away in the fourteenth aeon" (*Refut.* 5. 7. 20). At about the same time Origen mentions a Gospel of Thomas that he regarded as heterodox (*Hom. 1 on Luke*). Eusebius follows suit some decades later (*Eccl. Hist.* 3. 25. 6). Cyril of Jerusalem indicates that the Gospel was popular among the Manichaeans (*Catecheses* 4. 36 and 6. 31).

The details of the discovery of the Nag Hammadi Library as reconstructed by James Robinson are now widely known (see his Introduction to *The Nag Hammadi Library in English*). The find consisted of twelve relatively complete codices and the remains of a thirteenth. These books are anthologies of texts, a total of fifty-two writings altogether. Eliminating duplicates from the total, forty-six different texts were found; most of these, including the Gospel of Thomas, were either completely or mostly unknown before the find. The texts are all written in Coptic. The leather covers of most of the codices survive; these have been helpful for dating the manuscripts: the bindings were strengthened with scrap papyrus, some of which contained dated receipts. The books were manufactured in the second half of the fourth century. The writings they contained, therefore, must have been composed some time before then. There continue to be debates concerning the date of many of these writings, including the Gospel of Thomas (see below).

Thomas has been the most significant of the texts in the small "library." It is found in a single copy, bound as the second work of Codex 2, which contains the following writings, in this order, The Apocryphon of John, The Gospel of Thomas, The Gospel of Philip, The Hypostases of the Archons, On the Origin of the World, Exegesis of the Soul, and the Book of Thomas the Contender. Like the other texts of this codex, and indeed of the entire collection, Thomas appears to be a Coptic translation from a Greek original. While some scholars have argued for a Syriac original of Thomas, this has not proved convincing to most. At the least we can say that there was an early history of transmission of the book in Greek—witness the multiple copies from Oxyrhynchus, dating as much as a century and a half before the Coptic version.

A comparison of the Greek fragments with the Coptic text shows some variation in sequence and wording. Most striking is the circumstance that in P.Oxy. 1, Saying 77b of the Coptic text is located between what is now numbered Saying 30 and Saying 31. In terms of textual variation, sometimes the Greek form of the text has a longer version (saying 3), sometimes a shorter version (saying 2), and sometimes simply a different version (saying 6).

The Coptic version consists of 114 sayings of Jesus. It contains no narratives of any kind, no report of Jesus' activities, his healings, or his exorcisms, no accounts of his travels, his passion, or his resurrection. Most sayings are simply introduced with the words "Jesus said. . . ." In some instances, however, there is a dialogue, for example, when the disciples ask Jesus a question and he responds.

The division of the Gospel into 114 sayings is not found in the manuscript itself but goes back to the first edition published in 1959—fifteen years after the discovery—by A. Guillaumont et al. Within the Gospel there is no obvious organizational pattern of the various sayings, although on occasion it appears that smaller groups of sayings have been combined on the basis of catchwords (sayings 28–29; 36–37; 50–51) or themes (sayings 63–65; 68–69).

One of the reasons the Gospel evoked such scholarly interest upon its first publication was precisely that it contained nothing but sayings. New Testament scholars had long suspected that a similar kind of Gospel was used as a source for two of the Synoptics, Matthew and Luke, which combined a Sayings Gospel Source, called Q (from the German, Quelle, "source"), with the narratives of Mark to produce their fuller accounts. But a consistent objection to the one-time existence of this hypothetical Q source was that early Christians would (surely) never have composed a Gospel comprising only Jesus' sayings, without an account of his death and resurrection—since these events were, after all, the heart and soul of the Christian message. With the discovery of Thomas, all such doubts disappeared. It is not that Thomas could be the long-lost Q source: most of the sayings material in Matthew and Luke cannot be found in Thomas, just as many of Thomas's sayings cannot be found in the Synoptics. But it came to be thought that Q may have been a Gospel *like* Thomas, in structure and purpose.

It is possible to get a sense of the character of Thomas already from its prologue and first saying: "These are the hidden sayings that the living Jesus spoke and Didymus Judas Thomas wrote down. And he said, 'Whoever finds the interpretation of these sayings will not taste death.'" The sayings of Jesus recorded in this book are "hidden"—not available to people at large; and understanding their meaning will bring eternal life. Jesus himself is the one who can give life (he is the "living" Jesus); and he does so *not* through his death and resurrection (as, for example, in the writings of Paul or the Gospels of the New Testament), but through his secret sayings. The author claims to be Didymus Judas Thomas. Didymus is the Greek word for twin; Thomas is an Aramaic term for twin. The author's name is Judas, or Jude. In traditions known from early Christianity in Syria, Judas/Jude was thought to be a twin of none other than Jesus himself. It is no accident that he is the one charged with writing down the secret teachings: he is the one closest to Jesus who best understands his revelation.

One of the most disputed areas in the scholarship on the Gospel of Thomas is whether this revelation through secret teachings is best understood as gnostic or not. In recent years, some scholars have contended that we should do away with the category of "gnostic" altogether, since it has come to be used in such a wide variety of ways that it has virtually lost all specificity of meaning. On the other hand, it can be argued that the misuse of a term is not sufficient ground for disallowing its use altogether. The term "gnostic" comes from the Greek term for "knowledge" (GNOSIS), and can still be helpfully used to refer to a broad range of religious groups from at least the second Christian century onwards that emphasized the importance of secret knowledge for salvation. These groups varied greatly from one another (just as do groups within "Judaism" or "Christianity"—with which there is, of course, significant overlap). But they tended to devalue the material world as the creation not of the one true God, but of lower, inferior, often ignorant, or even evil divinities, who have used their creation as a place to imprison elements of the divine. People have a spark of the divine within them, trapped in the material shell of their body. By coming to know secrets from the divine realm, they can learn how to escape this world and return to the spiritual realm whence they came. Many gnostic texts (e.g., the Apocryphon of John, On the Origin of the World) describe in complex, graphic, and sometimes contradictory detail the myths underlying this world view.

With some such broad understanding of Gnosticism it is still possible to see the Gospel of Thomas as presenting an understanding of the world, Christ, and salvation that in broad outline can be considered gnostic, or at least gnostic-like. Those who have argued that Thomas is not gnostic have largely based their argument on the circumstance that nowhere does this Gospel elaborate the gnostic myth, and that, as a result, a gnostic view needs to be imported into the text rather than drawn out of it. In response it should be pointed out that gnostic texts do not need to lay out the gnostic myth, any more than ideological texts of any sort need to spell out in detail the ideology on which they are based (apocalyptic texts, for example, rarely explicate what exactly will happen at the end of time). And so the question is whether there are indications that a gnostic (or apocalyptic or any other particular ideological) set of assumptions lies behind the text, and whether the text itself suggests that orientation.

In fact there are clear and numerous indications in the Gospel of Thomas that some kind of gnostic world view—defined broadly—lies behind it. As already suggested, saying 1, with its emphasis on the need to understand the secret knowledge that Jesus conveys in order to have salvation, can be seen as a key to the gnostic function of the collection. For this Gospel, the material world is dead and useless (Saying 56); it is the realm of poverty into which the "wealth" of the spirit has unfortunately become entrapped (29); people have come into it from another realm, the realm of light (50), where they enjoyed a unified, rather than a bifurcated existence (i.e., as a mixture of spirit and matter; 11b). Now they are like drunk people who cannot see the truth (28); they need to be brought back to sobriety (28), to come to saving "knowledge" that Jesus alone provides (3b) through his secret teachings (1). When they do so they will discard the body of the flesh (38) and find their salvation.

The gnostic-like orientation is especially signaled by the repeated emphasis on the need for saving "knowledge" (Sayings 1, 3, 5, 16, 18, 39, 46, 56, 67, and so on), found implicitly even in sayings where the term "knowledge" or its verbal equivalent are not explicitly found (e.g., 2, 4, 13).

This is not to say that every saying of this collection needs to be forced into the procrustean bed of some pre-conceived understanding of the specific kind of gnosis it contains. But understanding that the collection, in its final form, is shaped by gnostic-like concerns can help make sense of many of its most obscure sayings.

At the same time, it is important to emphasize that the final author/editor of this text was not simply devising sayings to put on the lips of Jesus. Instead, a large number—possibly all—of the sayings came to him from the Christian oral and, perhaps, written tradition. One of the ongoing and heated arguments concerning this text involves its level of dependency on other known Gospel sources. Depending on how one counts, somewhere between half and two-thirds of the sayings have parallels in the Synoptic Gospels of the New Testament. In some instances the parallels are very close (sayings 20, 34, 54, for example); in other instances a saying starts off with a Synoptic ring, but then shifts to a gnosticized form of expression (saying 2: "Seek and you shall find"). Other sayings, of course, or parts of sayings, have no Synoptic parallel, and these are the ones that appear most clearly to express a gnostic perspective (e.g. Sayings 3b, 11b, 37b). And so the question: did this author/editor utilize the Synoptic Gospels as one of his sources?

Scholars have given every imaginable answer to the question, some thinking that the author is literarily dependent on the Synoptics, some that he is independent, some that he had read the Synoptics but did not use them as literary sources, some that he had heard the Synoptics read and that they influenced him in a secondary, oral way, and so on. Given the circumstance that even the sayings with clear Synoptic parallels differ, usually significantly, in their wording from the Synoptics, at the least we might be able to say that the author did not slavishly copy his sources, if indeed these were his sources.

Possibly it is best to say that both Thomas and the Synoptics had access to sayings of Jesus in the oral tradition and included the sayings in the forms familiar to them. If so, this raises the possibility that in some of the sayings of Thomas we may have access not just to later versions of Jesus' teachings, but to the actual teachings themselves—at least for those sayings that do not reflect the later concerns of whatever form of gnostic thought underlies much of the Gospel.

In the form it is now known to us, the Gospel of Thomas may have been composed in (bilingual) Syria. Among the reasons for thinking so is the circumstance that the name Didymus Judas Thomas is otherwise attested there in a number of important traditions. Given the date of the earliest surviving fragment of the text (P.Oxy. 1, from around 200 CE), the text must have been composed sometime in the second century at the latest. Attempts by J. D. Crossan and others to argue for a first-century date are generally recognized as inadequate, especially in light of the developed gnostic concerns of some of the sayings, which presuppose at the very least an early second century dating. And so the majority of scholars continue to place the text sometime around 100–150 CE.

The bibliography on the Gospel of Thomas is enormous (up to 1988, see Fallon/Cameron). Here we give only the most important works for dealing with the text we have used, along with other works cited above. We have translated the Coptic text (reformatted and slightly revised) from the edition of B. Layton.

Bibliography

Attridge, H. "The Greek Fragments," in B. Layton, ed., *Nag Hammadi Codex II, 2–7* (see below), 99–101.

Bernhard, A. E. *Other Early Christian Gospels: A Critical Edition of the Surviving Greek Manuscripts*. London: T&T Clark, 2006; pp. 16–19.

Blatz, B. "The Coptic Gospel of Thomas," in *New Testament Apocrypha*, ed. W. S.; trans. R. McL. Wilson. Louisville: Westminster/John Knox, 1991; vol. 1, pp. 110–16.

Crossan, J. D. *Four Other Gospels: Shadows on the Contour of the Canon*. Minneapolis: Winston Press, 1985.

Elliott, J. K. *The Apocryphal New Testament*. Oxford: Clarendon, 1993; pp. 123–35.

Fallon, F. T., and R. Cameron. "The Gospel of Thomas: A Forschungsbericht and Analysis," in *ANRW* 2. 25. 6 (1988), pp. 4196–4251.

Guillaumont, A., H.-C. Puech, G. Quispel, W. Till, and Yassah Abd al Masih. *The Gospel according to Thomas*. Leiden: E. J. Brill, 1959 (editio princeps).

King, K. *What Is Gnosticism?* Cambridge, MA: Belknap Press, 2003.

Klauck, H.-J. *Apocryphal Gospels: An Introduction*. London: T&T Clark, 2003; pp. 107–22.

Layton, B. *The Gnostic Scriptures*. New York: Doubleday, 1987; pp. 376–99.

Layton, B., ed. *Nag Hammadi Codex II, 2–7 together with XIII.2*, Brit Lib. Or 4926(1) and P. Oxy 1, 654, 655*. Leiden: E. J. Brill, 1987.

Robinson, J. " 'Logoi Sophon': On the Gattung of Q," in J. M. Robinson and H. Koester, *Trajectories through Early Christianity*. Philadelphia: Fortress, 1971; pp. 71–113.

Robinson, J. *The Nag Hammadi Library in English*. 4th ed. Leiden: E. J. Brill, 1996.

Williams, M. *Rethinking Gnosticism: An Argument for Dismantling a Dubious Category*. Princeton, N.J.: Princeton University Press, 1996.

The Gospel according to Thomas

These are the hidden sayings that the living Jesus spoke and Didymus Judas wrote down.

(1) And he said, "Whoever finds the interpretation of these sayings will not taste death."[1]

(2) Jesus said, "The one who seeks should not stop seeking until he finds.[2] And when he finds he will be disturbed; and when is disturbed, he will marvel. And he will rule over the all."

(3) Jesus said, "If your leaders say to you, 'Look, the kingdom is in the sky,' then the birds of the sky will precede you. If they say to you, 'It is in the sea,' then the fish will precede you. But the kingdom is within you,[3] and it is outside you. When you come to know yourselves, then you will be known, and you will understand that you are the children of the living Father. But if you will not know yourselves, then you are in poverty, and it is you who are the poverty."[4]

(4) Jesus said, "A person advanced in days will not hesitate to ask a little child of seven days about the place of life, and that person will live. For many who are first will be last[5] and so become a single one."

(5) Jesus said, "Know what is before your face, and what is hidden from you will be disclosed to you. For there is nothing hidden that will not be revealed."[6]

(6) His disciples questioned him and said to him, "Do you want us to fast? And how should we pray? Should we give alms?[7] And what kind of diet should we observe?" Jesus said, "Do not tell lies and do not do what you hate, for they are all disclosed before heaven. For there is nothing hidden that will not be revealed, and nothing that is covered will remain undisclosed."[8]

(7) Jesus said, "Blessed is the lion that the human will eat so that the lion becomes human. And cursed is the human whom the lion will eat, and the lion will become human."[9]

(8) And he said, "The human being is like a wise fisherman, who cast his net into the sea and dragged it up from the sea, full of little fish. Among them the wise fisherman found a fine large fish. He cast all the small fish back into the sea

1. See John 8:51–52.
2. See Matt. 7:7–8; Luke 11:9–10.
3. See Luke 17:20–21.
4. See Gal. 4:9.
5. See Matt. 19:30; 20:16; Mark 10:31; Luke 13:30.
6. See Matt. 10:26; Mark 4:22; Luke 8:17; 12:2.
7. See Matt. 6:1–8, 16–18.
8. See Matt. 10:26; Mark 4:22; Luke 8:17; 12:2.
9. See Plato, *Rep.* 9.588c7–589b6.

and chose the large fish without any effort. The one who has ears to listen had better listen!"[10]

(9) Jesus said, "Look, the sower came forth, took a handful, and cast. Now, some fell on the path, and the birds came and gathered them up. Others fell on the rock, and they did not take roots down into the ground and send up ears. And others fell on thorns, and they choked the seeds and the worm devoured them. And others fell on the good ground, and it sent up good fruit and yielded sixty per measure and a hundred-twenty per measure."[11]

(10) Jesus said, "I have cast a fire upon the world, and look, I am guarding it until it blazes."[12]

(11) Jesus said, "This heaven will pass away, and the one above it will pass away.[13] And the dead are not alive, and the living will not die. In the days you ate what is dead you made it alive; (but) when you come to be in light, what will you do?[14] On the day when you were one, you became two; but when you become two, what will you do?"

(12) The disciples said to Jesus, "We know that you will leave us. Who will be great among us?"[15] Jesus said to them, "Wherever you have come,[16] you will go to James the Righteous, for whose sake heaven and earth came to be."

(13) Jesus said to his disciples, "Make a comparison and tell me: who am I like?"[17] Simon Peter said to him, "You are like a righteous angel." Matthew said to him, "You are like a wise philosopher." Thomas said to him, "Teacher, my mouth cannot let me say at all what you are like." Jesus said, "I am not your teacher, for you have drunk and become intoxicated from the bubbling spring that I myself have measured out." And he took him, withdrew, and said three sayings to him. Now, when Thomas came to his companions, they asked him, "What did Jesus say to you?" Thomas said to them, "If I tell you one of the sayings he said to me, you will take up stones and cast them at me, and fire will come out of the stones and burn you."

(14) Jesus said to them, "If you fast, you will bring sin upon yourselves; and if you pray, you will be condemned; and if you give alms, you will do harm to your spirits.[18] And when you go into any land and walk in the countryside, if they receive you, eat whatever they place before you and heal the sick among them.[19]

10. See Matt. 13:47–50.

11. See Matt. 13:3–9; Mark 4:3–9; Luke 8:5–8.

12. See Luke 12:49.

13. See Matt. 24:35; Mark 13:31; Luke 21:33.

14. See Hippolytus, *Refut.* 5.8.32.

15. See Matt. 18:1; Mark 9:34; Luke 9:46.

16. Or "have come from."

17. See Matt. 16:13–17; Mark 8:27–30; Luke 9:18–21.

18. See Matt. 6:1–8, 16–18.

19. See Luke 10:8–9.

For whatever goes into your mouth will not defile you; rather, it is what comes out of your mouth that will defile you."[20]

(15) Jesus said, "When you see one who was not born from woman, fall upon your faces and worship him: that one is your father."

(16) Jesus said, "Perhaps people think that I have come to cast peace on the world, and they do not know that I have come to cast divisions on the earth: fire, sword, war. For there will be five in a house: three will be against two and two against three, the father against the son and the son against the father.[21] And they will stand as solitary ones."

(17) Jesus said, "I will give you what eyes have not seen, and what ears have not heard, and what hands have not touched, and what has not arisen in the human heart."[22]

(18) The disciples said to Jesus, "Tell us how our end will come about."[23] Jesus said, "Have you uncovered the beginning, then, that you are now seeking the end? For where the beginning is the end will come to be. Blessed is the one who stands at the beginning: that one will know the end and he will not taste death."

(19) Jesus said, "Blessed is the one who existed before coming to be. If you exist as my disciples and listen to my sayings, these stones will serve you. For you have five trees in paradise that do not move in summer or winter, and whose leaves do not fall. Whoever knows them will not taste death."

(20) The disciples said to Jesus, "Tell us: what is the kingdom of heaven like?" He said to them, "It is like a mustard seed. It is smallest of all seeds, but when it falls on tilled ground, it puts forth a great branch and becomes a shelter for the birds of the sky."[24]

(21) Mary said to Jesus, "Whom are your disciples like?" He said, "They are like children[25] dwelling in a field that is not theirs. When the owners of the field come they will say, 'Surrender our field to us.' They, for their part, strip in their presence in order to surrender it to them, and so give their field to them. For this reason I say, when the homeowner knows that the burglar is coming, he will keep watch before he comes, and will not let him dig through into his house, which belongs to his kingdom, to steal his possessions.[26] You, then, keep watch against the world. Gird your loins with great power,[27] so that the brigands may not find a way to come to you; for they will find the gain for which

20. See Matt. 15:11, 17–18; Mark 7:15, 18, 20.
21. See Matt. 10:34–35; Luke 12:51–53.
22. See 1 Cor. 2:9.
23. See Matt. 24:3; Mark 13:4; Luke 21:7.
24. See Matt. 13:31–32; Mark 4:20–32; Luke 13:18–19.
25. Or: "servants."
26. See Matt. 24:43–44; Luke 12:39–40.
27. See Exod. 12:11; Luke 12:35.

you are waiting.[28] Let there be among you a person of understanding. When the crop ripened, he came hastily with a sickle in his hand and reaped it.[29] The one who has ears to listen had better listen!"[30]

(22) Jesus saw some infants being nursed. He said to his disciples, "These infants being nursed are like those entering the kingdom." They said to him, "Shall we then enter the kingdom by being infants?"[31] Jesus said to them, "When you make the two one, and make the inside like the outside and the outside like the inside and the upper like the lower; and you make[32] the male and the female be a single one, with the male no longer being male and the female no longer female; when you make eyes in the place of an eye and a hand in the place of a hand and a foot in the place of a foot, an image in the place of an image—then you will enter the kingdom."

(23) Jesus said, "I will choose you—one out of a thousand and two out of ten thousand. And they will stand as a single one."

(24) His disciples said, "Show us the place where you are, since we must seek it." He said to them, "The one who has ears had better listen! There is light inside a person of light, and it[33] shines on the whole world. If it does not shine, it is dark."[34]

(25) Jesus said, "Love your brother like your soul; guard him like the pupil of your eye."[35]

(26) Jesus said, "You see the speck that is in your brother's eye, but you do not see the log that is in your eye. When you take the log out of your eye, then you will see well enough to take the speck out of your brother's eye."[36]

(27) "If you do not fast from the world, you will not find the kingdom. If you do not make the Sabbath a sabbath,[37] you will not see the Father."

(28) Jesus said, "I stood in the midst of the world and appeared to them in flesh.[38] I found them all drunk, and I did not find any of them thirsty. And my soul was anguished for the children of humankind, for they are blind in their hearts and do not see. For they came into the world empty, and empty again they

28. Or: "for they will find the necessities you are watching out for."

29. See Mark. 4:29.

30. See Matt. 13:9; Mark 4:9; Luke 8:8.

31. See Matt. 18:1–3; 19:13–15; Mark 9:33–36; 10:13–16; Luke 9:46–47; 18:15–17.

32. Lit. "and that you might make . . ."

33. Or: "and he . . . If he . . ."

34. See Matt. 6:22–23; 11:34–35.

35. See Matt. 22:39; Mark 12:31; Luke 10:27.

36. See Matt. 7:3–5; Luke 6:41–42.

37. The clause may mean two opposite things: either "if you do not observe the Sabbath day as a Sabbath," or "if you do not turn the Sabbath into a regular day (a sabbath)" that is, abstain from it. For the latter interpretation, see *above*, sayings (6) and (14).

38. See John 1:9–10, 14.

seek to depart from the world. Yet now they are drunk; when they shake off their wine, then they will repent."

(29) Jesus said, "If the flesh came into being because of the spirit, it is a marvel. But if the spirit (came into being) because of the body, it is a marvel of marvels. Yet I marvel at this, how this great wealth has come to dwell in this poverty."

(30) Jesus said, "Where there are three gods, they are divine. Where there are two or one, I am with that one."[39]

(31) Jesus said, "A prophet is not welcome in his village; a physician does not heal those who know him."[40]

(32) Jesus said, "A city built upon a high mountain and fortified cannot fall, nor can it become hidden."[41]

(33) Jesus said, "Whatever you hear with your ear, proclaim it into the other ear upon your rooftops.[42] For no one lights a lamp and places it under a bushel or sets it in a hidden place. But he puts it on the lampstand so that everyone who enters and leaves might see its light."[43]

(34) Jesus said, "If a blind person leads a blind person, they both fall into a pit."[44]

(35) Jesus said, "No one can enter the house of the strong and take it by force unless he binds his hands. Then he will plunder his house."[45]

(36) Jesus said, "Do not be concerned from morning to evening and from evening to morning about what you will wear."[46]

(37) His disciples said, "When will you appear to us and when shall we see you?" Jesus said, "When you strip naked without being ashamed and take your clothes and place them under your feet like little children and stamp on them, then you will see the Son of the Living One, and you will not be afraid."

(38) Jesus said, "Many times you have desired to hear these sayings that I am speaking to you, and you have no one else to hear them from. Days will come when you will seek me, and you will not find me."[47]

(39) Jesus said, "The Pharisees and the scribes have taken the keys of knowledge and hidden them. They have neither entered nor let those wishing to enter do so.[48] But you should be wise as snakes, and innocent as doves."[49]

39. See Matt. 18:20.
40. See Matt. 13:57–58; Mark 6:4–5; Luke 4:24; John 4:44.
41. See Matt. 5:14.
42. See Matt. 10:27; Luke 12:3.
43. See Matt. 5:15; Mark 4:21; Luke 8:16; 11:33.
44. See Matt. 15:14; Luke 6:39.
45. See Matt. 12:29; Mark 3:27; Luke 11:21–22.
46. See Matt. 6:25; Luke 12:22.
47. See Matt. 13:17; Luke 10:24; John 7:33–36.
48. See Matt. 23:13; Luke 11:52.
49. See Matt. 10:16.

(40) Jesus said, "A grapevine has been planted outside of the Father. And since it is not strong, it will be pulled up by its root and perish."[50]

(41) Jesus said, "The one who has something in his hand will be given (more); and the one who has nothing will have even the little that he has taken from him."[51]

(42) Jesus said, "Become passersby."

(43) His disciples said to him, "Who are you to say these things to us?" "You do not understand who I am from what I say to you.[52] Rather, you have become like the Jews; for they love the tree but hate its fruit; and they love the fruit but hate the tree."[53]

(44) Jesus said, "Whoever blasphemes against the Father will be forgiven; and whoever blasphemes against the Son will be forgiven; but whoever blasphemes against the Holy Spirit will not be forgiven, either on earth or in heaven."[54]

(45) Jesus said, "Grapes are not harvested from thorn bushes, nor are figs collected from thistles; for they do not yield fruit. A good person brings something good from his storehouse; a bad person brings vile things from his evil storehouse inside his heart and speaks vile things. For from the abundance of the heart he brings forth vile things."[55]

(46) Jesus said, "From Adam to John the Baptist, among those born of women there is no one greater than John the Baptist lest he should avert his eyes. [56] Yet I have said that whoever among you becomes a young child will know the kingdom; and he will become greater than John."[57]

(47) Jesus said, "No person can mount two horses and string two bows; and no servant can serve two masters, or he will honor the one and insult the other.[58] No person drinks aged wine and immediately desires to drink new wine. And new wine is not put into old skins, or they might burst. And aged wine is not put into new skins, or it might go bad. An old patch is not sown on a new garment, for there would be a tear."[59]

(48) Jesus said, "If two make peace with one another in a single house, they will say to the mountain, 'Move from here,' and it will move."[60]

50. See Matt. 15:13.
51. See Matt. 13:12; 25:29; Mark 4:25; Luke 18:18; 19:26.
52. See John 14:9.
53. See Matt. 7:16–18; 12:33; Luke 6:43.
54. See Matt. 12:31–32; Mark 3:28–29; Luke 12:10.
55. See Matt. 7:16; 12:34–35; Luke 6:44–45.
56. Or "lest he should keep his eyes down." Lit. "lest his eyes should be broken."
57. See Matt. 11:11; 18:3; Mark 10:15; Luke 7:28; 18:17.
58. See Matt. 6:24; Luke 16:13.
59. See Matt. 9:16–17; Mark 2:21–22; Luke 5:36–39.
60. See Matt. 17:20; 21:21; Mark 11:22–23; Luke 17:6.

(49) Jesus said, "Blessed are the solitary ones and the elect, for you will find the kingdom. For you have come from it and you will return there."

(50) Jesus said, "If they say to you, 'Where have you come from?' tell them 'We have come from the light, from the place where the light came to be on its own, established itself, and was revealed in their image.' If they say to you, 'Is it you?' say, 'We are its children, and we are the chosen of the living Father.' If they ask you, 'What is the sign of your Father in you?' say to them, 'It is movement and repose.'"

(51) His disciples said to him, "When will the repose of the dead take place? And when will the new world come?"[61] He said to them, "What you are looking for has come, but for your part you do not know it."[62]

(52) His disciples said to him, "Twenty-four prophets spoke in Israel, and they all spoke about you." He said to them, "You have abandoned the one who lives in your presence and have spoken of the dead."

(53) His disciples said to him, "Is circumcision beneficial or not?" He said to them, "If it were beneficial, their father would beget them already circumcised from their mother. But true circumcision in the spirit has become entirely profitable."[63]

(54) Jesus said, "Blessed are the poor, for the kingdom of heaven is yours."[64]

(55) Jesus said, "Whoever does not hate his father and his mother cannot be a disciple of mine; and whoever does not hate his brothers and his sisters and take up his cross the way I do, he will not be worthy of me."[65]

(56) Jesus said, "The one who has come to know the world has found a corpse; and the one who has found the corpse, the world is not worthy of that person."

(57) Jesus said, "The kingdom of the Father is like a person having some good seed. His enemy came at night and sowed weeds among the good seed. The person did not allow them to pluck the weeds. He said to them, 'Otherwise, you might go to pluck the weeds and pluck the wheat with it. For on the harvest day the weeds will be plainly visible: they will be plucked and burned.'"[66]

(58) Jesus said, "Blessed is the person who has suffered and found life."

(59) Jesus said, "Look to the living one while you are living, or you might die and then seek to see him; and you will not be able to see."[67]

61. See Matt. 24:3; Mark 13:4; Luke21:7.
62. See Luke 17:20–21.
63. See Rom. 2:25–29.
64. See Matt. 5:3; Luke 6:20.
65. See Matt. 10:37–38; 16:24; Mark 8:34; Luke 9:23; 14:26–27.
66. See Matt. 13:24–30.
67. See John 7:33–36.

(60) (They saw) a Samaritan carrying a lamb on his way to Judea. He said to his disciples, "That one is going around with the lamb." They said to him, "It is so he can kill it and eat it." He said to them, "While it is living he will not eat it, but only if he kills it and it becomes a corpse." They said, "He cannot do it otherwise." He said to them, "You, too, seek for yourselves a place for repose, lest you become a corpse and be eaten."

(61) Jesus said, "Two will be resting on a couch: one will die, one will live."[68] Salome said, "Who are you, O man? As if you are from someone,[69] you have climbed onto my couch and eaten from my table." Jesus said to her, "I am the one who comes from what is whole.[70] I was given some of the things of my Father."[71] "I am your disciple." "For this reason I say that the one who is whole[72] will be full of light, but that the one who is divided will be filled with darkness."

(62) Jesus said, "I am speaking my mysteries to those who are worthy of my mysteries.[73] Do not let your left hand understand what your right hand is doing."[74]

(63) Jesus said, "There was a rich person who had many possessions. He said, 'I will use my possessions: I will sow, harvest, plant, and fill my storehouses with crops, so that I no longer need anything.' These things he was thinking in his heart, but that very night he died. The one who has ears had better listen!"[75]

(64) Jesus said, "A person had some visitors. And when he prepared a dinner he sent his servant to invite the visitors. He went to the first and said to him, 'My master invites you.' He replied, 'Some merchants owe me money; they are coming to me this evening, and I must go to give them instructions. I ask to be excused from the dinner.' He went to another and said to him, 'My master has invited you.' He said to him, 'I have bought a house and need to be there for a day; I will not be free.' He went to another and said to him, 'My master invites you.' He said to him, 'My friend is getting married, and it is I who am to prepare the banquet. I cannot come; I ask to be excused from the dinner.' He went to another and said to him, 'My master invites you.' He said to him, 'I have bought an estate, and I am going to collect the rent. I cannot come: I ask to be excused.' The servant came and said to his master, 'The people you invited to the dinner have asked to be excused.' The master said to his servant, 'Go out to the streets; whomever you find, bring them in to have dinner.' Buyers and traders will not enter the places of my Father."[76]

68. See Matt. 24:40; Luke 17:34.

69. Or: "as a stranger"; or "as from whom."

70. Or: "the sameness."

71. See Matt. 11:27; Luke 10:22.

72. Or: "destroyed"; or "desolate," following the manuscript reading (see *Ap. Gos.*, p. 325).

73. See Matt. 13:11; Mark 4:11; Luke 8:10.

74. See Matt. 6:3.

75. See Luke 12:16–21.

76. See Matt. 22:1–10; Luke 14:15–24.

(65) He said, "A good man[77] owned a vineyard, and he leased it to tenant farmers so that they might work it and he might receive its produce from them. He sent his servant so the farmers might give him the produce of the vineyard. They seized the servant and beat him: they almost killed him. The servant went and told his master. The master said, 'Perhaps he did not know them.' He sent another servant, and the farmers beat this one as well. Then the master sent his son and said, 'Perhaps they will show respect to my son.' Since those farmers knew that he was the heir of the vineyard, they grabbed him and killed him. The one who has ears had better listen!"[78]

(66) Jesus said, "Show me the stone that the builders have rejected: that is the cornerstone."[79]

(67) Jesus said, "The one who knows the all but is lacking in himself lacks everything."[80]

(68) Jesus said, "Blessed are you whenever you are hated and persecuted;[81] and, wherever you have been persecuted, you will not be found there."

(69) Jesus said, "Blessed are those who have been persecuted in their heart: it is they who have come to know the Father in truth. Blessed are those who are hungry, so that the stomach of the needy may be satisfied."[82]

(70) Jesus said, "If you bring forth what is within you, what you have will save you; if you do not have that within you, what you do not have within you will kill you."

(71) Jesus said, "I will destroy this house, and no one will be able to build it . . ."[83]

(72) A person said to him, "Tell my brothers to divide my father's possessions with me." He said to him, "O man, who has made me a divider?" He turned to his disciples and said to them, "I am not a divider, am I?"[84]

(73) Jesus said, "The harvest is plentiful, but the workers are few. So pray to the Lord that he might send workers out to the harvest."[85]

(74) He said, "Lord, there are many around the drinking trough, but there is nothing in the cistern."

(75) Jesus said, "Many are standing at the door, but it is the solitary ones who will enter the bridal chamber."

77. Or: "a usurer."

78. See Matt. 21:33–39; Mark 12:1–8; Luke 20:9–15.

79. See Matt. 21:42; Mark 12:10; Luke 20:17.

80. Or: "The one who knows the all but is deficient in one thing has been deficient in everything."

81. See Matt. 5:11; Luke 6:22.

82. See Matt. 5:6, 8, 10; Luke 6:21.

83. See Matt. 26:61; Mark 14:58.

84. See Luke 12:13–14.

85. See Matt. 9:37–38; Luke 10:2.

(76) Jesus said, "The kingdom of the Father is like a merchant who owned merchandise and then found a pearl. That merchant was wise; he sold the merchandise and bought for himself the single pearl.[86] You, too, seek his unfailing and enduring treasure, where no moth comes in to devour and no worm destroys."[87]

(77) Jesus said, "It is I who am the light upon them all.[88] It is I who am the all. It is from me that the all has come, and to me that the all has extended.[89] Split a piece of wood: I am there. Lift up the stone and you will find me there."

(78) Jesus said, "Why did you come out into the country? To see a reed moved by the wind? And to see a person dressed in soft clothes, like your kings and your dignitaries, who are dressed in soft clothes and are unable to know the truth?"[90]

(79) A woman in the crowd said to him, "Blessed is the womb that bore you and the breasts that nourished you." He said to her, "Blessed are those who have heard the word of the Father and guarded it in truth. For days are coming when you will say, 'Blessed is the womb that has not conceived and the breasts that have not given milk.'"[91]

(80) Jesus said, "The one who has come to know the world has found the body; and the one who has found the body—the world is not worthy of him."

(81) Jesus said, "The one who has become rich, let him reign; and the one who has power, let him renounce (it)."

(82) Jesus said, "The one who is near me is near the fire; and the one who is far from me is far from the kingdom."[92]

(83) Jesus said, "The images are visible to humans. And the light that is within them is hidden in the image of the light of the Father. It[93] will be disclosed; and his image is hidden by his light."

(84) Jesus said, "When you see your likeness, you rejoice. But when you see your images that came into being before you and that neither die nor become revealed, how much you will bear!"[94]

(85) Jesus said, "Adam came into being from a great power and a great wealth; and he did not become worthy of you. For had he been worthy, he would not have tasted death."

86. See Matt. 13:44–46.
87. See Matt. 6:20; Luke 12:33.
88. John 8:12.
89. See John 1:3.
90. See Matt. 11:7–8; Luke 7:24–25.
91. See Matt. 24:19; Mark 13:17; Luke 11:27–28; 21:23; 23:29.
92. See Mark 12:34.
93. "It," viz. the hidden light. Or: "he."
94. See Gen 1:26–27; Philo, *Opif.* 69–71; *LA* 1.31–32.

(86) Jesus said, "The foxes have their dens and the birds their nests, but the Son of Man has no place to lay his head and rest."[95]

(87) Jesus said, "Wretched is the body that depends on a body; and wretched is the soul that depends on these two."

(88) Jesus said, "The angels[96] and the prophets are coming to you, and they will give you what you have. And you, too, give them what is yours and say to yourselves, 'When will they come and take what is theirs?'"

(89) Jesus said, "Why do you wash the outside of the cup? Do you not realize that the one who made the inside is also the one who made the outside?"[97]

(90) Jesus said, "Come to me, for my yoke is easy and my lordship is kind. And you will find repose for yourselves."[98]

(91) They said to him, "Tell us who you are, so that we may believe in you." He said to them, "You evaluate the appearance of the sky and of the earth, yet you have not come to know the one who is before you, and you do not know how to evaluate this moment."[99]

(92) Jesus said, "Seek and you will find.[100] Yet, the things you asked me about in the past and I did not tell you then, now I am willing to tell you; and you no longer seek after them."[101]

(93) "Do not give holy things to dogs, or they might throw them on the dung heap. Do not throw pearls to swine, or else they might make it . . ."[102]

(94) Jesus said, "The one who seeks will find; the one who knocks will have it opened."[103]

(95) Jesus said, "If you have money, do not lend it at interest, but give it to the one from whom you will not get it back."[104]

(96) Jesus said, "The kingdom of the Father is like a woman who took a small amount of yeast, hid it in dough, and made it into large loaves of bread. The one who has ears had better listen!"[105]

(97) Jesus said, "The kingdom of the Father is like a woman who was carrying a jar full of meal. While she was walking a great distance on the road, the handle

95. See Matt. 8:20; Luke 9:58.
96. Or "messengers."
97. See Matt. 23:25–26; Luke 11:39–40.
98. See Matt. 11:28–30.
99. See Matt. 16:1–3; Luke 12:56.
100. See Matt. 7:7; Luke 11:9.
101. See John 16:4–5.
102. See Matt. 7:6. There are several possible restorations of the end of this saying: "or they might bring it to naught"; "or they might grind them to bits"; "or they might make mud of it."
103. See Matt. 7:8; Luke 11:10.
104. See Matt. 5:42; Luke 6:34–35.
105. See Matt. 13:33; Luke 13:20–21.

of the jar broke off and the meal poured out behind her on the road. She was not aware of it: she had noticed no trouble. When she reached her house, she set the jar down and found that it was empty."

(98) Jesus said, "The kingdom of the Father is like a person who wanted to kill a dignitary. At home, he pulled the sword out and stuck it in the wall, to find out if his hand would be firm. Then he murdered the dignitary."

(99) The disciples said to him, "Your brothers and your mother are standing outside." He said to them, "Those here who do the will of my Father, they are my brothers and my mother. It is they who will enter the kingdom of my Father."[106]

(100) They showed Jesus a gold coin and said to him, "Caesar's people are demanding taxes from us." He said to them, "Give what is Caesar's to Caesar, and give what is God's to God; and what is mine, give it to me."[107]

(101) "Whoever does not hate his father and his mother the way I do cannot be a disciple of mine.[108] And whoever does not love his father and his mother the way I do cannot be a disciple of mine. For my mother did . . . [109] But my true mother gave me life."

(102) Jesus said, "Woe to the Pharisees, for they are like a dog sleeping in the cattle's feeding trough. For it neither eats nor lets the cattle eat."[110]

(103) Jesus said, "Blessed is the person who knows at what point the robbers are entering, so that he may rise up, muster his estate, and arm himself before they enter."[111]

(104) They said to Jesus, "Come, let us pray today and let us fast." Jesus said, "What is the sin that I have committed, or how have I been overcome? But, when the bridegroom comes out of the bridal chamber, then people should fast and pray."[112]

(105) Jesus said, "Whoever knows the father and the mother will be called the child of a prostitute."

(106) Jesus said, "When you make the two one, you will become children of humanity.[113] And when you say, 'Mountain, move away,' it will move."[114]

(107) Jesus said, "The kingdom is like a shepherd who had a hundred sheep. One of them, the largest, wandered away. He left the ninety-nine and looked for

106. See Matt. 12:47; Mark 3:32; Luke 8:20–21.
107. See Matt. 22:16–21; Mark 12:14–17; Luke 20:21–25.
108. See Matt. 10:37; Luke 14:26.
109. Possibly: "For my mother gave me falsehood."
110. See Matt. 23:13; Luke 11:52.
111. See Matt. 24:43; Luke 12:37–39.
112. See Matt. 9:14–15; Mark 2:18–20; Luke 5:33–35.
113. Or "sons of man."
114. See Matt. 21:21; Luke 11:23.

the one until he found it. After all his labor, he said to the sheep, 'I love you more than the ninety-nine.'"[115]

(108) Jesus said, "Whoever drinks from my mouth will become like me. I myself will become that person, and the hidden things will be revealed to that person."[116]

(109) Jesus said, "The kingdom is like a person who had a hidden treasure in his field without knowing it. And upon dying he left it to his son. The son did not know (about it). He took over the field and sold it. And the one who bought it came plowing and found the treasure. He began to lend out money at interest to whomever he wished."[117]

(110) Jesus said, "Whoever finds the world and becomes rich, let him renounce the world."

(111) Jesus said, "The heavens and the earth will roll up before you, and the one who lives from the living one will not see death." Does not Jesus say, "Whoever has found oneself, the world is not worthy of that person"?

(112) Jesus said, "Woe to the flesh that depends on the soul. Woe to the soul that depends on the flesh."

(113) His disciples said to him, "When will the kingdom come?"[118] "It will not come by waiting for it. They will not say, 'Look, here it is,' or 'Look, it is there.' Rather, the kingdom of the Father is spread out upon the earth, and people do not see it."[119]

(114) Simon Peter said to them, "Mary should leave us, for females are not worthy of the life." Jesus said, "Look, I am going to guide her in order to make her male, so that she too may become a living spirit resembling you males. For every female who makes herself male will enter the kingdom of heaven."

115. See Matt. 18:12–13; Luke 16:4–6.
116. See Matt. 10:26; Luke 12:2.
117. See Matt. 13:44.
118. See Matt. 24:3; Mark 13:4; Luke 21:7.
119. See Luke 7:20–21.

The Gospel of Thomas: The Greek Fragments

Prologue and Saying 1 (P. Oxy. n. 1–5)

These are the hidden sayings that
the living Jesus spoke and Judas,
who is also Thomas, wrote down. And he said, "Whoever
finds the interpretation of these sayings
will not taste death."

Saying 2 (P. Oxy. 654.5–9)

Jesus said,[120]
"Let the one who seeks not cease seeking until
he finds; and when he finds he will be amazed, and
when he has been amazed, he will rule, and when he has ruled,
he will rest."

Saying 3 (P. Oxy. 654.9–21)

Jesus said, "If
those who lead you say to you, 'See,
the kingdom is in the sky,'
the birds of the sky will precede you. But if they say that
it is under the earth, the fish
of the sea will enter (it) ahead of
you. Indeed, the kingdom of God
is both inside you and outside. Whoever
has come to know himself will find it; and when you
come to know yourselves, you will realize that
you are children of the living Father. But if you will not
know yourselves, you are in poverty,
and it is you who are the poverty."

120. Or "said," *passim*.

Saying 4 (P. Oxy. 654.21–27)

Jesus said,
"A person old in days will not hesitate
to ask a seven-day-old child
about the place of life, and
he will live. For many who are first will be last, and
the last first, and they will come to be one."

Saying 5 (P. Oxy. 654.27–31)

Jesus said, "Know what is before
your eyes, and what is hidden
from you will be disclosed to you. For there is nothing
hidden that will not become manifest,
and nothing buried that will not be raised."

Saying 6 (P. Oxy. 654.32–40)

His disciples asked him and
said, "How shall we fast, and how shall we
pray, and how shall we give alms,
and what rule shall we observe concerning
food?" Jesus said, "Do not lie, and
whatever you hate do not do, because everything
is revealed in the sight of truth. For nothing
is hidden that will not become manifest."

Saying (7 P. Oxy. 654.40–42)

. . . Blessed is . . .
. . . lion will be . . .
. . .

Possible restoration

. . ."Blessed is the lion that a human
eats, and the lion will be human; and
cursed is the human that a lion eats . . ."

Saying 24 (P. Oxy. 655 (d) Fragment d)

. . . is . . .
. . . of light . . .
. . . world . . .
. . .
. . . is . . .

Possible restoration

". . . There is light
within a person of light,
and it shines on the entire world.
If it does not shine,
then it is dark."

Saying 26 (P. Oxy 1 ↓ , 1–4)

". . .
and then you will see clearly
to take out the speck,
which is in the eye
of your brother."

Saying 27 (P. Oxy. 1 ↓, 4–11)

Jesus
said, "If you do not fast
as regards the world, you will not
find the kingdom
of God; and if you do not
keep the Sabbath as a sabbath,
you will not see the
Father."

Saying 28 (P. Oxy. 1 ↓, 11–21)

Jesus said, "I stood
in the midst of the world,

and in flesh I appeared
to them; and I found everyone
drunk and
I found no one
among them thirsting. And
my soul is distressed for
the children of humans,
for they are blind in
their hearts and they do not
see that . . ."

Saying 29 (P. Oxy. 1 →, 22)

". . .
inhabits this poverty."

Saying 30 and 77b (P. Oxy 1 →, 23–30)

Jesus said, "Wherever there are
three, they are without God. And
wherever there is one alone,
I say, 'I am with him.'
Lift up the stone
and you will find me there.
Split the wood and I
am there."

Saying 31 (P. Oxy. 1 →, 30–35)

Jesus said,
"A prophet is not welcome
in his own country,
nor does a physician
perform healings on those
who know him."

Saying 32 (P. Oxy. 1 →, 36–41)

Jesus said, "A city
built on the top

of a high mountain and
fortified can neither
fall nor
be hidden."

Saying 33 (P. Oxy. 1 →, 41–42)

Jesus said, "What you hear
in your one ear,
proclaim this . . ."

Saying 36 (P. Oxy. 655, col. i, 1–17)

Jesus said, "Do not be concerned
from early morning till late,
nor from evening
till early morning, either about
your food, what you should eat, or
about your clothing, what
you should wear.
You are worth
much more than the lilies,
which neither card
nor spin. If you
have no clothing,
what will you put on?
Who might add
to your stature?
He is the one who will give
you your clothing."

Saying 37 (P. Oxy 655, col. i. 17–col. ii.1)

His disciples
said to him,
"When will you be
visible to us, and when
will we see you?" He said,
"When you take off your clothing and

are not ashamed . . .
[ca. 6 lines]
and you will not be
afraid."

Saying 38 (P. Oxy 655, col. ii. 2–11)

. . . says . . .
[*lines 2–11 mostly wanting*]

Possible restoration

Jesus said, "Oftentimes
you have desired
to hear these
sayings of mine,
and you have no one
else from whom to hear (them).
And there will come
days when you will
seek me and you will not
find me."

Saying 39 (P. Oxy 655, col. ii. 11–23)

Jesus
said, "The Pharisees
and the scribes
have taken the keys
of knowledge; they themselves
have hidden them. Neither
have they entered, nor have they
permitted those entering
to enter. But you,
become wise
as snakes and
innocent as
doves."

21

Agrapha

The term "agrapha" has traditionally been applied to a group of "unrecorded" sayings allegedly delivered by the historical Jesus. The term is not altogether apt, since technically speaking these sayings have indeed been recorded—otherwise we would have no access to them. And so the term is more normally taken to mean sayings of Jesus that are not found in the canonical Gospels. Even this definition is problematic however, since it privileges books that eventually came to be included in the canon, a decision that involves theological, rather than historical judgments. And so perhaps it is best to understand the agrapha as comprising sayings allegedly spoken by the historical Jesus that are recorded in documents other than the surviving Gospels (canonical or non-canonical).

In the following listing of the agrapha several types of sayings have been excluded. Since the principal concern is with sayings that Jesus allegedly delivered during his lifetime, words attributed to the pre-incarnate or post-resurrection Christ are not included (e.g., Ignatius, Smyrneans 3:1–2; or the sayings of such "resurrection dialogues" as the *Epistle of the Apostles*). We have also not included sayings that appear to be quotations (loose or exact) of surviving Gospel sources (such as the strings of sayings found in the Didache or 1 Clement). We have also not included sayings from non-Christian sources, which require extensive attention in their own right (e.g., in the Talmud and the Quran).

The three principal sources for the agrapha, then, are (1) sayings of Jesus recorded in books outside the Gospel genre (e.g., the book of Acts); (2) manuscript variations of passages found within the Gospels; and (3) Patristic citations of no-longer surviving Gospels.

Most listings of the agrapha in collections of the early Christian apocrypha are notably sparse; a few collections are far more extensive than what we provide here. Our listing is meant to be full and representative, but not exhaustive. We do not give duplications of sayings (that is, additional sources that give the same saying, often in different words). Normally we cite either the earliest or clearest version of the saying.

In the history of scholarship, much of the interest in these materials has been to uncover authentic sayings of the historical Jesus from outside the Gospels. But this is a rather myopic concern: the agrapha are important not only for determining what the historical Jesus might have said but also for seeing how traditions about Jesus were circulated in oral and written form in the early centuries of the church. These agrapha are, in other words, directly germane to the interests and concerns of the early Christian apocrypha.

Bibliography

Delobel, J. "The Sayings of Jesus in the Textual Tradition: Variant Readings in the Greek Manuscripts of the Gospels," in J. Delobel et al., eds., *Logia: Les Paroles de Jésus / The Sayings of Jesus*. Leuven: Peeters, 1982; pp. 431–57.

Elliott, J. K. *The Apocryphal New Testament*. Oxford: Clarendon, 1993; pp. 26–30.

Hofius, O. "Isolated Sayings of the Lord," in *New Testament Apocrypha*, ed. W. Schneemelcher; trans. R. McL. Wilson. Louisville: Westminster/John Knox, 1991; vol. 1, pp. 88–91.

Jeremias, J. *Unknown Sayings of Jesus*. 2nd ed. London: S. P. C. K., 1964.

Agrapha

New Testament

Acts 20:35

We must . . . remember the words of the Lord Jesus, for he himself said, "It is more blessed to give than to receive."

1 Cor. 7:10

To those who are married I command—not I, but the Lord: "A woman should not be separated from her husband . . . and a man should not divorce his wife."

1 Cor. 9:14

So also the Lord ordered that those who proclaim the gospel should make their living from the gospel.

1 Cor. 11:22–24

The Lord Jesus, on the night in which he was handed over, took bread, and after giving thanks he broke it and said, "This is my body that is for you. Do this to remember me." Likewise also the cup after dining, saying, "This cup is the new covenant in my blood. Do this as often as you drink, to remember me."

Manuscript Variations in the NT

Matthew 20:28 in ms D (see Luke 14:8–10)

But you, seek to increase from what is small and to become less from what is greater. And when you enter in and are invited to eat, do not recline in the prominent place, or else someone more exalted than you might come in and the host of the dinner might come and say to you, "Go down lower"—and you would be put to shame. But if you recline in the lower spot and a lesser person enters, the host of the dinner will tell you, "Come up higher"; and this will be to your profit.

Mark 9:49 in ms D et al.

For every sacrifice will be salted with salt.

Mark 16:14 in ms W (Freer Logion)

And they defended themselves saying, "This age of lawlessness and unbelief is under Satan, who does not allow the truth and power of God to prevail over the unclean things of the spirits. And so, reveal your righteousness now." They were speaking to Christ. And Christ foretold to them, "The term for the years of Satan's authority has been fulfilled; but other terrible things draw near. And I was handed over to death for those who have sinned, in order that they might return to the truth and sin no longer, that they might inherit the spiritual and imperishable glory of righteousness that is in heaven."

Mark 16:15–18 in Later Greek Manuscripts

And he said to them, "Go into all the world and preach the gospel to all creation. The one who believes and is baptized will be saved; but the one who does not believe will be condemned. And these signs will follow those who believe. In my name they will cast out demons, they will speak in new tongues, and they will take up snakes in their hands; and if they drink anything poisonous it will not harm them; they will place their hands upon the sick and they will become well."

Luke 6:4 in ms D

On the same day, when he saw a certain man working on the Sabbath, he said to him, "O man, if you know what you are doing, you are blessed; but if you do not know, you are cursed, and a transgressor of the Law."

Luke 9:55b, 56a in K G Q and other manuscripts

And he said, "You do not know of what sort of spirit you are; for the son of man did not come to destroy human souls but to save them."

Luke 22:27, 28 in ms D

"For I came into your midst not as one who reclines at the table, but as the one who serves; and you have grown in my service as one who serves."

John 8:7; 10–11 in ms D and later Greek manuscripts

As they continued to question him, he stood up and said to them, "Let the one who has no sin among you be the first to cast a stone at her." . . . Standing up, Jesus said to her, "Woman, where are they? Has no one condemned you?" She said, "No one, Lord." Jesus replied, "Neither do I condemn you. Go, and from now on, sin no more."

Papias (according to Irenaeus, Against Heresies *5. 33. 3–4)*

Thus the elders who saw John, the disciple of the Lord, remembered hearing him say how the Lord used to teach about those times, saying:

The days are coming when vines will come forth, each with ten thousand boughs; and on a single bough will be ten thousand branches. And indeed, on a single branch will be ten thousand shoots and on every shoot ten thousand clusters; and in every cluster will be ten thousand grapes, and every grape, when pressed, will yield twenty-five measures of wine.

And when any of the saints grabs hold of a cluster, another will cry out, "I am a better cluster, take me; bless the Lord through me." So too a grain of wheat will produce ten thousand heads and every head will have ten thousand grains and every grain will yield ten pounds of pure, exceptionally fine flour. So too the remaining fruits and seeds and vegetation will produce in similar proportions. And all the animals who eat this food taken from the earth will come to be at peace and harmony with one another, yielding in complete submission to humans."

. . . And in addition Papias says "These things can be believed by those who believe. And the betrayer Judas," he said, "did not believe, but asked, 'How then can the Lord bring forth such produce?'" The Lord then replied, "Those who come into those times will see." (Ehrman, *Apostolic Fathers*, vol. 1, pp. 92–95)

Barnabas 7:11

And so he says: "Those who wish to see me and touch my kingdom must take hold of me through pain and suffering." (Ehrman, *Apostolic Fathers*, vol. 2, pp. 40–41)

2 Clement

3:2

For even he himself says, "I will acknowledge before my Father the one who acknowledges me before others."

4:2

For he says, "Not everyone who says to me, 'Lord, Lord' will be saved, but only the one who does righteousness."

4:5

The Lord has said, "Even if you were cuddled up with me next to my breast but did not do what I have commanded, I would cast you away and say to you, 'Leave me! I do not know where you are from, you who do what is lawless.'"

5:2–4

For the Lord said, "You will be like sheep in the midst of wolves." But Peter replied to him, "What if the wolves rip apart the sheep?" Jesus said to Peter,

"After they are dead, the sheep should fear the wolves no longer. So too you: do not fear those who kill you and then can do nothing more to you; but fear the one who, after you die, has the power to cast your body and soul into the hell of fire."

8:5

For the Lord says in the Gospel, "If you do not keep what is small, who will give you what is great? For I say to you that the one who is faithful in very little is faithful also in much."

12:2–6

For when the Lord himself was asked by someone when his kingdom would come, he said, "When the two are one, and the outside like the inside, and the male with the female is neither male nor female. . . . When you do these things," he says, "the kingdom of my Father will come."

13:2

For the Lord says, "My name is constantly blasphemed among all the outsiders." And again he says, "Woe to the one who causes my name to be blasphemed."

Clement 13:4

They hear from us that God has said, "It is no great accomplishment for you to love those who love you; it is great if you love your enemies and those who hate you." (All from Ehrman, *Apostolic Fathers*, vol. 1, pp. 153–99)

Justin, Dialogue with Trypho *47.5*

Therefore our Lord Jesus Christ said, "In whatever circumstances I overtake you, in those I will also judge you." (Goodspeed, *Die Ältesten Apologeten*, 146)

The Preaching of Peter

Clement of Alexandria, Stromateis *6.5.43*

For this reason Peter indicates that the Lord said to the apostles: "If then anyone in Israel wishes to believe in God after repenting through my name, his sins will be forgiven. But after twelve years go out into the world, so that no one can say, 'We did not hear.'" (Stählin-Früchtel, *Clemens* GCS 52 [15] p. 453)

Clement of Alexandria, Stromateis *6.6.48*

I chose you twelve, judging you to be disciples worthy of me, you whom the Lord desired; and considering you faithful apostles, I sent you into the world to proclaim the gospel to people throughout the earth, that they might know that there is one God, and to reveal the things that are about to take place through faith in me, the Christ, so that those who hear and believe may be saved, but those who hear and do not believe may bear witness that they have no excuse to say, "We did not hear."(Stählin-Früchtel, *Clemens* GCS 52 [15] p. 456)

Clement of Alexandria

Stromateis 1.24.158

"For," he says, "ask for the great things, and the small things will be given you as well." (Stählin-Früchtel, *Clemens* GCS 52 [15] p. 100)

Stromateis 5. 10. 63

For the Lord proclaimed in a certain Gospel, "My mystery is for me and the children of my house." (Stählin-Früchtel, *Clemens* GCS 52 [15] p. 368)

Exc. Ex Theod. 2.2

For this reason the Savior says, "Save yourself, you and your soul." (Stählin-Früchtel, *Clemens* GCS 52 [15] p. 106)

Origen

Commentary on John 19.7.2

Keeping the commandment of Jesus, which says, "Be skillful moneychangers." (Preuschen, *Origenes Johanneskommentar,* p. 307)

Commentary on Matthew 13.2

And Jesus indeed said, "I was weak because of the weak, and I was hungry because of the hungry, and I was thirsty because of the thirsty." (Klostermann, *Origenes Werke* 10.183)

Acts of Peter

10

For I heard that he also said this: "Those who are with me have not understood me." (Lipsius-Bonnet, *Acta Apostolorum Apocrypha* 1.58)

38

Concerning these things the Lord said, in a mystery, "If you do not make the things on the right like the things on the left and the things on the left like the things on the right, and the things above like the things below and the things behind like the things in front, you will not come to know the kingdom." (Lipsius-Bonnet, *Acta Apostolorum Apocrypha* 1:94)

Apostolic Church Ordinances

26

For he foretold to us when he was teaching: "The weak will be saved through the strong." (Preuschen, *Antilegomena,* 27)

Pseudo-Cyprian

De montibus Sina et Sion 13

For we, too, who believe in him, see Christ in ourselves as if in a mirror. As he himself instructs and admonishes us in a letter of his own disciple John to the people, "So you see me in yourselves, just as one of you sees himself in the water or in the mirror." (Hartel, *Cyprianus* 3:117)

De aleatoribus 3

The Lord admonishes and says, "Do not grieve the Holy Spirit who is in you, and do not extinguish the light, which shines in you." (Harnack, *Der Pseudocryprianische Tractat de Aleatoribus,* 17)

Psalms of Heracleides

187.27–29

Remember what I said, between you and me on the Mount of Olives: "I have something to say but no one to whom to say it." (Allberry, *Manichaean Psalm Book,* 187)

Manichean Psalms of the Bema

Ps. 239:23–24

He is not far from us, my brothers, as he said when he proclaimed, "I am near you, like the garment of your body." (Allberry, *Manichaean Psalm Book,* 39)

Acts of Philip

137

But the Savior said, "O Philip, Since you have abandoned and not fulfilled this my commandment, that you should not pay back evil for evil, for this reason you will be held back from eternity for forty days and will not come to the place that has been promised you." (Lipsius and Bonnet, *Acta Apostolorum Apocrypha,* 2.2:69)

Apostolic Constitutions

4. 2–3

For also again it was said by him, "Woe to those who (already) have and who receive in hypocrisy, or who are able to help themselves yet wish to receive from others. For each one will render an account to the Lord God on the day of judgment." (Funk, *Didascalia et Constitutiones Apostolorum,* 221)

Symeon of Mesopotamia

Homily 12.17

Finally the Lord was saying to them, "Why do you marvel at my signs? I am giving a great inheritance to you, which the entire world does not have." (Dorries, Klostermann, and Kroeger, *Geistliche Homilien,* 119)

Homily 37.1

. . . but hearing the Lord who says: "Pay attention to faith and hope, through which love—directed toward both God and others—provides eternal life." (Dorries, Klostermann, and Kroeger, *Geistliche Homilien,* 265)

PASSION, RESURRECTION, AND POST-RESURRECTION GOSPELS

22

The Gospel of Peter

The third-century Origen is the first patristic author to mention a Gospel allegedly written by Jesus' disciple Simon Peter. Origen indicates that the book may have spoken of Jesus' "brothers" as sons of Joseph from a previous marriage (*Commentary on Matthew* 10.17). It is not clear that Origen had actually read the book: nothing that we now know indicates that any such story was in it, and Origen also states that the information may instead have come from a "book of James"—presumably a reference to what is now called the Proto-Gospel of James, a book that does identify Jesus' brothers in this way. The next church father to mention a Gospel of Peter is the fourth-century "father of church history," Eusebius, who twice numbers the book among writings not accepted by the church as Scripture (*Church History*, 3. 3. 2; 3. 25. 6). On one other occasion, Eusebius discusses the book at some length, in order to show why it had been excluded from consideration from the canon.

The story involves Serapion, a bishop of Antioch at the end of the second century. Based on an account he had read from Serapion's own hand, Eusebius indicates that Serapion had firsthand knowledge of the Gospel of Peter and insisted that it not be used. As bishop over a large area, Serapion had made a trip among the various churches under his authority, including the church in the Syrian village of Rhossus. Upon arriving in Rhossus he learned that for their worship services the Christians there used a Gospel allegedly written by Peter. At first Serapion sanctioned the use of the book, sight unseen: if Peter had written a Gospel, then certainly it was appropriate for use in the church. After returning to Antioch, however, he learned from several informers that the so-called Gospel of Peter was in favor among a group of heretical believers known as the "Docetae."

We do not know exactly what this group was or what beliefs they held. It is usually thought that they subscribed to an alternative understanding of Christ. The term "Docetism" comes from the Greek term DOKEO, "to seem" or "to appear," and is usually applied to Christological views that maintained that Christ was not really human and did not really suffer and die, but only appeared to do so. We know of two major forms of docetic belief in the early church. One form, associated with figures such as Marcion of Sinope, held that Jesus was not a real human being but that he had come from heaven only in the "appearance" of human flesh. His body, in other words, was a phantasm. The other form of docetism, associated with a number of different Gnostic groups, maintained that Jesus himself was a flesh-and-blood human being, but that he was not to be identified with the Christ. The Christ was a divine being who descended from heaven and temporarily united with the man Jesus (at his baptism, for example) empowering him for his ministry of teaching and miracles. Then at the end of Jesus' life, before his death, the divine Christ once more separated from him, leaving him to die alone. Here again, Christ only "appeared" to suffer.

We do not know which, if either, of these beliefs was held by Serapion's Docetae. But once Serapion learned that the group revered the Gospel of Peter used in Rhossus, he obtained a copy for himself and read it. On the basis of this perusal he decided that even though most of its account was orthodox, there were some "additions" to the story that could indeed be used to support a heretical understanding of the gospel. Serapion wrote a small tractate detailing the problems of the book and sent it to the church in Rhossus, along with a letter forbidding their future use of the book.

Over a century later, Eusebius tells the story (*Church History* 6. 12) and quotes from the letter. But he does not quote any of the problematic passages that Serapion detailed in his tractate. This is much to be regretted, because it makes it impossible to know with absolute certainty that the Gospel of Peter that has now come into our hands is the one that Serapion had read at the end of the second century. In any event, the Gospel more or less disappeared from sight for seventeen hundred years.

What we now call the Gospel of Peter was found in one of the most remarkable archaeological discoveries of Christian texts in the nineteenth century. In the winter season of 1886–87 a French archaeological team headed by M. Grébant was digging in Akhmîm in Upper Egypt, in a portion of a cemetery that contained graves ranging from the eighth to the twelfth centuries CE. They uncovered the grave of a person they took to be a Christian monk, who had been buried with a book. Among other things, the book contained a fragmentary copy of a Gospel written in the name of Peter.

It is a parchment manuscript (P. Cair. 10759) of sixty-six pages, averaging 13 x 16 cm, containing a small anthology of four texts in Greek, all of them fragmentary (the manuscript itself is not fragmentary; the works copied into it are incomplete): the Gospel of Peter, the Apocalypse of Peter, the Book of Enoch, and the Martyrdom of St. Julian. The first page is adorned with a cross; the second page starts, at the top, in the middle of a sentence: ". . . but none of the Jews washed his hands, nor did Herod or any of his judges. Since they did not wish to wash, Pilate stood up." Since this is the beginning of the text (after a page of decoration) and yet starts in mid-sentence, it appears that the scribe producing this manuscript had before him only a fragmentary text. Pages 2–10 of the manuscript contain, then, an account of Jesus' trial, death, and resurrection, before ending, once again, in the middle of a sentence, which is followed then by two blank pages before the next text begins. It is impossible to know what else the "original" Gospel of Peter may have contained—whether it was simply a passion narrative (like the Gospel of Nicodemus, from later times; see later in this collection) or rather a complete Gospel of Jesus' life and ministry leading up to his passion, like the Gospels of the New Testament.

In the first published edition of the Gospel, U. Bouriant suggested that the Akhmîm manuscript could be dated anywhere from the eighth to the twelfth centuries. Since then scholars have argued for earlier dates; most recently T. Klaus and T. Nicklas have settled on late sixth or early seventh centuries.

The account provides us with an alternative version of the passion and resurrection of Jesus, similar in many respects to the accounts of the New Testament Gospels but with striking differences and few extensive verbatim agreements. As the opening line quoted above intimates, this Gospel is even more concerned than those of the New Testament to implicate "the Jews" for the death of Jesus. Here, in fact, it is not the Roman governor Pilate who orders Jesus' execution, but the Jewish King Herod. Throughout the text "the Jews" are vilified for demanding Jesus' death. After the crucifixion, for example, they realize just what they have done: "Then the Jews, the elders, and the priests realized how much evil they had done to themselves and began beating their breasts, saying, 'Woe to us because of our sins. The judgment and the end of Jerusalem are near'" (v. 25). Here then is the notion, found scattered throughout Christian sources of the second and third century, that the Roman destruction of Jerusalem in 70 CE was divine retribution for the execution of Jesus.

In addition to maligning the Jews (and exonerating Pilate), the text provides a number of narrative details not found in other Gospel accounts of the passion. On the cross, one of the robbers reviles not Jesus, but the Roman soldiers for killing Jesus. The soldiers respond by *not* breaking his legs, thus prolonging his suffering and forcing him to die in agony.

Most remarkable, and most famous, is the major episode near the end of the Gospel, an account of Jesus emerging from the tomb on the third day. The Gospels of the New Testament give no such report, but simply indicate that Jesus *had* been raised (when the women find the tomb empty). The report of the resurrection in the Gospel of Peter, on the other hand, is its best known and most commented feature: for here Jesus comes forth from the tomb as tall as a mountain, with the cross emerging behind him and speaking to the heavens, affirming that the message of salvation has been proclaimed in the realm of the dead.

The author of this account writes in the first-person on two occasions, once without identifying himself ("I and my companions" v. 26), but the other time indicating that he is none other than the disciple Peter: "But I, Simon Peter, and Andrew my brother . . ." (v. 60). Here then is a Gospel with the marks of antiquity, written in the name of Peter. Is it the Gospel of Peter known and proscribed by Serapion at the end of the second century?

Unfortunately, since Eusebius chose not to quote the passages of the Gospel that Serapion had found potentially offensive to orthodox faith, but open to docetic construal, it may be impossible ever to know. Scholars did identify this text with Serapion's almost immediately upon its discovery, for example, in U. Bouriant's first edition in 1892. The identification was accepted without question by the host of scholars who published editions or discussions of the find soon thereafter. In part the identification was obvious: Serapion spoke of a Gospel by Peter, we have record of only one such Gospel in the early church, and now we have an ancient Gospel that claims to be written by Peter. Contributing to the identification, however, was the sense that the theological emphases of this text coincide with what Eusebius tells us about the Gospel, for it was thought that it was indeed a docetic text. Particularly to be noted are the statements in v. 10, that Jesus "was silent as if he had no pain" (if he had no pain, he must not have had a real body); in v. 19 his cry "My power, O power, you have left me behind" (is this the divine Christ leaving the body of the man Jesus?); the statement that on the cross "he was taken up" (Jesus' body obviously wasn't "taken up," since it remained on the cross; was it his "spirit"—the divine Christ—that ascended?); and of course the resurrection narrative, where the body that emerges from the tomb is obviously not a normal, but a superhuman body.

A number of scholars later in the twentieth century, however, came to question whether these passages are necessarily docetic: v. 10 indicates that Jesus was silent "as if" he had no pain--not that he had no pain. The cry in v. 19 is just a paraphrase of the cry of dereliction in Mark 15:34. And his "being taken up" may simply be a euphemism for his "giving up his spirit"—that is, for dying. Moreover, even in the New Testament Gospels Jesus' resurrection body is not a normal human body (it can walk through walls and disappear at will, for example)—but that does not make these books docetic.

In trying to resolve these issues it is useful to return to what Eusebius indicates about Serapion and the Gospel of Peter. Nowhere does Eusebius (or Serapion) indicate that the Gospel was actually written from a docetic perspective, only that while the book was for the most part orthodox, it was open to a docetic interpretation (hence it was used by the Docetae). Certainly the Gospel we now have before us is all that. Much of the Gospel is comparable to the Gospels of the New Testament, and there are some passages that *could* be understood docetically (whether they were *meant* to be docetic is an entirely different question).

For these reasons, the majority of scholars today see this Gospel as the one referred to by Serapion in the late second century. Assuming that this identification is correct, what is the book's relationship to the Gospels of the New Testament, and what is its date? The first issue has occupied a large number of scholarly discussions over the years, with every possible relationship being proposed: (1) that the Gospel of Peter is a pastiche of the earlier canonical Gospels with legendary accretions; (2) that its author had read the earlier Gospels and constructed his own account based on his (somewhat faulty) recollection of them; (3) that the author was writing independently of the other Gospels and had derived his stories from the oral traditions about Jesus; (4) that the Gospel of Peter was based on a source that *antedated* the canonical Gospels, and that it preserved this source better than they, so that it, not they, represents the earliest form of the tradition of Jesus' death and resurrection. The final option has had the fewest adherents. On the other hand, since there are so few verbatim agreements with the other Gospels, it is hard to establish that the author actually used them as literary sources. And so it seems more likely that he constructed his Gospel on the basis of oral traditions and/or on recollections of accounts he had earlier read.

The question of the date of the Gospel is, of course, closely tied to the questions of whether it is the book known to Serapion and if its author was familiar with the Gospels of the New Testament. If both questions are answered in the affirmative then the book must date sometime in the middle of the second century—after the canonical Gospels and before Serapion. More recently Dieter Lührmann has argued that there is hard evidence for a second-century dating. In Lührmann's view, there are three other ancient fragments of the Gospel of Peter: P. Oxy 2949; P. Oxy. 4009; and the Fayûm Fragment P.Vindob. G 2325. He dates the first two of these to the second century, and the other to the third, so that if they belong to the Gospel of Peter, the book must have circulated nearly half a millennium before the Akhmîm codex. Few scholars have been convinced by Lührmann's identification of the Fayûm fragment as part of the Gospel of Peter, but his other two identifications may be correct (see introductions for each one above; for a contrary view see P. Foster and T. Kraus/T. Nicklas).

Whether or not these fragments go back to the Gospel of Peter, there are reasons for dating the text to a period after the canonical Gospels, probably sometime in the beginning or middle of the second century. In particular, the heightened animosity toward "the Jews" for their involvement with the death of Jesus and the legendary accretions to the stories of his death and resurrection fit well into that time frame.

In early editions, the Gospel was divided into either fourteen chapters (A. Harnack) or sixty verses (J. A. Robinson). Over the years, scholars have followed the confusing convention of using both enumerations, so that, for example, 4:14–15 is immediately followed by 5:16–17. For the sake of simplicity, only Robinson's verse divisions will be given here.

Bibliography

Bernhard, A. E. *Other Early Christian Gospels: A Critical Edition of the Surviving Greek Manuscripts*. London: T&T Clark, 2006; pp. 49–52.

Bouriant, U. *Fragments du texte grec du livre d'Énoch et de quelques écrits attribué à Saint Pierre*. Paris: E. Leroux, 1892; pp. 137–42.

Crossan, J. D. *The Cross That Spoke: The Origins of the Passion Narrative*. San Francisco: Harper & Row, 1988.

Ehrman, B. D. *Lost Christianities: The Battles for Scripture and the Faiths We Never Knew*. New York: Oxford University Press, 2003; pp. 13–28.

Elliott, J. K. *The Apocryphal New Testament*. Oxford: Clarendon, 1993; pp. 150–54.

Foster, P. *The Gospel of Peter: Introduction, Critical Edition, and Commentary*. Leiden: E. J. Brill, 2010.

Harnack, A. *Bruchstücke des Evangeliums und der Apokalypse des Petrus*. Leipzig: J. C. Hinrichs, 1893.

Klauck, H.-J. *Apocryphal Gospels: An Introduction*. London: T&T Clark, 2003; pp. 82–88.

Kraus, T. J., and Tobias Nicklas. *Die Petrusevangelium und die Petrusapokalypse*. Berlin: De Gruyter, 2004.

McCant, J. W. "The Gospel of Peter: Docetism Reconsidered," *NTS* 30 (1984): 258–73.

Robinson, J. A. "The Gospel according to Peter," in J. A. Robinson and M. R. James, *The Gospel according to Peter and the Revelation of Peter*. London: C. J. Clay, 1892.

Schneemelcher, W. "The Gospel of Peter," in *New Testament Apocrypha*, ed. W. Schneemelcher; trans. R. McL. Wilson. Louisville: Westminster/John Knox, 1991; vol. 1, pp. 216–22.

Swete, H. B. *The Akmîm Fragment of the Apocryphal Gospel of Peter*. London: Macmillan, 1893.

The Gospel of Peter

Jesus Put on Trial and Mocked

(1) . . . but none of the Jews washed his hands, nor did Herod or any of his judges.[1] Since they did not wish to wash, Pilate stood up. (2) Then King Herod ordered the Lord to be taken away and said to them, "Do everything that I ordered you to do to him."

(3) Standing there was Joseph, a friend of both Pilate and the Lord; when he knew that they were about to crucify him, he came to Pilate and asked for the Lord's body for burial.[2] (4) Pilate sent word to Herod, asking for his body. (5) Herod said, "Brother Pilate, even if no one had asked for him we would have buried him, since the Sabbath is dawning.[3] For it is written in the Law that the sun must not set on one who has been killed."[4] And he delivered him over to the people[5] the day before their Feast of Unleavened Bread.[6]

(6) Those who took the Lord began pushing him about, running up to him and saying, "Let us drag around the Son of God, since we have authority over him." (7) They clothed him in purple and sat him on the judgment seat, saying, "Give a righteous judgment, O King of Israel!"[7] (8) One of them brought a crown made of thorns and placed it on the Lord's head. (9) Others standing there were spitting in his face; some slapped his cheeks; others were beating him with a reed; and some began to flog him, saying, "This is how we should honor the Son of God!"[8]

The Crucifixion of Jesus

(10) They brought forward two evildoers and crucified the Lord between them. But he was silent, as if he had no pain. (11) When they had set the cross upright, they wrote an inscription: "This is the King of Israel." (12) Putting his clothes in front of him they divided them up and cast a lot for them.[9] (13) But one of the evildoers reviled them, "We have suffered like this for the evil things we did; but this one, the Savior of the people—what wrong has he done you?"[10] (14) They

1. See Matt. 27–24.
2. See Matt. 27:58; Mark 15:43; Luke 23:52; John 19:38.
3. See Luke 23:54.
4. Deut. 21:22–23; see John 19:31.
5. See Matt. 27:26; Mark 15:15; Luke 23:25; John 19:16.
6. See Matt. 26:17; Mark 14:12; Luke 22:7.
7. See John 19:13.
8. See Matt. 26:67–68; 27:27–31; Mark 14:65; 15:16–20; Luke 22:63–65; John 19:2–3.
9. See Matt. 27:33–37; Mark 15:22–26; Luke 23:33–34; John 19:17–27.
10. See Luke 23:39–43.

became angry at him and ordered his legs not be broken,[11] so that he would die in torment.

(15) It was noon and darkness came over all of Judea. They were disturbed and upset that the sun may have already set while he was still alive; for their Scripture says that the sun must not set on one who has been killed.[12] (16) One of them said, "Give him gall mixed with vinegar to drink." And they made the mixture and gave it to him to drink.[13] (17) Thus they brought all things to fulfillment and completed all their sins on their heads.

(18) But many were wandering around with torches, thinking that it was night; and they stumbled about. (19) And the Lord cried out, "My power, O power, you have left me behind!"[14] When he said this, he[15] was taken up.

(20) At that hour, the curtain of the temple in Jerusalem was ripped in half.[16] (21) Then they pulled the nails from the Lord's hands and placed him on the ground. All the ground shook and everyone was terrified.[17] (22) Then the sun shone and it was found to be three in the afternoon.[18]

The Burial of Jesus

(23) But the Jews were glad and gave his body to Joseph that he might bury him, since he had seen all the good things he did. (24) He took the Lord, washed him, wrapped him in a linen cloth,[19] and brought him into his own tomb, called the Garden of Joseph.[20] (25) Then the Jews, the elders, and the priests realized how much evil they had done to themselves and began beating their breasts, saying "Woe to us because of our sins. The judgment and the end of Jerusalem are near."[21]

(26) But I and my companions were grieving and went into hiding, wounded in heart. For we were being sought out by them as if we were evildoers who wanted to burn the temple. (27) While these things were happening, we fasted and sat mourning and weeping, night and day, until the Sabbath.

(28) The scribes, Pharisees, and elders gathered together and heard all the people murmuring and beating their breasts, saying, "If such great signs happened

11. See John 19:31–37.
12. Deut. 21:22–23; see John 19:31.
13. See Matt. 27, 34, 48; Mark 15:23, 36; Luke 23:36; John 29:28–30.
14. See Matt. 27:46; Mark 15:34.
15. Or: it.
16. See Matt. 27:51; Mark 15:38; Luke 23:45.
17. See Matt. 27:51, 54.
18. See Matt. 27, 45; Mark 15:33; Luke 23:44.
19. See Matt. 27:59; Mark 14:46; Luke 23:53; John 19:40.
20. See John 19:41.
21. See Luke 23:48; esp. note the variant reading in the Latin ms g[1:] dicentes: vae nobis quae facta sunt hodie propter peccata nostra; appropinquavit enim desolatio Hierusalem.

when he died, you can see how righteous he was!"[22] (29) The elders became fearful and went to Pilate and asked him, (30) "Give us some soldiers to guard his crypt for three days to keep his disciples from coming to steal him. Otherwise the people may assume he has been raised from the dead and then harm us."[23]

(31) So Pilate gave them the centurion Petronius and soldiers to guard the tomb. The elders and scribes came with them to the crypt. (32) Everyone who was there, along with the centurion and the soldiers, rolled a great stone and placed it there before the entrance of the crypt.[24] (33) They smeared it with seven seals, pitched a tent there, and stood guard.[25]

The Resurrection of Jesus

(34) Early in the morning, as the Sabbath dawned, a crowd came from Jerusalem and the surrounding area to see the sealed crypt. (35) But during the night on which the Lord's day dawned, while the soldiers stood guard two by two on their watch, a great voice came from the sky. (36) They saw the skies open and two men descend from there; they were very bright and drew near to the tomb. (37) That stone which had been cast before the entrance rolled away by itself and moved to one side; the tomb was open and both young men entered.[26]

(38) When the solders saw these things, they woke up the centurion and the elders–for they were also there on guard. (39) As they were explaining what they had seen, they saw three men emerge from the tomb, two of them supporting the other, with a cross following behind them. (40) The heads of the two reached up to the sky, but the head of the one they were leading went up above the skies. (41) And they heard a voice from the skies, "Have you preached to those who are asleep?"[27] (42) And a reply came from the cross, "Yes."

(43) They then decided among themselves to go off to disclose what had happened to Pilate. (44) While they were still making their plans, the skies were again seen to open, and a person descended and entered the crypt. (45) Those who were with the centurion saw these things and hurried to Pilate at night, abandoning the tomb they had been guarding, and explained everything they had seen. Greatly agitated, they said, "He actually was the Son of God."[28] (46) Pilate replied, "I am clean of the blood of the Son of God; you decided to do this."[29]

22. See Luke 23:47–48.
23. See Matt. 27:62–66.
24. See Matt. 27:60; Mark 15: 46; Luke 23:53.
25. See Matt. 27:66.
26. See Matt. 28:1–2.
27. See 1 Pet. 3:19.
28. See Matt. 27:54; Mark 15:39.
29. See Matt. 27:24.

(47) Then everyone approached him to ask and urge him to order the centurion and the soldiers to say nothing about what they had seen. (48) "For it is better," they said, "for us to incur a great sin before God than to fall into the hands of the Jewish people and be stoned." (49) And so Pilate ordered the centurion and the soldiers not to say a word.[30]

The Women at the Tomb

(50) Now Mary Magdalene, a disciple of the Lord, had been afraid of the Jews, since they were inflamed with anger; and so she had not done at the Lord's crypt the things that women customarily do for loved ones who die. But early in the morning of the Lord's day (51) she took some of her women friends with her and came to the crypt where he had been buried.[31] (52) And they were afraid that the Jews might see them, and they said, "Even though we were not able to weep and beat our breasts on the day he was crucified, we should do these things now at his crypt. (53) But who will roll away for us the stone placed before the entrance of the crypt, that we can go in, sit beside him, and do what we should? (54) For it was a large stone,[32] and we are afraid someone may see us. If we cannot move it, we should at least cast down the things we have brought at the entrance as a memorial to him; and we will weep and beat our breasts until we return home."

(55) When they arrived they found the tomb opened. And when they came up to it they stooped down to look in, and they saw a beautiful young man dressed in a very bright garment, sitting in the middle of the tomb. He said to them, (56) "Why have you come? Whom are you seeking? Not the one who was crucified? He has risen and left. But if you do not believe it, stoop down to look, and see the place where he was laid, that he is not there. For he has risen and left for the place from which he was sent." (57) Then the women fled out of fear.[33]

The Disciples after the Resurrection

(58) But it was the final day of the Feast of Unleavened Bread, and many left to return to their homes, now that the feast had ended. (59) But we, the twelve disciples of the Lord, wept and grieved; and each one returned to his home, grieving for what had happened. (60) But I, Simon Peter, and my brother Andrew, took our nets and went off to the sea.[34] And with us was Levi, the son of Alphaeus, whom the Lord . . .

30. See Matt. 28:11–15.

31. See Matt. 28:1; Mark 16:1–2; Luke 24:1; John 19:1.

32. See Mark 16:3–4.

33. See Mark 16:1–8.

34. See John 21:1–14.

23

The Gospel of Judas

The Gospel of Judas is the most recently discovered Gospel to be published and is arguably the most important and intriguing Christian text to appear since the discovery of the Nag Hammadi Library in 1945. Details of the discovery and the mishandling of the manuscript by antiquities dealers are provided in the exhaustive account of Herb Krosney. The manuscript containing the Gospel preserves three other gnostic works as well: the "Letter of Peter to Philip," known in a slightly different version from the findings at Nag Hammadi; the "(First) Apocalypse of James," also known from Nag Hammadi; and a treatise entitled the "Book of Allogenes," unrelated to the Nag Hammadi treatise also called "Allogenes" (= the Stranger). All four texts are in Coptic, but they are clearly translations of Greek originals. The manuscript was discovered by peasants rummaging through a burial cave in the Al Minya province of Egypt in 1978, but its existence was not known to the scholarly world at large until the Swiss Coptologist R. Kasser announced its discovery and pending publication at the Eighth International Conference of Coptic Studies in Paris, July 2004.

By this time Kasser and conservationist F. Darbre had been at work for three years conserving the text, after it had been subject to abuse by the overly zealous and poorly informed antiquities dealers who had, over the years, torn the manuscript straight through, rearranged its pages, frozen and then thawed it, and so on. As a result of this mishandling, something like 5–10 percent of the contents of the Gospel of Judas has been permanently lost. But enough remains to make this one of the truly significant finds of modern times.

It is a complete Gospel—with the beginning, end, and much of the middle preserved. The manuscript itself can be dated on palaeographic grounds to the fourth century (a carbon-14 dating puts it in the late third). The question, of course, is when the account was originally composed. The church father Irenaeus mentions the Gospel of Judas as a document used by a group of Gnostics later known as the Cainites. G. Wurst, along with others, has made a compelling case that the recently published text is the one known to Irenaeus, who was writing around 180 CE (see Wurst in Kasser, 2006). Since the book had been in circulation before it came to Irenaeus's attention, a date of 140–150 CE seems plausible.

The publication of an English translation of the Gospel created a media stir in April 2006. The Gospel was seen as having wide public appeal. Not only does it contain a gnostic revelation that explains the generation of the divine realm and the creation of this world (a cryptic revelation that, like most such gnostic accounts, is difficult to unpack), it contains a number of encounters between Jesus and his disciples, principally Judas Iscariot, prior to Jesus' arrest. What was most striking to the scholars who first investigated the text is that Judas is given such a high profile in the account. He alone among the disciples is portrayed as recognizing who Jesus really is (he is not from the world of the creator). Debates over the Gospel have turned on whether Judas is portrayed as the hero of the text, the one who both knows Jesus and does his will or if, instead, he is denigrated as an evil demon who may recognize aspects of the truth (gnosis) but is nonetheless condemned not to attain salvation. Quite possibly a mediating position is to be preferred, in which Judas is portrayed as a "psychic" Christian who is superior to the other disciples but is not a true "spiritual" Gnostic who will eventually ascend to the "heavenly generation."

In terms of its structure, the Gospel contains a series of dialogues between Jesus and his disciples during the Passover week, before the crucifixion. The crucifixion itself is not narrated in the account—indeed, for this anonymous author, the crucifixion is not the climax of the story of Jesus. What matters, instead, is the "secret" revelation (1.1) that Jesus delivers, as he unveils the hidden truths of salvation to his disciples, and especially to Judas. This text, in other words, embodies a gnostic understanding of Jesus, in which it is not his death and resurrection that bring salvation, but his secret teachings. The Gospel, accordingly, ends not with the passion but with the betrayal of Judas, when Jesus' discussions with his disciples come to an end.

The tone of the Gospel is set at the first encounter of Jesus with the disciples. He comes upon them while they are sharing a eucharistic meal—that is, a sacred meal in which they are "thanking" (the meaning of "eucharist") God for their food. When Jesus sees what they are doing, he laughs—much to their dismay. But for Jesus their actions are indeed risible, for the disciples have mistakenly assumed that the creator of this world (i.e., the one who provides food) is the God he himself represents. In fact, he is not related to the creator God—as Judas alone realizes, when he confesses that Jesus comes from the realm of Barbelo, the name of a gnostic deity known from other texts as the mother of all that exists. Judas is praised for his insight, and Jesus takes him aside to give him private instruction.

From this point on occur a number of discussions and dialogues, none more significant than the revelation about the creation of the world that takes up a large portion of the second half of the Gospel. While many readers will find this revelation bizarre and hard to understand (as well it should be, since it is part of the "secret" knowledge that only the insiders—the Gnostics—can fathom), its overarching point is not difficult to discern. There is more to this creation than meets the eye. Before the material world came into existence there evolved a higher, divine realm; the divine beings responsible for the creation of our material world were lower inferior deities: the creator of the world itself is Nebro, whose name means "rebel" and who is said to be stained with blood; the creator of human beings is his assistant, Saklas, whose name means "fool." In other worlds, this world and the humans who inhabit it were created by a bloodthirsty rebel and a fool.

This revelation leads to a further back and forth between Jesus and Judas, climaxing in the key line of the text, where Jesus indicates Judas's superiority to all the other disciples: "you will surpass them all" [a translation probably to be preferred to "you will do worse than all of them," for which see A. DeConnick, p. 58] "for you will sacrifice the human who bears me." This much-debated line may suggest that Jesus, like the Gnostics themselves, is only temporarily resident in the body; he needs to escape it in order to return, permanently, to his heavenly home. In this reading, Judas's act is thus not a nefarious betrayal but a beneficent deed done for the Savior—whose teachings (not death) are salvific. The Gospel ends, then, with an account of the betrayal itself.

If this Gospel is quite unlike most of the others presented in this collection, it is not unlike those preserved in gnostic documents found at Nag Hammadi. As Marvin Meyer has shown, in one of the trenchant early pieces of scholarship on the text, the Gospel of Judas is best seen as containing a version of the Sethian Gnostic myth. At the same time, the Gospel is rich with connections to other non-Sethian writings of Christian antiquity: Jesus' laughter is found in non-Sethian sources, the ignorance of the disciples was a key then in the teachings of Marcion, and there are even remnants of Jewish apocalyptic thought here. Still the scholarship on this important document has just begun, and no consensus has emerged on many aspects of its interpretation.

Our translation is based on the Coptic text of R. Kasser and G. Wurst, eds., *The Gospel of Judas: Critical Edition* (Washington, DC: National Geographic, 2007). New portions of the Gospel appeared in 2008, when the one-time owner of the manuscript, in connection with bankruptcy proceedings, turned over the remaining fragments of the Gospel of Judas that had been illicitly retained when he originally sold the manuscript. These have been photographed and they have begun to be studied; for our translation of the account here we have been able to take them into consideration (see the "Preliminary Report" by Krosney, Meyer, and Wurst in the bibliography).

Bibliography

Brankaer, J., and H.-G. Bethge. *Codex Tchacos: Texte und Analysen*. TU 161. Berlin-New York: Walter de Gruyter, 2007, pp. 255–372.

Ehrman, B. D. *The Lost Gospel of Judas Iscariot: A New Look at Betrayer and Betrayed*. New York: Oxford University Press, 2007.

Jenott, L. *The Gospel of Judas. Coptic Text, Translation, and Historical Interpretation of the "Betrayer's Gospel."* Tübingen: Mohr Sieback, 2011.

Kasser, R., and G. Wurst. *The Gospel of Judas, Together with the Letter of Peter to Philip, James, and a Book of Allogenes from Codex Tchacos: Critical Edition*. Introductions, Translations, and Notes by R. Kasser, G. Wurst, M. Meyer, and F. Gaudard. Washington, D.C.: National Geographic, 2007.

Kasser, R., M. Meyer, and G. Wurst. *The Gospel of Judas*. Washington, D.C.: National Geographic, 2006 (contains an English translation and interpretive essays by Kasser, Meyer, Wurst, and Bart Ehrman); the second edition, 2008, contains additional essays by C. Evans and G. Schenke Robinson.

Krosney, H. *The Lost Gospel: The Quest for the Gospel of Judas*. Washington, D.C.: National Geographic, 2006.

Krosney, H., M. Meyer, and G. Wurst. "Preliminary Report on New Fragments of Codex Tchacos," *Early Christianity* 1 (2010): 282–94.

Pleše, Z. "Gnostic Literature," in *Religiöse Philosophie und philosophische Religion der frühen Kaiserzeit Literaturgeschichtliche Perspektiven*. Ratio Religionis Studien I, ed. R. Hirsch-Luipold, H. Görgemanns, M. von Albrecht, and M. v. Tobias Thum. Tübingen: Mohr Siebeck, 2008; pp. 163–98, esp. 173–74.

Schenke Robinson, G. "Judas, a Hero or a Villain?" in Kasser, Meyer, and Wurst, *The Gospel of Judas*, pp. 155–68.

Scopello, M., ed. The Gospel of Judas in Context. Proceedings of the First International Conference on the Gospel of Judas. Paris, Sorbonne, October 27–28, 2006. NHMS 62. Leiden: Brill, 2008.

Wurst, G. "Gospel of Judas, New Fragment III." Paper presented at the Ninth International Congress of Coptic Studies, IACS, Cairo, September 2008.

The Gospel of Judas

33 The secret discourse of revelation that Jesus spoke with Judas Iscariot in the course of eight days, three days before he celebrated Passover.

Gospel Frame: Jesus' Ministry

When he appeared on earth, he performed signs and great miracles for the salvation of humankind. And since some walked on the path of righteousness and others walked in their transgression, the twelve disciples were called. He began to speak with them about the mysteries that are beyond the world and what will happen at the end. Oftentimes he would not disclose himself to his disciples, but when necessary,[1] you would find him in their midst.

First Day: Jesus Separates Judas from Other Disciples

One day he came in Judaea to his disciples, and he found them seated and gathered together, practicing godliness.[2] When he approached his disciples **34** as they were assembled together, seated and giving thanks over the bread, he laughed. But the disciples said to him, "Teacher, why are you laughing at our thanksgiving? What have we done? This is what is appropriate." He replied and said to them, "I am not laughing at you. You are not doing this out of your own will: rather, your god will receive praise through this." They said, "Teacher, you . . . are the son of God." Jesus said to them, "How do you know me? Truly I say to you that no generation will know me from the people that are among you."

Now when his disciples heard this, they began to feel irritated and angry, and to blaspheme against him in their hearts. And Jesus, when he saw their senselessness, said to them, "Why has this agitation produced wrath? Your god who is within you and his powers[3] **35** have become irritated with your souls. Let the one who is strong among you people bring forth the perfect human being and stand before my face!"

And they all said, "We are strong." Yet their spirit could not dare to stand before him, except Judas Iscariot. He was able to stand before him, yet he could not look him in his eyes, but rather turned his face away. Judas said to him, "I know who you are and where you have come from. You have come from the immortal aeon of Barbelo and from the one that has sent you, whose name I am not worthy to utter." But Jesus, knowing that he was thinking of something lofty,

1. Or, perhaps, "you would find him as an apparition," or "as a child."
2. See 1 Tim. 4:7; or: "disputing issues concerning God."
3. Or: "stars."

said to him, "Separate from them, and I will tell you the mysteries of the kingdom, not so that you may go there, but that you may grieve greatly. **36** For someone else will take your place, so that the twelve disciples may again be complete with their god."[4] And Judas said to him, "When will you tell me these things, and when will the great day of light dawn for that generation?" But when he said these things, Jesus left him.

Second Day: Jesus Appears to His Disciples Again

The next morning he appeared to his disciples, and they said to him, "Teacher, where did you go and what were you doing after you left us?" Jesus said to them, "I went to another generation, one that is great and holy." His disciples said to him, "Lord, what is the great generation that is superior to us and holy, but is not in these aeons?"

When Jesus heard this, he laughed. He said to them, "Why are you pondering in your heart about the strong and holy generation? **37** Truly I say to you, no one born of this aeon will see that generation, nor will any angelic host of the stars rule over that generation; and no person of mortal birth will be able to join it. For that generation is not from . . . that has come to be . . . the generation of humans . . . but it is from the generation of the great people . . . the powerful authorities . . . nor any power . . . those in which you rule."

When his disciples heard this, they each became disturbed in their spirit, and they did not find anything to say.

Another Day: Jesus Interprets to His Disciples Their Vision of the Temple

On another day Jesus came to them. They said to him, "Teacher, we saw you in a vision; for we saw great visions last night." Jesus said, "Why did you . . . and conceal yourselves?" **38** They said, "We saw a great house with a large altar in it, and twelve people—we would say they are priests—and a name. A crowd attended at that altar until the priests came out and received the offerings.[5] And we ourselves were in attendance." Jesus said, "What are . . .[6] like?" They said, "Some fast for two weeks, while others sacrifice their own children and others their wives, in praise and humility toward one another. Some sleep with men, others perform murder, and still others commit a multitude of sins and lawless acts; and

4. See Acts 1:15–26; John 17:13, 23; some scholars propose "elements" or "stars" instead of "disciples."

5. Or: "until the priests were done presenting the offerings."

6. The lacuna may be filled with the "priests," the "crowd," or the "people."

the people standing over the altar invoke your name. **39** And as they are occupied with all their acts of sacrifice,[7] that altar gets filled."

And when they said these things, they fell silent, for they were disturbed. Jesus said to them, "Why have you become disturbed? Truly I say to you, all the priests who stand over that altar are invoking my name; and I also say to you that my name has been written on this house of the generations of the stars by the generations of humans, and they have shamefully planted trees without fruit in my name."

Jesus said to them, "It is you who receive the offerings at the altar you saw. That one is the God you serve. And the twelve men you saw are you. And the animals brought in are the sacrifices you saw—these are the crowd you lead astray. **40** Over that altar . . .[8] will stand up, and thus he will make use of my name, and the generations of pious people will attend him. After him, another person will stand up for the fornicators, and another will stand up for the murderers of children, and yet another for those who sleep with men and those who fast, and the rest of the impurities, lawless acts, and errors, and also for those who say, 'We are like angels.'[9] And they are the stars that bring everything to completion. For they have said to the generations of humans, 'Behold, God has received your sacrifice from a priest'[10]—that is, the minister of error. But the Lord who commands is he who rules over the all; on the last day they will be put to shame."

41 Jesus said to them, "Stop sacrificing animals that you have offered upon the altar, for they are on your stars with your angels and have already come to completion there. So let them come to naught before you and become clear." His disciples said to him, "Lord, cleanse us from our sins that we have committed through the error of the angels." Jesus said to them, "It is impossible . . . Nor can a fountain extinguish the fire of the whole inhabited world; nor can a spring in a . . . water all the generations, except the great and stable one. And a single lamp will not shine on all the aeons, except on the second generation; nor can a baker feed the whole creation **42** under heaven." And when the disciples heard these things, they said to him, "Teacher,[11] help us and save us." Jesus said to them, "Stop contending with me. Each of you has his own star, and . . . of the stars will . . . what belongs to it. . . . I was not sent to the corruptible generation but to the generation that is strong and incorruptible. For no enemy has ruled over that generation, nor one of the stars. Truly I say to you, the pillar of fire[12]

7. Or: "deficiency."
8. The subject in the lacuna could be "your minister," "the lord of the world," or "the great bishop."
9. See Luke 20:36.
10. Or: "from the hands of priests."
11. Or, less likely, "Lord."
12. See Ex. 13:21–22; 14:24; 1 En. 18:11–12.

will fall quickly and that generation will not be moved by the stars." And after Jesus said these things, he departed and took Judas Iscariot with him. He said to him, "The water that is on the high mountain is from **43** the . . . It has not come to . . . spring . . . tree . . . fruit . . . time of this aeon. For . . . after a while . . . . Rather, it has come to water God's paradise and the fruit that will last; for it will not defile the journey of that generation, but it will be for ever and ever."

Jesus Discloses the Fate of Human Generations to Judas and Other Disciples

Judas said to him, "Tell me, what fruit does this generation have?" Jesus said, "The souls of every human generation will die. But these ones, in turn, when they have brought the time of the kingdom to its completion and the spirit parts from them, their bodies will die, but their souls will be alive and will be taken up."[13] Judas said, "So what will the remaining generations of people do?" Jesus said, "It is impossible **44** to sow upon a rock and receive fruit;[14] so also it is impossible to sow the defiled race, together with corruptible wisdom and the hand that has fashioned mortal people, so that their souls ascend to the aeons on high. Truly I say to you (pl.), no authority[15] or angel or power can see those places, which the great holy generation will see." After Jesus said these things, he departed.

Jesus Interprets Judas' Vision

Judas said, "Teacher, just as you have listened to all of them, now also listen to me; for I have seen a great vision." When Jesus heard this, he laughed and said to him, "Why do you trouble yourself, O thirteenth *daimon*?[16] But speak up for yourself, I will bear with you."

Judas said to him, "I saw myself in the vision as the twelve disciples threw stones at me and **45** persecuted me zealously. And I came again to the place where I had followed after you. I saw a house in that place, and its size my eyes could not measure. Some great people were surrounding it, and that house had a grass rooftop,[17] and in the midst of the house . . . Teacher, take me inside, too, together with these people."

Jesus replied and said, "Your star has led you astray, Judas. Indeed, no person born of any mortal is worthy to enter the house you saw. For that place is kept for

13. See below, **53**.

14. See Luke 8:6.

15. Or: "star."

16. See below, **46**. The number thirteen and the term *daimon* may have both positive and negative applications in the religious and philosophical texts of the period.

17. See 4 Kgdms. 19:16 LXX; Ps. 128:6 LXX; Isa. 37:27.

the holy ones, where neither the sun nor the moon will rule, nor will the day, but they will always stand firm there in the aeon with the holy angels. Look, I have told you the mysteries of the kingdom, **46** and I have taught you about the error of the stars. And . . . has been sent on high upon the twelve aeons."

Judas said, "Teacher, does this mean that my seed, too, is subordinate to the rulers?" Jesus replied and said to him, "Come, I will speak with you . . . not that . . . but that you may come to grieve even more when you see the kingdom and its entire generation." When Judas heard these things, he said to him, "What gain is there for me, since you have set me apart from that generation?" Jesus replied and said, "You will become the thirteenth, and you will be cursed by the remaining generations, and you will come to rule over them. In the last days they will . . . you shall not ascend[18] on high **47** to the holy generation."

Jesus' Revelatory Monologue: The Mystery of Creation

Jesus said, "Come, I will teach you about the things . . . that . . . human will see. For there exists a great and boundless aeon, whose size no angelic generation has seen, in which there is a great invisible Spirit that no eye of angel has seen and no thought of the mind comprehended,[19] and which has not been called by any name.

And a luminous cloud appeared there. And he[20] said, 'Let an angel come into being as my attendant.' And from the cloud there came forth a great angel, the Self-Originate, the god of the light. And on his behalf another four angels came into being from another cloud, and they came to be as attendants for the angelic Self-Originate. And **48** the Self-Originate said, 'Let there come to be a . . . ,'[21] and it came to be just as he said.[22] And he established the first luminary to rule over it,[23] and he said, 'Let angels come into being to serve it,' and countless myriads came to be.

18. All letter traces of this difficult passage have been deciphered, but its meaning remains ambiguous. The National Geographic critical edition (Kasser-Wurst 2007, 211n. 25) follows Nagel (2007) 249n. 108, and suggests that something might have dropped out by *homoioarcton*: "In the last days they <will ---> to you, and (that?) you will not ascend on high to the holy generation. As it stands, the extant manuscript text yields two possible translations: (1) "In the last days they will utter a curse (see Matt. 26:74; Mark 14:71). You shall not ascend on high . . ."; (2) "In the last days they will utter a curse that you may not ascend on high." If the former, then Jesus prohibits Judas' ascent into the spiritual realm; if the latter, Jesus only announces that the others will try to prevent him from ascending.

19. See 1 Cor. 2:9.

20. Or: "it," i.e., the Invisible Spirit.

21. Possibly "another aeon," or "Adamas."

22. Possibly "the procession occurred."

23. Or: "him."

And he said, 'Let there come to be a luminous aeon,' and it came to be. He established the second luminary to rule over it, along with countless myriads of angels to render service. And this is how he created the rest of the aeons of light, and he made them to be ruled over, and he created for them countless myriads of angels for their assistance.

And Adamas was in the first cloud of light, which no angel has seen among all those called 'divine.' And he **49** . . . that . . . image . . . and after the likeness of this angel he revealed the incorruptible generation of Seth to the twelve luminaries . . . He revealed the seventy-two luminaries in the incorruptible generation by the will of the Spirit. The seventy-two luminaries, for their part, revealed three hundred sixty luminaries in the incorruptible generation by the will of the Spirit, so that their number should be five for each.

And their Father consists of the twelve aeons of the twelve luminaries, with six heavens for each aeon, so that there are seventy-two heavens for the seventy-two luminaries, and for each **50** of them five firmaments, so that there are three hundred sixty firmaments.[24] They were granted authority and a great host of countless angels, for glory and service, and in addition some virginal spirits as well, for glory and service to all the aeons and the heavens and their firmaments.

Now the multitude of those immortal beings is called 'cosmos'—that is, corruption—by the Father and the seventy-two luminaries that are with the Self-Originate and his seventy-two aeons. There the first human being appeared together with his incorruptible powers.

And the aeon appeared with his generation, the one in which are the cloud of knowledge and the angel called **51** Eleleth . . . aeon . . . After these things he . . .[25] said, 'Let there come to be twelve angels and rule over chaos and the underworld.' And look, from the cloud there appeared an angel, whose face breathed out fire, and whose appearance was defiled with blood. His name was Nebro, meaning 'rebel' in translation,[26] but other people call him Ialdabaoth. And another angel also came forth from the cloud, namely Saklas. Nebro then created six angels, and Saklas,[27] to be attendants. And these gave birth to twelve angels in the heavens, and they each received a share in the heavens.

24. All these numbers have clear astrological connotations, denoting the hierarchy of heavenly beings, from twelve zodiacal constellations and seventy-two pentads (i.e., the stars presiding over the Egyptian week of five days) down to three hundred sixty zodiacal *monomoiriai*.

25. Probably "Eleleth."

26. In the *Gospel of the Egyptians* (NCH III,2, pp. 56–57), Nebruel is a great feminine demon who mates with Saklas and produces twelve aeons, and is probably related to Nebrod, "the first on earth to be a giant" (Gen 10:8–12 LXX), whose Hebrew name, viz. Nimrod, may mean 'rebel.'

27. The Coptic construction is unclear and may be rendered in the following ways: "Nebro and Saklas together created six angels"; "Nebro created six angels besides Saklas," i.e., the total of seven angels; "Nebro created six angels, and so did Saklas," i.e., they each created six angels, the total of twelve.

And the twelve rulers spoke with the twelve angels, 'Let each one of you **52** . . . and let them . . . generation . . . five angels.'

The first is Iaôth,[28] who is called 'the Christ'[29];
the second is Harmathôth, who is the eye of fire;
the third is Galila;
the fourth is Iôbel;
the fifth is Adônaios.

These are the five who have come to rule over the underworld, and first of all over chaos.

Then Saklas said to his angels, 'Let us create a human being after the likeness and after the image.'[30] And they in turn molded Adam and his wife Eve, who in the cloud is called 'Zoe.'[31] For by this name all generations seek him; and each of them calls her by their own names. Now Saklas did not **53** command . . . give birth . . . except . . . among the generations . . . which . . . And the angel said to him, 'The life of yours and your children shall last for a limited time.'"[32]

The Dialogue Resumed: The Destiny of Humankind and Judas

Then Judas said to Jesus, "How long will the human being live?" Jesus said, "Why are you surprised that Adam, along with his generation, received his time in a limited way, considering that he received his kingdom in the same limited way as his ruler?"

Judas said to Jesus, "Does the human spirit die?" Jesus said, "It is like this: God ordered Michael[33] to grant the spirits of humans to them as a loan, while they serve. But the Great One ordered Gabriel to grant spirits to the great generation with no king over it—the spirit along with the soul.[34] For this reason, the rest of the souls **54** . . . light . . . chaos . . . seek after the spirit within you (pl.), which you have made to dwell in this flesh from the generations of angels. [35] But God had knowledge brought to Adam and those with him, so that the kings of chaos and the underworld might not rule over them."

28. Or, less likely, "Seth."
29. Possibly a scribal error for "the Ram."
30. See Gen. 1:27.
31. See Gen. 3:20.
32. See Gen. 3:22.
33. See Dan. 10:31, 21; 12, 1.
34. See above, 43.
35. Or: "among."

And Judas said to Jesus, "So what will those generations do?" Jesus said, "Truly I say to you (pl.), the stars are bringing them all to completion. And when Saklas completes the span of time that was allotted to him, their first star[36] will come with the generations, and they will complete what has been said. Then they will fornicate in my name and slaughter their children,[37] **55** and they will . . . evil . . . and . . . aeons, bringing their generations and presenting them to Saklas. And after that Israel will come, bringing the twelve tribes of Israel from . . . And all the generations will serve Saklas, committing sins in my name. And your star will rule over the thirteenth aeon."[38]

And after that Jesus laughed. Judas said, "Teacher, why are you laughing at me?" Jesus replied and said, "I am not laughing at you, but rather at the error of the stars; for these six stars go astray with these five warriors,[39] and they all will be destroyed together with their creations."

And Judas said to Jesus, "So what will those who have been baptized in your name do?" Jesus said, "Truly I say to you (sg.), this baptism **56** . . . in my name . . . it will wipe out the whole generation of Adam. Tomorrow the earthly human, one who bears me, will be tortured. Truly I say to you (pl.), no hand of a mortal human will sin against me. Truly I say to you, Judas, those who offer sacrifices to Saklas . . . all . . . everything that is evil. But you yourself will surpass them all, for you will sacrifice the human that bears me.

Already your horn has been exalted,[40]
and your wrath has been kindled,[41]
and your star has passed through,
and your heart has grown strong.

57 Truly I say to you (sg.), your last . . . become . . . the thrones of the aeon have been . . . and the kings have grown weak, and the generations of the angels have grieved, and the evil ones . . . and the ruler is destroyed. And then the fruit of the great generation of Adam will be exalted, for before heaven and earth and the angels that generation exists from eternity.[42]

Look, you have been told everything. Lift up your eyes and see the cloud and the light therein, and the stars that surround it; and the star that leads the way is your star."

36. Possibly an oblique reference to Judas; see below, **55** and **57**.
37. See above, **38–39**.
38. See above, **44, 46**.
39. See above, **51–52**; see Rev 12:5–7.
40. See Ps. 74:11; 88:18; 148, 18 LXX.
41. See Ps. 2:12 LXX; or "your wrath has come to full," for which see Jer. 6:11.
42. Or: "from the aeons."

And Judas lifted up his eyes and saw the luminous cloud. And he[43] entered it. Those standing on the ground heard a voice coming from the cloud, saying,[44] **58** ". . . the great generation . . . and . . . which is in . . ." And Judas no longer saw Jesus.

Gospel Frame: Judas' Betrayal of Jesus

And immediately there was turmoil among the Jews. . . . Their high priests murmured, for he had entered the guestroom[45] for his prayer. But some of the scribes were there watching closely in order to arrest him during the prayer; for they were afraid of the people, because he was regarded by all as a prophet.[46] And they approached Judas and said to him, "What are you doing here? You are the disciple of Jesus!"[47] And he replied to them as they wanted. Then Judas received some money and handed him over to them.[48]

43. "He" stands probably for Jesus; see below, **58**: "And Judas no longer saw Jesus."
44. See Mark 9:7.
45. See Mark 14:14; Luke 22:11.
46. See Matt. 21:46; Luke 22:2.
47. See Matt. 26:14–15a; Mark 14:10; Luke 22:3–4; see also John 13:26–30.
48. See Matt. 26:15b–16; 27:3 ; Mark 14:11; Luke 22:5–6.

24

Jesus' Correspondence with Abgar

The apocryphal correspondence between Jesus and Abgar Uchama (= "the Black"), king of Edessa in eastern Syria (4 BCE–7 CE and 13–50 CE), is first mentioned in Eusebius (*Church History*, 1. 13. 5). Eusebius claims to have found the letters in the archives of Edessa and to have translated them literally from their original Syriac into Greek. The first is a short letter from the king, acknowledging Jesus' miracle-working powers and asking him to come to Edessa to heal him of his illness and, at the same time, to escape the animosity of the Jews in his homeland. In his reply, Jesus blesses Abgar for "believing without seeing" (an allusion to John 20:29), but informs the king that he cannot come because he needs to fulfill his mission, that is, by being crucified. After his ascension, however, he will send an apostle to heal the king.

This is the first instance of an apocryphal letter written in Jesus' name (for a later example, see the Narrative of Joseph of Arimathea). He is never said to have written anything in our earliest Gospels, apart from an episode in the apocryphal story of the woman taken in adultery, found in later manuscripts of John 7:53–8:11.

These two letters lie at the heart of a widely known legend about Abgar, ruler of Edessa. According to the story, known from both Eusebius and a Syriac source called the *Doctrina Addai*, after Jesus' death, his apostle and brother Judas Thomas sent a colleague Addai (named Thaddaeus by Eusebius) who heals Abgar and converts the city of Edessa to the Christian faith. There are grounds for thinking, however, that the fuller legendary narrative was composed after the apocryphal correspondence itself was known and circulated and that it is roughly based on the correspondence, or on story-tellers' "knowledge" of a similar correspondence. For one thing, there is a basic inconsistency between the letter and the legend: the former indicates that Jesus will send an apostle to Abgar, the latter indicates that his disciple Judas Thomas does so. Moreover, we have a historical account from the end of fourth century of the pilgrim Egeria who goes to Edessa and reports what she finds there. She knows about the correspondence but betrays no knowledge of the legend (*Travels of Egeria*, 17–19).

Finally, we know that the correspondence did circulate independently in a separate manuscript tradition. In fact, citizens of Edessa in later times considered the correspondence significant for its magical powers, as containing a letter from the Son of God himself. According to later tradition it was brought forward in times of war, miraculously scattering the armies laying siege to the city (thus *Travels of Egeria*, 18). Eventually a copy of the correspondence was affixed to the city gates to ward off its enemies. The miraculous character of the correspondence was based in no small measure on the last line of Jesus' letter, which is not found in Eusebius's account but is present both in the surviving Greek fragments of the letter and in the account found in the *Doctrina Addai*, where Jesus assures Abgar that "Your city will be blessed, and the enemy will no longer prevail over it." This line itself can still be found in inscriptions, ostraca, and amulets.

The legend as a whole was in wide circulation: it is preserved in Greek, Latin, Syriac, Coptic, Armenian, Arabic, Persian, and Slavonic. H. J. W. Drijvers makes a complex but convincing argument that it was generated at the end of the third century among the proto-orthodox minority of Christians in eastern Syria, to counter the religious claims of the Manichaeans for Mani, the founder of their religion.

If the letters are earlier than the full legend, they may have arisen sometime in the early part of the third century, possibly in Syriac. Eusebius and the surviving Greek fragments of the *Doctrina Addai* appear to represent two different Greek translations of the correspondence. The translation here is of Eusebius (from the edition of Schwartz) which is the earlier version.

Bibliography

Bauer, W. *Orthodoxy and Heresy and Heresy in Earliest Christianity*. Philadelphia: Fortress, 1971 (German original, 1934); pp. 1–43.

Drijvers, H. J. W. "The Abgar Legend," in *New Testament Apocrypha*, ed. W. Schneemelcher; trans. R. McL. Wilson. Louisville: Westminster/John Knox, 1991; vol. 1, pp. 492–500.

Elliott, J. K. *The Apocryphal New Testament*. Oxford: Clarendon, 1993; pp. 538–42.

Schwartz, E., ed. Eusebius *Kirchengeschichte* 5th ed. Leipzig: Hinrich, 1955; pp. 33–34.

Jesus' Correspondence with Abgar (Eusebius, E.H. I, 13)

Copy of the letter written by the Ruler Abgar to Jesus, and sent by him to Jerusalem through his courier Ananias.

The Ruler Abgar Uchama,[1] to Jesus the good Savior who has appeared in the region of Jerusalem, greetings. I have heard about you and your healings, which you perform without medications or herbs. As the report indicates, you make the blind see again and the lame walk, you cleanse lepers, you cast out unclean spirits and demons, you heal the chronically sick, and you raise the dead. Having heard all these things about you, I have concluded one of two things: either you are God and do these things having descended from heaven, or you do them as the Son of God. For this reason now I am writing you, asking that you take the trouble to come to me and heal my illness.[2] For I have also heard that the Jews are murmuring against you and wish to harm you.[3] My city is very small and esteemed, and it can accommodate us both.

The reply sent by Jesus to the Ruler Abgar through the courier Ananias.

Blessed are you who have believed in me without seeing me.[4] For it is written about me that those who see me will not believe in me, and that those who do not see me will believe and live.[5] But concerning your request for me to come to you: I must accomplish everything I was sent here to do, and after accomplishing them ascend to the One who sent me. After I have ascended I will send you one of my disciples to heal your illness and to provide life both to you and to those who are with you.

1. Uchama is a Syriac word that means "black." It is often used in texts to refer to people with African roots. Some manuscripts omit the word.

2. See 2 Kings 5:1–19.

3. See John 6:41.

4. See John 20:29.

5. See Isa. 6:9; Matt. 13:14–17; John 9:39; 12:39–40.

25

The Gospel of the Savior

The Gospel of the Savior is one of the most recent Gospels to become available to public view, having been first announced in the mid-1990s. It comes to us on seven fragmentary parchment leaves from a codex that is housed in the Egyptian Museum in Berlin; the manuscript is labeled P. Berol. Inv. 22220. The manuscript, written in Coptic, was purchased by the museum on March 20, 1967, and was classified by a curator there as allegedly containing sayings of Jesus—and then it was put into storage. It was not until 1991 that an American scholar, P. Mirecki, was shown the manuscript in the museum; it was seen later, but independently, by another American scholar, C. Hedrick. The "discovery" was announced by Hedrick in 1996 in a paper read at the Sixth International Congress of Coptic Studies. Hedrick and Mirecki collaborated in the publication of the Coptic text, along with an English translation, in 1999: *Gospel of the Savior: A New Ancient Gospel.*

There were problems with Hedrick and Mirecki's reconstruction of the Coptic text; these were corrected by the Coptologist S. Emmel in an important article in 2002. Emmel's reconstruction of the text is now generally followed.

At the same time, Emmel recognized that the text is even more fragmentarily preserved in a manuscript that was first published in 1900 and is preserved in Strasbourg, called the Strasbourg Coptic Gospel. Portions of the Strasbourg and Berlin texts overlap and are word for word the same. The Berlin codex probably dates to the sixth or seventh century and the Strasbourg fragments to the early fifth century.

The text contained in these Coptic manuscripts was almost certainly originally composed in Greek. The text begins in the middle of a discourse of "the Savior" (as Jesus is called in this text) to his disciples—a scene highly reminiscent of what is found in the Farewell Discourse of the Gospel of John (chs. 13–17). The scene then shifts to a mountain where the disciples describe, in the first person, a vision of Jesus appearing before God in his throne room in the seventh heaven, expressing his deep despair at having to die, and praying three times that God will "let this cup pass from me." Even more striking, God replies to Jesus, asking him why he is distressed. Jesus then returns to earth and speaks further with his disciples, launching into a long speech in which he gives a number of "I am" sayings that are followed by "Amen." In possibly the most intriguing portion of the text, Jesus then begins to address the cross itself: "I will mount you, O cross, I will be hung upon you. . . . Do not weep O cross, but rather rejoice. . . . You and I are together, O cross, we are brothers" (pp. 109–10). The text continues (in the Strasbourg fragments) with Jesus telling his disciples that the end is at hand, and then, after a gap, there appears to be a resurrection appearance. The rest of the text is missing.

There are debates among scholars over whether this surviving portion of Jesus' interactions with the disciples, God, and the cross originally formed part of a larger Gospel like those of the New Testament or instead came from something like a Passion Gospel (the Gospel of Nicodemus), or even from a non-Gospel book altogether, for example, an apocalypse, a church homily, or some other kind of writing. In any event it is clear that the text, whatever genre it may have originally been, was composed after the books of the New Testament, as it quotes and alludes to Matthew, John, and the book of Revelation. It must, then, have been written sometime after 100 CE, moreover, since the Strasbourg fragments date to around the year 400, it must have been composed in the second or third centuries. Scholars debate the more precise date, but there are strong reasons for dating it near the end of the second century (as shown, for example, by U.-K. Plisch, "Zu einigen Einleitungsfragen des Unbekannten Berliner Evangeliums," *ZAC* 9 [2005] 64–84).

As we indicated in the Preface on p. xiii, there are many gaps in these two highly fragmentary manuscripts, where numerous lines, words, and parts of words are missing at a stretch. In some places it is possible to reconstruct the missing words and parts of words with reasonable confidence. Those reconstructions are placed in brackets in the translation. Missing lines are indicated throughout. The pages of both the Berlin and Strasbourg manuscripts are indicated explicitly (so that B109 = Berlin manuscript, p. 109; and S5r = Strasbourg manuscript, p. 5, recto).

Bibliography

Emmel, S. "Preliminary Reedition and Translation of the *Gospel of the Savior*: New Light on the Strasbourg Coptic Gospel and the Stauros Text from Nubia." *Apocrypha* 14 (2003): 9–53.

Emmel, S. "The Recently Published Gospel of the Savior ("Unbekanntes Berliner Evangelium"): Righting the Order of Pages and Events." *HTR* 95 (2002): 45–72.

Emmel, S. "Unbekanntes Berliner Evangelium = The Strasbourg Coptic Gospel: Prolegomena to New Edition of the Strasbourg Fragments." In H.-G. Bethge et al., eds., *For the Children, Perfect Instruction: Studies in Honor of Hans-Martin Schenke*. Nag Hammadi and Manichaean Studies LIV. Leiden: E. J. Brill, 2002; pp. 353–74.

Hedrick, C. W., and P. A. Mirecki. *Gospel of the Savior: A New Ancient Gospel*. Santa Rosa, CA: Polebridge, 1999.

Piovanelli, P. "Thursday Night Fever: Dancing and Singing with Jesus in the Gospel of the Savior and the Dance of the Savior around the Cross." *Early Christianity* 3 (2012): 229–48.

The Gospel of the Savior

The Dialogue of the Savior and His Apostles

. . . (B[1] 97) [*ca. 12 lines untranslatable*] ". . . the kingdom of heaven at your right hand. Blessed is the one who will eat with me in the kingdom of heaven.[2] You are the salt of the earth,[3] and you are the lamp that shines on the world.[4] Do not sleep or slumber [until] you clothe yourselves with the garment of the kingdom, which I have purchased[5] with the blood of grapes."

Andrew replied and said, "My lord," [*ca. 22 lines untranslatable*] "Since I have cured those of the world, it is necessary that I also descend to Hades for the sake of the others who are bound there. So now what is necessary (B 98) [*23 lines untranslatable*] everything securely. I myself will appear to you with joy, for I know that you can do everything with joy. For a human being [is] free-willed. [*9 lines untranslatable*] Now then, as long as you [are] in the body, do not let matter rule over you. Rise, let us leave this place! For the one who will betray me is at hand. And you will all flee and stumble because of me.[6] You will all flee and [leave me] alone; but I do not remain alone because my Father is with me.[7] I and my Father are one and the same.[8] For it is written: 'I will strike the shepherd, and (B 99) the sheep of the flock shall be scattered.'[9] So I am the good shepherd: I will lay down my life for you.[10] You, too, lay down your lives for your friends,[11] so that you may please my Father; for no commandment is greater than this,[12] that I should lay down my life [for] humankind. For [this reason] my Father loves me[13] because I accomplished his will.[14] For [even though] divine, I have become [human] on account of [*4 lines untranslatable*]"

When [the Savior] [*6 lines untranslatable*] "How soon will you remember us and send for us, and take us from the world so that we come to you? [*26 lines*

1. B = Berlin manuscript (P. Berol. inv. 22220).
2. See Luke 14:15.
3. Matt. 5:13a.
4. See Matt. 5:14a.
5. Possibly a scribal error for "washed"; see Gen. 49:11b (LXX): "He shall wash his robe in wine and his garment in the blood of a bunch of grapes."
6. Matt. 26:31a; Mark 14:27a; see Matt. 26:56b; Mark 14:50.
7. John 16:32b.
8. John 10:30.
9. Zech. 13:7.
10. John 10:11.
11. John 15:13b.
12. Mark 12:31a
13. John 10:17a.
14. See John 4:34; 5:30; 6:38.

untranslatable] (B 100) The Savior said to us, "O my holy members, my blessed seeds, rise and . . . pray" [24 *lines untranslatable*]

A Vision on the Mount

. . . on the mountain.[15] We also became as spiritual bodies. Our eyes opened wide in all directions. The whole place was shown forth before us. We saw the heavens: they opened up one after another. The guardians of the gate became disturbed. The angels became afraid and [darted to] and fro, think[ing] that they all would be destroyed. We saw our Savior having traversed all gates, [his] feet [set firmly with us upon] the [mountain and his head penetrating the seventh] heaven.[16] [8 *lines untranslatable*] (B 101) from all the heavens. Then the world became as darkness before us, the apostles. We became as [those] in the [im]mortal aeons, with our [eyes] traversing all the aeons and clothed with the [power] of our apostleship.[17] And we saw our Savior after he had reached the [seventh] heaven [7 *lines untranslatable*] The [heavens] shook. [The] angels and archangels bowed down on their [faces. The] cherubim [bowed down] to his . . . [The seraphim] let down their [wing]s.[18] The angels that were [. . . the Father's curtain] sang praises. [The] elder[s, seated] on their [throne]s,[19] cast [their] crown[s down] before the Father's [throne].[20] All [the] saints[21] took a] robe, and when they had [wrapped him, the] Son [bowed down at his Father's feet.][22] [*ca.* 6 *lines untranslatable . . .*]

The Savior Prays to the Father

"Why are you weeping and [grieved][23] so that the whole angelic host is [disturbed]?"[24] And he replied [in this] way, "[5 *lines untranslatable*] (B 102) I am deeply [grieved that I will be] killed by the [people of] Israel.[25] My [Father], if it

15. Presumably the Mount of Olives (Matt. 24:3, 26:30; Mark 13:3, 14:26; Luke 22:39; see John 8:1).

16. For this visionary ascent of the disciples and their reception of the "power of apostleship," see esp. the Coptic *Book of the Resurrection of Jesus Christ by Bartholomew the Apostle*, also known as the *Gospel of Bartholomew* (*Gos. Barth.*) 18.1–17 (English translation in W. Schneemelcher, ed., *New Testament Apocrypha*, trans. R. McL. Wilson. Louisville: Westminster/John Knox, 1991, 537–57); see also Ps.-Cyril of Jerusalem, *On the Life and Passion of Christ* 24b-25a.

17. See Acts 1:25; compare the final section of the extant text below (S 6v:1-9).

18. See Ezek. 1:25.

19. See Rev. 4:4.

20. Rev. 4:10.

21. See Rev. 5:9.

22. *Gos. Barth.* 18.2 (manuscript C); see Matt. 26:39a; Mark 14:35a; Luke 22:41a.

23. See Matt. 26:37; Mark 14:33.

24. The question is posed by the Father.

25. See Matt. 26:38a; Mark 14:34a.

is [possible], let this [cup] pass from me.[26] Let [me] be [killed by some other [sinful] people who . . . if . . . Israel [*ca. 6 lines untranslatable*] [so that] salvation [might] come to the whole world." Then again the Son bowed down at his Father's feet, say[ing], "[My Father], [*5 lines untranslatable*] [that I may] die with joy and pour out my blood for the human race.[27] But I weep greatly on account of my beloved, namely A[braha]m, Isaac [and] Jacob, because they [will] stand [on the] day of judgment [while] I will sit upon [my] throne and [judge] the world, [and they will] say to me, [*ca. 8 lines untranslatable*] "[on account] of the glory that was given to me on the earth. My [Father, if it possible, let this cup] pass from me."[28] [The Father replied] to him for [the] second time, "My son, you do not (B 103) [*28 lines untranslatable*]." The Son [replied] for the [third] time, "My Father, if [*ca. 32 lines untranslatable*] (B 104) [*ca. 61 lines untranslatable*] he [has come to] complete [the] ministry until [he returns] to them.[29] (B 105) [*27 lines untranslatable*] prophet.

The Savior Comforts the Apostles

The [Savior] said to us, "There is no lot better than yours and no glory higher than [your] own." [*31 lines untranslatable*] (B 106) [*31 lines untranslatable*] O the entirety of [*21 lines untranslatable . . .*] cross [*5 lines untranslatable*] three days [I will] take you . . . with me and teach you what you desire (B 107) to see. So [do not] be disturbed when [you] see me."[30] We said to him, "Lord, in what form will you reveal yourself to us, or else in what kind of body will you come? Teach us!" John replied and said, "Lord, when you come to reveal yourself to us, do not reveal yourself to us in all your glory, but change your glory into another glory so that we may be able to bear it; otherwise we will see [you] and despair from fear." The Savior replied, "I [will take away] from you the fear that you are afraid of, so that you may see and believe. But do not hold me until I ascend to my Father and [your] Father, to [my God] and your God, and to my Lord and your Lord.[31] And if someone draws near unto me, he will be [burned]: I am the blazing [fire]. The [one who is near me] is near [the] fire; the one who is far from me is far from life.[32]

26. Mt. 26:39b; Mark 14:36a; Luke 22:42a; see John 18:11b.
27. See Matt. 26:28; Mark 14:24.
28. See n. 24.
29. See Luke 1:23.
30. See Matt. 26:32; Mark 14:28.
31. John 20:17.
32. See *Gos. Thomas* 82: "Jesus said, 'The one who is near me is near the fire; and the one who is far from me is far from the kingdom'; see also Origen, *Hom. Jer.* 3.3; Didymus, *Fr. Ps.* 883.

An Amen Responsory between the Savior and the Apostles

So now gather unto me, my holy members . . . and [*ca. 5 lines untranslatable*] as we [surrounded] him, [he] said to us, "I am [among] you [as] children." He said, "Amen. A little while I am among you."[33] [We] responded, "Amen." (B 108) "They are plotting against me, [those who] who wish [to set the] world against me because I am alien to it.[34] So behold, now I am grieving over the [sins] of the world. [Yet] I am rejoicing on [your] account: you have [fought] bravely in [the] world. So come to know yourselves so that you might benefit me, and I will rejoice over your work. I am the king." "Amen." "I am the [son] of the king." ["Amen."] "I am . . ." ["Amen."] "I am . . . and you have no [other." "A]men." "I am fighting [for] you: you also wage war!" "Amen." "I am being sent away: I also want to send you away."[35] "Amen." ". . . O [everyone] among you." "[Am]en." "I want to [bring] you joy [for] the world;[36] but you rather [grieve] for [the] world as if you had not entered it at all!" "Amen." "Do not weep from now on, but rather rejoice!" "Amen." "I have overcome the world;[37] but you do not let the world overcome you!" "Amen." "I have become free [from] the world; you also [become] free from [it]!" "Amen." "I myself [will be] given [vinegar and] gall to drink;[38] but [you], receive life and [rest for yourselves]!" "Amen." I will be [pierced] with a spear [in] my side. The one who will have seen it, let him bear testimony; and his testimony is true."[39] "Amen." (B 109) [*3 lines untranslatable*] "A[men]." [Whoever will] . . ., I for my part will . . . [him]." "[Ame]n." "Whoever has . . . me, I [for my part] will make him . . . with me." "Am[en]." "Whoever does not [receive] my body and my blood is a stranger to me."[40] "Amen." [*8 lines untranslatable*] you (*sg.*) . . ." "[Am]en."

The First Praise to the Cross

[*5 lines untranslatable*] . . . cross." "Am[en]." "I [will rush] toward you (*sg.*)." "Ame[n]."[41] . . . dispensation . . . [*5 lines untranslatable*]." "[Amen]." "You (*sg.*) are . . .

33. John 13:33a.

34. See the *Discourse upon the Cross*, pp. 24, 1–25, 12: "It happened one day that the Savior was sitting on the Mount of Olives, before the lawless Jews crucified him, and all of us were gathered with him. He replied and said, 'My holy members, gather unto me: I will sing the praise of the Cross and you respond after me.' And we made a circle and surrounded him. He said to us, 'I am among you as children.' He said, 'Amen. A little while I am with you in your midst: they are now plotting against me. Do not hold me back, O Cross!'"

35. See John 17:18, 20:21.

36. Or: apart from the world.

37. John 16:33.

38. See Matt. 27:34a and 48b; John 19:29; Ps 69:21.

39. John 19:34–45.

40. See John 6:53.

41. See the *Discourse upon the Cross*, p. 28, 9-12: "I will rush toward you, O cross." "Amen."

since . . . cross . . ." "Amen." [For] those on the [right will] take shelter [under you][42] apart from those on the [left], O cross, . . . [*4 lines untranslatable*] Rise up, rise, O cross, . . . you, [and you] . . . lift in . . . for this is your will, O cross. Do not be afraid! I am rich: I will fill you with my riches. [I] will mount you, O cross. I will be hung upon you (B 110) as a [testimony against them.]" "[Ame]n." "[Receive me to yourself,] O [cross]! [*5 lines untranslatable*] Do not weep, O [cross], but rather [rejoice][43] and know that [your] lord is coming [to] you, that he is [gentle] and humble."[44] "Amen."

The Second Praise to the Cross

[The] second [dance] [*3 lines untranslatable*] ". . . but [I am] rich. I will [fill you] with my riches.[45] A little while, O cross, and what is lacking will become perfect, and what is wasted will be replenished. A little while,[46] O cross, and what has fallen will rise. A little while, O cross, and the entire fullness will be complete." [*5 lines untranslatable*] [I see you and I] laugh: [many] people, [too,] have looked for you, one [laughing] and rejoicing, another weeping, [mourning], and grieving. Be eager for me, O [cross], and I also will be eager for you.[47] You and I together, O [cross], we are brothers; we are [strangers and] [*9 lines untranslatable*] [I] and [you together, O] cross: otherwise, whoever is far from [you] is far (B 111) [from] me." [*24 lines untranslatable*]

"[Glory] be to you, the three whose [fruit] has been shown forth so that it might be known [in the] lands of the [foreigners] and be [glorified by means of its fruit; for it . . . a multitude of . . ." "Amen."][48]

42. See the *Discourse upon the Cross*, pp. 16, 10–17:5: "Everyone who has believed in the cross will come under the shadow of the cross and stand there."

43. See the *Discourse upon the Cross*, pp. 25, 12–27, 1: "Rise up, rise, O holy cross, and lift me up, O cross! I am rich." "Amen." "I will mount you, O cross. I will be hung upon you as a testimony against them. Receive me to yourself, O cross!" "Amen." "Do not weep, O cross, but rather rejoice!" "Amen." See also pp. 28, 12–29, 5: "I will mount you as a testimony against them. Receive me to yourself, O cross! Do not reveal my body!" "Amen."

44. See Matt. 11:29b, and esp. 21:5 (Zech 9:9).

45. See the *Discourse upon the Cross*, pp. 29, 6–30, 3: "The fourth dance around the cross: 'I am not poor, O light-giving cross.' 'Amen.' 'I will fill you with my riches.' 'Amen.' 'Receive me to yourself, O cross!' "

46. See John 7:33; 12:35; 14:19; 16:16–18.

47. Or: "Precede me, O [cross], and I in turn will precede you."

48. See the *Discourse upon the Cross*, pp. 30, 4–31, 1: "Glory be to you, for you have obeyed your Father." "Amen." "Glory be to you, all sweetness." "Amen." "Glory be to the godhead." "Amen."

(S 5r:1-25)[49] "So[50] give me your [power], my Father,[51] so that [they might] endure [the world][52] with me." "Ame[n]." "I [have] taken [to myself the] scepter of kingship[53] . . . crown . . . them [in their humility]. Without their having . . . I have reigned . . ., my Father. You will have [my enemies] obey me."[54] ["Amen."] ["Through] whom will [the] enemy be [destroyed]? Through the [cross]." "Am[en]." Through whom [will] the sting of death [perish]?[55] [Through the] Only-Begotten." "A[men]." "To whom does [the] kingdom belong? It [belongs to the Son]." "Amen." "Where is [his kingdom] from? [It is from the wood." "Amen."] [*ca. 15 lines wanting*][56] . . .

The Savior Comforts the Apostles

(S 5v:1-24) Now [after Jesus] had finished [the] entire [glorification?] of [his Father],[57] he turned to us and said [to us], "[The] hour is at hand[58] when I will be taken [from you].[59] The spirit indeed [is eager], but the flesh [is] weak.[60] So [remain] and stay awake [with me]."[61] [But] we the apostles wept, saying [to him], "So [if you are afraid, [the Son] of God, [then] what are we [to do] in turn?" He replied and [said to us], "Do not be afraid [of] perishing, but rather [take heart].[62] [Do not be afraid] of the authority . . .[63] Remember all the things [I have

49. S = Strasbourg Coptic Gospel.

50. See the *Discourse upon the Cross*, pp. 30, 10–32, 6: "I have taken to myself the crown (or scepter) of kingship from the wood." "Amen." "I will have my enemies obey me." "Amen." "The enemy will be destroyed through the cross." "Amen." "The sting of death will perish through the Only-Begotten Son." "Amen." "To whom does the kingship belong? To the Son." "Amen." "Where is his kingship from? It is from the wood." "Amen."

51. See John 17:1–2.

52. See John 17:14-16; the phrase can also be rendered as "endure [the cross]; see Heb. 12:2.

53. See Ps. 45:7 (LXX) and Heb. 1:8. The phrase can also be rendered as "the crown of kingship"; see Isa. 62:3; Wis. 10:14.

54. See Ps. 109:1 (LXX); Matt. 22:44; Mark 12:36; Luke 20:42.

55. See Hos. 13; 14; 1 Cor 15:55–56.

56. For a possible content of the missing lines on this page, compare the *Discourse upon the Cross*, pp. 32, 6–33, 11: "'Who is it that sent him to the cross? It is the Father.' 'Amen.' 'What is the cross and where is it from? It is from the Holy Spirit.' 'Amen.' 'It exists from eternity and for all time, from the foundation of the world.' 'Amen.' 'I am the Alpha.' 'Amen.' 'And [the Omega].' 'Amen.' 'The beginning and the end.' 'Amen.' 'I am the ineffable beginning and the ineffable end, and the perfect one forever.' 'Amen.' When we heard these things, we gave glory to God."

57. See John 17:4.

58. Matt. 26:45.

59. See Matt. 9:15; Mark 2:20; Luke 5:35.

60. Matt. 26:41; Mark 14:38.

61. Matt. 26:38; Mark 14:34.

62. See Matt. 10:28, 14:27.

63. See Luke 12:5.

said] to you . . . For if they have persecuted [me, they will persecute you.[64] So [you] should rejoice, for I have [overcome the world].[65] I have [*ca. 5 lines untranslatable*] (B 112) . . . [66] shame. [Your names] have been written on your robes, com[ing] down and spreading[67] . . . [*B 113 ff. wanting; ca. 32 pages missing in S*]

The Savior Appears to the Apostles after the Resurrection

(S 6r:1-7) ". . . [reveal] my full glory to you (*pl.*) and teach you about your full power and the mystery [of] your apostleship."[68] ". . . reveal to us . . . [*1 line untranslatable*] . . . give us [*ca. 49 lines untranslatable*]

(S 6v:1-9) Our eyes traversed everywhere and we saw the glory of his lordship.[69] He clothed [us] with the power of our apostleship[70] . . . We became as . . . light . . . [with] him [ca. *7 lines untranslatable; the rest of the work is missing*].[71]

64. John 15:20.

65. John 16:33.

66. Only the last six lines of the right column of B 112 have been preserved.

67. See Rev. 6:11, 19:16.

68. See Acts 1:25.

69. See John 1:14.

70. See the parallel text in the visionary ascent on the apostles in B 101 and n. 17 above.

71. For a possible continuation of the text, see the Savior's commission to the apostles toward the end of the post-resurrection dialogue in the *Discourse upon the Cross*, pp. 20, 5–21, 3: "And now, my holy members, go and preach to the whole world so that they may follow the cross and attain the glory on that fearful day."

26

The Discourse upon the Cross

The construction of the Aswan High Dam in the 1960s led to enormous local difficulties. The dam was to create Lake Nassar by flooding some 500 kilometers of valley between Aswan and the wadi Halfa. This was to uproot some 120,000 people. Also serious, for those concerned about antiquity, it would destroy all the monuments and archaeological sites in that archaeologically rich region. Frantic but highly successful excavations were undertaken to salvage what was there before the waters came.

In 1965 archaeologists from the Oriental Institute of the University of Chicago worked on the site of Qasr el-Wizz ("Castle of the Geese") on the west bank of the Nile just north of the Sudan border, in what was once Nubia. There they discovered a Christian monastery that had been active from the seventh to the tenth centuries. In November of that year the workers found, inside a monk's cell within the monastery, a seventeen-page parchment manuscript, illuminated with fascinating pictures. It was completely intact, was written in Coptic, and was thought to date around 900 CE. The manuscript contained a text highly reminiscent of the Gospel of the Savior—in fact it is now widely believed that earlier Gospel supplied the material for the final portion of the manuscript's text. Here too Jesus speaks directly to the cross.

The manuscript was initially taken to the Coptic Museum in Cairo but was later transferred to the Nubian Museum in Aswan, where it is now kept. Eventually it was realized that the text it contains is attested as well in an old Nubian manuscript that had been purchased by a German scholar in Egypt in 1906. Scholars have debated whether the text should be thought of as having come from a Gospel, a homily, or some other kind of book.

The account begins by indicating that it contains a discourse that Jesus delivered on the Mount of Olives to his disciples four days before his ascension. Peter asks Jesus to reveal the mystery of the cross and why he will bring it with him on the day of judgment; Jesus explains about the cross and indicates the role it will play when people are judged at the end of time. The text then moves to the time before Jesus was crucified, and Jesus sings a hymn of praise to the cross; after each of his statements the disciples respond with "Amen" (see the Gospel of the Savior). Some of his words are directed to the cross itself, again with similarities to the Gospel of the Savior: "I will mount you as a testimony against them." The extensive similarities between these two texts makes it possible to use The Discourse upon the Cross to help fill in some of the missing words and phrases in the Gospel of the Savior.

Today the manuscript is thought to date no earlier than the eighth century, possibly the ninth or tenth. It is difficult to say when the text itself was composed, except that it must have been after the Gospel of the Savior, which it used as a source. The manuscript was published finally in 2009 by P. Hubai (*Koptische Apokryphen aus Nubien. Der Kasr el-Wizz Kodex* [trans. Al Balog; Berlin: De Gruyter, 2009; Hungarian original: Budapest, 2006]). For our translation we have used the available photographs of the manuscript directly, although Hubai's edition has been consulted.

Bibliography

Emmel, S. "Preliminary Reedition and Translation of the *Gospel of the Savior*: New Light on the Strasbourg Coptic Gospel and the Stauros Text from Nubia." *Apocrypha* 14 (2003): 9–53.

Heidorn, L., A. Obluski, N. Reshetnikova, and B. Williams. "Fulfilling the Rescue: Publication of Materials from the Nubian Salvage Campaign, 1960–68." *The Oriental Institute News & Notes* 214 (2012): 3–9.

Hubai, P. *Koptische Apokruphen aus Nubien. Der Kasr el-Wizz Kodex*, trans. A. Balog. Berlin: De Gruyter, 2009; Hungarian original: Budapest, 2006.

Piovanelli, P. "Thursday Night Fever: Dancing and Singing with Jesus in the Gospel of the Savior and the Dance of the Savior around the Cross." *Early Christianity* 3 (2012): 229–48.

The Discourse upon the Cross (the Stauros-Text)

(p. 3) A discourse that our Savior and our Master Jesus Christ delivered to his holy and glorious apostles before his ascension concerning the power and (p. 4) the might and the conduct of the glorious and life-giving cross. In the peace of God.

My beloved ones, one day our Savior was sitting on the Mount of Olives, (p. 5) four days before his ascension to the heavens, and his apostles gathered together with him. He spoke to them of the unfathomable mysteries in the heavens (p. 6) and upon the earth, and also of the way in which he will judge the living and the dead, and of the resurrection of the dead.

Peter replied and said, "Our Lord and our God,[1] and (p. 7) the Savior of the souls and of everyone who hopes in you, and the cure of the souls wounded by sins! You have disclosed to us all the mysteries; so now also (p. 8) reveal to us the mystery that we will ask you about."

The Savior answered and said, "O my chosen Peter and you, my fellow heirs,[2] surely I have never concealed (p. 9) from you a single word you have asked of me, nor will I conceal any from you. But ask me everything you want to know, and I will reveal them to (p. 10) you."

Peter answered and said, "Our Lord and our God and our Savior, we want you to teach us the mystery of the cross, namely why you will bring it along, (p. 11) the sign of the honorable cross, on the day you will judge in righteousness,[3] so that we may hear about it from you and preach it to the (p. 12) entire world."

The Savior answered and said, "My chosen Peter and you, my brothers, you know everything that the lawless Jews did to me and (p. 13) the blasphemies that they hurled at me upon the cross.[4] They spat at me and they struck me;[5] and they put upon my head the crown of thorns,[6] and the words of reviling they pronounced against me. (p. 14) For this reason I will bring along the cross, in order to disclose their shame, and I will bring their injustices upon their head.

"But now listen to me: I will teach (p. 15) you another great honor of the cross. When I am seated upon my throne of glory[7] to judge the entire world, the cross will stand at my right upon the valley of Josaphat,[8] (p. 16) with its roots

1. See John 20:28.
2. Rom. 8:17.
3. See Acts 17:31; Rev 19:11.
4. See Matt. 27:39; Mark 15:29; Luke 23:39.
5. Matt. 26:67; Mark 14:65.
6. Matt. 27:29–30; Mark 15:17; John 19:2.
7. Matt. 19:28; 25:31.
8. See Joel 3:12.

down in the ground and with its branches sprouting up again as before; and its branches will have cast a shadow on the earth, over the three parts of the earth. Everyone who has (p. 17) believed in the cross with their whole heart will come under the shadow of the cross and stand there—whoever has fed the hungry or given drink to the thirsty or clothed the naked,[9] and especially those (p. 18) who have written the books praising the cross—until I cease judging the entire world. And after I have judged the entirety of the just and the sinners, again the cross will have risen and (p. 19) ascended to the heavens. And everyone who has believed in it will return with it and enter the kingdom of the heavens,[10] and they will inherit eternal life.[11] I will not judge any among them either (p. 20) in word or in deed, but the power of the cross will save them.

"And now, my holy members,[12] go and preach to the whole world[13] so that they might follow the cross (p. 21) and attain the glory on that fearful day."

When we, the apostles, heard these things, we worshiped our Savior and said to him: "Glory be to you, Father who are in the Son, and Son who are (p. 22) in the Father,[14] and the Holy Spirit, for ever and ever. Amen. For you have always glorified those who have loved you."

May we find mercy and grace[15] on the day (p. 23) he will judge in righteousness,[16] now and always, and forever and ever. Amen.

(p. 24) One day the Savior was sitting on the Mount of Olives before the lawless Jews crucified him,[17] and all of us were gathered with him. He replied and said, "My holy members, gather unto me: I will sing a hymn to the cross and (p. 25) you respond after me." And we made a circle and surrounded him.

He said to us, "I am among you as children."[18] He said, "Amen! A little while I am with you in your midst;[19] they are now plotting against me.[20] Do not hold me back, O cross!

Rise up, rise, (p. 26) O holy cross, and lift me up, O cross! I am rich." "Amen." "I will mount you, O cross. I will be hung upon you as a testimony against them.

9. See Matt. 25:35–38.
10. See Matt. 5:20; 7:21; 18:3; 19:23.
11. See Matt. 19:29; Mark 10:17; Luke 10:25; 18:18.
12. See Rom. 12:4–5; 1 Cor. 6:15; 12:27; Eph. 5:30.
13. See Matt. 28:19; Mark 16:15.
14. See John 10:38; 14:10–13; 17:21.
15. See Heb. 4:16.
16. See Acts 17:31; Rev 19:11.
17. See Matt. 26:30; Mark 14:26; Luke 21:37; 22:39.
18. Matt. 18:3.
19. John 7:33; 12:35; 13:33; 14:19; 16:16–17.
20. See Matt. 26:4; Mark 14:1; John 11:53.

Receive me to yourself, O cross!" "Amen." "Do not weep, O cross, but rather rejoice!" (p. 27) "Amen." And when he finished his praises, we all responded after him: "Amen."

The second hymn to the cross: "I am the way of honorable life.[21] I am the immortal bread.[22] Eat until you are filled." We responded after him: "Amen."

Again he said to us, "Gather unto me, (p. 28) my holy members: I will dance to the cross for the third time and you will respond after me: 'Amen.'" "O cross, full of light, again you will bear the light. I will rush toward you, O cross." "Amen." "I will mount (p. 29) you as a testimony against them. Receive me to yourself, O cross. Do not reveal my body." "Amen."

The fourth dance around the cross: "I am not poor, O light-giving cross." "Amen." "I will fill you with my riches." (p. 30) "Amen." "I will mount you: receive me to yourself, O cross. Glory be to you, for you have obeyed your Father." "Amen." "Glory be to you, all sweetness." "Amen." "Glory be to the godhead." "Amen." "Show your grace, my Father, so that I might praise (p. 31) the cross." "Amen." "I have taken to myself the scepter of kingship[23] from the wood." "Amen." "I will have my enemies obey me."[24] "Amen." "The enemy will be destroyed through the cross." "Amen." "The sting of death will perish through the only-begotten Son."[25] "Amen." (p. 32) "To whom does the kingship belong? To the Son." "Amen." "Where is his kingship from? It is from the wood." "Amen." "Who is it that sent him to the cross? It is the Father." "Amen." "What is the cross and where is it from? It is from the Holy Spirit." "Amen." "It exists from eternity and for all time, from (p. 33) the foundation of the world."[26] "Amen." "I am the Alpha." "Amen." "And [the Omega]." "Amen." "The beginning and the end."[27] "Amen." "I am the ineffable beginning and the ineffable end, and the perfect one forever." "Amen."

When we had heard these things, we gave glory to God, to whom be glory forever and ever.[28] Amen.

21. See John 14:6.

22. See John 6:35.

23. See Ps. 45:7 LXX and Heb. 1:8. The phrase can also be rendered as "the crown of kingship"; see Isa. 62:3; Wis. 10:14.

24. See Ps. 109:1 LXX; Matt. 22:44; Mark 12:36; Luke 20:42.

25. See Hos. 13:14; 1 Cor. 15:55–56.

26. Matt. 13:35; Luke 11:50; John 17:24; Eph 1:4; Heb 4:3; 9:26; 1 Pet 1:20; Rev 13:8.

27. Rev. 21:6; 22:13.

28. Gal. 1:5; Phil. 4:20; 2 Tim. 4:18; Heb. 13:21.

27

The Gospel of Nicodemus (The Acts of Pilate) A

Scholars have long debated whether any of the earliest Gospel accounts of Jesus' life and death were devoted exclusively to his passion. Source critics in the nineteenth century argued that there were (no longer surviving) written accounts behind the passion narratives of Mark and of John. More recently, some scholars have seen a distinctive passion narrative lying behind the Gospel of Peter (see Crossan, *The Cross that Spoke*). When we move into later periods of Christianity, there can be no doubt about the matter. The Gospel of Nicodemus, also known as the Acts of Pilate, is preserved in multiple versions in the surviving manuscripts. But we have it as a complete text, from beginning to end, and it is a Gospel that deals exclusively with the events surrounding Jesus' trial, death, and resurrection.

The textual forms of this Gospel are so different from one another that it is best to present two different editions of it, neatly classified by Tischendorf—who is, remarkably, the most recent scholar to attempt anything like a critical edition of the Greek text (1853)—as the Acts of Pilate A and the Acts of Pilate B. The first sixteen chapters of the latter overlap with the former, with considerable textual variation; but then come an additional eleven chapters that relate the famous account of Jesus' descent to Hades (the "harrowing of hell" tradition), not found in A. Given the vast differences between these two textual forms, we will deal with them separately here—at present considering form A and in the next chapter setting out portions of form B.

One of the complications of this writing is knowing even what to call it. Ancient Christian sources mention an account of Jesus' passion told from the perspective of the Roman prefect of Judea, Pontius Pilate. In our earliest reference (ca. 160 CE), Justin Martyr refers to "the Acts drawn up under Pontius Pilate" (*First Apology* 35.9; see also 48.3). Two centuries later the heresy-hunter Epiphanius refers to an Acts of Pilate and indicates that it could be used to establish the date of Jesus' crucifixion on the eighth day before the Kalends of April

(March 25) (*Panarion* 50.1). Other references to an alleged Acts of Pilate clearly do not refer to our present work. Tertullian, for example, is the first author to mention some kind of official correspondence between the governor Pilate and the emperor Tiberius (*Apology* 21.24). This refers not to the present work but, possibly, to the Pilate correspondence dealt with later in this collection. A century later Eusebius indicates that a *pagan* composition known as the Acts of Pilate was promulgated during the reign of the Roman emperor Maximinus Daia (311–312), as part of the official opposition to the Christian religion (*Church History* 1.9.3–4; 9.5.1; 9.7.1). This too cannot be the present book, which is anything but anti-Christian.

These references show that several works were known (or thought) to be in circulation called the Acts of Pilate. There is some question, however, whether that is the most appropriate title for the present work, for this book deals with much more than Pilate's view of the passion. Nor does it claim to be written by Pilate, or even from his perspective. Moreover, whereas Pilate is one of the leading figures in the first half of the account, he virtually disappears from view in the second half. A number of our manuscripts begin with a prologue that indicates that the account was written by Jesus' Jewish follower Nicodemus. For this reason, it is perhaps best to give the book the title found throughout the medieval manuscript tradition, and call it the Gospel of Nicodemus.

Whatever one calls the text, it is very difficult to assign a date to it. There is no certainty that Justin actually knew a Gospel comparable to the one that lies before us, although he may have heard of the existence of one. If Epiphanius knew our text (what little he says about it corresponds to what we have here), then it must have been written by the middle of the fourth century. But given the extensive variation among the manuscripts of the text, it is also possible that there were multiple forms of the tradition circulating in different times and places. And so some scholars date the composition of the present work not until the fifth or sixth centuries, others put it in the middle of the fourth century, and yet others, somewhat optimistically, place it all the way back in the second century. Possibly Z. Izydorczyk is the most judicious in suggesting that the composition lying at the foundation of our surviving manuscripts was created in the fourth century, based on traditions in circulation already some two hundred years earlier.

The book was originally written in Greek, though it claims to have been composed in Hebrew. This claim serves an apologetic purpose, providing the account with the kind of antiquity and authenticity required of an eyewitness testimony (from Palestine) to the last hours of Jesus' life.

No one reading the account, however, will have any doubts about its legendary character. In simplest terms, the Gospel presents creative literary expansions of the accounts of Jesus' trial, death, and resurrection found in the four

Gospels of the New Testament. Each of the canonical Gospels comes to prominence in different portions of the narrative: Matthew and John, for example, in the trial scene, Luke in the crucifixion, and Mark in the "Great Commission" to the disciples following the resurrection (at least the last twelve verses of Mark from later manuscripts, which were not original to Mark's text).

The author used different methods for expanding the canonical narratives. Sometimes he provided imaginative details to their narratives, for example, in the discussions between Jesus and Pilate (from John), the dream of Pilate's wife (from Matthew), or the guard posted at the tomb (also from Matthew). At other times, and far more obviously, he added entire stories to underscore his overarching points, for example, in the wonderful and well-known account of the Roman standards bowing to worship Jesus and in Joseph of Arimathea's imprisonment and miraculous escape.

Taken together these narratives establish Jesus' divine character, Pilate's innocence in his execution, and the Jews' ultimate culpability. In terms of Jesus' character, from beginning to end the account marshals testimony that he was in fact divine, as witnessed by Pilate's courier, the Roman (and then Jewish) standard bearers, the twelve Jews who knew the details of his birth, Nicodemus before Pilate, Pilate himself, those healed by Jesus who come forward as witnesses, Joseph of Arimathea, the guards at the tomb, three Galilean Jews (Phineas, Adas, Angaius), and so on. The motif of Pilate's innocence is carried beyond even the later Gospels of the New Testament, where he three times declares Jesus innocent (Luke) or washes his hands of Jesus' blood (Matthew). Here he repeatedly declares Jesus' innocence and urges the Jews to try him according to their own law. Since Pilate is a witness to Jesus' divine character here, of course, then someone else must be at fault for his fate. The Jewish leaders and people come off especially poorly in the text as those who are out for blood. Three times the people are said to have cried out the horrible words of Matthew 27:25, "His blood be upon us and our children." But in the end, not even the Jewish leaders can deny Jesus' divine character: after the resurrection the evidence is too overwhelming even for them.

There may have been several motives behind the composition of this account. Some scholars have argued that it satisfies the natural Christian curiosity to know more about what happened at Jesus' death and its aftermath. This is certainly true, but it is also important to recognize that the new details in the account are not simply innocent expansions; they serve clear theological and ideological purposes, with respect, for example, to the divinity of Christ and the hateful rejection of the Jews. The account also serves to provide a first-hand (by Nicodemus) and "official" (by Pilate) testimony to what actually happened at Jesus' passion.

At the same time, there may have been something even more concrete lying behind the composition of this account. On the one hand, it may be that a later

Christian read about some such "Acts of Pilate" in the writings of Justin or others, and decided to compose just such a narrative. But it is also possible that after the publication of a pagan version of Pilate's account under Maximinus a Christian decided to write a "counter" version, a Christian narrative of what Pilate *really* said and did leading up to Jesus' death.

This would explain part of the composition—the first half—but probably not the entire work, since, as pointed out, the second half is not told from Pilate's perspective. And so it may be that different portions of this work came into existence at different times, and possibly for different reasons, so that the final product embodies a range of emphases and functions.

In any event, once it was written, this account proved to be enormously popular—nearly as influential on Christian understandings of Jesus' passion as was the Proto-Gospel for understanding Jesus' birth. It survives in over 500 manuscripts in a number of ancient languages (Greek, Latin, Syriac, Coptic, Aramaic, Armenian, Georgian, Old Slavonic) and in most of the major vernacular languages of medieval western Europe (High German, Low German, Dutch, Old French, Italian, Old English, Middle English, Norse, Welsh, Cornish, and so on). Its greatest impact was in the Latin-speaking world, as documented above all by the thorough analyses of Isydorkzyk (the vernaculars are translations from the Latin). There still survive 424 Latin manuscripts; twelve others known in the nineteenth and twentieth centuries have now been lost.

There has been far less work done on the Greek tradition and, as indicated, no modern critical edition exists, though one is reportedly underway for the Corpus *Christianorum Series Apocryphorum* (Association pour l'étude de la litterature apocryphe chrètienne). In lieu of such an edition, Tischendorf's "A" text, based on eight manuscripts of the 12th-16th centuries, continues to be used, as here.

Bibliography

Elliott, J. K. *The Apocryphal New Testament*. Oxford: Clarendon, 1993; pp. 164–69.

Izydorkzyk, Z. *Manuscripts of the Evangelium Nicodemi: A Census*. Toronto: Pontifical Institute of Mediaeval Studies, 1993.

Izydorkzyk, Z. *The Medieval Gospel of Nicodemus: Texts, Intertexts, and Contexts in Western Europe*. Tempe, Ariz.: Medieval & Renaissance Texts & Studies, 1997.

Klauck, H.-J. *Apocryphal Gospels: An Introduction*. London: T&T Clark, 2003; pp. 88–98.

Scheidweiler, F. "The Gospel of Nicodemus / Acts of Pilate and Christ's Descent into Hell," in *New Testament Apocrypha*, ed. W. Schneemelcher; trans. R. McL. Wilson. Louisville: Westminster/John Knox, 1991; vol. 1, pp. 501–5.

Tischendorf, C. von. *Evangelia Apocrypha*; reprint edition Hildesheim: Georg Olms, 1966; pp. liv-lxxvii; 210–86.

The Gospel of Nicodemus (Acts of Pilate) A

Public Records about our Lord Jesus Christ Composed Under Pontius Pilate

Prologue

I, Ananias, a member of the procurator's bodyguard, well versed in the law, came to know our Lord Jesus Christ from the divine Scriptures, coming to him by faith and being deemed worthy of holy baptism. I searched out the public records composed at that time, in the days of our master Jesus Christ, which the Jews set down under Pontius Pilate. These public records I found written in Hebrew, and with God's good pleasure I have translated them into Greek, so that all who call upon the name of our Lord Jesus Christ might know them. This I did in the seventeenth year of the reign of emperor Flavius Theodotius, the sixth year of Flavius Valentinianus, in the ninth indiction.[1]

All you who read these records and who copy them into other books, remember me and pray for me, that God may be merciful to me and have mercy on the sins I have committed against him.

Peace be to those who read and those who hear, along with their households. Amen.

These things took place in the fifteenth year of the rule of Tiberius Caesar, emperor of the Romans, and in the nineteenth year of the rule of Herod, king of Galilee, eight days before the Kalends of April—that is, on the twenty-fifth of March, during the consulate of Rufus and Rubellion, in the fourth year of the two hundred second Olympiad, when Joseph Caiaphas was the high priest of the Jews.

Nicodemus related all the things that happened after the crucifixion and suffering of our Lord and delivered them over to the high priests and the other Jews. The same Nicodemus compiled these writings in the Hebrew tongue.

The Jewish Leaders Accuse Jesus

1

1 The chief priests and scribes called a meeting of the council—Annas, Caiaphas, Semes, Dathaes, Gamalial, Judas, Levi, Nephthalim, Alexander, Jairus, and the other Jews—and they came to Pilate, accusing Jesus of many deeds: "We know that this one is the son of the carpenter Joseph and was born from Mary; yet he calls himself a Son of God and a king. Moreover, he profanes the Sabbath

1. I.e., 424–425 CE.

and wants to destroy our ancestral law." Pilate responded, "What does he do, and what does he want to destroy?" The Jews replied, "We have a law that no one may be healed on the Sabbath. But this one has performed evil deeds by healing the lame and crippled, the withered and the blind, the paralyzed, mute, and demon possessed on the Sabbath." Pilate said to them, "Then what are his evil deeds?" They replied, "He is a magician, and by Beelzeboul, the ruler of the demons, he casts out demons, and they all are subject to him." Pilate responded to them, "No one can cast out demons by an unclean spirit, but only by the god Asclepius."

The Roman Standards Worship Jesus

2 The Jews said to Pilate, "We ask your greatness to bring him before your judgment seat and put him on trial." Pilate called out to them and said, "Tell me, how can I, a mere governor, interrogate a king?" They replied, "We do not say he is a king; that is what he calls himself." So Pilate summoned his courier and told him, "Have Jesus brought in gently." The courier went out; and when he recognized who he was, he worshiped him. He then took his handkerchief and spread it out on the ground, and said to him, "Lord, walk here and enter, for the governor is calling you." When the Jews saw what the courier did, they cried out against Pilate, "Why did you not command him to be brought in by a herald, instead of the courier? For once the courier saw him, he worshiped him; and he spread his kerchief on the ground and had him walk in as a king."

3 Pilate called the courier back in and asked him, "Why did you do this, spreading your kerchief on the ground and having Jesus walk on it?" The courier replied, "Lord governor, when you sent me to Jerusalem to Alexander, I saw this one sitting on a donkey, and the children of the Hebrews were holding branches in their hands and crying out; and others were spreading their garments out and saying, 'Now save us, you who dwell in the heights. Blessed is the one who comes in the name of the Lord.'"[2]

4 The Jews cried out to the courier, "The children of the Hebrews were crying out in Hebrew; how do you know what they said in Greek?" The courier answered them, "I asked one of the Jews, 'What are they crying out in Hebrew?' And that one interpreted for me." Pilate said to them, "What were they crying out in Hebrew?" The Jews answered, "Hosanna, membrome barouchamma adonai."[3] Pilate said to them, "And the Hosanna, and the rest, what does it mean?" The Jews replied, "Now save us, you who dwell in the heights. Blessed is the one who comes in the name of the Lord." Pilate said to them, "If you testify that this

2. See Matt. 21:1–9; Mark 11:1–10; Luke 19:28–38; John 12:12–16.
3. Ps. 118:26.

is what the voices of the children said, what has the courier done wrong?" They gave him no reply. The governor said to the courier, "Go out and bring him in however you like." The courier went out and did the same as before, saying to Jesus, "Lord, enter, for the governor is calling you."

5 As Jesus entered, while the standard bearers were holding the standards, the images at the tops of the standards bowed forward and worshiped Jesus. When the Jews saw how the images on the standards bowed and worshiped Jesus, they cried out loudly against the standard bearers. Pilate said to the Jews: "Aren't you amazed at how the images bowed down and worshiped Jesus?" The Jews replied to Pilate, "We saw how the standard bearers bowed and worshiped him." The governor summoned the standard bearers and said to them, "Why did you do this?" They replied to Pilate, "We are Greek men and temple slaves. How could we worship him? While we were holding the images they bowed down by themselves and worshiped him."

6 Pilate said to the synagogue leaders and the elders of the people, "Select strong and powerful men, and let them hold the standards; then we will see if they bow down by themselves." The elders of the Jews took twelve powerful and strong men, six to hold each standard, and they stationed them before the governor's judgment seat. Pilate said to the courier, "Take him outside the praetorium and bring him in again, however you like." And Jesus and the courier went outside the praetorium. Pilate then summoned the men who had first held the images and said to them, "I swear by the salvation of Caesar, if the standards do not bow down when Jesus comes in, I will chop off your heads." The governor ordered Jesus to enter for the second time. And the courier did the same as before, strongly urging Jesus to walk upon his kerchief. He did so and entered. When he entered, again the standards bowed down and worshiped Jesus.

The Dispute Over Jesus' Character
2

1 When Pilate saw this happen, he was terrified, and tried to get up from his judgment seat. As he was still thinking about getting up, his wife sent word to him, "Have nothing to do with this righteous man; for I suffered many things throughout the night because of him."[4] Pilate called together all the Jews and said to them, "You know that my wife is a God-fearer and prefers to practice Judaism with you." They replied, "Yes, we know." Pilate said to them, "Just now my wife has sent word to me, 'Have nothing to do with this righteous man; for I suffered many things through the night because of him." The Jews replied to

4. See Matt. 27:19.

Pilate, "Did we not tell you that he is a magician? See, he has sent a bad dream to your wife."

2 Pilate summoned Jesus and said to him, "Why do these people speak out against you? Do you have nothing to say?" Jesus replied, "If they had no authority, they would not speak. For each of them has authority over his own mouth, to speak what is good and what is evil. Let them see to it themselves."

3 The Jewish elders replied to Jesus: "What is it we will see? First, that you were born from an act of fornication; second, that your birth led to the destruction of the infants in Bethlehem; third, that your father Joseph and mother Mary fled to Egypt because they were afraid to face the people."

4 Some of the pious Jews who were standing there said, "We do not say that he was born from fornication; rather, we know that Joseph was espoused to Mary, so that he was not born from fornication." Pilate said to the Jews who had said that he was born from fornication, "You have not spoken the truth, for they had a betrothal ceremony, as these, your fellow countrymen, have said." Annas and Caiaphas said to Pilate, "All of us—the entire multitude—have cried out that he was born from fornication and we are not believed. These others are proselytes and his disciples." Pilate summoned Annas and Caiaphas and said to them, "What are proselytes?" They replied, "They were born as children of Greeks, and now have become Jews." Those who said that he was not born from fornication—Lazarus, Asterius, Antonius, James, Annas, Zeras, Samuel, Isaac, Phineas, Crispus, Agrippus, and Judas—said, "We were not born as proselytes, but we are children of Jews and we speak the truth, for we were even there for the betrothal ceremony of Joseph and Mary."

5 Pilate summoned the twelve men who said that he was not born from fornication, and said to them, "I adjure you by the salvation of Caesar: is what you say the truth, that he was not born from fornication?" They replied to Pilate, "We are bound by law not to swear an oath, because it is a sin. But if these others will swear by the salvation of Caesar that it is not just as we have said, then we will deserve to die." Pilate said to Annas and Caiaphas, "Do you have no reply to make to these things?" Annas and Caiaphas replied to Pilate, "These twelve are believed when they say that he was not born from fornication; yet we, the entire multitude, are crying out that he was born of fornication and that he is a magician and that he calls himself a Son of God and a king. Yet we are not believed."

6 Pilate ordered the entire multitude to leave, except for the twelve men who said that he was not born from fornication; and he ordered Jesus to be set aside. He then said to them, "Why do these people want to kill him?" They replied to Pilate, "They are filled with religious zeal, because he heals on the Sabbath." Pilate said, "They want to kill him for doing a good deed?" They replied, "Yes."

Pilate, Jesus, and His Jewish Accusers

3

1 Pilate was filled with anger and went outside the praetorium and said to them, "The sun is my witness that I find nothing to charge this man with."[5] The Jews replied to the governor, "If he were not an evildoer, we would not have handed him over to you."[6] Pilate said, "Take him yourselves and judge him according to your law." The Jews said to Pilate, "We are not allowed to kill anyone."[7] Pilate replied, "God has told you not to kill anyone, but I am supposed to do so?"

2 Pilate again entered the praetorium and called Jesus to speak to him privately, and he said, "Are you the king of the Jews?" Jesus replied to Pilate, "Do you say this yourself, or have others told you about me?" Pilate responded to Jesus, "I am not a Jew am I? Your nation and the chief priests have handed you over to me. What have you done?" Jesus replied, "My kingdom is not from this world. For if my kingdom were from this world, my servants would have put up a fight, so that I would not be handed over to the Jews. But now my kingdom is not from here." Pilate replied to him, "So you are a king!" Jesus answered him, "It is you who say I am a king. This is why I was born and have come, that everyone who is from the truth might hear my voice." Pilate said to him, "What is truth?"[8] Jesus replied to him, "Truth is from heaven." Pilate said, "Is there no truth on earth?" Jesus said to Pilate, "You see how those who speak the truth are judged by those who have authority on earth."

4

1 Leaving Jesus inside the praetorium, Pilate went out to the Jews and said to them, "I find nothing to charge him with."[9] The Jews replied to him, "This one has said, 'I can destroy this temple and build it in three days.'"[10] Pilate replied, "What temple?" The Jews said, "The temple that Solomon built in forty-six years. But this man says he can destroy it and build it in three days." Pilate said to them, "I am innocent of the blood of this righteous man. You see to it yourselves." The Jews replied, "His blood be upon us and our children."[11]

2 Pilate summoned the elders, priests, and Levites and said to them privately, "Do not do this; for none of your charges against him deserves death. Your

5. See Luke 23:4, 14, 22; John 18:38; 19: 4, 6.
6. See John 18:30.
7. See John 18:31.
8. See John 18:33–38.
9. See John 18:38.
10. See Matt. 26:61; Mark 14:58.
11. See Matt. 27:24–25.

charges have only to do with healing and profaning the Sabbath." The elders, priests, and Levites replied, "If anyone blasphemes against Caesar, is he worthy of death or not?" Pilate answered, "He is worthy of death." The Jews replied to Pilate, "So—anyone who blasphemes against Caesar is worthy of death. But this one has blasphemed against God!"

3 The governor ordered the Jews to leave the praetorium, and he summoned Jesus and said to him, "What should I do with you?" Jesus answered Pilate, "Do as it has been given to you." Pilate said, "How has it been given?" Jesus replied, "Moses and the prophets preached ahead of time about my death and resurrection." The Jews inquired about what was said, and when they heard they said to Pilate, "What greater blasphemy do you need to hear?" Pilate said to the Jews, "If what he has said is a blasphemy, seize him yourselves for the blasphemy, take him to your synagogue, and judge him according to your law."[12] The Jews said to Pilate, "Our law stipulates that if a person sins against another person, he is to receive the forty lashes minus one; but the one who blasphemes against God is to be stoned."

4 Pilate said to them, "Take him yourselves and punish him in whatever way you see fit." The Jews replied to Pilate, "We want him crucified." Pilate said, "He does not deserve to be crucified."

5 When the governor looked around at the crowd of Jews standing there, he saw that many of them were weeping, and he said, "Not everyone in the crowd wants him to die." The elders of the Jews replied, "This is why we, the entire crowd, came—that he might die." Pilate said to the Jews, "Why should he die?" The Jews answered, "Because he said that he was a Son of God and a king."[13]

Nicodemus Gives His Testimony

5

1 A certain Jewish man named Nicodemus stood before the governor and said, "I ask you, most pious one, give the word and I will say a few things." Pilate said to him, "Speak." Nicodemus said, "I said to the elders, priests, Levites, and all the crowd of the Jews in the synagogue, 'What are you seeking from this man? This man does many signs and wonders, unlike anyone has done before or ever will do. Let him go, and do not plot any evil against him. If the signs he does are from God, they will stand on their own; but if they are human, they will come to nought.[14] For Moses was also sent from God to Egypt and did many signs, as God told him to do before Pharaoh, the King of Egypt. Jannes and Janbres were

12. See John 18:31.
13. See John 19:7.
14. See Acts 5:38–39.

also there, Pharaoh's servants; they themselves performed many of the signs that Moses did, so that the Egyptians considered them to be gods, this Jannes and Jambres. Since, however, the signs they did were not from God, they were destroyed—both they and those who believed in them. So now, let this man go; he is not worthy of death.'"

2 The Jews said to Nicodemus, "You have become his disciple and are trying to mount a defense for him." Nicodemus replied to them, "Has the governor also become his disciple? And is he trying to mount a defense for him? Did Caesar not appoint him to his position?" The Jews became incensed and were gnashing their teeth at Nicodemus. Pilate said to them, "Why are you gnashing your teeth against him, now that you have heard the truth?" The Jews said to Nicodemus, "May you receive his truth and share his fate." Nicodemus replied, "Yes indeed! May I receive it, just as you have said."

Other Witnesses Speak on Jesus' Behalf

6

1 One of the Jews ran up and asked the governor if he could say a word. The governor said, "If you want to say something, speak." And the Jew said, "For thirty-eight years I was confined to my pallet, in great pain. Jesus came and healed many demon possessed and those laid low by various illnesses. Several young men took pity on me and carried me, with my pallet, and brought me to him. When he saw me, he had compassion on me and said a word to me: 'Take your cot and walk.' And I took my cot and walked."[15] The Jews said to Pilate, "Ask him on which day he was healed." The one who was healed said, "On the Sabbath." The Jews said, "Is this not what we taught, that he heals and casts out demons on the Sabbath?"

2 Another Jew ran up and said, "I was born blind, able to hear a voice but not to see a face. When Jesus was passing by I cried out in a loud voice, 'Have mercy on me, Son of David.' He had mercy on me and laid his hands on my eyes. Suddenly I could see clearly."[16] Another Jew ran up and said, "I had a crooked back, and he straightened me with a word." And another said, "I became a leper, and he healed me with a word."

7

A certain woman named Bernice cried out from the distance, "I had a flow of blood, and I touched the hem of his garment, and the flow of blood I had for

15. See Matt. 9:1–8; Mark 2:1–12; Luke 5:17–26; John 5:1–7.
16. See Matt. 20:29–34; Mark 10:46–52; Luke 18:35–43.

twelve years was stopped."[17] The Jews said, "We have a law that a woman may not serve as a witness."

8

Others, a crowd of both men and women, began crying out, "This man is a prophet, and the demons are subject to him." Pilate said to those who told him that the demons were subject to him, "Why then are your teachers not subject to him?" They replied to Pilate, "We do not know." Others said that he had raised Lazarus from the tomb after four days. The governor trembled and said to the entire crowd of the Jews, "Why do you want to shed innocent blood?"

Pilate Is Compelled to Condemn Jesus

9

1 He summoned Nicodemus and the twelve men who had said that he was not born from fornication, and he said to them, "What should I do? The people are starting a riot." They replied to him, "We don't know; they will see to it themselves." Again Pilate summoned the entire crowd of the Jews and said, "You know that you have a custom that one prisoner be released to you at the Feast of Unleavened Bread. I have a condemned murderer in prison, named Barabbas, and this Jesus who is standing before you, against whom I have found nothing to charge. Which one do you want me to release for you?" They cried out, "Barabbas." Pilate said, "What then shall I do with Jesus, who is called the Christ?" The Jews replied, "Let him be crucified."[18] Some of the Jews then answered, "You are no friend of Caesar if you release this one, because he called himself a son of God and a king.[19] You, therefore, want this one to be king instead of Caesar."

2 Pilate became angry and said to the Jews, "Your nation is always causing riots, and you oppose those who are your own benefactors." The Jews replied, "What benefactors?" Pilate said to them, "I have heard how your God delivered you from harsh slavery in the land of Egypt and saved you through the sea, as if on dry land; and in the wilderness he nourished you with manna and gave you quail; and from a rock he provided you with water to drink and he gave you his law. And in spite of all this, you enraged your God and sought after a molten calf. You provoked your God to anger and he sought to kill you. But Moses interceded for you, so that you were not put to death. And now you charge me with hating the king."

17. See Matt. 9:20–21; Mark 5:25–29; Luke 8:42–46.
18. See Matt. 27:15–23; Mark 15:6–14; Luke 23:17–23; John 18:39–40.
19. See John 19:12.

3 He rose up from his judgment seat and was trying to leave. But the Jews cried out, "We know Caesar is our king—not Jesus. For even the magi brought him gifts from the east as for a king. When Herod heard from the magi that a king had been born, he tried to kill him. But when his father Joseph learned of it, he took him and his mother, and they fled to Egypt. When Herod found out, he murdered the Hebrew children that had been born in Bethlehem."[20]

4 When Pilate heard these words, he became afraid. Pilate silenced the crowds, because they were crying out, and said to them, "So this is the one sought by Herod?" The Jews replied, "Yes, he is the one." Then Pilate took water and washed his hands before the sun and said, "I am innocent of the blood of this righteous one. See to it yourselves." Again the Jews cried out, "His blood be upon us and our children."[21]

5 Then Pilate ordered the curtain be drawn before the judgment seat on which he sat, and he said to Jesus, "Your nation has convicted you for being a king. For this reason I pronounce sentence: first you will be flogged according to the decree of the pious kings; and then you will be hanged on the cross in the garden where you were seized. And let the two criminals Dysmas and Gestas be crucified with you."

The Crucifixion of Jesus
10

Jesus went out from the praetorium, along with the two criminals. When they came to the place, they stripped him of his clothes and put a linen cloth on him. Then they placed a crown of thorns around his head. So too they hanged the criminals. But Jesus said, "Father, forgive them; for they do not know what they are doing."[22] The soldiers divided his clothes, and the people stood by watching him. The chief priests and the leaders with them began mocking him: "He saved others; let him save himself. If he is the Son of God, let him descend from the cross."[23] The soldiers also ridiculed him, approaching him, offering him vinegar mixed with gall, and saying, "You are the king of the Jews: save yourself!" After the sentence, Pilate commanded that the charge against him be inscribed as a title in Greek, Latin, and Hebrew, just as the Jews had said: "This is the king of the Jews."[24]

20. See Matt. 2:1–18.
21. See Matt. 27:24–25.
22. Luke 23:34.
23. See Matt. 27:38–43; Mark 15:27–32; Luke 23:35–38.
24. See Matt. 27:37; Mark 15:26; Luke 23:38; John 19:17–22.

2 But one of the criminals being hanged said to him, "If you are the Christ, save yourself and us." But Dysmas responded and rebuked him, "Don't you fear God at all? You are under the same judgment. We deserve our fate, for we are being fairly punished for the things we did. But this one did nothing wrong." Then he said to Jesus, "Remember me, Lord, in your kingdom." Jesus said to him, "Yes indeed, I tell you, today you will be with me in paradise."[25]

11

1 It was about the sixth hour, and darkness came over the land until the ninth hour, with the sun being darkened. And the curtain of the temple was ripped in half. Then Jesus cried out with a great voice: "Father, baddach ephkid rouel," which means, "Into your hands I hand over my spirit." Once he said this, he handed over his spirit. When the centurion saw what had happened, he glorified God and said, "This man was righteous." All the crowds who had come to this sight, seeing what had happened, turned away beating their breasts.[26]

2 The centurion reported what had happened to the governor. When the governor and his wife heard, they were deeply grieved, and they ate and drank nothing that day. Pilate sent for the Jews and said to them, "Have you seen what happened?" They replied, "It is just a natural eclipse of the sun."

3 Jesus' acquaintances stood off at a distance, along with the women who accompanied him from Galilee, who saw these things. But a certain man, named Joseph, a member of the council from the city of Arimathea, who was anticipating the kingdom of God, approached Pilate and asked for the body of Jesus. He took him down, wrapped him in a clean linen cloth, and placed him in a stone-hewn tomb, where no one had ever been placed.[27]

The Jewish Leaders Confront Nicodemus and Joseph of Arimathea

12

1 When the Jews heard that Joseph had asked for the body of Jesus, they began looking for him, and for the twelve who had said that Jesus was not born from fornication, and for Nicodemus and many others who had run up to Pilate to reveal the good deeds he had done. But since all the others were in hiding, Nicodemus alone appeared to them, because he was a ruler among the Jews. Nicodemus said to them, "How is it that you have come into the synagogue?" And the Jews responded: "How is it that *you* have come into the synagogue? For you

25. See Luke 23:39–43.
26. See Luke 23:44–48.
27. See Matt. 27:57–60; Mark 15:42–46; Luke 23:50–53; John 19:38–42.

sympathize with him and will share his fate in the world to come." Nicodemus replied, "Yes indeed!" So too Joseph stepped forward and said to them, "Why were you aggravated with me for asking for the body of Jesus? See, I have placed him in my new tomb, after wrapping him in a clean linen cloth; and I rolled the stone before the door of the cave. You did not behave well, opposing the righteous one. You crucified him with no remorse and even pierced him with a spear."

The Jews seized Joseph and ordered that he be locked away until the first day of the week. They said to him, "You know that we cannot do anything against you because of the hour, since the Sabbath is dawning; but know also that you will not even be granted a burial, but we will give your flesh over to the birds of the sky." Joseph replied to them, "This is how the haughty Goliath spoke, who reproached the living God and the holy David. For God spoke through the prophet: 'Vengeance is mine, and I will repay, says the Lord.'[28] Now the one who is uncircumcised in the flesh but circumcised in heart has taken water to wash his hands before the sun, saying, 'I am innocent of the blood of this righteous one; see to it yourselves!' And you replied to Pilate, 'His blood be upon us and our children.'[29] Now I am afraid that the wrath of the Lord may come upon you and your children, just as you have said." The Jews were deeply embittered when they heard these words and they attacked Joseph, seized him, and locked him in a house with no window, setting guards at the door. They then sealed the door where Joseph was locked in.

2 On the Sabbath the leaders of the synagogue, priests, and Levites decreed that everyone should come to the synagogue on the first day of the week. Rising early, the entire crowd in the synagogue planned how they should kill Joseph. When the council was seated they ordered him to be brought in with great disgrace. But when they opened the door they did not find him. The entire crowd was amazed and astonished, because they found the seals still sealed, and Caiaphas had the key. They no longer dared to lay a hand on any of those who had spoken on behalf of Jesus before Pilate.

The Guard at the Tomb
13

1 While they were still sitting in the synagogue amazed about Joseph, there appeared some of the guards whom the Jews had requested from Pilate to guard Jesus' tomb, to keep his disciples from coming to steal him away. They reported to the leaders of the synagogue, the priests, and the Levites what had happened:

28. See Deut. 32:35; Rom. 12:19.
29. See Matt. 27:24–25.

"There was a great earthquake and we saw an angel descending from heaven; he rolled away the stone from the mouth of the cave and sat on it. He was shining like snow, like lightening. We were terrified and lay on the ground like corpses.[30] We then heard the voice of the angel speaking to the women who were waiting at the tomb: 'Do not fear. I know that you are looking for Jesus, who has been crucified. He is not here. He has been raised, just as he said. Come, see the place where the Lord lay. Now, go quickly and tell his disciples that he has been raised from the dead, and he is in Galilee.'"[31]

2 The Jews asked, "Which women was he speaking to?" The guards replied, "We don't know which ones they were." The Jews said, "What time was it?" The guards replied, "It was the middle of the night." The Jews said, "Why did you not seize the women?" The guards replied, "We became like corpses out of fear; we lost all hope of seeing the light of day. How could we have seized them?" The Jews replied, "As the Lord lives, we do not believe you." The guards said to the Jews, "You did not believe when you saw all those signs happen to that man; how would you be able to believe us? You were right to swear 'As the Lord lives'—for he is indeed alive!" Then the guards said, "We heard that you locked up the one who asked for the body of Jesus, and sealed the door, but then did not find him when you opened it. You produce Joseph and we will produce Jesus." The Jews replied, "Joseph has returned to his city." The guards replied to the Jews, "And Jesus has arisen, just as we heard the angel say, and he is in Galilee."

3 The Jews were terrified when they heard these words, and said, "What if word gets out and everyone turns to Jesus?" The Jews formed a plan and pooled sums of money to give to the soldiers. They told them, "Say this: 'We fell asleep and his disciples came at night and stole him.' If this report reaches the governor, we will persuade him and keep you blameless."[32] They took the money and spoke as they were instructed.

Phineas, Adas, and Angaius Witness to the Resurrection
14

1 But a certain priest Phineas, a teacher Adas, and Angaius, a Levite, came down from Galilee to Jerusalem and reported to the leaders of the synagogue, the priests, and the Levites, "We have seen Jesus and his disciples sitting on the mountain called Mamilch; and he was telling his disciples, 'Go into all the world and preach to all creation. The one who believes and is baptized will be saved, but the one who disbelieves will be condemned. These signs will accompany

30. See Matt. 28:2–4.
31. See Matt. 28:5–7.
32. See Matt. 28:12–14.

those who believe: they will cast out demons in my name; they will speak in new tongues; they will pick up snakes; and if they drink anything poisonous, it will not harm them; they will lay their hands on the sick and they will become well.'[33] While Jesus was speaking to his disciples we saw him taken up into heaven."

2 The elders, priests, and Levites said, "Give glory to the God of Israel and confess to him: did you hear and see these things you have described?" Those who described them replied, "As the Lord lives, the God of our fathers Abraham, Isaac, and Jacob, we heard these things and saw him taken up into heaven." The elders, priests, and Levites said to them, "Is this why you came, to preach to us? Or did you come to pray to God?" They replied, "To pray to God." The elders, chief priests, and Levites responded to them, "If you came pray to God, why are you speaking such nonsense in the presence of all the people?" Phineas the priest, Adas the teacher, and Angaius the Levite said to the leaders of the synagogue, priests, and Levites, "If what we have said and seen is in error, see, we are standing before you: do to us as you see fit." And they took the book of the Law and put them under oath to describe none of these matters to anyone. Then they gave them food and drink, and cast them out of the city, after giving them money and three men to accompany them. They sent them back to Galilee, and they set out in peace.

3 Once those men set out to Galilee, the chief priests, leaders of the synagogue, and elders in the synagogue gathered together, shut the gate, and began to mourn greatly: "Why has this sign happened in Israel?" But Annas and Caiaphas said, "Why are you disturbed? Why do you weep? Don't you know that his disciples gave a sum of gold to the guards at the tomb and instructed them to say that an angel descended from heaven and rolled the stone away from the door of the tomb?" But the priests and elders replied, "Even if his disciples stole the body, how did his soul return to the body, so that he is spending time in Galilee?" And they could scarcely make any answer, but said "We are not allowed to believe those who are uncircumcised."

The Search for Jesus
15

1 Nicodemus rose up and stood before the council and said, "What you have said is right. You know full well, people of the Lord, that these men who came down from Galilee fear God and are men of high standing who hate greed; they are peaceful men. They themselves have explained under oath that 'We saw Jesus on the mountain of Mamilch with his disciples,' and that he taught them everything that you heard from them, and that 'we have seen him being taken up into

33. See Mark 16:15–18.

heaven.' Yet no one asked them in what form he was taken up. For just as the book of the holy Scriptures teaches us, Elijah was also taken up into heaven and Elisha called out with a great voice; then Elijah cast his sheepskin cloak upon Elisha. And Elisha cast his cloak upon the Jordan, then crossed over the river and came into Jericho. The children of the prophets came to him and said, 'Elisha, where is your master Elijah?' And he said that he had been taken up into heaven. They replied to Elisha, 'Is it possible that a spirit has seized him and cast him onto one of the mountains? Let us go out with our servants and look for him.' And they persuaded Elisha, and he went with them. They looked for him for three days without finding him, and so knew that he had been taken up.[34] So now listen to me: let us send forth to every mountain of Israel to see whether Christ has been taken up by a spirit and cast onto one of the mountains." This idea was pleasing to everyone. They sent forth to every mountain of Israel to look for Jesus, but they did not find him. They did, however, find Joseph in Arimathea. But no one dared to seize him.

Joseph of Arimathea Is Found and Summoned

2 They reported to the elders, priests, and Levites: "We passed through every mountain in Israel and we did not find Jesus. But we did find Joseph in Arimathea." When they heard about Joseph, they rejoiced and gave glory to the God of Israel. The leaders of the synagogue, the priests, and the Levites considered how they should deal with Joseph, and they took a roll of papyrus and wrote to Joseph as follows: "Peace be with you. We know that we sinned against God and against you, and we pray to the God of Israel that you think it worthwhile to come to your fathers and your children; for we are all deeply grieved. For we opened the door and did not find you. We know that we devised an evil plot against you, but the Lord helped you, and the Lord himself thwarted our plan against you, O honored father Joseph."

3 Then they chose seven men from all of Israel who were friends of Joseph, whom Joseph himself knew. The leaders of the synagogue, priests, and Levites said to them, "See now: if he receives our letter and reads it, you will know that he will come with you to us. But if he does not read it, you will know that he holds a grudge against us. If so, greet him in peace and return to us." They then blessed the men and sent them out. The men came to Joseph and bowed down before him, and said to him, "Peace be with you." He replied, "Peace be with you and with all the people of Israel." They handed him the letter, which he read and then rolled it up, blessing God: "Blessed be the Lord God, who delivered Israel from shedding innocent blood. And blessed be the Lord who sent his angel and

34. See 2 Kings 2:1–18.

protected me under his wings." He then laid out a table for them, and they ate and drank, and slept there.

4 They rose early in the morning and prayed. Then Joseph saddled his donkey and went out with the men, and they came to the holy city Jerusalem. All the crowd met Joseph and cried out, "Peace on your arrival!" He replied to all the people, "May peace be with you." And all the people kissed him. The people prayed with Joseph and they were astonished at his appearance. Nicodemus welcomed him into his house and made a great feast, and he invited Annas and Caiaphas, along with the elders, priests, and Levites to his house. They rejoiced while eating and drinking with Joseph, and after singing a hymn each went away to his own house. But Joseph stayed in the house of Nicodemus.

Joseph of Arimathea Testifies Before the Jewish Leaders

5 On the next day, which was the day of preparation, the leaders of the synagogue, the priests, and the Levites rose early and went to the house of Nicodemus. Nicodemus met them and said, "May peace be with you." They replied, "May peace be with you and with Joseph, and with all your house and with all the house of Joseph." Then he brought them into his house. When the entire Council was seated, Joseph sat between Annas and Caiaphas. No one dared say a word to him. So Joseph said, "Why have you called me?" They motioned to Nicodemus to speak to Joseph. Nicodemus opened his mouth and said to Joseph, "Father, you know that the revered teachers, and priests, and Levites are seeking to learn something from you." Joseph replied, "Go ahead and ask." Annas and Caiaphas then took the book of the Law and placed Joseph under an oath, saying, "Give glory to the God of Israel and make a confession to him. For also when Achar was placed under an oath by the prophet Joshua, he did not violate his oath but reported to him everything, and hid from him not a word. You too, do not hide from us a single word." Joseph replied, "I will not hide one word from you." They said to him, "We were greatly grieved because you asked for the body of Jesus and wrapped it in a clean linen cloth and placed it in a tomb. That is why we shut you up in a house with no window, and locked and sealed the door, and guards were watching where you were shut in. When we opened it up on the first day of the week and did not find you, we were exceedingly grieved. And amazement fell on all the people of the Lord until yesterday. Now, tell us what happened."

6 Joseph said, "On the day of preparation, around the tenth hour, you locked me in, and I stayed there the entire Sabbath. In the middle of the night, while I was standing in prayer, the house where I was locked in was raised by its four corners, and I saw something like a flash of lightning with my eyes. Full of fear, I fell to the ground. Someone took me by the hand and brought me out from the

place I had fallen. A mist of water poured out from my head to my feet; and a scent like myrrh reached my nose. He wiped off my face, kissed me, and said, 'Do not fear, Joseph. Open your eyes and see who is talking to you.' When I looked up, I saw Jesus. I was trembling and began to think it was a phantom; so I began reciting the commandments. But he was speaking with me. Now, as you well know, if a phantom meets someone and hears the commandments, he flees straight off. But when I saw that he was speaking with me I said, 'Rabbi Elijah!' He replied to me, 'I am not Elijah.' I said to him, 'Who are you Lord?' He said to me, 'I am Jesus, whose body you requested from Pilate. You clothed me in a clean linen cloth and placed a cloth upon my face, and lay me in your new cave, and rolled a great stone across the mouth of the cave.' So I said to the one speaking with me, 'Show me the place where I laid you.' He brought me out and showed me the place where I had laid him, and the linen cloth was lying in it, as was the cloth that had been on his face. Then I knew that it was Jesus. He took my hand and put me inside my own house, while the doors were still locked. He brought me to my bed and said, 'May peace be with you.' Then he kissed me and said to me, 'Do not leave your house for forty days; for see, I am going to my brothers in Galilee.'"

Levi Testifies
16

1 When the leaders of the synagogue, the priests, and the Levites heard these words from Joseph, they became like corpses and fell to the ground; and they ate nothing until the ninth hour. Then Nicodemus, along with Joseph, exhorted Annas and Caiaphas, the priests, and the Levites, "Rise up and stand on your feet. Eat some bread and strengthen your souls, for tomorrow is the Sabbath of the Lord." They arose and prayed to God, and ate and drank. Then each one went away to his own home.

2 On the Sabbath our teachers, the priests, and the Levites were sitting and discussing with one another, "What is this wrath that has come upon us? For we know his father and mother." Levi the teacher said, "I know that his parents fear God; they do not refrain from prayer and they pay their tithes three times a year. When Jesus was born, his parents brought him to this place, and they gave sacrifices and whole burnt offerings to God. When the great teacher Simeon took him in his arms, he said, 'Now release your slave in peace, O Master, according to your word. For my eyes have seen your salvation, which you prepared before all the people, a light of revelation for the nations and a glory for your people Israel.' Simeon blessed them and said to Mary, his mother, 'I tell you the good news about your son.' Mary replied, 'Is it good, my lord?' Simeon said to her, 'It is good. See, this one is appointed for the falling and rising of many in Israel, and for a

sign that will be disputed. And a sword will pass through your own soul, so that the thoughts of many hearts might be revealed.'"[35]

3 They responded to the teacher, Levi: "How do you know these things?" Levi replied to them, "Do you not know that I learned the law from him?" The council said to him, "We want to see your father." So they sent for his father. When they questioned him, he said to them: "Why have you not believed my son? The blessed and righteous Simeon himself taught him the law." The council said, "Rabbi Levi, are you speaking the truth?" Levi replied, "It is the truth." And the leaders of the synagogue, the priests, and the Levites said to one another, "Come, let us send to Galilee to the three men who came and described his teaching and his ascension, and they will tell us how they saw him taken up." This word was pleasing to everyone. So they sent the three men who had already gone to Galilee with them, and they said to them, "Say to Rabbi Adas, Rabbi Phineas, and Rabbi Angaeus, 'May peace be to you to all who are with you. Because a great dispute has occurred in the council, we have been sent to you to call you to this holy place, Jerusalem.'"

Adas, Phineas, and Angaius Testify Again

4 The men went to Galilee and found them sitting and studying the law. They greeted them in peace. The men who were in Galilee said to those who had come to them, "May peace be with all Israel." And they replied, "May peace be with you." Then they said to them, "Why have you come?" Those who were sent said, "The council is calling you to come to the holy city Jerusalem." When the men heard that they were being sought by the council, they prayed to God, and then reclined for a meal with the men, and ate and drank. Then they arose and went in peace to Jerusalem.

5 On the next day the council was seated in the synagogue, and they questioned them, "Did you really see Jesus seated on the mountain Mamilch, teaching his eleven disciples? And did you see him being taken up?" The men answered them, "We saw him taken up, as we have told you."

6 Annas said, "Separate them from one another and let us see if their accounts agree." They separated them from one another and first called Adas. They said to him, "How did you see Jesus being taken up?" Adas responded, "While he was sitting on the mountain Mamilch, teaching his disciples, we saw a cloud overshadow both him and his disciples. The cloud then took him up to heaven, and his disciples lay flat on the ground." They called Phineas, the priest, and asked him also, "How did you see Jesus being taken up?" He gave them a similar response. Then they asked Angaeus, and he also gave a similar response. The

35. See Luke 2:28–35.

council said, "The law of Moses indicates, "Every word will be established from the mouths of two or three people."[36] Bouthem the teacher said, "It is written in the law, 'Enoch walked with God, and he was no longer, for God took him.'"[37] Jairus the teacher said, "And we have heard of the death of the holy Moses, but we have not seen him. For it is written in the law of the Lord, 'Moses died by the mouth of the Lord, and no one has known where his tomb is to this day.'"[38] Rabbi Levi said, "Why is it that the Rabbi Simeon said, when he saw Jesus, 'See, this one is appointed for the falling and rising of many in Israel, and for a sign that will be disputed'?"[39] Rabbi Isaac said, "It is written in the law, 'See, I am sending my messenger before you; he will precede you to guard you in every good path, for my name has been called in it.'"[40]

The Jewish Leaders Themselves Testify

7 Then Annas and Caiaphas said, "You have rightly said that it is written in the law of Moses that no one saw the death of Enoch and no one named the death of Moses. But Jesus made a defense before Pilate; and we have seen that he received blows and was spit in the face; and that the soldiers placed a crown of thorns on him; and that he was scourged and received a sentence from Pilate; and that he was crucified on the place of the skull, along with two brigands; and that he was given vinegar with gall to drink, and that Longinus the soldier pierced his side with a spear, and that our honored father Joseph requested his body; and that, as he now says, he has been raised; and that, as the three teachers have said, 'We saw him being taken up to heaven,'; and that Rabbi Levi spoke bearing witness to what was said by Rabbi Simeon, 'See, this one is appointed for the falling and rising of many in Israel, and for a sign that will be disputed.'"

All the teachers said to the entire people, "If what has happened has come from the Lord, and it is a marvel in our eyes, you should know for certain, O house of Jacob, that it is written: 'Cursed is everyone who hangs on a tree.'[41] And another scripture teaches, 'The gods who did not make heaven and earth will be destroyed.'"[42] The priests and Levites then said to one another, "If his remembrance extends until the year[43] which is called Jubilee, know that he will prevail forever and will raise a new people for himself." Then the leaders of the synagogue,

36. Deut. 19:15.
37. Gen. 5:24.
38. Deut. 34:5–6.
39. Luke 2:34.
40. Exod. 23:20–21.
41. Deut. 21:23.
42. Jer. 10:11.
43. Greek: SŌMMOU; possibly corrupt, or possibly a form of the Hebrew term *šanah* for "year."

the priests, and the Levites proclaimed to all Israel, "Cursed is that man who worships what is made by human hands, and cursed is the man who worships creatures alongside the one who created them." And all the people replied, "Yes indeed!"

8 And all the people sang a hymn to the Lord and said, "Blessed is the Lord, who gave rest to the people of Israel, according to everything that he has said. Not one word failed of all the good words he spoke to Moses, his slave. May the Lord our God be with us just as he was with our fathers. May he not destroy us. May he not destroy us so that we might incline our hearts to him, to walk along all his paths and to keep his commandments and the decrees that he commanded our fathers. The Lord shall be king over all the earth in that day; and the Lord will be one and his name will be one, the Lord our king. He will save us. There is no one like you, O Lord. You are great, O Lord, and great is your name. Heal us by your power, O Lord, and we will be healed. Save us, O Lord, and we will be saved. We are your portion and inheritance. The Lord will not forsake his people, on account of his great name; for the Lord has begun to make us his people."

When all had sung this hymn, each one returned to his home, glorifying God—for his glory is forever and ever. Amen.

28

The Gospel of Nicodemus (Acts of Pilate) B

(Including the Descent into Hades)

The narrative preserved in Tischendorf's B text of the Gospel of Nicodemus (Acts of Pilate) is a later reworking of the A text, and includes an entirely new narrative, in eleven chapters, of the "Descent into Hades." This account became the basis of much of the later speculation concerning the "harrowing of hell" (in which Jesus descended to hell and took the saints away from it). As an entire narrative, the Gospel of Nicodemus B deals with Jesus' trial before Pilate, his crucifixion, resurrection (and its "proofs" in his resurrection appearances), and a post-resurrection recollection of what occurred during the days of his death, when he set free the captives of Satan in Hades.

This alternative version of the Gospel of Nicodemus shows how fluid and utterly malleable these traditions were. There was no fixed text; rather, the stories recounted were told and retold, written and rewritten, over the centuries. This makes it difficult—well nigh impossible—to speak about an "original" form of these traditions. We have Latin attestation of the extended narrative (the B text) dating from the ninth century; and in fact the recent scholarship of R. Gounelle has argued that the Greek B text, found in about thirty manuscripts, represents a translation *back* into Greek from the Latin. In any event, the long addition of the Descent into Hades appears to have reached some kind of written form sometime in the fifth or sixth centuries.

The reasons for the creation of Greek B were much the same as those for the older form A (see Introduction there): to proclaim the divinity of Christ, the innocence of Pilate, and the culpability of the Jews. But the Descent to Hades embodies still other concerns. Most obviously, it provides a narrative elaboration of the terse statement of 1 Peter 3:19, which indicates that after his death Christ "went and made a proclamation to the spirits who were in prison."

This elaboration came in response to questions that had long tantalized Christians familiar with the traditions of Jesus' death and resurrection. If Jesus died on Friday, but was not raised until Sunday, what was he doing during the interim? And if his death brings salvation—what about those who died before his appearance on earth? Do they too receive salvation? When, and how? Taken together, these questions led to stories told of Jesus' journey to the realm of the dead, to "lead captivity captive" (Eph. 4:8). The account of the Descent in the Gospel of Nicodemus B is our oldest surviving record of these stories.

Like Nicodemus A, however, it was not written purely to answer speculative questions, as it too contains clear theological teachings, for example, explaining why the Son of God had to become human (in order to dupe Satan and so bring salvation to the dead), and to exalt his incomparable divine character, as again attested by a string of impeccable witnesses: the two sons of Simeon now raised from the dead and a number of occupants of Hades (John the Baptist, Abraham, Isaiah, Seth, David)—not to mention Satan and Hades itself.

Since the first sixteen chapters of Nicodemus B repeat material in Nicodemus A, although often in highly variant form, they will not be reproduced in full here. Instead, simply to give a sense of how malleable the tradition was over time, even in written form, we have provided just the end of the account, from the report of the Roman guard of what happened at the resurrection to the account of the three Jewish witnesses from Galilee to Jesus' ascension (where Greek A ends; in both A and B this is chapters 13–16). Then will be given, in toto, the new material of chapters 17–27, which recount the Descent.

The translation is of Tischendorf Greek B, which is based on four manuscripts.

Bibliography

See the bibliography given for Gospel of Nicodemus A.

The Gospel of Nicodemus

Not given: chaps 1–12

The Report of the Guard at the Tomb
13

1 Then one of the soldiers who had been guarding the tomb arrived in the synagogue and said, "You should know that Jesus has arisen." The Jews said, "How?" He replied, "First there was an earthquake. Then an angel of the Lord, flashing like lightning, came from heaven, rolled the stone away from the crypt, and sat on it. Struck by fear before him, all of us soldiers became like corpses; we could neither flee nor speak. But we heard the angel speaking with the women who had come there to see the tomb: 'Do not fear! I know that you are looking for Jesus. He is not here, but he has risen, just as he told you in advance. Stoop down and look into the tomb where they laid his body. Go and tell his disciples that he has been raised from the dead. They should go to Galilee, for they will find him there. This is why I am speaking with you first.'"[1]

2 The Jews said to the soldiers, "Who were the women who came to the grave? And why did you not seize them?" The solders said, "We were terrified just by the appearance of the angel, and were able neither to speak nor to move."[2] The Jews said, "As the God of Israel lives, we do not believe anything you are saying." The soldiers replied, "Jesus did such amazing deeds, and you did not believe; how would you be about to believe us now? You speak the truth when you say 'As God lives,' for truly indeed, the one you crucified lives. But we have heard that you were holding Joseph, locked in prison. Then when you opened the doors, you did not find him. So then, you give us Joseph and we will give you Jesus." The Jews said, "Joseph has fled from prison; you will find him in his own land of Arimathea." The soldiers replied, "And if you go to Galilee you will find Jesus, just as the angel said to the women."

3 Frightened by these words, the Jews said to the soldiers, "See that you report this to no one else, or everyone will believe in Jesus." To this end they gave them a large sum of money. But the soldiers said, "We are afraid that Pilate will hear that we took money and will execute us." The Jews replied, "Take it, and we promise to defend you before Pilate. Just say that you fell asleep, and while you slept Jesus' disciples came and stole him from the grave." Then the soldiers took

1. See Matt. 28:1–7.
2. See Matt. 28:4.

the money and said what they were ordered to say. And to this day this false account is given by the Jews.[3]

Phineas, Angaeus, and Adas Witness to the Resurrection
14

1 After a few days three men came from Galilee to Jerusalem. One of them was a priest named Phineas, another was a Levite named Angaeus, and the other was a soldier named Adas. These came to the chief priests and said to them and to the people: "We saw Jesus, the one you crucified, in Galilee with his eleven disciples, on the Mount of Olives; he was teaching them and saying, 'Go into all the world and preach the gospel. Whoever will believe and be baptized will be saved; but whoever will not believe will be condemned.'[4] When he said these things he went up into heaven. We ourselves saw this from afar, as did many others of the five hundred."[5]

2 When the chief priests and the Jews heard these things, they said to these three men, "Give glory to the God of Israel and retract these false words." They answered, "As the God of our fathers lives, the God of Abraham, Isaac, and Jacob, we are not speaking falsely; we have told you the truth." Then the high priest spoke, and they brought the ancient book of the Hebrews from the temple; and he made them swear an oath. He then gave them money as well, and sent them to another place, to keep them from preaching the resurrection of Christ in Jerusalem.

3 When all the people heard these various accounts, a crowd gathered in the temple, and there was a great disturbance. Many of them were saying, "Jesus has risen from the dead, just as we have heard. So why did you crucify him?" But Annas and Caiaphas said, "O Jews, do not believe everything the soldiers are saying, nor believe that they saw an angel coming down from heaven, for we gave the soldiers money to keep them from telling these things to anyone. So too Jesus' disciples also gave them money to say that Jesus rose from the dead."

Nicodemus and Joseph of Arimathea with the Jewish Leaders
15

1 Nicodemus said, "O children of the Jerusalemites! The prophet Elijah went up to the heights of heaven with a fiery chariot[6]; and so, it would be nothing incredible if Jesus also arose. For the prophet Elijah was a foreshadowing of Jesus. So,

3. See Matt. 28:11–15.
4. See Mark 16:15–16.
5. See 1 Cor. 15:6.
6. 2 Kings 2:1–18.

when you hear that Jesus arose, do not disbelieve it. I give this advice: it would be fitting for us to send soldiers to Galilee, where the men testify that they saw him with his disciples; they can wander around and find him; and then we can ask his forgiveness for the evil you did against him." This idea was pleasing to them; they selected soldiers and sent them to Galilee. They did not find Jesus, however; but they did find Joseph, in Arimathea.

2 When the soldiers returned, the chief priests learned that Joseph had been found; they gathered the people and asked, "What can we do to induce Joseph to come to us?" After talking it over, they wrote him a letter, which read as follows: "Father Joseph: may peace be with you, with all your house, and with your friends. We know that we sinned against God and against you, his slave. For this reason we ask you to come here to us, your servants. For we were greatly astonished that you managed to flee from prison; and we speak the truth when we say that we were planning to do you harm. But God saw that our plot against you was unjust; and so he rescued you from our hand. But come to us, for you are the honor of our people."

3 The Jews sent this letter to Arimathea with seven soldiers who were friends of Joseph. When they came and found him, they greeted him honorably, as they were instructed, and gave him the letter. When he took it and read it, he gave glory to God and embraced the soldiers. And he prepared a table and ate and drank with them the entire day and night.

4 On the next day he went with them to Jerusalem. The people came out to meet him and embraced him. Nicodemus welcomed him in his house. The following day the chief priests Annas and Caiaphas summoned him to the temple and said to him, "Give glory to the God of Israel and tell us the truth. For we know that you provided a burial for Jesus, and that is why we arrested you and locked you in prison. When we tried to bring you out in order to execute you, we did not find you, and we were astonished and terrified. But we prayed to God that we could find you for questioning. And so, tell us the truth."

5 Joseph said to them, "On the evening of the day of preparation, when you secured me in prison, I fell on my face in prayer through the entire night and the entire day of the Sabbath. In the middle of the night I saw that four angels had raised the house of the prison, holding it by its four corners. And Jesus entered like a flash of lightening. I fell to the ground out of fear. He grabbed me by the hand and raised me up, saying, 'Do not fear, Joseph.' Then putting his arms around me he kissed me and said, 'Turn around and see who I am.' When I turned and saw him I said, 'Lord, I do not know who you are.' He said, 'I am Jesus, whom you buried yesterday.' I said to him, 'Show me the tomb and then I will believe.' He took me by the hand and led me to the tomb, which stood open. When I saw the linen cloth and the head cloth, I recognized him and said, 'Blessed is the one who comes in the name of the Lord.' And I worshiped him.

Then he took me by the hand, with angels following us, and led me to my house in Arimathea; and he said to me, 'Sit here for forty days; for I am going to my disciples, to give them the confidence to preach my resurrection.'"

Other Witnesses to Jesus
16

1 When Joseph said these things the chief priests cried out to the people, "We know that Jesus had both a father and mother; how they are we to believe that he is the Christ?" One of the Levites responded, "I know Jesus' family. They are noble people, great slaves of God who obtain tithes from the Jewish people. I also know that the old man Simeon received him when he was a child and said to him, 'Now release your slave, O Master.'"[7]

2 The Jews said, "Let us find the three men who saw him on the Mount of Olives, so that we can question them and learn more accurately the truth." They found them and brought them before the multitude, and put them under oath to speak the truth. And they said, "As the God of Israel lives, we saw Jesus alive, on the Mount of Olives, and going up into heaven."

3 Then Annas and Caiaphas separated the three men from one another and questioned each one individually. Then they agreed with one another and all three gave the same account. The chief priests responded, "Our Scripture says that every word given by two or three witnesses will be established.[8] Joseph therefore admits that he buried and entombed him with the help of Nicodemus; and he states that it is true that he was raised."

7. See Luke 2:29.
8. Deut. 19:15.

The Descent of Christ to Hell

The Sons of Simeon come to Jerusalem
7

1 Joseph said, "And why are you amazed that Jesus has been raised? This is not amazing. What is amazing is that he was not raised alone, but that he raised many other dead, who have appeared to many people in Jerusalem. Even if you do not know the others, for some time you have known Simeon, who received Jesus, and his two sons, whom he raised. For we buried them a short while ago. But now their tombs can be seen to be opened and empty, and they are alive and living in Arimathea." And so they dispatched some people who found their crypts open and empty." Joseph said, "We should go to Arimathea and find them."

2 Then the chief priests Annas and Caiaphas, along with Joseph, Nicodemus, Gamaliel, and others with them rose up and went off to Arimathea, and they found the ones Joseph had mentioned. And so they prayed and greeted one another; then they came with them to Jerusalem and brought them into the synagogue; they secured the doors, and placed the ancient Law of the Jews in their midst. The chief priests said to them, "We want you to swear an oath to the God of Israel, Adonai, and so speak the truth about how you arose and who raised you from the dead."

3 When those who had arisen heard this they made the sign of the cross on their faces and said to the chief priests, "Give us paper, ink, and pen." They brought these things. When they sat down, they wrote as follows:

Witnesses to Christ in Hades
18

1 O Lord Jesus Christ, the resurrection and the life of the world, give us grace that we may describe your resurrection and the amazing deeds you performed in Hades. We then were in Hades with all those who had fallen asleep from the beginning. But when it was middle of the night, into that darkness there arose as it were the light of the sun, and it shone and enlightened everyone; and we saw one another. Immediately our father Abraham was united with the patriarchs and the prophets. At once filled with joy, they said to one another, "This light is from the great enlightening." The prophet Isaiah who was there said, "This is the light from the Father and from the Son and from the Holy Spirit, about which I prophesied while still living: 'O land of Zebulon and land of Naphtali, the people who sit in darkness, see a great light!'"[9]

9. Isa. 9:1–2.

2 Then there came into their midst another figure from the wilderness, an ascetic. The patriarchs said to him, "Who are you?" He replied, "I am John, the last of the prophets, who made straight the paths of the Son of God and who proclaimed to the people a repentance for the forgiveness of sins.[10] The Son of God came to me and when I saw him from a distance I said to the people, 'See the Lamb of God who takes away the sin of the world.'[11] With my hand I baptized him in the Jordan river, and I also saw the Holy Spirit like a dove coming upon him. And I heard also the voice of God the Father speaking thus, 'This is my beloved Son in whom I am well pleased.'[12] For this reason he has sent me to you, that I might preach how the unique Son of God is coming here, that whoever puts faith in him will be saved, but whoever will not believe in him will be condemned. For this reason I say to all of you, when you have seen him, you should worship him, all of you; for now alone do you have the occasion to repent for having worshiped the idols in the futile world above, and for having sinned. This will be impossible at some other time."

19

1 While John was teaching these things to those in Hades, Adam the first to be formed, and father of all, heard and spoke to his son Seth: "My son, I want you to tell the forefathers of the human race and the prophets where I sent you when I had fallen down and was about to die." Seth said, "Prophets and patriarchs, listen. My own father Adam, the first formed, when he had fallen to the point of death, sent me to make a petition to God, near the gate of paradise, that he might guide me through an angel to the tree of mercy, that I might take away some oil and anoint my father, that he might rise up from his weakness. And I did what he asked. After my prayer an angel of the Lord came and said to me, 'Seth, what are you asking? Are you asking for the oil that can raise the weak or the tree from which this oil flows, because of the weakness of your father? You will not be able to find this now. Go away and tell your father that five thousand five hundred years after the creation of this world, the unique Son of God will descend to earth, having become human, and he will anoint him with this oil. He will then arise; and he will wash him in water and the Holy Spirit—both him and those who descend from him. Then he will be healed from all illness. But this is not possible now.'"

When the patriarchs and prophets heard these things, they rejoiced greatly.

10. See Matt. 3:3; Mark 1:3–4; Luke 3:3–4.
11. John 1:29.
12. Matt. 3:16–17.

Satan Speaks with Hades
20

1 While all of them were filled with such joy, Satan, the heir of darkness came and said to Hades, "O all-devouring and insatiable one, listen to my words. There is a certain one named Jesus from the nation of the Jews, who calls himself the Son of God. But this one is a human, and because of our joint efforts the Jews crucified him. Now that he has died, be prepared so that we can keep him securely here. For I know that he is human, as I heard him saying 'My soul is deeply grieved unto death.'[13] Still, he did much mischief against me in the world above, while living with the mortals. For when he found my slaves, he persecuted them, and everyone that I made crippled, blind, lame, leprous, or any such thing, he healed through a word alone. And when I prepared many for their burial, through a word alone he also brought them back to life."

2 Hades said, "Is this one so powerful that he did these things through a word alone? Can you oppose him, if he is so great? It seems to me that no one can oppose him, he is so great. But if you say that you heard him fearing death, he said this to mock and deride you, wanting to seize you by his powerful hand. Woe, woe to you for all ages to come." Satan replied, "O all-devouring and insatiable Hades, are you so frightened by hearing about our common enemy? I did not fear him, but I empowered the Jews, and they crucified him, and they also gave him gall mixed with vinegar to drink.[14] And so be prepared to seize him forcefully when he comes."

3 Hades answered, "O heir of darkness, son of destruction, Devil, just now you told me that when you prepared many for their burial, by a word alone he brought them back to life again. If he set others free from the grave, in what way and by what power will he be seized by us? Not long ago I devoured a certain dead man named Lazarus, and soon afterwards someone from the living forcefully dragged him from my intestines through a word alone.[15] I suppose this was the one about whom you are speaking. If then we receive that one here, I am afraid that we might somehow be in danger with all the others. For see, I can sense that all those whom I devoured from the beginning are stirred up, and I am pained in my belly. It does not seem to me to be a good sign that Lazarus was previously snatched from me. For he flew out from me not like a corpse but like an eagle, so quickly did the earth cast him forth. For this reason I adjure you, for both your benefit and mine, do not bring him here. For I think he is coming here to raise all the dead. And this I tell you, by the darkness we enjoy, if you lead him here, none of the dead will be left to me."

13. See Matt. 26:38; Mark 14:34.
14. See Matt. 27:34.
15. See John 11:1–44.

Christ Comes to Hades

21

1 While Satan and Hades were saying such things to one another, a great voice like thunder was heard, saying, "O you rulers, lift the gates! Ancient gates, rise up, and the King of glory will enter."[16] When Hades heard this he said to Satan, "Go out, if you are able, and oppose him." Satan then went out. Then Hades said to his demons, "Make the bronze gates and the iron bars fully and strongly secure,[17] and hold my deadbolts fast. Stand upright and keep watch. For if that one comes in here, disaster will overtake us."

2 When the forefathers heard these things they all began to malign him, saying, "O all- devouring and insatiable one, open up that the King of glory may come in." David the prophet said, "Do you not know, O blind one, that while I was still living in the world I prophesied this very call: 'O you rulers, lift the gates!'?" Isaiah said, "I saw this in advance and wrote through the Holy Spirit, 'The dead will arise and those in their tombs will be raised, and those in the earth will rejoice.'[18] And also, 'O death, where is your sting? O Hades, where is your victory?'"[19]

3 And then a voice came again, saying "Lift up the gates." When Hades heard the voice the second time, he answered as if he did not know, and said, "Who is this King of glory?" The angels of the Master said, "He is a Lord who is mighty and powerful, a Lord powerful in war."[20] And immediately then at this word the bronze gates were crushed and the iron bars were smashed, and all the dead who were bound were released from their bonds, and we along with them. And the King of glory came in, as a human; and all the dark places of Hades were enlightened.

22

1 Immediately Hades cried out, "We have been defeated. Woe to us! But who are you who has such authority and power? What sort of being are you who comes here without sin, you who seem small yet has power to do great things, the one who is humble yet exalted, the slave and the master, the soldier and the king, the one who has authority over the dead and the living? You were nailed to the cross and placed in the grave, and now you have become free and have destroyed all our power. Are you then Jesus, whom the chief ruler Satan told us is about to inherit the entire earth through the cross and death?"

16. See Ps. 24:7.
17. See Isa. 45:1–2; Ps. 106:16.
18. Isa. 26:19.
19. See Isa. 25:8; Hos. 13:14; 1 Cor. 15:55.
20. Ps. 24:8.

2 Then the King of glory seized the chief ruler, Satan, by the head and handed him over to the angels, and said, "Bind his hands, feet, neck, and mouth with iron." Then he handed him over to Hades and said, "Take him and hold him fast until my second coming."

23

1 Hades took Satan and said to him, "O Beelzeboul, heir of fire and torment, enemy of the saints, why were you compelled to arrange for the King of glory to be crucified, so that he could come and strip us of our power? Turn and see: none of the dead is left in me. But everything you gained through the tree of knowledge you have lost through the tree of the cross. All your joy has turned to grief. Wanting to kill the King of glory, you have killed yourself. For since I have received you to hold you fast, you will learn by experience all the evil things I am about to do to you. O chief devil, the beginning of death, the root of sin, the goal of all evil, what evil did you find against Jesus that moved you to destroy him? How could you dare to do such an evil thing? How could you think to bring such a man in this darkness, through whom you have been deprived of all those who have died since the beginning?"

The Release of the Captives in Hades

24

1 While Hades was talking with Satan in this way, the King of glory stretched out his right hand to grasp and raise up Adam, the father of all. Then he also turned to the others and said, "Come with me all you who experienced death through the tree that this one touched; for now see, I am raising all of you up through the tree of the cross." After saying this, he sent all of them out; and the father of all, Adam, appeared, filled with joy, and said, "I thank your magnificence, O Lord, because you led me forth from the lowest depths of Hades."[21] So too all the prophets and saints said, "We give you thanks, O Christ, Savior of the world, because you led our lives forth from corruption."[22]

2 When they said these things, the Savior blessed Adam by making the sign of the cross on his forehead. He then did the same for all the patriarchs, prophets, martyrs, and ancestors; then taking them he sprang up from Hades. And as he went, the holy fathers followed him singing a hymn, saying "Blessed is the one who comes in the name of the Lord. Hallelujah! To him be the glory of all the saints."[23]

21. See Ps. 86:13.
22. See Ps. 16:10.
23. See Pss. 118:26; 149:9.

The Saints Arrive in Paradise
25

And then, going into paradise, while holding the father of all, Adam, by the hand, he delivered him over to the archangel Michael, along with all the righteous. While they were entering the door of paradise, two elderly people met them. The holy fathers said to them, "Who are you, who have not seen death and have not descended into Hades, but live in your bodies and souls in paradise?" One of them answered, "I am Enoch, the one who was pleasing to God, and I was transported here by him. And this is Elijah the Thesbite. We will continue to live until the completion of the age. Then we will be sent by God to oppose the Antichrist, and be killed by him. Then after three days we will arise and be snatched up in the clouds for a meeting with the Lord."[24]

26

While they were saying these things, another, humble person came, bearing a cross on his shoulders. The holy fathers said to him, "Who are you, who has the appearance of a robber; and what is the cross you are carrying on your shoulders?" That one answered, "Just as you have said, I was a robber and thief in the world, and for this reason the Jews seized me and handed me over to death on a cross, along with our Lord Jesus Christ. And so, while he was hanging on the cross, I saw the signs that happened and believed in him; and I urged him, saying, 'Lord, when you rule as king, do not forget me.' And he immediately replied, 'Truly, truly I say to you today, you will be with me in paradise.'[25] And so, bearing my cross I came into paradise, and when I found the archangel Michael I said to him, 'Our Lord Jesus, who has been crucified, sent me here. Lead me, therefore, to the gate of Eden.' When the flaming sword saw the sign of the cross, it opened up for me, and I entered. Then the archangel said to me, 'Stay here for a little while, because the forefather of the human race, Adam, is coming as well, along with the righteous, that they too might enter in.' And now when I saw you I came to meet you."

When the saints heard these words they all cried out with a loud voice, "Great is our Lord, and magnificent is his strength."

The Sons of Simeon
27

We saw and heard all these things, we two brothers. We also were sent by the archangel Michael and were appointed to proclaim the resurrection of the Lord, but first to go to the Jordan to be baptized. We went there and were baptized along

24. See Rev. 11:3–14; 1 Thess. 4:17.
25. See Luke 23:42–43.

with others who had been raised from the dead. Then also we came to Jerusalem and completed the Passover of the resurrection. But since we are not long able to tarry here long, we are leaving. May the love of God the Father and the grace of our Lord Jesus Christ and the communion of the Holy Spirit be with all of you.[26]

When they wrote these things and sealed the books, they gave half to the chief priests and half to Joseph and Nicodemus. They then immediately became invisible, to the glory of our Lord Jesus Christ. Amen.

26. See 2 Cor. 13:13.

29

The Report of Pontius Pilate

(Anaphora Pilati)

The "Report" of Pontius Pilate to the Emperor Tiberius (the "Anaphora Pilati") relates the events of Jesus' trial, death, and resurrection from the perspective of the Roman governor. We learn that despite his many divine deeds, Jesus was condemned by the Jews, who compelled Pilate to have him crucified. But in the presence of many supernatural signs, Jesus was raised from the dead, leading to the damnation of his Jewish opponents. The obvious motives behind the account are to celebrate Jesus' miraculous character, to exonerate Pilate for his death, and in so doing to inculpate the Jews.

The first half of the document is largely devoted to an account, delivered by Pilate himself, of the wondrous deeds Jesus performed during his public ministry. These should have convinced anyone with eyes to see and ears to hear of Jesus' divine character. But the "whole multitude of the Jews" was hardened to these signs, and so they turned Jesus over to Pilate without being able to "convict him of a single crime." The earthly deeds of Jesus are surpassed only by the miracles that transpired at his death and resurrection, which take up most of the second half of the narrative (there is only a terse account of the trial and crucifixion themselves). Some of the tales scattered throughout the text are summaries of biblical narratives; others provide creative expansions: Lazarus, for example, came forth from the grave after he "was already undergoing corruption by the worms that had sprouted from his ulcers."

Tischendorf presented two different forms of the Greek text, each based on five manuscripts, ranging in date from the twelfth to the fifteenth centuries. His "B" text is the more coherent and interesting of the two, with fewer secondary accretions. It is the one translated here. A third form of the text was discovered by Abbott in a very late (eighteenth-century) manuscript. This appears to be a still later version that supplements the accounts of the earlier ones, especially by detailing the gory deaths of Jesus' Jewish opponents.

It is impossible to date the Report with any confidence. Some scholars have seen it as an expansion of the Letter of Pilate to Claudius (see introduction there). Already by the end of the second century some such letter was thought to exist, as evidenced in Tertullian's *Apology*: "Pilate, who was himself already a Christian with respect to his most innermost conviction, made a report of everything that happened to Christ for Tiberius, the emperor at the time" (*Apol.* 21.24). Still, it is doubtful that the surviving Report is the one referred to by Tertullian—if in fact he really knew of an actual document. In the form presented here, the Report may well derive from a later period, possibly the fourth or fifth century.

Bibliography

Abbott, G. F. "The Report and Death of Pilate," *JTS* 4 (1903:) 83–86.

Elliott, J. K. *Apocryphal New Testament*. Oxford: Clarendon, 1993; pp. 211–12.

Scheidweiler, F. "The Gospel of Nicodemus / Acts of Pilate and Christ's Descent into Hell," in *New Testament Apocrypha*, ed. W. Schneemelcher; trans. R. McL. Wilson. Louisville: Westminster/John Knox, 1991; vol. 1, pp. 530–31.

von Tischendorf, C. *Evangelia Apocrypha*. Leipzig: H. Mendelssohn, 1853 (2nd ed. 1876); pp. lxxvii-lxxviii; 443–49.

The Report of Pontius Pilate Governor of Judea, Sent to Tiberius Caesar in Rome (Anaphora Pilati)

To the most excellent, revered, awe-inspiring, and divine Emperor, from Pontius Pilate, who administers the rule in the East.

(1) Although I have been constrained by great trembling and fear, most excellent king, I have undertaken to reveal to your piety, through this my writing, the present state of affairs, as their outcome has shown. According to your most gentle directives, O master, I was administering my province, which includes one of the cities of the East, called Jerusalem, where the temple of the Jewish people is built. The entire multitude of the Jews gathered together and handed over to me a certain man named Jesus, bringing endless charges against him. They were not able to convict him of a single crime. But they held one false teaching against him: he claimed that the Sabbath day was not a proper rest for them.

The Miracles of Jesus

Now that man performed many healings as well as good works. He made the blind see, he cleansed lepers, he raised the dead, he healed paralytics—who were not able to move at all, having only the their voice and their bones intact. But he gave them the power both to walk and to run, relying on his word alone. He did an even more powerful deed, which not even our own gods can do. He raised from the dead a certain man named Lazarus, who had been dead for four days. It was by his word alone that he commanded the dead man to be raised, even though his body was already undergoing corruption by the worms that had sprouted from his ulcers. And he commanded that stinking body lying in the grave to move quickly; and it came forth from the tomb as if from a bridal chamber, filled with the powerful smell of perfume.[1]

(2) And there were others who were mercilessly possessed by demons, who made their homes in wilderness areas and ate the flesh of their own limbs, living with reptiles and the wild beasts. These he restored to their own homes, as city-dwellers; and through a word he made them reasonable, and those who had been troubled by unclean spirits he turned into intelligent and honorable people; and he cast the demons in them into a herd of swine, and drowned them in the sea.[2]

1. See John 11:1–44.
2. See Matt. 8:28–34; Mark 5:1–20; Luke 8:26–39.

(3) And there was another man who had a withered hand; he lived in pain, with not even half of his body healthy; but he restored him to health with a word alone.[3]

(4) There was also a woman who had experienced a flow of blood for many years; this discharge of blood was so severe that her entire skeletal frame was visible and was as transparent as glass. No doctor could heal her; she was written off as a hopeless case. For she indeed had no hope of finding a cure. But once Jesus was passing by she touched the hem of his garments from behind, and at that very instant the vigor of her body was restored, and she became well, as if she had nothing wrong with her. And she began to run at full speed back to her city, Paneas.[4]

Jesus' Trial and Crucifixion

(5) So these are the things that have happened. But the Jews informed me that Jesus accomplished these deeds on the Sabbath. For my part, I know that the gods we worship have never performed such astounding feats as his.

(6) Still, Herod, Archelaus, Philip, Annas, and Caiaphas, along with all the people, handed this man over to me for questioning. And because many stirred up a rebellion against me, I ordered him to be crucified.

(7) But when he was crucified, a darkness came over all the earth; the sun was completely hidden from view and the vault of the sky was darkened, even though it was day, so that the stars appeared, even though their brilliance was obscured. I am sure that even you were not unaware of this, O pious one, because throughout the world people lit lamps from noon until evening. The moon appeared as blood and it did not shine all night long, even though it was completely full. The stars and the Orion were in mourning over the Jews, because of the lawless deed they had done.

The Miracles at the Resurrection

(8) Then on the first day of the week, around three in the morning, the sun appeared, shining like never before, and the entire sky was brightened. Several exalted men appeared in the air, like lightning that strikes in winter, wearing dazzling garments full of indescribable glory; and a multitude of angels without number cried out and said, "Glory be to God in the highest, and on earth peace and good will among all.[5] Come up from Hades, you who have been enslaved in

3. See Matt. 12:9–14; Mark 3:1–6; Luke 6:6–11.
4. See Matt. 9:20–22; Mark 5:24–34; Luke 8:42–48.
5. See Luke 2:14.

the nether world of Hades." And at the sound of their voice, all the mountains and hills were shaken and the rocks were split apart and great chasms formed in the earth, so that even the realms of the abyss could be seen.[6]

(9) At that fearful moment there appeared the dead who had been raised,[7] as the Jews themselves observed, saying "We have seen Abraham, Isaac, Jacob, and the twelve patriarchs, who died more than two thousand five hundred years ago. And we clearly saw Noah in the body." And the entire multitude walked and sang a hymn to God with a great voice: "The one who is risen from the dead, the Lord our God, has made all the dead alive; despoiling Hades, he has put it to death."

(10) The light did not cease that entire night, O King, my master. And many of the Jews died, being engulfed and swallowed up in the chasms in that night, so that their bodies could no longer be found. I mean to say that those Jews who spoke against Jesus suffered. But one synagogue was left in Jerusalem, since all the synagogues that opposed Jesus were engulfed.

(11) Paralyzed with fear and overwhelmed with trembling, at that very hour I ordered the things done by all of them to be recorded, and have reported them to your Majesty.

6. See Matt. 27:51.
7. See Matt. 27:52.

30

The Handing Over of Pilate

(Paradosis Pilati)

"The Handing Over of Pilate" is a fictitious account of Pilate's being recalled to Rome and censured by the Emperor Tiberius for his role in having the divine man, Jesus, crucified. Pilate pays the ultimate price for his heinous behavior by being beheaded—but only after he has repented of his deed and turned to Christ for salvation.

The narrative is closely related to the "Report of Pontius Pilate": it refers back to the account, given there, of the darkness and earthquake at Jesus' crucifixion; the same five Jewish leaders are named as culpable in Jesus' death; and the emperor refers to the "report" itself, when he speaks of Jesus as "one who was so righteous and did such good signs, as you yourself indicated in your report" (= anaphora—the title of the "Report"). The two documents are stylistically different, however, and were probably written by different authors.

The Handing Over is closely tied to other Pilate literature as well. The aim is to magnify the character of Christ and to malign the Jews responsible for his death. As in the Acts of Pilate (the Gospel of Nicodemus), Jesus is revered by Roman divinities: here it is not the standards bearing the image of the divine Caesar that bow down to him; it is the gods in the temple of Caesar who fall at the mention of his name, turning to dust.

Ultimately it is not Pilate but the hateful Jews who bear ultimate responsibility for Jesus' death. Both Pilate and his wife become believers. Traditions of Pilate's conversion were already in circulation by the late second century, as evidenced in the *Apology* of Tertullian, who indicates that "Pilate, who was already a Christian with respect to his most inner conviction, made a report of everything that happened . . ." (*Apol.* 21.24). This reverence for Pilate could be found in various churches of the East; in the Coptic church Pilate was eventually recognized as a Christian saint. The "Handing Over of Pilate" seems to be leaning in that direction, as Pilate hears a voice from heaven: "All the races and families of the nations will bless you, because under your rule everything spoken about me through the prophets was fulfilled. You yourself will appear as my witness at my second coming, when I judge the twelve tribes of Israel and those who do not confess my name." At Pilate's death an angel receives his head, presumably to carry it up into heaven.

On these grounds it may be that the text was written somewhere in the eastern part of the empire. As with so much apocryphal literature, the text is riddled with historical problems (not just Pilate's alleged conversion): the author, for example, appears to confuse the destruction of Jerusalem under Titus in 70 CE with a (nonexistent) decree from Tiberius forty years earlier, allegedly ordering the governor of Syria to lay the nation waste.

The following translation is of the Greek text found in Tischendorf's edition, which is based on five manuscripts, all of which also contain an account of the Report. The earliest of these manuscripts is from the twelfth century. Like the Report, this account may have originated sometime in the fourth or fifth century.

Bibliography

Elliott, J. K. *Apocryphal New Testament*. Oxford: Clarendon, 1993; pp. 208–9.
von Tischendorf, C. *Evangelia Apocrypha*. Leipzig: H. Mendelssohn, 1853 (2nd ed. 1876); pp. lxxviii–lxxix; 449–55.

The Handing Over of Pilate (Paradosis Pilati)

(1) When the letter arrived in the city of Rome and was read to Caesar, with a large crowd standing by, everyone became amazed that the darkness and the earthquake had struck the whole world because of the lawless deed of Pilate. Caesar was filled with anger and sent soldiers with orders to bring Pilate as a prisoner.

(2) When Pilate was brought to the city of Rome and Caesar heard that he was there, he sat in the temple of the gods before the entire senate, with all the people and all the multitude of his armed forces, and he ordered Pilate to stand in the entrance. Caesar then said to him, "How could you dare to do such things, you most impious man, after seeing such great signs accompanying that man? By daring to do this wicked deed you have destroyed the entire world."

(3) Pilate replied, "Sovereign King, I am innocent of these things; it is the multitude of the Jews who are reckless and guilty." Caesar asked, "Who are they?" Pilate said, "Herod, Archelaus, Philip, Annas, and Caiaphas, and the entire multitude of the Jews." Caesar said, "Why did you do what they wanted?" Pilate replied, "Their nation is rebellious and unruly, and refuses to be subject to your power." Caesar said, "The moment they handed him over to you, you should have kept him safe and sent him on to me, instead of being persuaded by them to crucify such a righteous man, who also did such good signs, as you yourself indicated in your report. For it was clear from such signs that Jesus was the Christ, the King of the Jews."

(4) When Caesar said these things and spoke the name of Christ, the entire multitude of the gods fell down and turned to dust, where Caesar was sitting with the senate. And all the people who were standing there near Caesar were shaking because of the word he spoke and the falling of their gods, so that each one went home overtaken by fear, amazed at what had happened. Caesar ordered Pilate to be kept securely under guard, so that he could learn the truth about Jesus.

(5) On the next day when Caesar sat in the capitol with the entire senate, he again tried to question Pilate. Caesar said, "Speak the truth, you impious man; for through your profane act against Jesus, even here your wicked deed was revealed, as the gods were cast down. And so, speak: who is that one who was crucified, that his name has destroyed all the gods?" Pilate said, "Yes indeed, the accounts about him are true. For I myself was persuaded by his works that he is greater than all the gods we worship." Caesar replied, "Then why did you perform such an audacious act against him, if you knew who he was? Or were you indeed plotting to harm my kingdom?" But Pilate replied, "I did this because of the anarchy and rebelliousness of the lawless and godless Jews."

(6) Filled with anger, Caesar took council with the entire senate and all his armed forces and he ordered a decree to be written against the Jews, as follows: "To Licianus, who rules supreme in the eastern region, greetings. I have learned of the rash and lawless deed performed recently by the inhabitants of Jerusalem and the surrounding cities of the Judeans, how they compelled Pilate to crucify a certain god, who was called Jesus. Through this sinful act of theirs, the world was darkened and dragged towards its destruction. Seek, therefore, to go there in haste with a large army and take them captive, authorized with this decree. Be obedient and move against them; send them into dispersion and enslave them among all the nations. Banish them from all of Judea and make their nation of no account, so that it can no longer be seen at all, since it is so full of wickedness."

(7) When this decree arrived in the eastern region, Licianus obeyed it out of fear and laid waste the entire nation of the Jews. And he took those who survived in Judea and sent them into dispersion among the nations, to serve as slaves. Everything Licianus did against the Jews in the eastern region was made known to Caesar, and it pleased him.

(8) Once again Caesar decided to interrogate Pilate; and he ordered a commander named Albius to behead him, saying, "Just as this one laid hands on the righteous man named Christ, so too he will fall and miss any chance of deliverance."

(9) When Pilate went off to the place of execution, he began to pray silently, "Lord, do not destroy me with the wicked Hebrews; for I could not have lifted my hand against you if it were not for the nation of godless Jews, as they were starting a rebellion against me. But you know that I acted out of ignorance. Do not, therefore, destroy me for this sin I committed, and remember no wickedness against me, Lord, or against your slave Procla who is standing with me here in this the hour of my death. For you appointed her to prophecy that you were to be nailed to a cross. Do not hold her, too, accountable for my sin, but forgive us both, and number us among your righteous ones."

(10) And behold! When Pilate finished his prayer, a voice came from heaven: "All the races and families of the gentiles will bless you, because under your rule everything spoken about me by the prophets was fulfilled. You yourself will appear as my witness at my second coming, when I shall judge the twelve tribes of Israel and those who do not confess my name." Then the executioner[1] severed Pilate's head, and behold! An angel of the Lord took it. When Procla his wife saw the angel coming and taking his head, she was filled with joy and immediately gave up her spirit. And she was buried with her husband.

1. Or: commander; literally: prefect.

31

The Letter of Pilate to Claudius

The letter allegedly written by Pontius Pilate to the emperor Claudius comes to us in several textual forms. A Latin version accompanies the Latin accounts of the Descent to Hades from the Acts of Pilate/Gospel of Nicodemus. In Greek it is quoted in Pseudo-Marcellus, *The Passion of Peter and Paul.* We have it in yet different forms in Armenian and Syriac. The form presented here comes to us from the fifth-century *Acts of Peter and Paul* (chs. 40–42). It has probably been incorporated from an earlier source.

The letter is cited in the following context in the *Acts*. Years after Jesus' death, the apostle Simon Peter and the heretic Simon Magus appear before the Emperor Nero. When the emperor hears about Christ, he asks Peter how he can learn more about him. Peter tells him to retrieve the letter sent by Pilate years earlier to the emperor Claudius, and to have it read out. He does so, and then the text of the letter is reproduced.

It is not clear what to make of the anachronistic reference to Claudius as the emperor at the time of Jesus' death (rather than Tiberius; Claudius would not assume the throne for another decade). The author of this letter, living so long after the fact, may simply not have known the facts of Roman imperial history. It is also possible that this was originally a letter that Pilate allegedly sent to Tiberius (comparable to the "Report of Pilate"), and that a later author/editor, possibly even the author of the fifth-century *Acts* in which the text is found, altered the name of the addressee (for unknown reasons). In the opinion of Dubois and Gounelle, the letter was originally composed as part of the (Latin) "Passion of Peter and Paul"; in that context—set in the time of Nero—the letter was more naturally placed in the reign of Nero's immediate predecessor, Claudius. In any event, we do learn of a letter sent by Pilate to the reigning emperor explaining Jesus' death already in Tertullian (*Apology* 21.24) and later in Eusebius (*Church History* 2.2). The letter we now have appears to be later than Tertullian. Possibly it was composed because some such letter was believed once to have existed.

The themes of this letter resonate with other works found in the Pilate cycle. Pilate himself was not responsible for Jesus' death; the stiff-necked and godless

Jews were. In this instance the theme is heightened: Pilate does not crucify Jesus to placate the Jewish leaders; they do the foul deed themselves. At the same time, the account differentiates between the Jewish people, who believed in Jesus, and the Jewish leaders, who hated him.

The letter may have been written any time between Tertullian at the very end of the second century and its incorporation in the fifth-century *Acts of Peter and Paul.* If it served as the basis for the "Report of Pilate," as some scholars have contended, then it may be situated in an earlier part of this period.

We have translated the text from the edition of the Acts of Peter and Paul by Lipsius-Bonnet.

Bibliography

Elliott, J. K. *Apocryphal New Testament.* Oxford: Clarendon, 1993; pp. 205–6.

Dubois, J.-D., and R. Gounelle. "Lettre de Pilate à l'empereur Claude," in *Écrits apocryphes chrétiens,* vol. 2, ed. P. Geoltrain and J-D. Kaestli. Paris: Gallimard, 2005; pp. 357–63.

Lipsius, R. A., and M. Bonnet. *Acta Apostolorum Apocrypha.* Leipzig: H. Mendelssohn, 1891; vol. 1, pp. 196–97.

Scheidweiler, F. "The Gospel of Nicodemus / Acts of Pilate and Christ's Descent into Hell," in *New Testament Apocrypha,* ed. W. Schneemelcher; trans. R. McL. Wilson. Louisville: Westminster/John Knox, 1991; vol. 1, pp. 530–31.

Letter of Pilate to Claudius

Pontius Pilate, to Claudius. Greetings.

I myself have uncovered what has just now happened. For the Jews, out of envy, have brought vengeance both on themselves and on those who come after them by their terrible acts of judgment. Indeed their ancestors had the promises that God would send them his holy one from heaven, who would rightly be called their king; he promised to send this one to earth through a virgin. And now this one has come to Judea, during my governorship.

They saw that he brought light to the eyes of the blind, that he cleansed lepers, healed paralytics, drove demons out from people, raised the dead, rebuked the winds, walked on the waves of the sea, and did many other miracles; and that all the people of the Jews called him the son of God. For this reason the chief priests were moved by envy to seize him and deliver him over to me; and they told lie upon lie, saying that he was a magician and that he acted contrary to their law.

Since I believed their accusations, I delivered him over to their will, after having him flogged. And they crucified him. Then when he was buried they set guards over him.[1] But while my soldiers were guarding him, on the third day he arose. The wickedness of the Jews was set aflame by this, so that they gave money to the soldiers, telling them to say that his disciples had stolen his body.[2] But when they took the money they were not able to keep what had happened a secret. For they themselves testified that they saw him raised, and that they had taken money from the Jews. That is why I have reported these things to your Majesty, in case someone else might lie about it and you be led to believe the false reports told by the Jews.

1. See Matt. 27:62–66.
2. See Matt. 28:11–15.

32

The Letter of Herod to Pilate

This apocryphon is allegedly a letter written by Herod Antipas—known from the Gospels for having beheaded John the Baptist—to Pontius Pilate, soon after the death of Jesus. In it Herod affirms the divine principle that "each will receive his due" for the evil deeds he has done. In his case, his actions toward John are reciprocated in the grisly death of his stepdaughter, Herodia, who literally loses her head in a flood. Herod too is faced with God's judgment; as he writes, "already worms are coming up from my mouth." Here the author of the text appears to confuse Herod the tetrarch of Galilee with Herod Agrippa, who according to the book of Acts was eaten by worms and died (Acts 12). So too, the soldier Longinus, who stuck a spear in Jesus' side on the cross, meets a grisly fate, condemned to be torn apart by a lion every night, only to have his body restored during the day in preparation for another night's agony—much as Prometheus of Greek legend.

There are clear connections between this text and the "Gospel of Nicodemus," the "Report of Pilate," and the "Taking Up of Pilate": here the Roman governor Pilate is portrayed in a positive light, representing the gentiles who will receive the future kingdom, as opposed to the Jews, represented by Herod, who have been rejected by God.

The earliest attestation of the letter is a Syriac version of the sixth or seventh century, although the original language was Greek. The Greek text, which we have translated here, was published by M. R. James on the basis of a fifteenth-century manuscript from Paris, which gives as well the Report and the Taking Up of Pilate.

Bibliography

Elliott, J. K. *Apocryphal New Testament.* Oxford: Clarendon, 1993; pp. 222–23.

James, M. R. *Apocrypha Anecdota.* Cambridge: Cambridge University Press, 1893; vol. 2, pp. xlv–xlviii, 66–70.

The Letter of Herod to Pilate

Herod, tetrarch of Galilee, to Pontius Pilate, governor of Judea, greetings.

I am in profound grief, as the divine scriptures say, over the things I write you. Surely you too will grieve when you hear what has happened. My beloved daughter Herodia was killed while playing by the water, when it flooded over the bank of the river. For suddenly the water rose up to her neck, and her mother grabbed her by the head to keep her from being swept away by the water. The head of the child was severed, so that my wife held only the head, while the water took the rest of her body. And so my wife held her head on her knees, weeping, and all my household fell into incessant grief.

I too am enmeshed in many misfortunes, having heard about Jesus that you have destroyed him—when I was wishing to come and see him alone, and to fall before him, and to hear a word from him, since I did so many evil things against him and against John the Baptist. And see, I am receiving my just deserts. For my father created a great outpouring of blood on the earth from other people's children because of Jesus.[1] Then I myself cut off the head of John, who baptized him.[2] Righteous are the judgments of God, for each will be repaid in accordance with his thoughts. Since therefore you are able to see the man Jesus again, this time exert yourself for me and speak a word with him as my representative. For the kingdom has been given to you gentiles, according to the prophets and Christ. Even my son Lesbonaks is near the end of his life in agony, overcome with a wasting illness now for many days. I myself am gravely ill, beset by dropsy, so that worms are coming out of my mouth. Even my wife has become blind in her left eye, on account of the grief that has befallen my household. Righteous are the judgments of God, for which we have mocked the righteous eye.

There is no peace for the priests, says the Lord. Death will soon overtake the priests and the ruling council of the children of Israel, because they unjustly laid hands on the righteous Jesus. These things will be fulfilled in the culmination of the age, so that the gentiles will become heirs of the kingdom of God, but the children of light will be cast out, because we did not keep the commandments of the Lord nor those of his Son.

So now, gird your loins. Take up your righteousness night and day, remembering Jesus, with your wife. And the kingdom will be yours. For we have treated the righteous one with disrespect.

But if I can make a petition, O Pilate, since we have been contemporaries, bury the members of my household with care. For it is better for us to be buried

1. See Matt. 2:16–18.

2. See Matt. 14:1–12; Mark 6:14–29; Luke 3:19–20; 9:7–9.

by you than by the priests, who will soon fall under the judgment of Jesus, in accordance with the Scriptures. Farewell. I am sending you my wife's earrings and my own signet ring. If you are ever remembered in the last day, you will give them back to me. For already worms are coming up from my mouth and I am receiving my judgment in this world.[3] But I fear the judgment that will be there even more. For the judgments of the living God are about to come upon me in double measure. For we flee in the present life, being here only for a short time. But in that place is eternal judgment and retribution for the things we have done.

Now concerning Longinus, the one who stuck the side of Jesus with a spear[4]: at this hour an angel of the Lord took him by his head and carried him across the Jordan to a wilderness place, and brought him further into the cave, and stretched him out on the ground in full view. And a lion was assigned to come forth at night and to destroy his body until dawn. The lion went away at dawn, and his body again became whole. This is the punishment he receives until the second coming of the Lord Jesus Christ.

These records were set down by Nicodemus and Joseph of Arimathea, the one who asked for the body of the Lord Jesus Christ. To him be the glory and the power, together with the Father, and the Son, and the Holy Spirit, now and always, forever and ever. Amen.

3. See Acts 12:20–23. The author of this letter apparently confuses Herod Antipas (tetrarch of Galilee in the days of Jesus) with Herod Agrippa, referred to in Acts.

4. See John 19:34.

33

The Letter of Pilate to Herod

This fictitious letter from Pontius Pilate, governor of Judea, to Herod, tetrarch of Galilee, is principally concerned with showing how he, Pilate, along with his wife Procla and the soldier Longinus, who was responsible for stabbing Jesus with a spear on the cross, all converted to become followers of Christ after the resurrection. One might expect the letter to have close connections with the Letter of Herod to Pilate (see preceding text), but in fact, despite the titles and the appearance of some of the same names (Herod, Pilate, Longinus), the letters have almost nothing to do with one another and stand at odds in their views. Nowhere is this more clear than in their respective accounts of Longinus. In the Letter from Herod, he is subject to cruel and lasting torment as an unbeliever; in the Letter from Pilate he converts to become a blessed devotee of Jesus after being confronted by him, personally, after the resurrection. It may be that the two letters were combined in the textual tradition simply because of their comparable titles. In any event, this text shares more with the "Handing Over of Pilate," where also Pilate and his wife, Procla, are portrayed as Christian converts—a theme, at least with respect to Pilate, that can be found in Christian sources as early as Tertullian (*Apology* 21.24).

The text for our translation is provided by M. R. James, on the basis of the same fifteenth-century manuscript that he used for the Letter of Herod to Pilate. It too is found in a Syriac manuscript of the fifth or sixth century; James hypothesized that both letters were composed, originally, some two hundred years before that.

Bibliography

Elliott, J. K. *Apocryphal New Testament.* Oxford: Clarendon, 1993; pp. 222–23.

James, M. R. *Apocrypha Anecdota.* Cambridge: Cambridge University Press, 1893; vol. 2, pp. xlv–xlviii, 66–70.

The Letter of Pilate to Herod

Pilate, governor of Jerusalem, to Herod the tetrarch, greetings.

Persuaded by you, I did a terrible thing on that day the Jews brought to me Jesus, the one who is called the Christ. They, along with the centurion, reported to me how he was crucified and arose from the dead on the third day. But I myself was persuaded to send messengers to Galilee. They saw him in the same flesh and in the same appearance; and he revealed himself in the same voice and with the same teachings to more than five hundred godly people,[1] who as witnesses have brought forth their testimony about this, expressing no doubts in the matter but preaching extensively the resurrection and declaring the eternal kingdom—so that the heavens and the earth appeared to rejoice at his holy teachings.

My own wife Procla came to believe because of the visions in which he appeared to her when I was about to hand him over to be crucified because of your advice. She left me, taking ten soldiers with her and Longinus, the faithful centurion, and went to catch sight of him—as if going to a great spectacle. They saw him seated in a plowed field, with a great crowd surrounding him; he was teaching the mighty works of the Father, so that all were amazed and astounded at how this one who suffered and was crucified was raised from the dead.

While everyone was watching and observing him, he became aware of their presence and spoke to them: "Do you still not believe in me, Procla and Longinus? Are you not the one who watched over my suffering and tomb? And you, woman, did you send a message to your husband about me?[2]

. . .[3] the covenant of God that the Father made. Through my own death, which you have perceived, I will bring to life every fleshly being that has perished—I the one who was lifted up and suffered many things. Now, therefore, listen: every fleshly being who believes in God the Father and in me will not perish. For I have set loose the birth pangs of death and have slain the many-headed dragon. In my second coming that is about to occur, everyone will be raised in the body and mind that they now have, to praise my Father—I who was crucified under Pontius Pilate."

When he said these things, my wife Procla heard them, along with the centurian Longinus, who had been entrusted to watch over the suffering of Jesus, and the soldiers who accompanied them. They all came, weeping and grieving, to proclaim these things to me. Once I heard them, I proclaimed them to my chief officers and fellow soldiers. And they were grieving and weeping throughout the day, trying to explain away the evil they had done to him. I myself was wrapped up in the pain of my wife, while we fasted, cast on the ground. . . .[4]

1. See 1 Cor. 15:6.

2. See Matt. 27:19.

3. There is no lacuna here in the manuscript, but some amount of text has obviously dropped out.

4. A significant portion of the text appears to be missing here (cf. the Syriac version), although there is no lacuna in the manuscript.

And the Lord came and raised my wife and me from the ground. Gazing at him I saw his body, still with its scars. He placed his hands on my shoulders and said, "All generations and nations will bless you, because in your time the son of man died and arose, and he will ascend into heaven and sit in the highest places. And all the tribes of earth will know that I am the one who is about to judge the living and the dead, in the final day."

34

The Letter of Tiberius to Pilate

This letter was allegedly written by the emperor Tiberius to Pontius Pilate in response to an earlier communication by the governor of Judea. But Pilate's earlier letter cannot be identified with any of the documents that we now have: it cannot have been the "Report of Pilate," since, unlike the present document, that latter portrays Pilate in a favorable light. Moreover, the "Handing Over of Pilate," closely connected with the "Report," has an entirely different account of Pilate's death from the one presented here. Nor do any of the other writings connected with Pilate answer to this one, as here Tiberius refers to Pilate's claim that Christ "is greater even than the gods we worship." This is comparable to a line found in the "Handing Over of Pilate," but there the statement is delivered at Pilate's trial, not in his letter. And no such line is found in the Letter of Pilate to Claudius, which may, in an earlier form, have been addressed to Tiberius (there is, however, a similar line in the "Report"). As a result, we may never know whether there was a companion letter to this reply of Tiberius or if the allusion is simply part of the fictional framework of the reply.[1]

As it stands, the current document is more than simply a letter: it is also a description of what happened in its aftermath: the grisly deaths of all those responsible for the death of Jesus. In the letter itself the emperor lashes out at Pilate for his impious act: "Even if you did not receive him as a god, at least you should have sympathized with him as a physician." He sends, then, for Pilate and the others who were responsible for the heinous crime of Christ's death: Archelaus, Philip, Annas, Caiaphas, and all the leaders of the Jews (not Herod, however, as in the "Report of Pilate"). Moreover, Tiberius orders the devastation of Judea by his courier Rahab, who carries out the order with a vengeance: all other Jewish men are slaughtered (not exiled, as in the "Handing Over of Pilate") and the women raped.

1. There is a Latin letter of Pilate to Tiberius that Tischendorf, following Fabricius, prints from late manuscripts; it may be that this apocryphon was created to fill the gap created by the reference to an earlier correspondence in the letter of Tiberius to Pilate.

The account concludes with descriptions of the vile deaths of the opponents of God, including Pilate's own death not by beheading (as in the "Handing Over") but inadvertently by Caesar's own hand.

Since Pilate appears here as a criminal rather than a saint, some scholars (e.g., Elliott) have contended that the book must have been written somewhere in the West rather than the East. The text is not found in Tischendorf, but is provided by M. R. James, based on the earlier editions of A. Birch and F. Fleck. On linguistic grounds, Gounelle thinks it cannot be dated much before the eleventh century.

Bibliography

Elliott, J. K. *Apocryphal New Testament*. Oxford: Clarendon, 1993; pp. 211–12.

Gounelle, R. "Rapport de Pilate, réponse de Tibère à Pilate, comparution de Pilate," in *Écrits apocryphes chrétiens*, vol. 2, ed. P. Geoltrain and J.-D. Kaestli. Paris: Gallimard, 2005; pp. 304–7.

James, M. R. *Apocrypha Anecdota*. Cambridge: Cambridge University Press, 1893; vol. 2, pp. xlix–l; 78–81.

The Letter of Tiberius to Pilate

This is the reply of Caesar Augustus and sent to Pilate Pontius, who holds the rule in the eastern part of the kingdom. He also wrote his judicial decision and sent it with the courier Rahab, to whom he gave two thousand soldiers as well.

"Because you condemned Jesus of Nazareth to a violent death that was completely unjust, and before condemning him to death you handed him over to the insatiably furious Jews, and you showed no sympathy for this righteous man, but dipping your pen you delivered a disastrous judicial decision, and having him flogged you handed him over to be crucified, without cause, and you received gifts for condemning him to death, sympathizing with him in what you said, but in your heart handing him over to the lawless Jews—for all this you will be brought to me as a prisoner to defend yourself and render to me an account of what you have done, on behalf of this one whom you handed over to death without cause. Oh your shamelessness and hardness! When I heard about this in a report, I was moved in my soul and cut to the core. For a certain woman has come to me, calling herself a disciple of this man; she is Mary Magdalene, from whom others testify that he had cast out seven demons.[2] She has testified that this one performed great healings: he made the blind see, the lame walk, and the deaf hear; he cleansed lepers and, to put it simply, as she herself testified, he performed these healings by a word alone.

How could you permit him to be crucified without cause? Even if you did not receive him as a god, at least you should have sympathized with him as a physician. But even from your own treacherous writing that has come to me you have pronounced your penalty, since you write that he is greater even than the gods that we worship. How could you deliver him over to death? But just as you condemned this one unjustly and delivered him to death, I in term will deliver you to death justly. And not only you, but also all your councillors and companions, from whom you received the gifts for his death."

As he gave the letter to the letter carriers, Augustus's judicial sentence was also given them in a written order, that they were to kill the entire race of the Jews with the sword, and that Pilate was to be brought to Rome as a condemned prisoner, along with the leaders of the Jews, those who were then the rulers of the region, Archaelaus, the son of the despised Herod, and his companion Philip, and those who were their chief priests, both Caiaphas and his father-in-law, Annas, and all the leaders of the Jews.

When Rahab went forth with the soldiers, he did as he was commanded, and slew the entire male race of the Jews with the sword, and the gentiles sexually

2. See Luke 8:2; Mark 16:9.

defiled their profane wives; and the loathsome posterity of their father, Satan, came to life and rose up. The courier took Pilate, Archaelaus, and also Philip, Annas, and Caiaphas, and all the leaders of the Jews, and led them as prisoners to Rome. But it came about that while they were passing through a certain island named Crete, Caiaphas was miserably and violently severed from life. When they took him in order to bury him, the ground would not receive him at all, but cast him out. Seeing this, the entire multitude took stones with their own hands and cast them on him, and so buried him. But the others came to anchor near Rome.

Now there was a custom among the ancient rulers that if someone was condemned to death but should happen to see their face, he would be spared from his condemnation. And so Caesar ordered that Pilate not see him, so that he might not be saved from death. Because of this command, they bricked him up in a certain cave, and left him there.

But they rolled Annas up in the skin of an ox, and as the leather dried out under the sun, he was pressed tightly in it, so that his intestines came out through his mouth, and it violently tore away his wretched life. But all the other Jews who were given over to him he delivered to death. They killed these by the sword. But Archelaus, son of the despised Herod, and his companion Philip, he ordered to be impaled.

One day the king went out to hunt and was pursuing a certain deer. The deer came to the opening of the cave and stood there. Now Pilate was about to be killed by the hand of Caesar. That the inevitable might be fulfilled, Pilate moved forward to see the ruler, while the deer was standing in front of him. Caesar placed an arrow on his bow to shoot the deer, and the arrow passed through the opening and killed Pilate.

All who believe in Christ, our true God and savior, give him glory and greatness. For to him is due the glory, honor, and worship, with his Father who is without beginning, and the Spirit who is of his same nature, now and always, even unto the ages. Amen.

35

The Vengeance of the Savior (Vindicta Salvatoris)

The Vengeance of the Savior (Vindicta Salvatoris) is normally included in the Pilate cycle—the Gospels dealing with the fate of Pilate after the crucifixion of Jesus—even though Pilate plays only a minor role in the account. The narrative does tell of his imprisonment and condemnation, but it is more especially concerned with the fate of the Jewish people, who are condemned for their role in the death of Jesus and inflicted with horrible punishments, including the violent destruction of Jerusalem by the Roman rulers Titus and Vespasian (who are not understood to be related; Titus, moreover, is portrayed, anachronistically, as a client king of the emperor Tiberius).

The framework for the story is provided by two accounts of Roman rulers, the king Titus and the emperor Tiberius, who are healed from horrible afflictions by the power of Christ after his death and resurrection (see the Abgar legend). Titus, a king in Libya, north (!) of Judah, learns of the miraculous ministry of Jesus, and of the horrific actions of the Jews against him, from a Roman envoy Nathan, who has just visited Palestine and is now returning to Rome. Titus is deeply moved and offended by what the Jewish people have done in executing their own savior, and he threatens violent reprisals against them. As soon as he utters his dire condemnations he is immediately healed: the cancer that has long disfigured his face falls away and he is restored to pure health. Converted and baptized, he and his colleague Vespasian launch a violent assault on the Jews in their homeland until they destroy Jerusalem and slaughter the opposition. News of the events is taken back to Rome by a special envoy, Volosianus, who brings with him a follower of Christ, Veronica, who has with her an image of Jesus' face on a sacred cloth. Once they arrive in Rome they meet with Tiberius, who is told of Christ's miraculous life and the destruction of his enemies, the Jews. He is then shown the image of Christ's face and as he worships it, he is cleansed of his leprosy. He too then comes to believe in Christ and is baptized, along with his household, bringing the story to an end.

Among the sources that have influenced this narrative are the Acts of Pilate (the Gospel of Nicodemus), the Abgar legend, and an early medieval tale (seventh or eighth century) known as the "The Cure of Tiberius"—the latter of which is taken over and significantly expanded in the Vengeance. Although the earliest manuscript of the Vengeance is from the ninth century, E. von Dobschütz has made a plausible argument that it was composed in the beginning of the eighth century.

The manuscript tradition of the Vengeance is highly complex, and the issues surrounding it have not yet been unraveled. Izydorczyk has identified sixty manuscripts of the Gospel, one third of them also containing the Gospel of Nicodemus. Tischendorf based his edition on two manuscripts, one of the fourteenth and one of the fifteenth century, but noted variations in the tradition supplied by an Old English version based on an earlier form of the text. Since his day the actual manuscript from which this version was made has been discovered and has been analyzed by Cross; it is called the Saint-Omer manuscript (O), of the ninth century. This is the manuscript we have translated here.

Bibliography

Cross, J. E. *Two Old English Apocrypha and Their Manuscript Source: The Gospel of Nicodemus and the Avenging of the Saviour*. Cambridge: Cambridge University Press, 1996.

Tischendorf, C. von. *Evangelia Apocrypha*; reprint edition Hildesheim: Georg Olms, 1966; pp. lxxxii–lxxxiv; 471–86.

von Dobschütz, E. *Christusbilder. Untersuchungen zur christlichen Legende*. TU 18. Leipzig: J. C. Hinrichs, 1899; pp. 214–17, 232–34, 239–40, 276–77.

The Vengeance of the Savior

Here begins the passion of our Lord Jesus Christ, how he suffered in Judea.

Conversion and baptism of Tyrus-Titus

1. In the days of the emperor Tiberius under the tetrarch Pontius Pilate,[1] he was betrayed by the Jews, unbeknownst to Tiberius. In those days, there was a certain man, Tyrus by name,[2] a court official of Tiberius for the kingdom of Aquitania, for the city of Libia called Burdigala;[3] he was ill, having a cancer on his right nostril and his face mangled up to the eye.

2. A certain man whose name was Nathan, son of Naum, left Judea, for he was an Ishmaelite going from land to land, from sea to sea, from the limits of the earth to the edge of the world. He was sent by the emperor Tiberius to bring a tribute to the city of Rome. The emperor Tiberius himself was ill with ulcers, very full of scars, which is the ninth kind of leprosy.[4]

3. And Nathan wanted to go to Rome. The north wind, which is called "auster,"[5] blew and directed his ship, and brought it to the gates of the city of Libia. Tyrus saw him and the ship coming and recognized in amazement that it was from Judea as everyone was saying: "We have never seen something like this, ever!"

4. Tyrus bid him to come to him and asked who he was; and he said: "I am Nathan, son of Nau, from the kingdom of the Greeks,[6] a subject of Pontius Pilate in Judea. I have been sent to Tiberius in the city of Rome to bring his tribute from Judea. A strong wind raged on the sea and turned me to this place, and I do not know where I am."

5. Now Tyrus said to him: "If you had ever been able to find anything, either an ointment or the names of herbs, that would cure the wound on my face, I would deliver you at once before Tiberius."

6. Nathan declared to him with an oath, "My lord, I really cannot find what you request of me. To be sure, had you been in Judea you would have found there

1. The title "tetrarch" is not applicable to Pontius Pilate, who was a governor (ἡγεμών, *praeses*) according to Matt. 27:2 and a prefect according to an inscription discovered in Caesarea. Tischendorf follows the reading in M, *Herode tetrarcha sub Pontio Pilato*, "while Herod was tetrarch under Pontius Pilate."

2. Tyrus's name is changed into Titus, following his baptism in §10.

3. Latin for Bordeaux. The Old English version has "the city called Lybie (Libie, Libia)," possibly Latin for the city of Albi in Southern France.

4. For Tiberius's disease see Tac. *Ann.* 4.57.3, and Suet. *Tib.* 58.3.

5. "(H)auster" is, in fact, the south wind blowing from the shores of Africa.

6. Two manuscripts of the longer version, M and V, have "from the race of I(sh)maelites."

a man, a chosen prophet, whose name is Jesus Christ. Indeed, he shall make his people healed of their sins,[7] who by his word cleansed the leprous, restored sight to the blind, raised the dead,[8] and performed many other signs and miracles in the presence of his disciples which are not written in our book.[9] He raised Lazarus from the tomb on the fourth day;[10] likewise, he raised a dead girl in the house of her father;[11] he mercifully freed in the temple a woman caught in adultery, who was already sentenced to death by stoning.[12] In like manner, he immediately healed another woman suffering from hemorrhages for twelve years, Veronica by name, who came up behind him and touched the fringe of his garment;[13] and with five loaves and two fishes he fed five thousand men.[14]

7. He fulfilled all these and many other things before the passion, when the Jews and the leaders of priests, stirred by envy[15], arrested and flogged him, requesting from Pilate that they might kill him. They then hanged him on the tree and gave him wine mixed with vinegar[16] to drink. But he gave up his spirit on the cross and descended to hell, and freed the saints detained there, and visited and saved the human race. Joseph, a just man, buried his body. And the Jews sent guards to watch lest he rise again.[17] We have seen him and witnessed him, just as he had himself foretold, in that very flesh in which he was born, in which he suffered, in which he was buried, in which he lay two days in the tomb, in which on the third day he rose from the dead as true God and true man, and in which for forty days he appeared to his disciples[18] and then, in our sight, ascended to the heavens with great might and power,[19] saying: 'Men of Galilee, why are you amazed, looking up to heaven? So will he come as you saw him go into heaven.'"[20]

8. Immediately Tyrus and the whole of his entire household believed in Christ, and he said in his own words: "Woe to you Tiberius, covered with ulcers and seized by leprosy for the scandal you caused. For you had sent your

7. See Matt. 1:21.

8. See Matt. 11:5; Luke 7:22.

9. See John 20:30.

10. See John 11:11–17.

11. See Matt. 9:18–19, 23–36; Mark 5:22–24, 38–43; Luke 8:49–56.

12. See John 8:1–11.

13. See Matt. 9:20–22; Mark 5:25–34; Luke 8:43–48; the hemorrhagic woman is also called "Veronica" in the *Gospel of Nicodemus* 6:3.

14. See Matt. 14:13–21; Mark 6:10–44; Luke 9:12–17; John 6:5–13.

15. See Matt. 27:18; Mark 15:10.

16. See Matt. 27:34.

17. See Matt. 27:62–66; 28:11–15.

18. See Acts 1:3.

19. See Acts 1:9.

20. See Acts 1:11, where it was "two men in white robes," and not Jesus, who said these words.

kings[21] into the land of my Lord's birth, who killed the king, the liberator and ruler of all the people, and did not allow him to come from us to cure you from leprosy and us from sores. So if we had been before his face and known him, we would have avenged him with the greatest vengeance, and we would be obliged to kill his enemies and hang their bodies on a dry tree, because they took our Lord, whom our eyes were not worthy to see."

9. As soon as he said this, the sore called "cancer" fell from his face, and his flesh that had been eaten up by it was restored like the flesh of a small boy. And behold, he became healthy and cried out with a loud voice, saying: "Lo, he is the true judge, the great king and the just God, for I have never seen him nor believed, and now I have just heard his name and become healthy." And prostrate on the ground, Tyrus himself prayed to the Lord with tears, saying: "Lord God almighty, king of kings and lord of lords, allow me to go into the land of your nativity to see your enemies and destroy their names and bodies and all that belongs to them, and avenge your death, so that nothing remains of them except what is[22] handed over to me."

10. When he said this, he summoned Nathan and said to him: "In what way did you see those who believed in Christ give baptism? Come and baptize me so that I may believe in all my heart in him whom I never saw and who made me healthy, Jesus Christ, our Lord." Then Nathan baptized him in the name of the Father and of the Son and of the Holy Spirit,[23] and changed his name from Tyrus to Titus, who was surnamed 'pious.' Then Titus sent his messengers to Vespasian to come prepared for the battle.

The Siege and Fall of Jerusalem

11. Vespasian hastened to meet him with seven thousand men. When he had come to the city of Libia, he asked Titus what was the reason he had sent for him. And he said, "Why do you not consider in your heart so that you believe in God the almighty Father, and see how Jesus Christus was born in Judea, in Bethlehem of Judah, the city of David,[24] to save the human race; how the Jews flogged and killed him out of jealousy; how he rose on the third day from the dead, and his disciples saw on that day the very flesh[25] in which he had been before; how, after his resurrection, he appeared to his disciples for forty days; and how afterwards,

21. As the subsequent chapters make it clear (12–17, 19, 29–30), Tiberius's "kings" are Herod, Archelaus, Caiphas, and Pilate.

22. Or, following Cross' conjecture, "except those handed over to me."

23. See Matt. 28:19.

24. See Matt. 2:5–6.

25. Or, following Cross' proposal, "and his disciples saw [Him] in the same flesh . . ."

before their eyes, he ascended to the heavens with great power as true God and true man. And we now wish to become his disciples; let us go and take revenge and destroy his enemies from the land of the living, and let them know that he has no equal on earth."

12. Once the plan was made, they left the city of Libia, which is called Burdigala, and went aboard ship and descended to Jerusalem: they besieged that kingdom and began to destroy them. When the kings of that land heard that this was happening, they were greatly disturbed and frightened to death. King Herod became disturbed, and all Jerusalem with him,[26] and he said to Archelaus, his son:[27] "My son, accept our kingdom, judge over it, and take counsel with other neighboring kings in order to free it from your enemies, for they want to destroy both us and our kingdom." Herod himself broke off his spear, fixed it in the ground, and threw himself over it and died.

13. Archelaus, his son, then came to other kings, and they convened together and shut themselves in Jerusalem with all the nobles who were with them. And they all remained within the city[28] and stayed there for seven years.

14. Titus and Vespasian, in their turn, came up with a wise plan that they might surround the kingdom, and they did so. After eight years had passed, famine came into that land, and they all began to eat the earth for want of bread.[29]

15. The soldiers, therefore, who were from eight regions,[30] made together an ominous decision, saying: "Truly we are going to die; see what God is doing to us. What use is our life? The Romans have come and taken our kingdom, place, and people. Indeed, it is better for us to kill ourselves to prevent them from saying that they killed us and gained a victory over us." Then they pulled out their swords and killed themselves and died, about eleven thousand of them; and their stench rushed into the city.[31]

16. The kings were frightened to death and could in no way escape from the furor of that event. Neither were they able to bury the bodies nor did they throw them outside, saying among themselves, "What should we do?" They groaned among themselves and cried out that, because they had delivered Christ to death, they would also die, and deserved so. "Let us bow our heads and hand over the keys of this city to the Romans because we are soon to die." And they

26. See Matt. 2:3.

27. Anachronisms in the passage are blatant: Herod the Great died in 4 BCE, and his son Archelaus was exiled to Gaul in 7 CE. In M and V, it was Archelaus who, being greatly disturbed, asked his unnamed son to rule the kingdom and thereupon committed suicide.

28. Literally, "nothing at all remained of them except those within the city." For the construction see also *above*, §9.

29. See Josephus, *B.J.* 6.3.

30. M and V have "from four kings."

31. The fall of Jerusalem is confused with that of Massada, on which see Josephus, *B.J.* 6:3.

went out on the walls, saying: "Let us hand over the keys of this city to our lords Titus and to Vespasian, which God has given to you from above. For we knew beforehand that this kingdom was no longer ours, but was given to you through the Messiah, whom you call Christ."

17. Thus they came under the sway of Titus and Vespasian and handed over themselves, as well as all the land of Judea, and said to them, "Judge for us how we ought to die because we delivered Christ to death." When they said this, they seized and bound them. Some of them they stoned and some they hanged on a dry tree, head down; some they speared and others they handed over for sale; and some among them they divided into four parts just as they had done with the tunic of Jesus.[32] And Titus and Vespasian gave to one another, from the Jews who remained, thirty for one denarius, just as they gave thirty silver pieces for Christ,[33] and, taking possession of all their land, they sent out an inquiry as to where they could find a portrait of Christ.

18. They found a woman whose name was Veronica, and found the face of the Lord with her. And they seized Pilate and put him in an iron cage in prison in Damascus, and before the door of the prison they placed as guards four squads of four soldiers.[34]

Tiberius Sends Volusianus to Judea

19. They sent envoys to the emperor Tiberius in the city of Rome to send over Volosianus into Judea and to learn everything that had happened in Judea concerning Jesus, for the emperor had heard none of these things beforehand. Then Tiberius said, "Volosianus, come and take all supplies that are necessary at sea, and go down into Judea and ask of one of the disciples of Jesus, in the name of the Lord his God, to come to me and cure my wounds from which I suffer greatly. Moreover, pass judgment on the kings among them as they also passed judgment on Christ, and destroy them. If indeed you bring here a man who may cure my wounds, I will believe in Jesus, the son of God, and be baptized in his name." Volosianus said to him, "My lord, if I find such a man, what reward should I promise him?" Then Tiberius said, "Thereafter he will be the king of his own land."

20. Then Volosianus went on a one-day journey and, when he arrived at the seaport called Licostratus,[35] he boarded a ship, hoisted the sails with his steersmen, and set the ship on course. After a year and seven days, he descended into Judea and came to Jerusalem. He ordered that everyone who had

32. See John 19:23–24; see Matt. 27:35, Mark 15:24, Luke 23:34.
33. See Matt. 26:14–15.
34. See Acts 12:4.
35. See John 19:13.

known Christ come to him, and he asked them everything that had happened concerning him.

Joseph of Arimathea, Nicodemus, and Simeon Give Testimony on Jesus

21. Joseph, however, came from Arimathea and Nicodemus with him; they told him everything they knew about him. Nicodemus said, "I saw him and I know that he is the savior of the world."[36] Joseph, in his turn, said to him, "I took him down from the cross and placed him in a tomb that I had hewn in the rock,[37] and I guarded him until the third day and bowed my head to see him,[38] and I found nothing of him there. But I saw two angels in white, who were sitting, one at the head and one at the feet,[39] and they asked me whom I was looking for.[40] And of truth, I said, 'Jesus, crucified.' But they said, 'Go to Galilee, there you will find him just as he foretold you.'[41] Afterwards I saw him in the flesh he had before, and he gave me something to eat and drink from his hands. And he revealed himself to his disciples and dined with them, and he broke bread with his hands and gave to them, saying, 'These are the words that I spoke to you while I was still with you.[42] And I believe that my redeemer himself lives, and that I will rise from the earth on the last day, and that in my flesh I will see God himself, my Savior."[43] But Simeon came, too, and said to him, "For my part, I saw and knew him as an infant and held him in the temple,[44] and I worshiped him on the cross and thereafter he resurrected in his body. For I recognized him afterwards, and I saw him ascend to heaven and sitting on the right hand of God the Father. And I truly know that he is true God and that he was made a human being of his own will."

Volusianus Obtains Jesus' Portrait from Veronica and Returns to Rome

22. But the woman Veronica came and said to him, "I touched the hem of his garment in the crowd, I who had suffered from a flow of blood for twelve years, and immediately I was completely cured, and I believe that he himself lives as God in eternity."[45]

36. See John 4:42.
37. See Luke 23:53; Matt. 27:60.
38. See John 20:5; 20:11.
39. See John 20:12.
40. See John 20:15.
41. See Matt. 28:5, 7, 10; Mark 16:7.
42. See Luke 24:44.
43. See Job 19:25–26.
44. See Luke 2:25–28.
45. See Matt. 9:20–22; Mark 5:25–34; Luke 8:43–48.

23. Volosianus said to Pilate, "Why did you kill the son of God?" Pilate said, "His people and the priests handed him over to me." Volusianus said angrily, "He himself lives as god; you will certainly die; you will not live because you killed a perfect man without guilt." And again he ordered him to be sent into the iron cage and thrown in prison.

24. And he asked the woman, Veronica by name, for the portrait of Jesus. She refused, saying that she did not have it. Then he sent her into the torture-chamber until she would hand over the portrait of the Lord. She said under constraint, "I have it indeed, locked in my chamber, where I worship my Lord every day." Volosianus said, "Give it over to me, and I will worship it." Then Veronica handed over the portrait of the Lord. As soon as he saw it, Volusianus fell flat on the ground and worshiped it with an upright mind. Then, rising with great trembling, he took it and wrapped it in a purple cover embroidered with gold and placed it in a golden vessel, sealed it with his ring, and said with a vow, "The Lord lives and my soul lives; I will not see the face of my Lord until I see my lord Tiberius!"

25. When he said this, he ordered all his nobles to come and he said to those who were in Judea, "I declare to you a great thing: I will not release you before I take you before my lord Tiberius and you declare to him all that you have witnessed to me." He ordered that they punish Pilate with the foulest death. And he took the portrait of the Lord, along with all his disciples and his supplies, and they went aboard the ship the same day.

26. Veronica also abandoned everything for the name of Christ and followed him, and went aboard the ship with them. Then Volosianus said, "Woman, whom are you seeking?"[46] And she said, "In truth, I am looking for (the image of) my Lord that the Lord gave to me, not for my merits but out his mercy, and which you have taken away from me against the law—just as the Jews had taken Christ, whom neither you nor your people have seen, from the world. Even though I have deserved ill, hand back to me my Lord! And if you do not hand him back to me, I will not release him until I see where they have laid him down. And I will worship him and serve him as long as I live because my redeemer himself lives, and on the last day I shall see God, my savior."[47] Now all of her men[48] began to weep, her sons and daughters, neighbors and all who knew her. Then Veronica said, "Daughters of Jerusalem, do not weep for me but for yourselves, and weep for your daughters.[49] For have you never heard God saying, 'Everyone who has left everything for the name of Christ will receive a hundredfold and will possess eternal life'?"[50]

46. See John 20:15.
47. See Job 19:25–26.
48. Another manuscript witness (P) has "her husband."
49. See Luke 23:28.
50. See Matt. 19:29.

27. Then Volosianus bid all his sailors to ply their oars and hoisted his sails in the name of his Lord God. And he sent Titus and Vespasian to Judea and steered his course on the sea. When his ship was in the Tiber, he entered the city called Lateran and sent his messengers to Tiberius.

Volusianus Gives Report to Tiberius

28. When he had heard, Tiberius ordered him to come to him: "Volosianus, what indeed have you found in Judea about Jesus Christ and his disciples? Tell me everything! But let one of his disciples come with you as well and, in the name of his Lord God, I will come and worship him, and let him place his hand over me, in the name of his Lord God, and cure my wounds, and I will give him the kingdom where he was born."

29. Then Volosianus said, "My Lord, you will now see everything I found, and you will gain your health and salvation. I found Titus and Vespasian, your faithful ones, fearing God. I found your worst and wicked kings: the emperor hanged,[51] Caiphas stoned, Archelaus stoned, and Pilate tied up and fastened in an iron cage, and thrown into prison in Damascus. Thus because the Jews stifled Jesus Christ with spears, torches, and lanterns,[52] and killed our light that illuminated and saved the human race, and did not grant him freedom to come to us, for this reason Titus and Vespasian, your faithful ones, killed them with the foulest death, a great host of Jews. And God's faithful people, Joseph of Arimathea and Nicodemus with him, came and asked for the body of Jesus and took him down from the cross and buried him in a new tomb.[53] But Jesus himself rose on the third day from the dead and revealed himself to his disciples in the same flesh which he had beforehand; and his disciples saw him ascend into heaven. To be sure, Jesus performed many other signs prior to his passion. He raised the dead, cleansed the lepers, gave sight to the blind, cured paralytics, cast out demons, gave hearing to the deaf, made the mute speak.[54] He raised Lazarus from the tomb on the fourth day[55] and the young girl in the house of her father in the arms of her mother;[56] and the woman suffering from hemorrhages for twelve years, who touched the hem of his garment from behind, he immediately cured her.[57]

51. P identifies this "emperor" with Herod.

52. See John 18:3.

53. See John 19:38–42.

54. See Matt. 11:5, 15:30–31; Mark 7:37; Luke 7:22.

55. See John 11:11–17.

56. See Matt. 9:18–19, 23–36; Mark 5:22–24, 38–43; Luke 8:49–56.

57. See Matt. 9:20–22; Mark 5:25–34; Luke 8:43–48.

30. He himself sent his angel, and he entered into Titus and Vespasian because we knew them to be worthy,[58] and he ordered them to go into Judea to avenge his death, and they did so. And they went down to Judea and arrived in Jerusalem, and seized your kings and sent them to judgment, saying as follows:

31. 'Just as they did with Christ, so also let us do to them. They hanged our Lord on a green tree, and we will hang them on a dry one.[59] They killed him without fault, and so let us kill them with the foulest death. They took his tunic and made four parts out of it,[60] and so let us rend them into four parts and give their bodies to the beasts on earth and birds in heaven.[61] They sold Christ for thirty silver pieces,[62] and we give thirty of them for one silver piece. And let their names be erased from the earth.' And they did just as they said.

32. Afterwards they sent a search for a portrait of the Lord and found the woman, Veronica by name, who had it because she had painted it.[63] Now, I have here the portrait of the Lord and the woman with it."

The Healing and Baptism of Tiberius

33. Then Tiberius said, "With great desire I wish to see it and worship and guard it." Then Volosianus spread out that cover in which was the portrait of the Lord, and Tiberius saw it and worshiped it. And at once his leprosy fell from him and his flesh was cleansed like the flesh of a small child.

35.[64] He believed and was baptized with his entire household into our Lord Jesus, to whom be honor and glory and rule and praise forever and ever. Amen.[65]

58. P has "because we were not worthy" (*quia nos indigni eramus*).

59. See Luke 23:31.

60. See John 19:23–24; see Matt. 27:35; Mark 15:24; Luke 23:34.

61. See 1 Sam 17:44–46.

62. See Matt. 26:14–15.

63. Or, following O, "who had him who painted it," implying that Jesus was the author of his own portrait.

64. Chapter 34 is wanting in O.

65. The end of the *Vindicta Salvatoris* is abridged in O; other redactions and their manuscript witnesses contain longer and more elaborate narratives.

36

The Death of Pilate Who Condemned Jesus (Mors Pilati)

The "Death of Pilate" is an intriguing account of Pilate's ignominious fate after he had Jesus crucified. The ailing emperor Tiberius learns that Jesus is able to heal him but discovers that Pilate has already had him executed. The emperor is eventually cured by the supernatural image of Jesus' face on the cloth of Veronica, but he is filled with wrath over Pilate's unjust action, and orders him to be imprisoned and executed. Pilate ends his own life in prison, but his corpse continues to defile everything it touches.

Tischendorf based his text of the account on a fourteenth-century manuscript from Milan. What Tischendorf did not realize is that the manuscript is simply an abstract taken from the famous *Golden Legend* of Jacob of Voragine (edited between 1252 and 1260). Only at the beginning and the end of the account has the scribe of the Milan manuscript modified the *Legend*'s narrative of Pilate (ch. 51). Starting with the words of Veronica, the texts are virtually identical.

This was first recognized and convincingly demonstrated by E. von Dobschütz in 1899. But Dobschütz also pointed out that Jacob of Voragine had utilized an earlier source for his account—a fuller life of Pilate, drawn from a Latin narrative called the *Historia Apocrypha*. This text describes, among other things, the horrible fates of all those closely involved with the death of Jesus: Judas Iscariot, "the Jews," and Pilate himself (basing its stories on earlier sources, starting with those of the New Testament).

The "Death of Pilate," then, represents only the final portion of this longer tale that had been taken over by Jacob of Voragine. The *Historia Apocrypha* was evidently produced in the eleventh–twelfth centuries; according to Pérès, it reflects the concerns of the Christian crusades, especially the importance of Christ's enemies and their just punishments. J. Knape in turn has argued that the author of the *Historia* utilized "The Vengeance of the Savior" and, for the suicide of Pilate, the account found in the church father Rufinus's Latin translation of the *Church History* of Eusebius.

Our translation is based on the text in Tischendorf.

Bibliography

Knape, J. "Die 'Historia apocrypha' der "Legenda aurea," *Zur Deutung von Geschichte in Antike und Mittelalter*, ed. J. Knape and K. Strobel. Bamberg: Bayerische Verlagsanstalt, 1985; pp. 113–72.

Pérès, J.-N. "Mort de Pilate," in *Écrits apocryphes chrétiens*, vol. 2, ed. P. Geoltrain and J.-D. Kaestli. Paris: Gallimard, 2005; pp. 401–5.

Schönbach, A. Review of *Evangelia apocrypha*, ed. Tischendorf, in *Anzeiger für deutsches Altertum und deutsche Literatur* 2 (1876): 149–212.

Tischendorf, C. von. *Evangelia Apocrypha*; reprint edition Hildesheim: Georg Olms, 1966; pp. lxxx–lxxxi; 456–58.

von Dobschütz, E. *Christusbilder. Untersuchungen zur christlichen Legende*. TU 18. Leipzig: J. C Hinrichs, 1899; pp. 230–39.

The Death of Pilate Who Condemned Jesus

Tiberius's Illness and the Mission of Volusianus

Now when Tiberius Caesar, emperor of the Romans, was seized with a grievous illness and found that there was at Jerusalem a certain physician, Jesus by name, who cured all diseases by his word alone, not knowing that the Jews and Pilate had killed him, he ordered one of his attendants, Volusianus by name: "Go overseas as quickly as possible and tell my servant and friend Pilate to send me this physician to restore me to my previous health." Volusianus, on hearing the emperor's order, departed at once and came to Pilate as he was commanded. And he told the same Pilate what Tiberius Caesar had committed to him, saying, "Tiberius Caesar, emperor of the Romans, your lord, having heard that there is a physician in this city who cures diseases by his word alone, earnestly requests that you duly send this man to him to cure his disease." Pilate was greatly abashed on hearing this, for he knew that he had slain him through envy.[1] Pilate answered the envoy: "This man was a criminal [2]and a man who attracted to himself all the people;[3] so, after taking counsel with the city's sages, I had him crucified."

Volusianus Encounters Veronica

Returning to his lodging, the envoy met a certain woman, Veronica[4] by name, who had been well acquainted with Jesus, and he said, "O woman, there was a certain physician in this city, who cured the sick by his word alone—why have the Jews slain him?" She began to weep, saying, "Ah, wretched me,[5] my lord, it was my God and my Lord[6] whom Pilate through envy delivered up,[7] condemned, and commanded to be crucified!" Then he said, grieving excessively, "I grieve immensely because I cannot do what my lord has sent me to do." Veronica replied to him, "When my Lord went about preaching and I was, very much against my will, deprived of his presence, I wished to have his image painted for me, that when I was deprived of his presence, at least the figure of his image might give me some solace. As I was taking a linen-cloth to

1. See Matt. 27:18, Mark 15:10.
2. John 18:30, 23:32.
3. See Luke 23:2–5.
4. For Veronica, see *Vindicta Salvatoris* 6, 18, 22–26, 32.
5. Starting with Veronica's response, the text follows almost verbatim that of the *Golden Legend*, chap. 51 (*De passione Christi*), 218–55, ed. Maggioni 1:350–352.
6. John 20:28.
7. John 19:16; see Luke 23:25.

the painter to paint it, my Lord met me and inquired where I was heading. When I disclosed to him the reason for my journey, he asked me for the kerchief and handed it back to me printed with the image of his venerable face. Therefore, if your lord will devoutly behold the sight of this, he will immediately receive a clean bill of health." Then he asked, "Can an image of this sort be bought with gold or silver?" She replied, "No, but with a pious affection of devotion. I will therefore go with you and bring the image for Caesar to see, and then return."

The Healing of Tiberius

So Volusianus arrived with Veronica in Rome and said to Tiberius the emperor, "This Jesus, whom you have long desired, Pilate and the Jews delivered to an unjust death and through envy fastened to the wood of the cross. Therefore, a certain matron is come with me bringing the image of the same Jesus. If you devoutly behold it, you will soon obtain the benefit of your health." So Caesar had the path spread with cloths of silk and ordered that the image be presented to him. As soon as he looked upon it, he regained his previous health.

Pilate Taken Prisoner to Rome

Then Pontius Pilate was taken prisoner by command of Caesar and brought to Rome. Caesar, hearing that Pilate had arrived in Rome, was filled with exceeding wrath against him and had him brought to him. But Pilate carried with him the seamless tunic of Jesus,[8] which he put on and wore before the emperor. As soon as the emperor saw him, he laid aside all his ire and instantly rose to him, unable to speak harshly to him about anything. And the one who seemed so terrible and cruel in his absence, now appeared somewhat gentle in his presence. As soon as he had dismissed him, he grew terribly inflamed against him, declaring himself wretched because he had not at all expressed to him the wrath of his mind. Straightaway he had him recalled, swearing and protesting that he was a child of death and too abominable to live upon earth. But when he saw him, he immediately greeted him and laid aside all the fury of his soul. Everyone was astonished, as he was himself, that he was so inflamed against Pilate while he was absent, yet could say nothing harsh to him when present. Finally, either by divine intervention or by chance, by the persuasion of a certain Christian, he had Pilate stripped of that tunic and soon resumed against him the previous fury of mind. Since the emperor was very much astonished about this, he was told that that tunic had belonged to the Lord Jesus.

8. John 19:23.

The Condemnation and Suicide of Pilate

Then the emperor ordered Pilate to be put in prison until he should take counsel with the wise men[9] as to what should be done with him. After a few days sentence was thus given against Pilate that he should be condemned to a most shameful death.[10] Hearing this, Pilate slew himself with his own dagger and by such a death ended his life. When Pilate's death was made known, Caesar said, "Truly he has died of a most shameful death; his own hand has not spared him."

The Fate of Pilate's Corpse

Pilate was consequently fastened to a huge millstone and sunk into the Tiber river. But all the wicked and foul spirits, rejoicing in his wicked and foul body, moved in the water[11] and produced in the air dreadful lightning and tempests, and thunder and hail, so that everyone was seized with terrible fear. For this reason, the Romans dragged the body out of the Tiber, and in derision took it away to Vienne and sunk it in the river Rhône; for Vienne, as it were, means 'Way of Gehenna' (*via gehennae*), because it was then a place of malediction.[12] But evil spirits were present there, doing the same things in that place, too. Now the people there, unable to bear such a great onslaught of demons, put that vessel of malediction[13] away from them and sent it to be buried in the territory of Losania.[14] But since these people were exceedingly wearied by the aforementioned onslaughts, they put it away from them and sunk it in a certain pool surrounded by mountains, where even now, according to some reports, certain diabolical contrivances are said to boil up.

9. See Matt. 26:3–5, Mark 14:1–2, Luke 22:1–2.

10. See Wis 2:20.

11. This sentence is an abridged version of the account given in the *Golden Legend*, chap. 51, 250, ed. Maggioni 1:352.

12. This fanciful etymology is probably derived from *Vigenna*, the Latin name for the river Vienne in the Poitou-Charentes region.

13. See Acts 9:15, where Paul is called "the vessel of election."

14. Latin for Lausanne.

37

The Narrative of Joseph of Arimathea

This apocryphon provides an alternative version of the passion narrative, emphasizing the betrayal of Judas and the events that transpired both at the crucifixion and after the resurrection. Particular attention is paid to one of the two robbers crucified with Jesus—a man named Demas—who is vividly portrayed as having entered paradise after his repentance on the cross. The account is told in the first person, much like the Gospel of Peter, only now by Joseph of Arimathea. This legendary expansion sometimes supplements and sometimes contradicts the canonical Gospels, on which it is partially based.

The first half of the narrative focuses on Judas's false accusations leading to Jesus' arrest. We are told that in exchange for thirty pieces "of gold" (!) Judas charges that Jesus had plundered the law of Moses from the temple, when in fact it was the robber Demas who had done so. Here is a not-so-subtle statement that Jesus died for the sin of another. In contrast to the canonical narratives, there is a particularly full account of both robbers, Gestas who is violent, wicked, and godless, and Demas, a Robin Hood figure who steals from the rich but behaves kindly to the poor. Demas repents of his sins on the cross and receives the gift of paradise, becoming, at the end of the narrative, a powerful ruler in the world beyond.

Included in the narrative is a remarkable account in which Jesus writes a letter of recommendation for Demas from the cross, addressed to the cherubim and powers in charge of paradise; he later receives a letter back from them in response.

The account of Joseph's arrest, imprisonment, and escape from prison appears to be dependent on the Gospel of Nicodemus, expanded here with yet more legendary detail.

The anti-Jewish character of the account is consistent with other works in the Pilate cycle (with which this account is generally included because of its emphasis on Joseph of Arimathea). The author speaks of the "murderous Jews who wage war against God" and indicates that "they crucified him . . . because they do not know God." At the end he states his anti-Jewish reason for writing: "When I had seen these things I wrote them down, so that all may believe in the crucified Jesus Christ, our Lord, and no longer serve the law of Moses."

Tischendorf edited the text from four manuscripts, one of the twelfth century, one of the fourteenth, and two of the fifteenth; we have translated his text here. The narrative does not appear to have been written early in the Christian tradition; it could date any time after the circulation of the Gospel of Nicodemus (fourth or fifth century?) up to its own earliest attestation in the twelfth century, possibly earlier in that period than later.

Bibliography

Elliott, J. K. *Apocryphal New Testament*. Oxford: Clarendon, 1993; pp. 208–9; 217–18.
von Tischendorf, C. *Evangelia Apocrypha*. Leipzig: H. Mendelssohn, 1853 (2nd ed. 1876); 459–70.

The Narrative of Joseph of Arimathea

The Narrative of Joseph of Arimathea, who asked for the Body of the Lord. In Which also are Related the Charges brought against the Two Robbers.

1

(1) I am Joseph of Arimathea, the one who asked Pilate for the body of the Lord Jesus for burial.[1] For this reason I was shackled and imprisoned by the murderous Jews who wage war against God; even though they cling to the law, they have caused affliction for Moses himself. After infuriating the lawgiver, and being ignorant of God they crucified him, revealing to those who know him that it was the Son of God who was crucified. Seven days before Christ suffered, two condemned robbers were sent to the governor Pilate from Jericho. The charge against them was as follows.

The Two Robbers

(2) The first, named Gestas, use to murder travelers with the sword and he stripped others naked; he hanged women head downwards from their ankles and cut off their breasts; he drank blood from the limbs of infants. He never knew God, did not follow his laws, and showed his violent character from the beginning in deeds such as these.

The charge against the other was this. He was called Demas and was a Galilean by race, the owner of an inn. He used to despoil the rich, but he behaved well toward the poor. He was a thief like Tobit, for he used to bury the poor who died. He tried to rob the multitude of the Judeans by carrying off the law itself in Jerusalem, stripping naked the daughter of Caiaphas who was the priestess of the sanctuary, and removing the mysterious deposit of Solomon that had been entrusted to that place. Such were his deeds.

Judas Arranges the Betrayal

(3) Now Jesus also was arrested three days before the Passover, when it was evening. But there was no Passover for Caiaphas and the multitude of the Jews, but great mourning instead, because of the plundering of the sanctuary by the robber. They called Judas Iscariot and spoke to him, for he was the son of the brother of Caiaphas, the priest. Now he was not openly a disciple of Jesus, but all

1. See Matt. 27:57–58; Mark 15:42–43; Luke 23:50–52; John 19:38.

the multitude of the Jews had persuaded him by stealth to follow Jesus—not that he might adhere to the signs that he did or confess him, but that he might hand him over to them, as he wanted to catch him speaking a false word. They gave gifts to him for this brave deed, paying him two pieces of gold every day. So he spent two years with Jesus, as one of his disciples named John says.

(4) On the third day before Jesus was arrested Judas said to the Jews, "Come, let us hold a council: for it was not the robber who plundered the law, but Jesus himself. And I am bringing the charge." But when these words were spoken, Nicodemus entered our midst. He is the one who holds the keys to the sanctuary. He said to all, "Do no such deed!" For Nicodemus held to the truth more than the entire multitude of the Jews. The daughter of Caiaphas, named Sara, cried out: "But he himself spoke before all the people against this sanctuary, saying 'I am able to destroy this temple and raise it in three days.'"[2] The Jews replied to her, "All of us believe you"—for they considered her to be a prophet. And so, once they held their council, Jesus was arrested.

Jesus Put on Trial
2

(1) At three o'clock on the next day, the fourth day of the week, they brought him into the courtyard of Caiaphas. Annas and Caiaphas said to him, "Tell us, why did you carry off our law? And why have you preached against the promises of Moses and the prophets?" But Jesus made no answer. Again a second time, when the multitude was also present, they said to him, "Why do you want to destroy in a single moment the sanctuary that Solomon constructed in forty-six years?" Again Jesus made no answer to these things—for the sanctuary of the synagogue had been plundered by the robber.

(2) When the evening of the fourth day had come to an end, the entire multitude began looking for the daughter of Caiaphas, to burn her at the stake because of the destruction of the law, since they would not be able to celebrate the Passover. But she said to them, "Wait, children; let us destroy Jesus: then the law will be found and the holy feast can certainly be observed. Annas and Caiaphas secretly gave Judas Iscariot a large sum of gold and told him, "Say what you told us before: 'I know that the law was stolen by Jesus.' Then the accusation will be leveled at him rather than this innocent young girl." Judas agreed with the plan and said to them, "We do not want the entire multitude to know that you instructed me to level this charge against Jesus. But release Jesus and I will persuade the multitude that this is how it happened." So they released Jesus by stealth.

2. See Matt. 26:61; Mark 14:48.

Judas Betrays Jesus

(3) Judas came in to the sanctuary at dawn on the fifth day, and said to all the people, "What do you want to give me if I hand over to you the destroyer of the law and the plunderer of the prophets?" The Jews said to him, "If you hand him over to us, we will give you thirty pieces of gold." But the people did not know that Judas was speaking about Jesus, for many of them held that he was the Son of God. Judas took the thirty pieces of gold.[3]

(4) He went out at ten o'clock in the morning, and at eleven he found Jesus walking on the street. When it was nearly evening, Judas told the Jews, "Give me a contingent of soldiers with swords and clubs, and I will hand him over to you." And so they gave him servants in order to apprehend him. And while they were heading out, Judas said to them, "The one I kiss—arrest him![4] For he is the one who plundered the law and the prophets." He then came up to Jesus and kissed him, saying, "Greetings, Rabbi." This was during the evening of the fifth day. They arrested him and handed him over to Caiaphas and the chief priests, while Judas told them, "This is the one who plundered the law and the prophets." They then subjected Jesus to an unfair interrogation, asking him, "Why did you do these things?" Yet he gave no answer.

But Nicodemus and I, Joseph, seeing the "seat of the pestilent" stood apart from them, not wanting to be perish "in the council of the impious."[5]

Jesus and the Robbers Are Crucified

3(1) They did many other terrible things to Jesus that night, and handed him over to the governor Pilate as the day of Preparation was dawning,[6] so that he might crucify him. And all of them gathered together for this purpose. After the trial was over, the governor Pilate ordered him to be nailed to the cross, along with two robbers. And so they were nailed up together with Jesus, Gestas to his left and Demas to his right.

(2) The one on his left began to cry out, saying to Jesus, "See how many evil deeds I have done on the earth! If I had known that you were the king, I would have tried to kill you as well. But why do you call yourself the son of God, when you cannot even help yourself in your time of need? How can you help someone else who prays to you? If you are the Christ, come down from the cross, that I might believe in you.[7] But now I see you not as a human, but as a wild beast,

3. See Matt. 26:15; Mark 14:11; Luke 22:5.
4. See Matt. 26:48; Mark 14:44.
5. See Psalm 1:1.
6. See John 19:14.
7 See Luke 23:34.

destroyed along with me." And he began to say many other things against Jesus, blaspheming and grinding his teeth against him. For the robber was caught in the snare of the devil.

(3) But the robber on his right, named Demas, when he saw Jesus' divine grace, cried out, "I know you, Jesus Christ—you are the son of God! But I see you worshiped as Christ by a myriad of myriads of angels. Forgive my sins that I committed. At my trial, do not allow the stars or moon to come against me when you are about to judge the entire earth, for I carried out my evil plans at night. And the sun that has grown dark because of you, do not move it to speak the evil doings of my heart. For I can offer you no gift for the forgiveness of my sins. Death is already coming upon me for my sins. But expiation belongs to you. Save me from your fearful judgment, Master of all. Do not give the enemy authority to devour me and to inherit my soul, like that of the one hanging to your left. For I see how the devil rejoices, taking his soul, and his fleshly parts are disappearing. Do not order me to depart to the portion allotted to the Jews, for I see Moses and the patriarchs in great weeping, while the devil rejoices over them. And so, before my spirit departs, Master, command my sins to be wiped away and remember me, the sinner, in your kingdom, when upon the great throne of the Most High you shall judge the twelve tribes of Israel, for you have prepared a great punishment for your world, for your own sake."[8]

(4) When the robber had said these things, Jesus said to him, "Truly, truly I say to you, Demas, today you will be with me in paradise.[9] But the sons of the kingdom, the children of Abraham, Isaac, Jacob, and Moses will be cast into the outer darkness. In that place there will be weeping and gnashing of teeth.[10] But you alone will dwell in paradise until my second coming, when I am about to judge those who do not confess my name." And he said to the robber, "Go and speak to the Cherubim and the powers, to those who turn the flaming sword, who have been guarding paradise from the time that Adam, the first-formed, was in paradise and transgressed, and did not guard my commandments, whom I cast out from there. None of those who lived before will see paradise until I come a second time to judge the living and the dead." Then he wrote to them as follows: "Jesus Christ, the Son of God, who came down from the heights of heaven, who came forth from the womb of the invisible God without separating from him, who came down into the world so as to be made flesh and to be nailed to the cross, so that I might save Adam, the very one whom I made, to my archangelic powers, the gatekeepers of paradise, servants of my Father. I wish and order that the one who was crucified with me should enter, that he should

8. See Luke 23:40–42.

9. See Luke 23:43.

10. See Matt. 8:11–12.

receive forgiveness of sins on my account, and that putting on an immortal body he should enter paradise and dwell there where no one at any time has been able to dwell."

And behold, when these words were spoken, Jesus handed over his spirit, on the day of Preparation at three o'clock. Darkness came over all the earth; and a large earthquake struck, causing the sanctuary to fall, along with the pinnacle of the temple.[11]

Joseph is Imprisoned and Freed
4

(1) I, Joseph, requested the body of Jesus and placed it in a new tomb where no one had ever yet been laid. But the body of the robber to his right could not be found; the one on his left had the appearance of a dragon—that is what his body looked like.

Because I requested Jesus' body for burial, the Jews were borne away by zealous anger and locked me in prison, where force is used against those who have done evil deeds. This happened to me when it was evening on the Sabbath, when our nation was violating the law. And behold, our nation itself endured terrible afflictions on that Sabbath.

(2) When it became late on the first day of the week, at around eleven at night, Jesus came to me in prison with the robber who had been crucified on his right side, whom he had sent into paradise. There was a great light in the building. And the house was suspended by its four corners, and the place was destroyed; so I went out. I recognized Jesus first, and afterwards the robber who was bringing a letter to Jesus. While we were making our way in Galilee a great light shown, more than the creation could bear, and a great sweet aroma from paradise exuded from the robber.

The Letter of the Cherubim

(3) When Jesus sat in a certain place, he read out from the letter, as follows: "We the Cherubim and the Six Winged Creatures who were commanded by your divinity to guard the garden of paradise are declaring this through the robber who was crucified with you according to your plan. When we saw the mark of the nails on the robber crucified with you and the splendor of your divine being in the letter that was sent, the fire that is here was extinguished, as it could not bear the brightness of the mark; and we were terrified, overcome with great fear—for we heard that the maker of heaven, earth, and all creation moved his

11. See Matt. 27:51.

dwelling from the heights to the lowest regions of the earth, on account of Adam, the first formed. For when we saw the undefiled cross shining like lighting through the robber, its light seven times brighter than the shining sun, trembling overtook us, while we held fast the upheavals of the netherworld. With a great cry, the ministers of Hades, together with us, cried out, 'Holy, holy, holy, the one who is in the beginning, in the highest places.' And the powers sent forth a cry, 'O Lord, you have appeared in heaven and on earth, and provided joy to the ages, having saved your own creation from death.'"

Jesus, Joseph, the Robber, and John in Galilee

5

(1) When I had seen these things I proceeded into Galilee with Jesus and the robber; and Jesus was transformed so that he no longer appeared as he did before he was crucified, but was entirely light. Angels were constantly ministering to him, and Jesus was speaking with them. I spent three days with him; but none of his disciples was with him, except the robber alone.

(2) When the Feast of Unleavened Bread was half over, his disciple John came; and we could no longer see what the robber was like. John asked Jesus, "Who is this? For you have not allowed me to appear to him." Jesus gave him no answer. Then he fell before him and said, "Lord, I know that you loved me from the beginning. Why do you not reveal this man to me?" Jesus said to him, "Why do you seek after what is hidden? Are you still ignorant? Do you not recognize the sweet smell of paradise that fills the place? Do you not know who this was? The robber from the cross has become the heir of paradise. Truly, truly I tell you, it is his alone until the great day arrives." John replied, "Make me worthy to see him."

(3) While John was still speaking, the robber suddenly appeared. Greatly astonished, John fell to the ground. But the robber did not appear as he did at first, before John had come; he looked like a king in great power, and he was wearing the cross. The voice of a great multitude came forth, "You have come to the place of paradise that has been prepared for you. We have been appointed by the one who sent you, to serve you until the great day." When this voice spoke, both the robber and I, Joseph, became invisible, and I was found to be in my own house, but I no longer saw Jesus.

(4) When I had seen these things I wrote them down, so that all may believe in the crucified Jesus Christ, our Lord, and no longer serve the law of Moses, but may believe in the signs and wonders that occurred through him—that by believing we might inherit eternal life and be found in the kingdom of heaven. For to him are due glory, power, praise, and greatness unto all the ages. Amen.

38

The Gospel according to Mary

We have no record of a Gospel according to Mary (Magdalene) from the early church (although see the lost Greater Questions of Mary cited by Epiphanius, later in this collection). The book was, in fact, unknown until its discovery at the end of the nineteenth century. Despite the sensational nature of the find, the book was not widely known for many decades: its first publication did not come until 1955—a marked contrast to the treatment accorded other Gospels discovered in the late nineteenth and early twentieth centuries, such as the Gospel of Peter, Papyrus Egerton 2, or even the Fayûm Fragment. Some of these are of less inherent intrigue than the Gospel of Mary, but they all were published almost immediately upon discovery. Whether the relative lack of scholarly interest in the Gospel of Mary was related to (1) the fact that this was a Gospel allegedly by, or about, a woman disciple, (2) the circumstance that it embodied a relatively complex gnostic cosmology rather than a more straightforward narrative, or (3) something else, is hard to determine.

It is clear, in any event, that the publication of the text was hopelessly delayed by a string of unfortunate and highly regrettable circumstances. The manuscript containing the Gospel was purchased by a German scholar, C. Reinhardt, in Cairo in January 1896. The seller of the book, whose identity is no longer known, informed Reinhardt that the book had been discovered by a peasant in the niche of wall, a claim that is today discredited. The manuscript was a papyrus codex, written in Coptic, with its leather and papyrus cover still in place; the pages measured 12.7 x 10.5 cm; it is dated to the fifth century. It contained four texts: The Gospel of Mary, the Apocryphon of John, The Sophia of Jesus Christ, and the Act of Peter (a separate work from the better known Acts of Peter).

Reinhardt brought the manuscript back to Berlin and deposited it in the Egyptian museum. Because it was known to contain gnostic texts, it was given the name The Berlin Gnostic Codex, and provided with the designation BG 8502. The German Coptic scholar C. Schmidt prepared an edition of the text, along with a German translation, completing his work in 1912. Unfortunately, when the edition was in production at the Prießen Press, a water main burst, destroying all the pages. Schmidt had no choice but to begin afresh, but he was hindered by the First World War and its aftermath. He died in 1938 without having completed the project.

W. Till took over where Schmidt had left off and completed the edition by 1943. But now it was the time of the Second World War and again publication was, for the moment, impossible. Not long after the war, news of the discovery of the Coptic documents at Nag Hammadi infiltrated the scholarly community, and Till decided to wait to publish his edition in case one or more other copies of the work should turn up in the Nag Hammadi library. When it turned out that this was not the case, Till finally published his edition in 1955—a lifetime after the discovery had first been made.

In the meantime, a small fragment of the Gospel in Greek—the original language of the text—had been discovered and published. The papyrus was acquired by the John Rylands Library in Manchester, England, in 1917. It probably was among the papyri discovered at Oxyrhynchus. This was a solitary papyrus leaf, written on both sides, measuring 8.7 x 10 cm, and containing portions of pages 17–19 of the corresponding Coptic text, with some notable variants. The fragment dates to the third century, possibly the early third century; it was published in 1938 by C. H. Roberts (and was utilized by Till).

Years later another Oxyrhynchus papyrus appeared. P.Oxy. 3525 was discovered by Grenfell and Hunt, probably in the early part of the twentieth century, but was not published until 1983 by P. J. Parsons. It too is from the third century, but it comes from a roll rather than a codex; it is written in a cursive script, that is, a documentary rather than a literary hand. Measuring 11.7 x 11.4 cm, it contains portions of pages 9–10 of the corresponding Coptic text.

It is in some ways unfortunate that neither Greek fragment gives us a portion of the text not also preserved in the Coptic of BG 8502, for that longer version is missing the opening six pages of the text (pp. 1–6) and four pages of the middle (pp. 11–14)—so that with all the surviving witnesses taken into account, we are still missing over half of the original (which took up just over 18 pages in BG 8502).

The Coptic text thus begins *in medias res*, with Jesus responding to a question from the disciples about whether "matter [will be] destroyed or not." Jesus' reply shows the gnostic orientation of the text from the outset. All things, including especially this material world, will be dissolved into their primal elements. Matter itself is evil, or at least susceptible of evil, in this text; its co-mingling with spirit is termed "adultery" and is what leads to "sin." But all things, Jesus indicates, will return to their original state.

After delivering several exhortations to his disciples, Jesus departs. Immediately forgetting what Jesus has just taught them—that this material world is not what ultimately matters—the male disciples are overcome with fear that they may share Jesus' fate and also be executed. Mary (almost certainly Mary Magdalene—the Coptic text calls her MARIHAM, the Greek MARRIAMÊ; neither spelling was normally used for Jesus' mother) then appears and comforts them. Peter asks her, as the one "the Savior loved . . . more than the other women" to tell them, the male disciples, the revelation Jesus had given to her alone. She complies by beginning to describe a vision that she had of Jesus, but that is where the second major lacuna of four pages occurs.

When the text resumes Mary is in the middle of a gnostic discourse describing the ascent of the soul back to its heavenly, spiritual, home, by escaping the "powers" of the heavenly spheres separating this world from the divine world above. These powers, in fact, are emblematic of the material trappings of the body, its desires, ignorance, and passions. Escaping this material prison of the body is to find eternal rest at last.

When Mary has finished relating this revelation a dispute breaks out among the male disciples, who wonder if it is possible that Jesus would reveal his truths to a woman. Andrew and Peter in particular doubt it, Peter somewhat hypocritically, given the circumstance that he was the one who asked Mary to tell them about her secret revelation in the first place. The apostle Levi finally intervenes, upbraiding Peter for his anger and his mistreatment of Mary, and pointing out that the Savior "knows her perfectly. That is why he loved her more than us." He urges them to go forth to preach the gospel, which they then do.

It may be difficult to assign a precise date to the composition of the Gospel. It certainly must have been written prior to the early third century, the date of the Rylands papyrus fragment. Its gnostic orientation suggests that it could not be earlier than the beginning of the second century, and so scholars have settled on a variety of dates within that range, either early in the second century or late.

We have translated the text found in the edition of Pasquier.

Bibliography

King, K. *The Gospel of Mary of Magdala: Jesus and the First Woman Apostle.* Santa Rosa, CA: Polebridge, 2003.

Klauck, H.-J. *Apocryphal Gospels: An Introduction.* London: T&T Clark, 2003; pp. 160–68.

Parsons, P. J. "3525. Gospel of Mary." *The Oxyrhynchus Papyri.* London: Egypt Exploration Society, 1983, vol. 50; pp 12–14.

Pasquier, A., ed. *L'Évangile selon Marie (BG 1). Édition revue et augmentée. Bibliothèque copte de Nag Hammadi,* Section "Textes" 10. Laval: Les Presses de l'Université Laval, 2007.

Puech, H.-C., and B. Blatz. "The Gospel of Mary," in *New Testament Apocrypha,* ed. W. Schneemelcher; trans. R. McL. Wilson. Louisville: Westminster/John Knox, 1991, vol. 1; pp. 391–95.

Roberts, C. H. *Catalogue of the Greek and Latin Papyri in the John Rylands Library Manchester,* vol. 3. Manchester: University of Manchester Press, 1938; pp. 18–23.

Till, W. C. *Die gnostischen Schriften des koptischen Papyrus Berolinensis 8502,* 1955; 2nd edition with H.-M. Schenke. Berlin: Akademie Verlag, 1972.

Wilson, R. McL., and G. W. MacRae. "The Gospel of Mary," in *Nag Hammadi Codices V, 2–5 and VI with Papyrus Berolinensis 8502, 1 and 4,* ed. D. M. Parrott. Leiden: E. J. Brill, 1979; pp. 453–71.

The Gospel according to Mary

The Nature of Matter and Sin

7 . . . Will matter then be destroyed or not?" The Savior said, "Every nature, everything fashioned, and all creation exist together in one another, and they will dissolve again into their own root. For the nature of matter dissolves into what belongs to its own nature. The one who has ears to hear should hear."[1]

Peter said to him, "Since you have taught us everything, tell us also this thing. What is the sin of the world?"

The Savior said, "Sin does not exist; rather, it is you who produce sin when you do what is in accordance with the nature of adultery, which is called 'sin.'[2] For this reason, the good has come among you, to those of every nature, in order to restore each to its own root." He then continued by saying, "For this reason you are sick and are dying, because you love **8** that which deceives you. The one who understands should understand. Matter has given birth to a passion that has no resemblance, for it has come forth in a way contrary to nature. A disturbance then occurs in the entire body. This is why I told you, 'Be content at heart.'[3] And if you remain discontent, surely you should be content in the presence of each and every image of nature. The one who has ears to hear should hear."

Jesus' Final Words and Departure

When the blessed one has said these things, he greeted them all, saying, "Peace be to you, may my piece be born to you.[4] Be on guard lest one leads you astray by saying, 'Look here' or 'Look over there.' For the Son of Man is within you.[5] Follow him! Those who seek him will find him. Go, then, and preach the gospel of the kingdom.[6] Do not **9** lay down any rules beyond what I have set for you, nor set forth any law like the lawgiver, or else you may be ruled by it."[7] When he said these things, he departed.

1. Matt. 11:15; Mark 4:9.

2. See Gos. Philip (NHC II, 3) 61, 10–12: "Every union that has occurred between those unlike each other is adultery."

3. See Luke 24:38; John 14:27.

4. See Luke 24:37; John 14:27; 20:19, 21, 26.

5. Luke 17:21, 24.

6. Matt. 4:23; 9:35; 24:14.

7. See Matt. 28:20. The Savior seems to condemn here the Mosaic law and its divine legislator.

Mary Comforts the Apostles

But they were distressed and wept greatly, saying, "How can we go to the gentiles and preach[8] the gospel of the kingdom of the Son of Man? If did they did not spare him, how will they spare us?"

Then Mary arose and greeted them all, saying to her brothers, "Do not weep or grieve or be of two minds,[9] for his grace will be with all of you and will protect you. Rather, let us praise his greatness, for he has prepared us and made us human beings."

When Mary said these things, she turned their hearts toward the good, and they began to discuss the Savior's words.

Peter Bids Mary to Teach

10 Peter said to Mary, "Sister, we know that the Savior loved you more than the other women.[10] Tell us the words of the Savior that you remember, which you know and we do not, since we did not hear them."[11]

Mary Recounts Her Vision

Mary replied, "What is hidden from you I will tell you." And she began speaking these words to them. "I," she said, "saw the Lord in a vision and said to him, 'Lord, I saw you in a vision today.' He answered me, 'You are blessed, because you do not falter at seeing me. For where the mind is, there is the treasure.'[12] I said to him, 'Now, Lord, does the one who sees a vision see it with the soul or with the spirit?' The Savior replied, 'He does not see it with the soul or with the spirit; but the mind that is between the two is what sees the vision, and it is that which . . .'"

The Ascent of the Soul

15 . . . it.[13] And Desire said, 'I did not see you descending, but now I see you ascending. So why are you lying, since you belong to me!' The soul replied, 'I saw you. You did not see me, nor did you recognize me. You possessed me as a

8. See Matt. 28:19–20.
9. See Matt. 28:17.
10. Gos. Philip (NHC II.3) 63,30–64,9.
11. See John 20:18.
12. See Matt. 6:21; Luke 12:34.
13. Or "him." Mary's report on the Savior teaching resumes after a long lacuna with a description of the heavenly ascent of the soul. The name of the first authority, which is lost in the lacuna, is most likely "Darkness"; see the list of the seven forms of the fourth authority below.

garment,[14] and you did not know me.' When she said these things, she left, rejoicing greatly.

Again, she came to the third authority, which is called Ignorance. [It] examined the soul, saying, 'Where are you going? You have been ruled by wickedness. Surely you have been ruled, so do not judge!' And the soul said, "Why do you judge me, when I have not judged? I was ruled, without having ruled. I was not known, but I myself have come to know that all is being dissolved, both the things of earth **16** and those of heaven.'

When the soul had brought to naught the third authority, she ascended and saw the fourth authority. It took seven forms: the first form is Darkness; the second, Desire; the third, Ignorance, the fourth is the Envy of Death; the fifth is the Kingdom of the Flesh; the sixth is the Foolish Wisdom of the Flesh;[15] the seventh is the Wrathful Wisdom. These are the seven authorities of Wrath. They queried the soul, 'Where are you coming from, slayer of humans, and where are you going, destroyer of realms?' The soul replied, 'What has ruled me has been slain, and what has surrounded me has been destroyed, and my desire has been brought to an end, and my ignorance has died. In a world, I have been released **17** through another world, and in an image, through a superior image. The bond of forgetfulness is temporary. From now on, I shall receive repose in silence for the duration of the time of the age.'"

The Apostles Dispute Mary's Authority

When Mary said these things, she fell silent, as though the Savior had spoken to her up to this point. Now Andrew[16] responded and said to his brothers, "Say what you will about what she has said, but I do not believe that the Savior said these things. For these teachings are strange thoughts indeed."[17] Peter replied and spoke about these things as follows. He asked them about the Savior, "Did he really speak with a woman secretly from us, not openly? Should we turn about, too, and all listen to her? Did he choose her over us?"[18]

14. The clause is ambiguous, as it may mean both "I (i.e., the soul) served you as a garment" (Wilson-MacRae) and "You (i.e., Desire) possessed me as my garment" (see Till-Schenke). The second translation seems more likely; see Numenius, test. 47 Leemans: "For in each of the spheres below heaven it (i.e., the soul) is clothed with an ethereal envelope, so that through the spheres it is gradually reconciled to its association with this garb. And so it passes by as many deaths as it does spheres, and comes to what on earth is called life."

15. See 1 Cor 1:19–20, 26; 2 Cor 1:12.

16. On Andrew, see Matt. 10:2; Mark 1:16–18; 3:18; Luke 6:14; John 1:35–42, 44; Acts 1:13.

17. See Luke 24:10–11.

18. See Gos. Thom. 114.

18 Then Mary wept and said to Peter, "My brother Peter, what are you thinking? Do you think that I have thought up these things alone in my heart or that I am telling lies about the Savior?" Levi[19] responded and said to Peter, "Peter, you are always angry. Now I see you disputing with this woman like the adversaries. If the Savior made her worthy, who are you then, for your part, to cast her aside? Surely the Savior knows her full well. That is why he has loved her more than us. Let us rather be ashamed, and put on the perfect human[20] and bring it forth for ourselves, just as he commanded us; and let us preach the Gospel, laying down no rule or law other than what the Savior has spoken." When **19**
Levi said these things, they began to go out to teach and proclaim.

The Gospel according to Mary

19. On Levi, see Matt. 9:9; Mark 2:14.
20. See Gal 3:27; Eph 4:13; Col 1:28; Jas 3:2.

The Gospel according to Mary: Greek Fragments

Papyrus Oxyrhynchus 3525

. . . nor have I set forth any law like the lawgiver

. . . .

When he said these things, he departed. But they were distressed, weeping greatly and saying, "How can we go to the nations preaching[21] the gospel of the kingdom[22] of the Son of Man? If indeed they did not spare him, how will they spare us?" Then Mary arose and, greeting them, kissed each one and said, "Brothers, do not weep nor grieve nor be of two minds.[23] For his grace will be with you, watching over you. Rather, let us give thanks to his greatness, for he has joined us together and made us human beings." Having said this, Mary turned their mind over to the good, and they began to discuss with one another the sayings of the Savior. Peter said to Mary, "Sister, we know that you were greatly loved by the Savior, as no other woman.[24] Tell us, therefore, whatever you know of the words of the Savior, which we have not heard."[25] Mary replied, saying, "Whatever is hidden from you and I remember, I will proclaim to you." She began with these words to them: "One time when I saw the Lord in a vision, I said, 'Lord, today I saw you.' He replied, saying, 'Blessed are you . . .'"

Papyrus Rylands 463 →
21

("'. . . I will receive,)

for the remaining course of the appointed time of the age, repose in silence.'" Having said these things, Mary fell silent, as though the Savior had spoken up to this point. Andrew[26] said, "Brothers, what do you think about that which has been said? I for one do not believe that the Savior said these things; for they seem

21. See Matt. 28:19–20.
22. Matt. 4:23; 9:35; 24:14.
23. See Matt. 28:17.
24. Gos. Philip (NHC II.3) 63,30–64,9.
25. See John 20:18.
26. On Andrew, see Matt. 10:2; Mark 1:16–18; 3:18; Luke 6:14; John 1:35–42, 44; Acts 1:13.

different from what he himself taught."[27]
Pondering these matters,
(Peter said,) "Did the Savior
speak secretly to a woman and not
openly, that we all might hear?
That she was more worthy than us,
is this what he wished to show?"][28] . . .

Papyrus Rylands 463 ↓
22

. . .

of the Savior?" Levi[29] said to Peter,
"Peter, you are always prone to anger.
And now you are disputing with
this woman as if you were her adversary.
If the Savior considered her worthy,
who are you to despise her?
For surely he knew her,
and loved her dearly. Let us rather
be ashamed and, clothed with the
perfect human,[30] do what
we have been commanded. Let us
preach the Gospel, setting no rules
nor establishing any laws, as
the Savior said. Having said these things,
Levi left and began to
preach the Gospel.

The Gospel according to Mary.

27. See Luke 24:10–11.
28. See Gos. Thom. 114.
29. On Levi, see Matt. 9:9; Mark 2:14.
30. See Gal 3:27; Eph 4:13; Col 1:28; Jas 3:2.

39

The Greater Questions of Mary

Some books from ancient Christianity have come down to us in manuscript form but are never mentioned in the writings of the church fathers (e.g., the Letter to Diognetus in the Apostolic Fathers). Others were previously known *only* from writings of church fathers, only to be rediscovered in modern times (e.g., the recently discovered Gospel of Judas). Yet others are mentioned by church fathers but have never been discovered. This is the case with the present apocryphon, "The Greater Questions of Mary" (i.e., of Mary Magdalene).

One of the "great questions" for scholars is whether such a book ever existed. It is mentioned only once in ancient literature, in a highly charged polemical context by Epiphanius of Salamis, a heresy-hunter prone to exaggeration and fabrication, who was incautious at best in his attacks against heretical sects in his book the *Panarion* (= "Medicine Chest"; in it Epiphanius supplies the "antidotes" for the "snake-bites of heresy").

The most notorious of the groups that Epiphanius attacks were known by a variety of names, including the "Phibionites." According to Epiphanius—our sole source of knowledge about the group—these gnostic believers engaged in nocturnal sex rituals that involved indiscriminate sex, coitus interruptus, and the consumption of semen and menstrual blood, all in a bizarre act of Christian worship (a sacred eucharist). Moreover, they allegedly possessed apostolic books that supported their outrageous rituals, including one known as the "Greater Questions of Mary" (*Panarion* 26, 8).

Epiphanius claims to have had access to this, and the other, Phibionite books. But this one he actually quotes. If the quotation does indeed go back to an actual document, as opposed to Epiphanius's fertile imagination, it is no wonder that the book never survived, as it recounts an episode in which Jesus himself engages in a sex act before a very bewildered Mary Magdalene.

For the Gnostic Phibionites, this text, and their corresponding rituals, related to their doctrinal views that humans represent divine sparks entrapped in human bodies, which need to escape. Human procreation perpetuates this state of entrapment, by providing an endless supply of bodies as prisons for the sparks of the divine. The "solution" to the problem, then, was to engage in non-procreative sex, as shown to Mary Magdalene by the Savior himself, one odd night on a mountaintop.

We have translated the text from the edition of Williams.

Bibliography

Benko, S. "The Libertine Gnostic Sect of the Phibionites," *VigChr.* 21 (1967): 103–19.

Ehrman, B. D. *Lost Christianities: The Battles for Scripture and the Faiths We Never Knew*. New York: Oxford University Press, 2003; pp. 198–201.

Gero, S. "With Walter Bauer on the Tigris. Encratite Orthodoxy and Libertine Heresy in Syro-Mesopotamiam Christianity," in C. Hedrick and R. Hodgson, *Nag Hammadi, Gnosticism, and Early Christianity*. Peabody, MA: Hendrikson, 1986; pp. 287–307.

Williams, F. *The Panarion of Epiphanius of Salamis*. NHS 35. Leiden: E. J. Brill, 1987.

The Greater Questions of Mary

For in the book called The Greater Questions of Mary (they have also forged one called the Lesser), they indicate that he [Jesus] gave a revelation to her [Mary]. Taking her to the mountain he prayed and then extracted a woman from his side and began having sexual intercourse with her; then he gathered his semen in his hand, explaining that "This is what we must do in order to live." When Mary became disturbed and fell to the ground, he again raised her and said to her, "Why do you doubt, you of little faith?"[1]

1. See Matt. 14:31.

Printed in the USA/Agawam, MA
December 7, 2017

664847.008